OPIUM SEASON

OPIUM SEASON

A YEAR ON THE AFGHAN FRONTIER

JOEL HAFVENSTEIN

The Lyons Press

Guilford, Connecticut

An imprint of The Globe Pequot Press

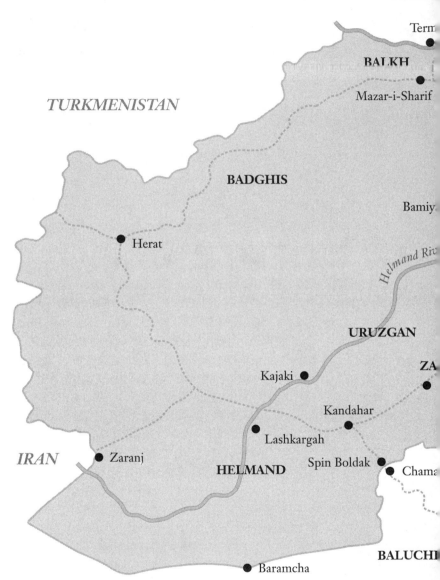

UZBE.

Term

BALKH

Mazar-i-Sharif

TURKMENISTAN

BADGHIS

Bamiy

Herat

Helmand Riv

URUZGAN

ZA

Kajaki

Kandahar

IRAN Zaranj

Lashkargah

Spin Boldak Chama

HELMAND

BALUCHI

Baramcha

The Lyons Press is an imprint of The Globe Pequot Press.

10 9 8 7 6 5 4 3 2 1

Printed in the United States of America

Library of Congress Cataloging-in-Publication Data

Hafvenstein, Joel.
  Opium season : a year on the Afghan frontier / Joel Hafvenstein.
    p. cm.
  ISBN 978-1-59921-131-2
  1. Afghanistan--History--2001- 2. Afghanistan--Description and travel. 3. Economic assistance, American--Aghanistan. 4. Opium trade--Afghanistan. 5. Hafvenstein, Joel--Travel--Afghanistan. I. Title.
  DS371.4H32 2007
  958.104'7--dc22

                    2007034177

Contents

Prelude: The End   1

PART ONE: PLANTING   5
Little America   7
Yaqub   14
City of Dust   26
Mullah Omar's Drought   36
Into the Minefield   46
Salaam to Helmand   58
A Million Dollars a Mile   67
The Place of the Soldiers   80
Jack of All Trades   91
The Babaji Abduction   103
Christmas in Helmand   115
The Warlords' Vendetta   127

PART TWO: FLOWERING   139
Guns and Poppies   141
New California   153
Traveling Difficulties   162
The Way of Love   176
Good Cop, Bad Cop   187

CONTENTS

Politics as Usual   198

The Royal Bungalow   210

The Indispensable Warlords   223

Back on Track   234

Gunfire in the Backyard   242

PART THREE: HARVEST   253

Valley of Death   255

Defining Success   266

Three Days in May   277

In Limbo   290

Helmand at War   304

Badakhshan   316

Sources   327

Index   329

OPIUM SEASON

The End

Lashkargah, Helmand—May 19, 2005

"We're getting out, mate." Charles's composure was belied by the taut lines in his face and the two Afghan guards flanking him, their rifles unslung and ready. "Get your things. If what we're hearing from Zabul is true, we've been sitting here like bloody ducks for too long already."

We had never been safe in this massive government of Afghanistan building on the banks of the Helmand River. Our project offices were on the top floor, with no reliable escape route if attackers breached the main door. We couldn't control the flow of visitors to the government offices in the building, and we didn't have enough guards to patrol the long fence. Our windows faced the forest on the far side of the river, where any would-be sniper could hide, strike, and make a clean getaway. Those had been acceptable risks before our project was targeted for murder.

If true, the rumors from Zabul province confirmed that someone was trying to kill us, but we didn't yet know who: the struggling remnants of the Taliban, opium smugglers who found our work an inconvenience, or local militia commanders with some unknown grudge. We didn't know if they planned more attacks, or if they could strike us in the city of Lashkargah itself. So we were running. There was a small U.S. military outpost on the edge of town, next to the graveyard. By the afternoon our office and staff houses would be empty of everyone but guards, and our Western staff would be inside a bunker.

I hadn't grasped yet that this was the end, that our six months of hard work could be undone so quickly and brutally. I did fleetingly think, *If we can't even protect ourselves here anymore, at the center, how on earth can we protect our workers way out in upper Helmand?* It was a logistical question, not a rhetorical one. I still believed there had to be a way to keep the project going. My thoughts were distracted, drawn sidelong to one eclipsing fear: If the rumors were true, another good friend was dead.

As I numbly packed essential files into a box, my mobile phone rang. I didn't recognize the number.

"Joel speaking."

"Is this Mr. Joel Hafvenstein of the Alternative Income Project?" The voice on the other end of the line was crisp, professional.

"May I ask who's calling?"

"This is Noor Khan of the Associated Press. I am calling from—"

I cut him off as quickly and politely as I could. "Mr. Noor Khan, I'm very sorry to tell you that I can't answer any questions about the attacks. Please let me refer you to our chief of party, Ms. Carol Yee. Her number is—"

"No, sir. I am not calling with questions." The journalist was calm but insistent. Even before he continued, I felt my throat constrict. "I am calling because your business card is the only identifying mark on the six murdered men we have here in Qalat Hospital. Two of them had it in their pockets. Everything else was taken."

For a moment my mind struggled to form words. "Six men, you said."

"Yes, sir."

"Six, including the . . ." I didn't know how to articulate the unlikely hope that somehow one of them had escaped.

"Seven bodies, but one of them was already dead, in a shroud and casket. They were attacked on the road. Before dawn, the police believe."

I had not believed the rumors, I realized. It had not seemed possible that after one friend's murder, another should follow so quickly and unsparingly. "I . . . Mr. Noor Khan, do the police know who did this?" Now I physically felt the belief settle into me—a sick, heavy compression in my chest.

"They have not said. Perhaps bandits, or Taliban. I thought you should know. After yesterday." He paused. "It is quite hot here, sir. Something must be done."

"Thank you, Mr. Noor Khan." Though shattered, I understood the urgency. "We'll notify their families and try to send someone to Qalat to identify and collect the bodies as soon as possible."

"Thank you, sir."

I hung up. Charles and Farid had paused in their work as I talked, and now I met their eyes. They handled security for our project. For months they had been striving to get the resources we needed to keep this very thing from happening. They had worked endlessly to discipline and equip our guards, to get us radios, to make sure our far-flung payroll trips and engineering inspections went out with plenty of police and little advance warning. Now the gunmen had gotten through—not once, but twice. I could see the bitterness in their eyes.

I told them what they already knew.

PART ONE: PLANTING

Little America

Lashkargah, Helmand—November 27, 2004

"You know, they used to call this place Little America."

The night sky was cloudless, but the moon had already set. Ray and I were walking by starlight through the dusty back streets of Lashkargah. Far away, a single lightbulb burned above the closed wooden shutters of a fruits and spices vendor. The earth-walled compounds on either side of the road were silent and dark. We had been in town for two days and had no idea who lived on the other side of those walls. Last night, we had walked back by a slightly different route to throw off anyone tracking us—a gesture at the basic security precautions we had chosen to ignore by traveling on foot, in the dark, through an unfamiliar bit of Afghanistan.

"Americans built this whole city," Ray explained. "Back in the 1950s. It was where the Morrison-Knudsen engineers lived while they were working on the canals. People remember that here. They basically like us."

Ray Baum always varied his route, and he always walked. He didn't like to keep the Afghan drivers around after the end of the work day, so whenever he worked late he would dismiss them and walk home. Even on evenings when we all finished work at six or seven o'clock, the rest of us would pile into our rented Toyota Land Cruisers in front of our Lashkargah office, while Ray handed one of us his laptop bag and struck out on foot. The drivers couldn't believe it; for the first two or three blocks outside the office, they cruised alongside Ray while he waved them away and did his best to ignore them. They didn't speak English, and none of us spoke Pashto, so it was beyond us to explain what possessed this grizzled American to walk home through the lightless alleys of Lashkargah.

"It's not like in Jalalabad. The whole of eastern Afghanistan was under Russian influence back in the '50s and '60s. Up there, the Russians built the roads and bridges and dams, and everyone went to study in Russia. Americans are still unpopular up there even today. But in Helmand, we were the good guys."

I had begun joining Ray on his walks home—not always, but usually on nights when we both stayed late at the office. I didn't like keeping the drivers waiting at night any more than he did, and I thought I understood a few other reasons why he chose to walk. Ray liked to know the places where he worked, to explore the geography and understand the people. Every day, he walked up the street, bought a pomegranate at the fruit stand, and ate it at meticulous length while conversing with the locals in fragments of English, Dari, and Pashto. Yet even though virtually no one was on the streets after dark, Ray made a point of always walking home at night. Another crucial principle was at stake: show no fear. Ray was a hardy man, spending his holidays on hunting expeditions in remote bits of his native Alaska, and he didn't want anyone to mistake him for a mere development bureaucrat. More importantly, Ray knew what he represented in Helmand province—America, development, the new Afghan order—and he didn't believe we could succeed if we were held back by fear of possible disaster.

"I think this is going to be a really good project, Joel. We've just got to get things approved and started quickly. We can adjust them later if we need to. We can't get scared or let things get bogged down."

Ray spoke at a deliberate pace, his eyes intense and searching beneath furrowed brows. He had a thick-tongued voice, a weathered, crumpled face, close-cropped gray hair, and a mustache. He was more a practical than an intellectual man, his conversation circling unadorned around whatever was most on his mind; when he came across an idea or phrase that resonated with him, he would bring it up verbatim and often. Yet Ray was the canniest development swashbuckler I knew. Back in the 1980s he had figured out how to get aid to areas of Nicaragua and Honduras dominated by anti-Communist guerrillas, and when the fighting was over, he helped talk the guerrillas down out of the hills. For that accomplishment, the United States Agency for International Development (USAID) awarded Ray its highest honor. He won it again, later, for his deft management of a counter-narcotics project in Bolivia.

I had worked with Ray before in Afghanistan, on my previous short trips to the country. I had seen him lead a team and handle the ever-shifting demands of the USAID mission in Kabul, and I admired his judgment and gruff diplomacy. In mid-2004 he had left Afghanistan, resigning from a long-term position to spend more time with his family. My boss had pleaded with Ray to come back for one month to lead the start-up team on our most challenging project yet.

We were working for Chemonics International, USAID's largest private contractor. A few weeks earlier, USAID had given Chemonics an urgent assignment: to create tens of thousands of jobs in remote southern Afghanistan. Our target area was Helmand province, which was both an oasis of relative calm in the heart of the Taliban resistance and the foremost drug-producing region in the country. The Afghan government had promised to eradicate the opium poppy fields of Helmand this year. USAID had promised to create enough temporary, cash-paying work to cushion the economic damage. Chemonics had promised to make it happen with eighteen million dollars.

Of course, all that money was in Washington, and we weren't sure how we were going to get it to Helmand. There were no banks in Lashkargah, the provincial capital. We had no staff yet, no reliable phone or Internet connections, no radios or project vehicles. All we had was the start-up Go Team, an all-star ensemble of the most relevant experts from Chemonics headquarters. Plus me.

I had been working with Chemonics for a year and a half, helping to "backstop" its existing Afghan agriculture projects. That is, I provided administrative support from the Washington office: getting visas for our consultants, buying plane tickets, handling the USAID paperwork. I had flown out to Afghanistan a couple of times, but those trips didn't really qualify me to help launch a project deep in Taliban country. What they did give me was the Afghanistan bug. I was captivated by the arid, serrated mountains and green valleys, the ruins left by foreign armies from Genghis Khan to Gorbachev, the generosity and resilience of my Afghan friends. I made sure my bosses knew that I would take any Afghan field assignment—even a one-year assignment to a dusty provincial center that made Kabul look like a cosmopolitan paradise.

As it turned out, my most important qualification was the willingness to stay longer than Christmas. We were launching this project on unusually short notice and the all-star team all wanted to be home for the holidays. The only other member of the start-up group who was in for the long haul was our government liaison, Yaqub Roshan, an affable Afghan-American with a vaguely defined job. If Chemonics couldn't replace Ray and the other Go Team members in the next few weeks, by Christmas Day it would just be Yaqub and me.

I was nervous—but mostly about my own ability to do the job. I had no idea I would end up as the *de facto* second-in-command, or that our project would succeed beyond our wildest dreams, employing thousands of men in some of the farthest corners of Helmand province. The Afghan friends who would make it happen—Habibullah, Khair, Raz, Ehsan, and dozens of others who would join us to struggle against problems both petty and lethal—were still strangers to me. And I didn't really understand that our success might make us a target. That night, as I followed Ray through the alleys of Lashkargah, I believed him when he said we shouldn't be afraid. Like him, I was more preoccupied with the seemingly impossible goal that had brought us to Helmand.

• • •

How do you convince a farmer to give up the perfect crop?

Picture a rugged, desert country in which a seven-year drought has emptied the canals and a twenty-five-year war has wrecked roads, schools, and markets. Orchards and vineyards have been bombed, fields and pastures mined. The millions of farmers and farm workers in this country have few sources of credit, no banks, and a national currency that until very recently was worthless. Many don't actually own land, and in fertile areas the competition for sharecropping work is intense.

Now imagine a drought-resistant cash crop. It grows during the wheat season but fetches a much higher price than wheat—anywhere from five to twenty-five times higher, depending on the year. This crop doesn't bruise or require refrigeration, so the lack of reliable roads and electricity is no obstacle. Once harvested, its gum can be kept for months or years before processing, so villagers stockpile the gum and use it as cash. The traders in this crop are a sophisticated, internationally connected bunch who offer credit; they'll pay farmers in the winter for a certain amount of gum in the spring. Landowners are more likely to accept sharecroppers who agree to cultivate this crop. It offers the most reward for the fewest risks, with one significant exception: The government might plow up your fields if it catches you. The government is weak, though, and plenty of local authorities are involved in the trade themselves.

The country is, of course, Afghanistan, and the crop is opium poppy, the raw material for heroin. Opium has been grown in the Afghan mountains for millennia, but it took two and a half decades of civil war to turn poppy into the country's economic mainstay—and to turn Afghanistan into the heart of the global heroin trade. During the long war that began in 1979, the country's government slowly disintegrated, local warlords began to support themselves by trafficking opium, and brutalized farmers turned to poppy as their best chance of escaping poverty. By 1992, Afghanistan had passed Burma as the world's largest opium exporter. By 2004, the largest sector of the Afghan economy was narcotics (generating well over one-third of its gross domestic product), and Afghanistan produced a staggering 87 percent of the world's illegal opium.

Opium brought me back to Afghanistan in November 2004. On my previous trips, I had worked with Chemonics' projects to restore the once-thriving Afghan agricultural sector. None of those programs had focused specifically on poppy. We hoped that by helping Afghan farmers cultivate and market legal crops, we would eventually give them a ladder out of poverty that didn't involve opium. We called it a *strategy*, but it was just a simple, plausible justification for leaving poppy out of our plans for the next few years.

The scale of the 2004 opium harvest wrecked that strategy. For the first time in history, farmers in all thirty-four Afghan provinces chose to plant the perfect crop. They carpeted an unprecedented 323,000 acres of land with poppy, which was 126,000 acres more than the previous year, and almost 99,000 acres above 1999's prior record. The harvest of opium gum fell just short of record levels, thanks to bad weather, disease, and poppy-munching parasites. Still, by the end of the season in summer 2004, Afghanistan's addiction to opium had unmistakably reached a new peak.

As the extent of the harvest became clear, the political rumbling from Washington and Kabul grew thunderous. George Bush and Hamid Karzai both had elections to win in the fall. Both knew their rivals would use the high poppy crop against them, though in rather different senses: Bush could expect a rhetorical bruising from the Democrats, while Karzai risked losing provincial control entirely to rich and well-armed drug lords. Neither president had the patience to rely on long-term projects of agricultural development. As the yearly report of the United Nations Office on Drugs and Crime euphemistically declared, Afghan farmers would require "more robust forms of persuasion" to give up opium. A comprehensive poppy eradication campaign was on the way.

Just before the fall 2004 poppy-planting season began, USAID frantically called its Afghanistan contractors with a new assignment: to keep the bottom from dropping out of the rural economy when the poppies were destroyed. In the top opium-cultivating provinces, hundreds of thousands of Afghans depended on opium for their livelihoods. If the American and Afghan governments were going to plow up the poppy fields, we needed to create enough jobs to plug the gap with cash.

Nobody mistook this kind of mass job creation program for a long-term solution. It was an emergency response, a bandage on the eradication campaign. The British government had been struggling for three years to come up with a serious substitute for poppy, and in 2004 USAID joined in, offering hundreds of millions of dollars for "alternative livelihoods" projects. The problem was that no one really knew what a long-term solution would look like. A bevy of agricultural specialists tried to come up with "silver bullet" alternative crops that were almost as lucrative as poppy: saffron, rose oil, black cumin. Others argued that instead of introducing a novel crop, it would be better to revive Afghanistan's traditional export business in dried fruits and almonds. Microfinance experts devised schemes to provide credit with no opium strings attached.

All this would take years to get off the ground, however; in the meantime, cash-for-work had to smooth the way. USAID ordered a few of its big private-sector contractors to head immediately into the Afghan provinces with the most poppy cultivation. Chemonics was told to redirect money from one of its existing projects to create jobs in Helmand, Afghanistan's opium heartland. The farmers of Helmand's central plains benefited from a massive irrigation canal network built with American money and engineering between the 1940s and the 1960s. During Afghanistan's decades of war, the farmers of "Little America" had switched wholesale from cotton to poppy, spurred on by local warlords who built shaky, violent baronies on a foundation of drug money. Now the Americans were back, hoping to transform Helmand again.

To compensate for the loss of poppy income in the province, USAID estimated, over the next year we would need to create two and a half million days of paid work. It wasn't entirely clear what assumptions about the poppy trade had inspired that peculiar number, but that was our only solid target: two and a half million days. Everything else—the amount of money we spent, the total number of people we hired, the nature of the jobs we created—was flexible. The "magic number" had some inescapable consequences, though. Given a six-day work week, we would need to have an average of eight thousand men at work every day for the whole year. With every day that we didn't meet that target, it would increase.

So we needed to quickly identify large-scale public works projects that would involve lots of pick and shovel work. To monitor our thousands of laborers, we needed to hire qualified engineers and project managers, in a province where a twelfth-grade diploma represented exceptionally high education. We needed somehow to get a million dollars in cash down from Kabul every month and safely distribute it all over a province still awash with guns from the long, American-funded jihad against the Soviet Union. No one was sure how the local drug traffickers or nearby insurgents would respond to us. The project was simple in conception, crazy in reality.

But as with the overall project of rebuilding Afghanistan, time was essential. Everyone involved in the Afghan reconstruction talked about windows of opportunity that would soon close. Ours was the window between the time we arrived in the country and the time the eradication tractors started rolling. Like Ray said, if we spent too long preparing, we'd lose our chance to make a difference. So we jumped in.

Yaqub

Lashkargah, Helmand—November 27, 2004

Yaqub Roshan liked to say that he first met me on his first day of work in our cramped Lashkargah office. Our government landlords had granted us five enormous, dusty desks, handcrafted by local carpenters for American engineers in the 1950s. Until our consignment of Pakistani plastic-and-plywood desks arrived from Kandahar, our staff would be working elbow to elbow. That first day, I had set up my laptop on the southeast corner of a desk with a nice view of the Helmand River. Yaqub surveyed the room and pulled his chair up to the northwest corner.

I was wearing my single set of traditional Afghan clothes, known in the south as *kaali* or *kamiz partoog*—a shin-length blue tunic with matching baggy trousers—and a gray waistcoat of a hundred pockets. Yaqub greeted me jovially in Pashto: "*Tsanga ye? Jor ye? Pu khair ye?*" (How are you? How is your health? Is it well with you? In any language, Afghan conversations generally begin with a stream of polite, rapid-fire inquiries into one's health.) When I didn't look up, he chidingly continued, "*Hay haleka! Taa ta sa paisha da?*" (Hey, man, what's the matter with you?) I looked up, blinked, and said, "Oh, sorry, I don't speak Pashto." Yaqub, by his account, had mistaken me for a local, so well did I blend in with my Afghan garb.

Yaqub Roshan was a born diplomat. Some Afghans did have a fair complexion that came close to my Scandinavian pallor, and blue eyes weren't uncommon in northern Afghanistan. I had been letting my beard grow long for a couple of weeks. Still, I betrayed my foreign origin by a dozen signs—from my white sports socks to the way I uncomfortably shrugged my heavy-laden waistcoat back off my neck every few minutes. I had no illusions of blending, especially given my ignorance of both major Afghan languages, Dari and Pashto. I wore Afghan clothes partly as a gesture of respect, partly for their mild exoticism, and mostly because they were comfortably cool and voluminous (uncinched, the trousers had a six-foot waist). Yaqub, not I, was the bridge between cultures: born and raised in Afghanistan, a refugee in Pakistan for seven years during the Soviet invasion, and since 1989 a U.S. resident and citizen.

Yaqub might not have noticed me before we became deskmates in Lashkargah, but I remembered first seeing him across a different table a month or two earlier. We had been in Chemonics' Washington, D.C., office with senior staff from the Asia division, tossing around strategies for winning USAID contracts in Afghanistan. Yaqub, a round-faced, barrel-chested, mustached man in his early fifties, was the only outsider in the conference room. Listening avidly, sweating generously, he made a couple of comments about the importance of Islam and getting moderate mullahs behind our projects, but otherwise he came across as uneasily out of place. Afterward, one of my colleagues whispered to me, "Who was he, and what was he doing here?"

I later learned that a few weeks earlier Yaqub had arrived in the office of the senior vice president of Chemonics' Asia division and declared, "I understand you are doing good work in Afghanistan. I am here to offer my services in any capacity you may need." We were always after people who would look good on an Afghanistan proposal, so even though neither Yaqub nor Chemonics were quite sure how to apply his skill set to our projects, he began showing up in the Afghanistan war room.

In November, when USAID gave its emergency call for alternative livelihood ideas, we wrote Yaqub Roshan into our proposal as the government liaison. We highlighted his past experience on other USAID projects, his good relationships with Afghan government officials, and his fluency with the local languages and culture. His job description was somewhat nebulous, but we expected to flesh it out on the ground.

I wrote Yaqub's biography for that proposal. At the time I didn't know the man at all or appreciate what had brought him to the Chemonics office. I had studied a bit of Afghanistan's history, but Yaqub had lived through it—and he was determined to stay in the middle of the latest phase.

• • •

Yaqub Roshan was born in the early 1950s in Wardak province, a cluster of fertile, relatively prosperous valleys just south of Kabul. At the time,

Afghanistan was a monarchy under King Zahir Shah, and Yaqub's father was a provincial governor, or *wali*. Governors tended not to govern for long in any one place, especially in their home province; the king moved them around to keep them from getting too tied into local power structures or feuds. So Yaqub enjoyed a nomadic youth, from the remote, beautiful mountain ravines of Badakhshan and Uruzgan to the broad river valley of Helmand. In each province he watched his father try to foster rural development while wrangling tribal leaders (*khan*s) and other local strongmen in the name of King Zahir.

The walis, and indeed the monarchy itself, did not "govern" rural Afghanistan in the full modern sense of the word. Like every other Afghan ruler of the last hundred years, King Zahir was at once strong and weak. He had enough authority to appoint and sack governors, enough resources to carry out a few big development projects, and enough guns and troops to repel most Afghan rivals for power. The monarchy was well funded and armed by foreign sponsors; the king's predecessors had enjoyed a subsidy from the British Empire, and throughout Zahir Shah's reign the United States and Soviet Union competed to offer aid money to the Afghan government.

The monarchy's power, however, was limited to large, blunt instruments. It could send in the army, but was much feebler when it came to sending in teachers, police, judges, doctors, and tax collectors. On a day-to-day basis, 90 percent of Afghans had more to do with purely local authority figures—tribal khans, big landowners, moneylenders, mullahs—than with any representative of the state. The king had limited control over these feudal authorities. A royal wali like Yaqub's father had to manage the local power brokers: co-opting them, punishing them, manipulating social divisions to pit them against each other instead of against the monarchy.

Afghanistan's society has no shortage of divisions to spark feuds and grudges. Afghans classify themselves in intricate, overlapping, and often bewildering categories of religion, language, region, and kinship. Yaqub and his family were members of the Pashtun ethnic group, as was King Zahir; for the last few centuries the Pashtuns have been Afghanistan's dominant group, providing nearly all of its kings, amirs, and presidents. Yet the Pashtuns alone can be carved up by dialect (most easterners speak Pakhto, most southerners Pashto), clan and tribe (two tribal confederacies, Ghilzai and Durrani, comprise scores of smaller tribes), livelihood (urban, rural, nomadic), and, over the last hundred years, ideology (traditionalists, modernizers, Communists, Islamists). For centuries, Afghan rulers have tried to find a balance between bridging these divisions to govern the country and manipulating the feuds to weaken and distract potential rivals.

Throughout Yaqub's childhood, Afghanistan enjoyed a certain stability with its detached monarchy, unruly tribes, and powerful local khans. Yaqub was born halfway through the forty-year reign of King Zahir and came of age during the royal family's cautious campaign to develop the country without losing control. Throughout the 1950s, the king's modernizing cousin Daud served as prime minister. An Afghan nationalist with Russian sympathies, Daud channeled foreign aid into a modern army, an expanding bureaucracy, and the universities needed to feed these modern institutions with educated young Afghans.

The jewel of the new higher education system was the Kabul Polytechnic, a showcase for Soviet foreign aid. Yaqub's uncle, an engineer trained in the USSR, declared admiringly that the labs and facilities at the Polytechnic were superior to anything he had seen in Russia itself. It was the obvious place for any young Afghan who wanted to be part of the modernization of the country, and in the early 1970s Yaqub successfully applied to study geological engineering there. He arrived in Kabul in 1973—the year that King Zahir's long reign ended—as former Prime Minister Daud smoothly ousted his royal cousin and declared Afghanistan a republic.

Kabul in those days was an intellectual hothouse centered on the Polytechnic and nearby Kabul University, where a generation of ambitious young Afghans first encountered the currents of international Communism and Islamism. The ideological quarrels of these students had an impact far beyond the lecture halls of Kabul. The wars that would wrack Afghanistan for the following two decades were largely driven by Yaqub's school friends and contemporaries.

For some students, higher education sparked a religious awakening. These students had grown up with the folk Islam of Afghan village mullahs or the ancient Sufi orders, whose *pirs* (leaders) were revered by their followers as living saints. At university, these students discovered the rigorously orthodox theologies taught at places like Cairo's grand al-Azhar University—theologies that took a dim view of Sufism, folk traditions, and veneration of sacred sites or holy men. Many students simultaneously discovered Islam as a political ideology. Afghan professors of *shari'a* (religious law) such as Burhanuddin Rabbani taught the political creed of Islamists in Egypt and Pakistan who insisted on the unity of *din wa dawla*, religion and state.

Other students discovered Marx, Mao, and the Communist critique of feudalism. These students knew the ugly face of feudalism from daily experience; many of their fathers were poor farmers whose land, water, wives, and lives could be taken away by powerful local khans and landlords. The leftist students also knew firsthand the ugliest face of the monarchy and Daud's republic—the secret police, censorship, and the beatings, torture, and murder deployed against serious critics of the government. Communism offered a vision of a new, revolutionary Afghanistan that would be both modern and just.

Still other students identified themselves simply as Afghan nationalists, the doctrine of the government. Prime Minister Daud was a fervent nationalist with an assertive, popular foreign policy. He refused to recognize the border between Pakistan and Afghanistan, disdaining it as a British colonial artifact that artificially divided the Pashtun and Baluch tribes. To the dismay of the Pakistani government, he gave shelter to ethnic insurgents from Pakistan's side of the border. No patron or neighbor was above Daud's criticism. On Daud's final visit to Moscow in 1977, Russian Premier Leonid Brezhnev complained that Afghanistan had allowed too many NATO aid experts into the country. Daud brusquely retorted that Brezhnev did not run Afghanistan and stalked out of the meeting. Many Afghan students shared their prime minister's tough national pride and admired his modernizing vision.

Yaqub's ideologically divided classmates skirmished verbally and sometimes physically on the streets of Kabul. At Kabul University, a hulking medical student and weight lifter named Muhammad Najibullah led the Communist students in debates, demonstrations, and brawls. An ambitious young engineering undergraduate, Gulbuddin Hekmetyar, was doing the same for the Islamists. Decades later, the legend of Gulbuddin's monstrosity would include tales of him throwing acid in the faces of unveiled female students, but Yaqub didn't remember hearing such lurid reports at the time. "He was always vicious, but back then he lacked any real ability to harm."

During those years in the Kabul intellectual and political scene, ideology was more significant than ethnicity. Pashtun students like Gulbuddin studied under the ethnically Tajik professor Rabbani and accepted his leadership in their covert political activities. There were two Communist factions, the *Khalq* (people) and *Parcham* (banner) groups, that coalesced around eponymous party newspapers. Pashtuns were slightly more common in the hardline Khalq group, while the Parcham base included more Tajiks and ethnic minorities, but an ethnic Pashtun like the student organizer Najibullah could be perfectly comfortable in the Parcham leadership.

Given his father's government job and his naturally conciliatory personality, Yaqub was little inclined to the radical fringes of student politics. He graduated from the Polytechnic in 1976 and launched his career as an engineer in a copper mine in eastern Logar province. Afghanistan's untapped copper deposits were world-class, and remain so today; mineral wealth might have driven Afghanistan's economic development if the country's politics hadn't veered into nightmare. Yaqub was still working in Logar in 1978 when he heard that the prime minister had been overthrown and killed in a Communist coup. Daud had launched a crackdown on the Afghan left but discovered too late that many university-trained army officers were also members of the party.

One of Yaqub's Communist classmates blacklisted him as a potential counterrevolutionary, so he was summoned back to Kabul by the new government and put under surveillance. Yaqub's father, now more than seventy years old and suffering from diabetes and heart disease, was thrown into the grim Pul-i-Charki Prison for his connections to the old royal and republican regimes. Three of Yaqub's brothers fled the country, leaving him the main breadwinner for his family. He discreetly quit his low-paying government job and studied English at the British Consulate while earning money as a language teacher and taxi driver.

Meanwhile, the country was being turned upside down. In the first flush of the 1978 revolution, the Afghan Communists were determined to break the power of the feudal elites and become the first government to truly control rural Afghanistan. They launched a brief but devastating campaign of land redistribution, resettlement, revised family law, and debt cancellation. To their shock and anger, the university-educated Communists found that not only the khans but also the peasants they wanted to liberate were zealously resisting their agenda, especially the partial emancipation of women under the new family law. The revolutionary government tried to reinforce its reforms with torture, terror, and a cult of personality around the "Great Leader." Instead, it sparked rebellions throughout the countryside and a series of mutinies in the army.

The Soviet Union's leaders watched with growing dismay as Afghanistan spiraled into chaos. They had never supported the radical agenda of the Afghan Communists, fearing correctly that it would destabilize the country. If the Afghan revolution now failed, it would not only be a propaganda defeat for Communism; it might also encourage similar rebellions in the USSR's Muslim-majority republics, several of which bordered on Afghanistan. After leaders from rival Afghan Communist factions began murdering each other, the Soviet Union finally sent the Red Army into Afghanistan on Christmas Eve 1979. Its mission was to restore order, install a stable, sensible Afghan government, and get out.

The invasion of Afghanistan by thousands of Soviet troops changed the whole nature of the fight. University-educated Islamists, exiled Sufi pirs, mutinous army leaders, and rural rebels throughout the country all declared themselves to be *mujahidin* (fighters in a *jihad*, or sacred struggle) against the avowedly atheist superpower. Many Afghans who might otherwise have ignored the government's ideology were outraged by the foreign occupation of their country and supported the resistance.

The mujahidin took full advantage of Afghanistan's harsh terrain, striking Soviet targets and melting quickly back into the desert or mountains. The Russians resorted to carpet-bombing the rural communities that sheltered the guerrillas, killing hundreds of thousands of Afghans and sending millions more as refugees into neighboring Pakistan and Iran. At the height of the fighting, the Red Army had roughly 120,000 troops in Afghanistan, supported by tens of thousands of Afghan government soldiers. The Afghan mujahidin, meanwhile, were shored up by billions of dollars from America and Saudi Arabia and thousands of zealous volunteers from all over the Muslim world.

Kabul saw relatively little actual fighting, but it was a city of dread nonetheless. The Soviets organized a ubiquitous secret police, KHAD, headed by the former student leader Najibullah. Hundreds of Kabulis disappeared into KHAD dungeons without explanation. Maybe some stranger passing their house had reported overhearing a Voice of America or BBC radio broadcast. Maybe a KHAD officer had simply decided that he wanted their property. Without warning or pretext, anyone might be taken away and tortured, shot, or buried alive.

Yaqub was jailed twice during those years in Kabul. The first time was after he learned that his father had been beaten in Pul-i-Charki and was languishing in the prison infirmary. Yaqub hurriedly brought a petition to the general commander of the security services, requesting his father's transfer to a better hospital. After standing for hours in a queue with forty or fifty other supplicants, Yaqub had to make his case publicly, in front of all the other petitioners. The commander, a Communist of the hardline Khalq faction, barked that Yaqub's father was a bloodthirsty criminal. "He is alive, which is more than he deserves. Why do you expect me to care about his health?"

Despite being generally mild-mannered and diplomatic to a fault, Yaqub detested losing face even more than the average Afghan. Twenty-five years later, telling me the story, the memory still twisted his lips in bemused pique. "That Khalqi could say what he wanted about my family, but why did he have to say it in front of all those people? I asked him if he could speak more quietly, but he kept shouting these things about my father and my family. Everyone in the office was listening while he used these insults no one could bear. Finally I began shouting back. I told him, 'You use whatever words you want, but what matters for my family is the judgment of the Afghan people, not that of a worthless person like you!'"

The commander's henchmen jumped forward, drawing their pistols. Yaqub remembered being clubbed with a gun and receiving two or three punches and kicks that drove him to the floor. The next thing he knew, he was groaning his way back to consciousness while a cellmate poured cold water over his contusions. For two weeks, he shared a small, dark room in the back of the Ministry of the Interior with eighty other prisoners. They could all hear the screams from distant interrogation chambers. No one ever came to question Yaqub.

At the end of the two weeks, all the detainees were brought out into a twilit courtyard and lined up by soldiers with bayonets. A KHAD man declared that the detention center was getting too crowded and they were moving some people to "a different place." He pulled Yaqub and five or six other men from the end of the line, escorted them through the ministry compound, and herded them impatiently into a Russian jeep, its engine already running. Yaqub was the last to board the vehicle. A mere second before the door closed, a guard emerged from the building and yelled, "Yaqub Roshan! Get that man off the truck." Yaqub stumbled out, the door slammed behind him, and the jeep drove away.

Yaqub had no idea what to expect until he turned a corner and saw a blessedly familiar face: an official of the criminal section in the Ministry of the Interior who was a longtime friend of his father. The official walked Yaqub to a side gate and said, "Go, quickly—leave. You're free." Yaqub tried not to tremble too visibly as he walked home. Later, he tried to find out what had become of the other detainees who had been taken away in the jeep. As he had half-suspected, none of them were seen again.

Shaken but undeterred, Yaqub continued to try to get his ailing father out of Pul-i-Charki. A year later, his petitions got Yaqub thrown in jail again. Again his family friend managed to get him released, unharmed. In 1982, Yaqub's father was finally freed from prison. Yaqub sent word to his elder brother, who was working with the mujahidin in Pakistan. His brother sent back a guide who helped the rest of the Roshan family flee the country. Yaqub and his father arrived that autumn in Peshawar, the capital of Pakistan's Northwest Frontier Province and the unofficial headquarters of the Afghan mujahidin.

The Afghan resistance had never been a unified force, but by the time Yaqub arrived in Peshawar, deep divisions were coming to the fore. The Pakistani army controlled all American and Saudi funds for the resistance, and

Pakistan's generals were determined not to strengthen any mujahidin faction that might one day want to redraw the Afghan-Pakistan border or get too friendly with India. So Pakistan poured foreign guns and money into the most radical Islamists (for whom national borders were of secondary importance and to whom India was a secular, infidel power) and shut out moderate, nationalist, and royalist mujahidin. The former student leader Gulbuddin Hekmetyar was Pakistan's favorite, both for his religious fanaticism and for his fearsome reputation as a killer of Soviets. Among Russian troops, the name *Gulbuddin* became a byword for Afghan cruelty.

As war and personal rivalries destroyed trust on both sides, ethnicity came to dominate Afghan politics. The Afghan Communist government began hiring tribal militias in lieu of a national army, and the ethnic divide between the two Communist factions grew more pronounced. In Peshawar, Gulbuddin broke with Professor Rabbani's Islamist party to found a radical splinter group, the Hizb-i-Islami party, which was increasingly dominated by Pashtuns. Rabbani relied instead on a young Tajik commander, Ahmad Shah Massoud—another of Yaqub's classmates at the Kabul Polytechnic, who had dropped out in 1974 to help rally Islamist dissidents. Massoud was a peerless tactician but also a pragmatist, willing to cut deals with the Russians to protect his home valley of Panjsher. His archrival Gulbuddin accordingly continued to get the lion's share of American money and guns.

By the time Yaqub arrived in Peshawar, it was clear that those guns weren't just being used on Communists. Gulbuddin's rivals and critics were disappearing in Peshawar, just as dissidents were disappearing in Kabul. "That was when we saw the real face of the beast," Yaqub later told me. "Gulbuddin is not like the Taliban, who at least fight for an idea, the role of women and all that. Gulbuddin serves his own ambition first and foremost."

Gulbuddin would personally test Yaqub's diplomatic skills over the next few years. After ensuring that his father and family were safe in Pakistan, Yaqub took up the cause of bringing education to the millions of Afghans in refugee camps and the "liberated areas" of Afghanistan. USAID intended to fund a major education program run by the University of Nebraska's Tom Gouttierre, a former Peace Corps volunteer and high school teacher in Kabul. Yaqub had been one of Gouttierre's students, and with his fluent English, he was the ideal liaison between American donors and the mujahidin. Some of the mujahidin, however, were unexpectedly hostile to the whole idea.

Gulbuddin was willing to accept weapons and cash from America, but he refused to countenance U.S.-funded schools or textbooks. His hardline Hizb-i-Islami fighters had been busily demolishing government schools in Afghanistan for teaching un-Islamic course material. The last thing the Islamist mujahidin wanted was to replace Soviet blasphemies with American blasphemies. Yaqub ended up as the main negotiator between the religious hardliners and the moderate mujahidin on the issue of education funding.

The compromise Yaqub eventually brokered would draw plenty of criticism in years to come. The Islamists agreed to accept American education funding as long as they had a say in the textbook content. Thousands more Afghan kids accordingly got schools and books, but their education was colored by violence and conservative religiosity. Their math textbooks taught them to calculate how many seconds it would take for a speeding Kalashnikov bullet to reach a Russian and pierce his head. Children memorized spelling lessons like: "*J* is for jihad. Jihad is an obligation. My mom went to the jihad. Our brother gave water to the mujahidin . . ."

Yaqub considered this a victory. The curriculum could have been much more Islamist, and once the schools were safely established there would be chances to revise the worst texts later. Over the next few years, Yaqub repeatedly went back to Afghanistan to set up education centers in areas under effective mujahidin control. On these journeys he would travel on foot with teams of guerrillas, carrying all their supplies on their backs, dodging Soviet planes and patrols. His longest trip, in the mountains of Kunar province, lasted thirty-nine days.

After seven years in Pakistan, Yaqub applied to Georgetown University and was admitted on a merit scholarship. He and his family moved to the USA in 1989. That same year, the Soviet Union finally accepted that no amount of military pounding was going to crush the Afghan insurgents and create a stable Communist government. The mujahidin were routinely bringing down Soviet aircraft and helicopters with American-provided Stinger missiles; on the ground, the Russians had seen fifteen thousand soldiers killed and more than fifty thousand wounded. Ten years after invading Afghanistan, the Soviets finally withdrew their troops in the winter of 1989. They left Najibullah, the former student organizer and secret police chief, as the unlucky president of the Republic of Afghanistan. Najibullah declared that the government no longer considered itself Communist and called in vain for national reconciliation.

The mujahidin had won an astonishing victory against a superpower, but a decade of infighting had left them hostile and polarized along ethnic lines. Massoud and Gulbuddin besieged Kabul from opposite sides but could not overcome their mutual distrust long enough to actually take the city. In the first sign of the coming civil war, Gulbuddin's Hizb-i-Islami forces assisted the hardline Khalq faction of the Communists in a failed coup attempt against President Najibullah. In theory, you couldn't have found two groups less likely to cooperate than Khalq and Hizb-i-Islami. In reality, their ethnic Pashtun identity had become both groups' most significant trait.

By the time Yaqub completed his Georgetown master's thesis on "Afghan Refugees' Attitudes Toward Repatriation," Afghanistan was slipping swiftly into anarchy. President Najibullah finally lost power in 1992, when his most powerful ethnic militia switched to fight alongside the mujahidin. The West tried to coax the major resistance leaders into a national power-sharing government in Kabul. Instead, Massoud, Gulbuddin, and several other militia commanders began battling for control of the capital. Yaqub's former classmates once again clashed in the streets around Kabul University, except this time they were fighting with rocket launchers, mortars, and Kalashnikovs.

The mujahidin leaders had become *jangsalaran*—warlords. The new era of "rule of the gun" not only destroyed any pretense of a central government, but it also provided the final deathblow to the network of local authorities that had existed before the war. The old tribal khans came from families that had built up wealth and a network of relationships for generations. The new warlords were engineering students or simple local thugs empowered by foreign weapons and the war economy. Their rule didn't bring Afghanistan back to its traditional tribal habits; the old ways were shattered beyond repair, and the horrors of the civil war proved that in the new Afghanistan, anything was possible.

In the same way, the old village mullahs had usually incorporated some degree of Sufism and superstition into their religious practice. During the war a new breed of mullahs grew up in Pakistan's refugee camps, cut off from Afghan culture and history, steeped instead in dogmatic political Islam. Eventually these mullahs acquired a name—Taliban—and swept across Afghanistan to briefly reimpose some form of order.

Yaqub avoided his shattered homeland for more than a decade. He found work with the World Bank in other bits of central Asia and spent some pleasant years in Tashkent. He had just moved back to Washington, D.C., in 2001, when a young man trained in a militant camp in Afghanistan flew a plane into the Pentagon. Yaqub followed the news after September 11 with mingled horror and hope. Perhaps at last the rest of the world would unite to support a new order in Afghanistan.

He got in touch with his old friends at the University of Nebraska. While America was dropping bombs on the Taliban front lines—and more importantly, handing sacks of dollars to local Afghan leaders who agreed to break with the Taliban—Yaqub and his colleagues were working painstakingly to update their old textbooks. They scrubbed all references to Kalashnikovs, dead Russians, and other gratuitous violence, though plenty of conservative religious references remained. With the help of USAID funding, a thoroughly venal Pakistani publisher, and a team of UNICEF pilots, they managed to get an emergency print run of 1.2 million textbooks distributed throughout the country within three months of the Taliban's defeat. Unfortunately for Yaqub, the University of Nebraska lost the long-term USAID education project to a specialized contractor, one of the big for-profit companies that increasingly dominate American foreign aid.

In 2002 and 2003, Yaqub took short assignments with the World Bank and the UN, helping them navigate the Kabul government. He wasn't satisfied with these brief missions after so many years away, and he asked his friends at USAID to recommend contractors with long-term Afghanistan projects. They referred Yaqub to Chemonics.

City of Dust

Shash Darak, Kabul—October 19, 2003

Chemonics dispatched me on my first, monthlong Afghan assignment in the autumn of 2003. As I flew into Afghanistan for the first time, my mind wandered apprehensively back to my father's photographs. My father had worked for much of his life along the great mountain spine of Asia, spending ten years as a civil engineer in the Nepali Himalayas and thirteen more years as Asia coordinator for the Lutheran mission that had supported our family in Nepal. These days he traveled twice a year to visit the mission's overseas personnel, including the staff of a hospital in the Pakistan borderlands and a handful of health care workers in Afghanistan. Dad had driven from Pakistan to Kabul a few times during the Taliban era in the late 1990s. He had come back with photos of a dry, rugged landscape wracked by war, of women in full-body *burqa* shrouds and unsmiling men brandishing Kalashnikovs. His pictures shaped my enduring associations with Afghanistan: desiccation, danger, claustrophobia. I couldn't recall any of the stories that went with the photos; I didn't remember whether he'd found a happier side to the country, something that the images alone didn't communicate.

From the air, Afghanistan seemed even more of a wilderness than I'd imagined. Our Ariana Afghan Airlines flight occasionally passed over a green ribbon of valley where I could make out tiny huts and roads, but the landscape from my window to the horizon was for the most part a vast, dry sea, its white-crested ridges and jagged gulfs devoid of plants or people. Eventually I drowsed off; I had been in the air for more than fifteen hours, with only a couple hours of fitful sleep in a Dubai hotel before catching the 5:00 a.m. flight to Kabul.

When I woke we were spiraling down over a densely populated flatland between mountain walls. The Ariana seatbacks flopped around with alarming abandon; as we angled sharply downward, the neighboring seat almost took my shoulder off. The jet hit the ground with a shudder and a squeal, sending up clouds of dust on all sides. The Kabul runway was lined with rusted wrecks of other planes cannibalized for parts. In the grassy fields to either side, I could see lines of white rocks marking the progress of landmine removal.

It was a sunny but blustery morning, and we were whipped by a dirty wind as we strode from the plane to the terminal. A large poster of the late Tajik warlord Ahmad Shah Massoud in a declamatory pose welcomed us to Afghanistan. Inside the airport, every surface was coated in a film of white, powdery dust. It took a long time for our luggage to arrive, and longer still before the last bag was tossed onto the belt and I could confirm that my crate of office supplies and files had never left Dubai. I wearily reported it missing and walked out into a cacophony of hopeful porters and taxi drivers. In the middle of the crowd, a tall, weathered Afghan man with graying hair and mustache was holding a sign with my name on it. When I approached him, he laconically introduced himself as Basir. He took my sole suitcase and led me to a Toyota Land Cruiser.

As we drove into Kabul I gazed around, trying to get my bearings. The sky was a gray-brown haze, and dust clouds whirled across the road. Stony mountains shot up on every side. Some were barren, while others had an astonishing clutter of mud-brick houses clinging to their steep, craggy slopes. Trees were scarce, green grass even scarcer. The roads were clogged with yellow Corolla taxis, dirty buses, and trucks painted too gaudily for the dust to mute them. Some of the trucks were loaded so high with bundles and boxes I could hardly believe they stayed upright. One pickup had a camel hog-tied and tossed in the back, its head and neck lolling ridiculously over the side. Basir wove through the dense traffic with alarming velocity and consummate skill, outrunning swarms of Corollas, dodging lumbering trucks. I caught glimpses of the shops on either side of the road: turbaned mechanics surrounded by grimy motor parts, stacks of brightly painted metal gates outside welders' workshops, tall rolled carpets in crimson and ocher, gyms with lovingly detailed paintings of muscle-bound men. I saw only a handful of women walking along the roadside, all of them hidden behind sky-blue burqas.

The bazaars eventually gave way to high-walled compounds: embassies, ministries, UN and aid agency offices. Their compounds were fortified with razor wire and boom gates; at the top of the walls, most had attached an extra two or three yards of opaque plastic sheeting to keep hostile outsiders from spying in. Outside, their concrete and earth buttresses spilled into the road. Several streets were closed off entirely with sandbags and wire. Near the heavily barricaded U.S. Embassy, a disgruntled Afghan organization had hung a large banner in English that read HONORABLE INTERNATIONAL SOCIETIES! HAVE YOU COME TO KABUL TO BLOCK OUR CROSSROADS AND ROADS?

After several minutes of winding through back streets, Basir drove down a long cul-de-sac and halted in front of an unmarked metal gate. An Afghan guard emerged with a mirror at the end of a long stick and perfunctorily scanned the underside of our vehicle for bombs. He nodded, the gate opened, and we rolled into the International Rescue Committee's Kabul compound. A couple of large concrete buildings rose out of the dust and scraggly brown grass, with a valiant attempt at a garden below the west wall. A satellite perched on the roof provided an erratic broadband Internet connection. Chemonics was renting three or four rooms in one wing for the headquarters of its Afghanistan Quick Impact Project, a small, one-year reconstruction project that was drawing to a close.

I found Zulaikha Aziz first, after overhearing a stream of imperious Dari from a side office. A diminutive Afghan-American woman, Zulaikha had huge brown eyes, slender, expressive hands, and a dense mane of black hair. Back in the States, with her rapid-fire conversation, stylish clothes, and fast car, Zulaikha was the model of a suburban American twenty-something. In Kabul, she was a brisk and confident operations manager, fluent in Dari, claiming respect from Afghan coworkers who were unaccustomed to women in positions of authority. She looked up to see me listing against the doorframe. "Joel! We were wondering when you were going to get here. Welcome to Afghanistan. How was your trip? How are you?"

"Hey, Zee." I was exhausted and ravenous, and I told her so. She called the cook in and told him to warm up some of today's lunch for me. Quickly, she introduced me to the project's six or seven remaining Afghan employees. Most of the others had already moved over to jobs on Chemonics' newest project, the biggest in the company's history: the Rebuilding Agricultural Markets Program, or RAMP, a $130 million USAID contract to support Afghanistan's farm sector. Our Quick Impact Project, with a mere $2.7 million budget, had been left to the kids. All the remaining managers were less than thirty years old—including me, the serious-looking young Afghans in the main office, Zulaikha, and even the chief of party, USAID's peculiar jargon for project leader.

I had never met Pete Siu in person, but within a few days of arriving at Chemonics I had learned to envy him. He was a company prodigy, the youngest chief of party in Chemonics history and surely one of the youngest on any USAID project. At twenty-six years old, he had been given the reins of the Quick Impact Project when Ray Baum, the initial chief, switched over to a top deputy position on RAMP. Pete had done such an exceptional job as Ray's second-in-command that USAID approved his promotion immediately, complimenting Chemonics on its good sense. Pete was rumored to have a sharp wit and an impish sense of fun—and to be somewhat embarrassed by his "youngest COP" poster-boy status. I figured I'd like him.

In person, Pete Siu turned out to be tall and skinny, with spiky black hair and clad in a comfortable-looking brown kamiz partoog. He stood up and extended his hand as I entered. "Dude. Welcome to Kabul." His voice was strikingly deep, coming from such a spare frame. "Glad they sent you out. We've got a lot for you to do." I did my best to pay attention through jet lag and hunger while he gave me a quick rundown of my duties.

There was nothing glamorous about my first Afghanistan assignment. I was responsible for dozens of little close-out jobs and one big, time-consuming task: procuring $200,000 in road construction equipment as a parting gift for the four Afghan aid organizations that had partnered with us. The four groups had been using begged, borrowed, or rented equipment for the duration of the project. Since the project had hit all its targets with more than $200,000 left in the budget, we wanted to buy our partners their own equipment to continue with similar work.

After giving me the briefest outline of what I'd be doing, Pete took me into the conference room that would serve as my office. The chairs and shelves were thick with dust and dozens of flies were busily patrolling the room. A few minutes after Pete left for his office next door, the cook brought me an oily lamb stew, served in standard Afghan style with rice, raisins, and sweetened carrot shavings. He also handed me a stack of flatbread, and for the first time I got to sample Afghan *naan*—great corrugated diamonds of bread two feet long, flatter and chewier but more hearty than the Indian naan with which I was familiar. I scattered the flies as best I could and bolted the food down with gusto. Pete popped his head through the window between our offices when I was nearly done. "Hey, careful with the meat, dude. It made Zee sick last week. You might want to wait till we get home."

Around sunset we headed to the Land Cruisers for our drive back to our project guesthouse. Zulaikha shrugged on her headscarf and buttoned up her long tawny coat as we left the office. I stared out the car window into a city I didn't know at all, wondering how likely we were to be shot or bombed. Our Land Cruiser lurched along the deeply pitted asphalt, past wooden stalls where late shoppers haggled over vegetables and naan. The incandescent white glow of the shopkeepers' gas lanterns vied with the pungent, meaty smoke rising from the streetfront grills of kebab restaurants. There weren't many pedestrians out in the dusk, just an abundance of cars and motorcycles choking the narrow streets. I tried to keep track of our route but was soon thoroughly lost.

Eventually we passed a small mosque and drove down a street of high, bare walls and featureless gates—the type of place I would learn to think of as a residential area. The Land Cruiser pulled up to one gate and honked three times. A guard emerged to let us in, one of three unarmed Afghan watchmen who took turns manning the guesthouse gate. As we got out of the car, Pete acknowledged the driver and guard with grave, uncharacteristic formality: "Thank you, Mr. Ainodeen. Good evening, Mr. Homayoon." The guesthouse was a two-story building with all the modern amenities of expatriate housing in Kabul: a generator, a more or less functional water heater, a large refrigerator, a comfortably carpeted living room with satellite television and a heap of pirated DVDs. Pete and Zulaikha had become improbably addicted to Korean soap operas, and after dinner I passed out to the querulous, unintelligible chatter of the TV.

• • •

In those first few days in Afghanistan, I was more disoriented than ever before in my life. Every day, I woke up jet-lagged at four or five in the morning. Lying there in the predawn shadows, I was seized by panic. *What are you doing here? You have no idea what you're supposed to be doing—no experience with any of this, no qualifications, no reference points.*

I hadn't come completely unprepared to my first field assignment. Poverty, culture shock, the routine complications of life in South Asia—those had all been familiar since I was three years old in Nepal. My formal qualifications for international development work were a little more tenuous, though. When I was job hunting, I had glossed over my years of waiting tables in Minneapolis and typing up corporate data in New York City and emphasized the six months I had spent traveling around Asia in 2000, working with poverty relief and human rights groups. I had a newly minted, one-year master's degree in international relations from Boston University, where I had worked as a teaching assistant for a class on Afghanistan. That had been enough to help me talk my way into an entry-level administrative job with Chemonics. Within three months, while I was still scrambling up the learning curve, they had sent me to close out the Afghanistan Quick Impact Project.

During my first week in Kabul, I shelved my other assignments and devoted myself to my biggest, simplest task: buying the road construction equipment for our Afghan partners. It was an escape, really—a retreat from my task list. I spent most of those days driving around Kabul's bazaars in search of people who could buy, ship, or build us the equipment within three weeks. Our logistics assistant Aziz did most of the real work. He knew where to go and what to look for; I was just the guy who kept notes on it all, asked one or two slightly informed questions, documented the price quotes, set a delivery timetable. Meanwhile, hours flew by on the traffic-throttled streets while I slowly grew accustomed to the look and feel of urban Afghanistan.

Kabul was a boomtown and a war ruin. Most of the houses were either half-built or half-destroyed. The physical scars of the long war were profound and inescapable: pockmarked walls, shredded shipping containers once used as barricades, gutted buildings topped with deformed rebar wreckage. Yet construction was booming. Well-connected government and aid agency managers were throwing up concrete mansions with lots of tinted glass and marble on display. Ordinary Kabulis were plastering up the shell holes in their brick walls and extending their homes with flimsy-looking new rooms on the roof or side. The piles of colorful metal gates for sale at every streetfront welder's stall suggested that a lot of people were renovating their outer walls. The north and northwest of the city had gotten off relatively lightly in the war, and their neighborhoods of simple mud or cinder-block huts were expanding at breakneck pace to accommodate millions of newcomers. Far above us, squatter families were stacking stones on the mountainsides to create enough level ground for a small shack. Much of Kabul now looked like any other poor, teeming city on the Indian subcontinent, with only occasional, incongruous reminders of the city's recent horrors. Few other Asian capitals use empty artillery shells as traffic lane dividers on major roads.

Which face of Kabul you saw depended very much on where you went. The most glamorous redevelopment examples, a popular topic for foreign press pieces, were concentrated in the central neighborhoods. The first of a handful of multistory, glass-fronted buildings was going up in the Shahr-i-Nau area. As several amused journalists pointed out, this was a remarkable act of faith in a city still riddled with bullet holes. Scores of new businesses had sprung up to capitalize on the surge in international aid: computer supply stores, travel agencies, shipping and logistics firms, grocers offering imported peanut butter and breakfast cereal, and an international cornucopia of restaurants. In late 2003, the Kabul gourmand could choose between Italian, Indian, French, American, Thai, German, Croatian, and Chinese eateries (the last reportedly a front for a less respectable profession). Once I thoughtlessly asked our driver Basir whether he knew if an Italian place I had spotted was any good; it was the first time I saw him come close to a smile. "I have never been there, Mr. Joel. One meal there costs the same as all the naan I will eat this month."

The glamour wasn't aimed exclusively at internationals. The profusion of big new wedding halls in northwest Kabul with their garishly painted, or namental concrete facades and broad, tinted glass windows—was clearly meant to charm aspiring middle-class Afghans whose tastes had been shaped in Pakistani exile. But most of Kabul's boom involved no glamour at all. Most of it was simply a population explosion, with millions of Afghans fleeing absolute poverty or foreign sojourn for the relative security and opportunity of the capital. Kabul's informal cash economy offered little dependable long-term work, but it offered more than most mountain villages or refugee camps.

The population surge was most obvious on the teeming, chaotic streets. Battered German buses rolled along with people hanging off the roof and out the windows. Whenever we reached a roundabout, traffic came to a standstill; cars attempted to drive both ways around while intrepid cyclists, hand-carts, and pedestrians sifted into the momentary gaps between vehicles. Thousands of petty vendors lined the roads: moneychangers selling prepaid mobile phone cards; "bucket pharmacists" with a plastic pail full of assorted medications; gaunt young *spandi* smoke-sellers, waving censers of burning, bitter-scented leaves to fend off the evil eye from passing Corollas. Beggars of all ages chased after vehicles, tapping on the door until the driver or passenger handed over a few afghanis. Burqa-clad figures appeared ghostlike at our window, faceless and unnerving, pleading for money.

In many neighborhoods, the devastation of the 1990s remained far more tangible than the ongoing expansion. The great central avenue of old Kabul, Jada-i-Maiwand, was the starkest juxtaposition of the capital's two faces. At eye level, it was a busy commercial boulevard, teeming with yellow Toyota taxis and stalls selling everything from turkeys to ironmongery. If you looked up, though, almost all the grand concrete buildings sagged around cavernous gaps in their upper stories, the legacy of mujahidin street battles using purloined Soviet tanks and U.S.-financed rocket launchers. I recalled reading that 60 percent of Kabul's houses had been shelled during the last decade—in particular, the houses of West Kabul, which had the geographical misfortune to be a front line for five or six of the city's major militias.

The first time I rode into West Kabul, across from the shattered campus of the Kabul Polytechnic, I noticed a massive array of concrete silos attached to an imposing square tower. It was the largest structure I'd seen in the city, and looking at it, I felt an unexpected, fond nostalgia for the old grain elevators of my native Minneapolis. Here, someone had blasted away at the upper levels with artillery or rockets, leaving a half-dozen small craters. A fragile-looking scaffold clung to one side of the tower. "Aziz," I craned my neck back to see our project's logistics assistant, "what was that place?"

"The Silo? The Russians built it. It was for keeping wheat and making bread," Aziz confirmed. He was young and nervous, with fair, ruddy skin and a straggling beard. Today, as on most work days, he was wearing a light blue polyester three-piece suit. "But when the mujahidin came to Kabul, it was used for fighting."

I tried to imagine it—snipers on top of the grain towers, a perfect vantage point from which to observe a major highway and the residential neighborhoods all around, until a rival militia brought rockets to bear on their perch. Or maybe not; Aziz didn't know the details. Maybe all the fighting was done with small arms, and the shell holes were just target practice on a monument to Russian development aid. Aziz shrugged. "It is *kherab*—wrecked. Everything here is kherab."

The gentle bitterness in his voice echoed a near-universal Kabuli sense of betrayal. The sack of Kabul was the great perfidy of modern Afghanistan, poisoning the country's victory over the Soviets. When the mujahidin finally ousted President Najibullah's government in 1992, no one imagined they would go on to make KHAD's reign of abduction, torture, and murder look like a golden age. Afghanistan's self-proclaimed saviors swiftly divided Kabul (and the country) into heavily fortified zones and began fighting for control. From the beginning, the predatory gunmen focused their violence as much on civilians as on rival militias. Gulbuddin Hekmetyar, who had been shut out of the first fragile post-Communist government, withdrew to the south and began indiscriminately shelling the city. The militias inside the city all fortified the highest ground they could claim and fired their artillery back at Gulbuddin, each other, and the helpless neighborhoods in between. Kabul had remained largely intact through a decade of Soviet occupation. Within two years of mujahidin "rule" it was a ruin, and tens of thousands of its civilians were dead.

We turned off the highway at an electrical pole buckled into the shape of a sharp 7, its metal length perforated with holes the size of my fist. The residential road we now drove down was lined with waist-high rubble. Through the debris heaps, mounded like snowdrifts, people had carved paths to the gates of their homes. The houses themselves were roofless skeletons; what little plaster still clung to their brick facades had been riddled with bullets. "Who fought in this area?" I asked quietly.

"The Wahdat Party was here. They were Hazara," Aziz said. The Hazara held the distinction of being the most-oppressed Afghan ethnic group, facing discrimination pretty much everywhere outside their central mountain homeland. They were the only major Afghan group that was religiously Shi'a rather than Sunni, and their facial features—tending toward gold-tinged skin, epicanthic folds, and thin beards, like Mongolians or Central Asian Turks—made it easy to set them apart. The Hazara claimed ancestry from Genghis Khan; during the jihad against the Russians, they had armed themselves for the first time in a century, and in the ensuing civil war they fought with a ferocity that recalled their Mongol forebears.

The post-Communist war had blazed up here, in West Kabul, when a particularly fundamentalist group of Pashtun mujahidin took on the "heretical" Shi'a from the strongest Hazara militia. Their battles eventually drew in all the other mujahidin forces. The Hazara and Pashtun militias alike resorted to civilian hostage-taking, rapes, mass executions, and other terror tactics to gain an edge. Their wretched conflict ended only when the Taliban rolled over Gulbuddin and stormed into West Kabul in 1995, displacing the other Pashtun forces, capturing the leader of the Hazara militia, and tossing him out of a helicopter.

As Aziz and I drove through the ruins, I tried to think of something hopeful to say. "There was a scaffold up on the Silo. Maybe some aid agency will get it working again."

"Maybe." Aziz did not sound optimistic. I couldn't blame him for withholding his trust from Afghanistan's new crop of ostensible saviors.

Some Western and Afghan critics had already suggested that the tragedy of 1992 was repeating itself as farce. An oppressive regime had fallen; a rescuing army had arrived in Kabul, sparking hopes of a new, free, and prosperous Afghanistan. A year and a half later, though, the shine was starting to come off the rescuers. The legions of Western aid agencies and their Afghan partners weren't murdering each other in the streets like the mujahidin, but the new Afghanistan was otherwise looking a bit too much like the old one: poor, hungry, and dominated by strongmen.

Most of the foreign projects for the first year and a half after the fall of the Taliban had been, like our Quick Impact Project, small-scale, emergency stuff. Their point was to provide short-term employment and meet immediate, local needs: give people enough cash to survive the winter, get a canal running properly again, dig a sewer ditch in one of Kabul's swelling slums.

These projects had tangible benefits, especially in the easy-to-reach areas around the capital; many were essential humanitarian efforts. But they weren't the sort of thing that would get Afghanistan on a road out of poverty.

The second generation of projects would be the real testing ground for the reconstruction effort. These were grand schemes with multiyear timescales, hundred-million-dollar budgets, and painstakingly chosen acronyms. Some aimed at building and rebuilding major national infrastructure, like power plants to serve Afghanistan's largest cities or the badly decayed "ring road" highway that circled the country. Other projects were meant to transform entire sectors of the Afghan economy, like the banking and credit system, hospitals and rural health care, or the agriculture sector (Chemonics' responsibility, under the RAMP program). After more than a year of planning, competitive bidding, and mobilization, the megaprojects were only now getting under way.

Meanwhile, scores of international contractors and aid organizations had set up their offices and guesthouses in central Kabul, driving property prices to astronomical levels. Rents on some of the nicer houses in the Wazir Akbar Khan neighborhood were described as "Manhattanesque." Foreign agencies had hired away the cream of Kabul's skilled labor force; a teacher or doctor could make more money driving a Land Cruiser for a UN or USAID project than working in any government school or hospital. The mujahidin warlords who had been forced out by the Taliban were back, staking claim to much of the capital's most valuable land. They dominated the new government and the police force and drew a steady stream of income from development contractors' rents and security payments. Ordinary Afghans were increasingly worried that the benefits of reconstruction would end up going only to their compatriots who were already rich, educated, or well armed.

For the most part, though, the Kabulis I spoke to were patient; the most common worry I heard was of a premature Western withdrawal. Few had expected an instant transformation of their country. Many had enjoyed some sort of direct benefit, however small, from international aid. Almost none had a kind word for the Taliban. The Islamic movement had brought peace of a sort, but at a price most Kabulis were unwilling to pay.

Mullah Omar's Drought

"In the days of the Taliban government, when no radio or TV was allowed, I used to listen to BBC World Service at night," confided our project's cheery office manager, Jahan. "One time I heard that there were big floods in Mexico, from too much rain. They were getting international assistance, but no one could stop the flood. And I realized that for this problem, Afghanistan had one very useful export."

After the final Taliban conquest of Kabul in 1996, the rains had stopped in several regions of Afghanistan. By 2001, the wracking drought had extended to the whole country and was the worst in living memory. Mullah Omar, the Taliban's reclusive, one-eyed leader, declared that it was a punishment from God for the continuing resistance to his rule. Jahan, like many other Afghans, quietly harbored another explanation. "We should just export Mullah Omar to Mexico. No other international assistance would be required. And it would solve our problems, too." The drought broke in 2002, the year after the Taliban were ousted.

Notwithstanding Mullah Omar's Drought, the extent of the Taliban's unpopularity in Kabul was a little surprising. After all, their seizure of the capital had ended a four-year nightmare of shelling and street combat. The last mujahidin warlord left standing, Ahmad Shah Massoud, had retreated north to his home valley of Panjsher, shifting the war's front line out of Kabul. The Taliban promised to bring Islamic justice and order to a city desperately lacking both. From the outset, however, there had been little love lost between the mullahs and the people of the capital.

Partly, this was because the new rulers quickly belied their promise of a just order. Plenty of Talib commanders indulged in extortion, burglary, and rape in Kabul like any mujahidin warlord. The mullahs' hasty, violent justice also won them as much revulsion as praise, beginning with their castration and hanging of former Communist President Najibullah (who had spent the previous four years hiding in a UN compound) and continuing with their notorious Friday public executions in Kabul's football stadium. Much of the Taliban's brutality, however, stemmed from their already intense contempt for Kabul—it did not explain it.

The mutual hostility also had a partly ethnic dimension. The Taliban were at their core a Pashtun movement, while Kabul had a multiethnic, mostly Persian-speaking population. Yet even many religiously devout Pashtuns like Jahan (who did sincerely believe that God was behind the long drought) disliked the invading mullahs. The greater clash was cultural, between the relatively cosmopolitan ethos of Kabul and the asceticism of the Taliban movement. By American or European standards, the values of most Kabulis were scarcely liberal, but to the Taliban, the northern city was a font of Western corruption and laxity.

The Taliban's answer to corruption was fervent, baroque legalism. To prevent the worship of images, they shut the cinemas and destroyed televisions. Shopkeepers had to completely black out any recognizable image of a living being on the packaging of their imports: the human faces on shampoo sachets from India, the cartoon children on Chinese candy packets, the laughing cow head on *La Vache Qui Rit* cheese wedges. The Taliban banned anything that could possibly induce men to gamble, including cards, chess, and bird-keeping (many Afghans bet on partridge and quail fights). They banned music and hobbies like kite-fighting that were deemed "distracting" from religious obligations. They banned weather forecasting, because telling the future was the exclusive prerogative of God.

The Taliban also demanded that men wear proper Islamic dress and beard. All men were required to don turbans and let their beards grow until they were long enough for a mullah to grab them and see hair protruding from the bottom of his fist. Men who failed the fist test were beaten, jailed, or both. My friend Hashem told me of a Talib commander who strictly enforced another recommendation of the traditional Muslim cleanliness code: that all devout men ought to shave their armpits at least once a month. "After he checked your beard, he would look under your arms. If your hair was long enough, he would take a stick and . . ." Hashem picked up a pencil, mimed winding body hair around it, and yanked his wrist sharply downward.

Finally, and to their lasting international infamy, the Taliban enforced a raft of restrictions on women. They ordered women to stay in the household as much as possible; any work or study outside the home was deemed unnecessary and unrighteous. If women did need to venture outside their compound walls, they had to wear the whole-body burqa, a pleated blue mantle that hid even their eyes behind an embroidered grillwork. They were also expected to go in the company of a male relative, which left the thousands of widows who had lost their husbands and sons to the Afghan-Soviet War at constant risk of either private starvation or public castigation. Female gathering places like hairdressing salons and the women's baths were closed. The Taliban tolerated cosmetics and "colorful clothes" in private, but any glimpse of them outside the home could lead to a whipping or worse. Women who laughed, spoke audibly, or even walked too loudly in public could be beaten for immorality by the ever-present religious police. Women found guilty of fornication were stoned to death, or (if unmarried), beaten with one hundred blows.

These edicts had a real impact in a city where, under the Communists, women had been able to work in government ministries and walk the streets with their faces uncovered. Many Kabulis had lived in foreign exile and were accustomed to the less demanding public modesty codes of conservative Muslim countries like Pakistan or Iran. Even traditionalists who agreed with the Taliban in principle were often put off by their crude, violent enforcement of women's roles. My colleague Mumtaz liked to tell a story that illustrated both the mullahs' inflexibility on gender issues and their frequent, startling coarseness.

Immediately after the Taliban took Kabul, a United Nations negotiating team met with the mullahs to reestablish access for the humanitarian UN organizations that had been keeping much of the population of Kabul alive. Mumtaz was the UN's Pashto-language interpreter. At the outset of the first meeting, the Taliban minister of planning gestured menacingly toward the UN delegation. "We are willing to discuss these Westerners' aid programs," he barked. "But tell them that if they so much as mention gender, I will fuck their mothers. Translate!"

The unflappable Mumtaz turned to his UN employers. "He says that the Taliban will consider your programs. But you must not mention the subject of gender. He simply will not hear it." The UN staff nodded gravely, and Mumtaz looked back to the minister.

"Did you tell them?" the minister bellowed. "Did you tell them that I would fuck their mothers?"

"Of course I did," Mumtaz replied mildly.

"They do not look very upset," said the dubious Talib.

"They are Westerners," Mumtaz shrugged. "Such things do not bother them."

• • •

Mumtaz, of course, spoke with tongue in cheek (and fortunately, the Taliban minister was amused). Yet the gap between Western values and common Afghan ideas of honor was genuinely wide, and as I got to know my young Kabuli friends better, I sensed just how uneasily they were stretched across that gap.

The Taliban's austere interpretation of Islam had not been wholly alien even in Kabul. Most Afghan families already lived by a demanding modesty code that separated men and women, the street and the household, and public and private life, with a few carefully controlled points of passage and interaction. The Pashtuns tended to build exceptionally high walls (both literal and metaphorical) between public and private domains, and the Pashtun-dominated Taliban movement had tried to control every glimpse and whisper across the boundary. But nearly all Afghan ethnic groups admitted the principle of segregation in one form or another. If an Afghan man could not control his home and his women, if other men could disregard his walls, most Afghans would agree that that man had lost honor. In a time of war and banditry, he would likely lose his life.

The burqa was a wall, a physical way to extend protection, invisibility, and control over women when they left the household. It was also a traditional symbol of male status. Most farm work was impossible in a burqa, so only wealthy or urban Afghan men could afford to keep their women fully veiled. Hamid Karzai, the interim president of post-Taliban Afghanistan, had hastened to declare it nonobligatory. Nonetheless, over half of the women I saw on the streets of Kabul in 2003 still wore a burqa. We drove past plenty of female clothing stores displaying brightly colored, embroidered, sequined shirts and trousers, but those were for the private sphere.

The Western media's strong association between the Taliban and the burqa was misleading; in Kabul, the "battle of the burqa" had been under way for nearly a century. The reformist King Amanullah was ousted in a 1929 uprising after he proposed to make the capital a veil-free zone. Prime Minister Daud declared the burqa optional in 1959 and successfully deployed his secret police to quell rebellious mullahs who disagreed. By the 1970s, however, Daud was sending his police to quell demonstrations by female high school students against the still-widespread burqa and other symbols of oppression.

Under the Soviet, mujahidin, and Taliban governments, the Revolutionary Association of the Women of Afghanistan (RAWA) had used the full-body mantle to hide in plain sight as they organized subversive women's groups and literacy classes. The Taliban's uncompromising, intricate rules on music, games, and kites had been bizarre to most Afghans, but on the issue of female veiling, Mullah Omar was just a particularly harsh advocate of a widespread, time-honored practice.

The passionate minority viewpoint of RAWA and those 1970s demonstrators was still alive, though, especially in Kabul. "The Qur'an only says that women should hide *their charms*," declared Zulaikha with frustration verging on fury. "It doesn't say anything about making them hide their arms, ankles, and eyes. That just has nothing to do with Islam." Zulaikha was a devout Muslim; in the Qur'an and traditions of the Prophet she found models of female leadership and justification for not covering her head at the office. A significant minority of educated Afghans, male and female, shared her interpretation. Many more Afghans, especially in Kabul, felt that a tightly wrapped headscarf and loose-fitting clothes should be enough to meet the modesty code.

The demands of modesty nonetheless preoccupied even the most liberal of my young Kabuli friends. They knew what they rejected on either extreme—Taliban asceticism and Western libertinism—but were not sure where to draw the line between freedom and sin. After years of being cut off from the rest of the planet save for a few furtive hours with BBC World Service, the youth of Kabul had been abruptly immersed in a delightful, unnerving torrent of new aesthetic and romantic possibilities. The mullahs called it Western, but the cultural deluge came mostly from the east: from Mumbai's prolific movie studios, the *filmi* playback songs of Bollywood, and the pretty celebrities associated with both. India and (to a lesser extent) Pakistan provided new models of fashion, with floppy hairstyles and tight jeans for men, lots of makeup and exposed elbows and ankles for women, and big sunglasses all around. They also offered new cinematic plots: young urban lovers dancing seductively, carrying on romances via mobile phone, and eventually finding happiness in love marriages (as opposed to the parentally arranged norm).

By 2003, the nonstop sermons and diatribes of the Taliban's Radio Shari'ah had been replaced by Radio Arman, a commercial station that played the hits of Tehran, Lahore, and Delhi, along with long-silenced Afghan singers. Radio Arman had just come up with what would soon be its most popular program, *Young People and their Problems*. The show encouraged Kabul's youth to write in with stories of heartbreak: young men frantically trying to arrange a second glimpse of their beloved; young women forced to marry an older cousin instead of the beautiful boy next door. Stories that would never have been whispered outside the family compound were now read on the air to millions of listeners.

Caught up in this cultural shift, tentatively flirting with each other by text message, my Kabuli friends were ever-conscious that powerful issues of honor and shame were at stake. "I would not marry a woman who had kissed another man. Nor would any of my friends," one of my clean-shaven young friends said with conviction. He considered, then qualified: "But I do not think she should be killed. That is the difference between us Kabulis and the Taliban."

A few of my friends wholeheartedly embraced what they took to be the Western moral standard: love justifies all. Hashem, for example, preached the virtues of love marriage and had refused to relinquish his gold wedding ring at a Taliban checkpoint, accepting a beating with knotted cords instead for wearing an un-Islamic adornment. After recounting this story with pride, he earnestly (and privately) asked us how many girlfriends we thought he could ethically have in addition to his wife, as long as he was in love with them all.

Shahr-i-Nau, Kabul—October 23, 2003

Kabul's sizable expatriate community was froth on this cultural sea change. The combined American and European population of Kabul didn't have the transformative impact of the latest Bollywood megahit, let alone the disc jockeys and talk show hosts of Radio Arman. We had an effect on the minority of Kabulis who worked with us, of course, but for the most part the high walls that shielded Afghan modesty also insulated us from our neighbors. Most young expats were chauffeured daily from office to guesthouse, relaxed in garden restaurants, enjoyed the occasional game of soccer, rugby, or poker in somebody else's compound, and met up every Thursday night to ring in the weekend (Friday being the Muslim day of communal prayer). This lifestyle involved only tangential contact with most Afghans other than our colleagues and our long-suffering drivers.

Pete took me out on my first Thursday in town. We met a couple Aussie girls for dinner at the dingy Mustafa Hotel, at the time a favorite haunt of foreign journalists and mercenaries. A sign at the bar informed all concerned parties that under no circumstances would alcohol be served to Afghan citizens. After devouring a chicken tikka pizza, we piled into a convoy with an international array of aid workers and began our quest for parties in a city without addresses. Our Danish navigator squinted into each dark alleyway for landmarks, while our tipsy, expostulating Scottish chauffeur tried to stay ahead of an aggressive local taxi driver. "Love the Afghans. Couldna find a kinder, more hospitable people. But get them behind the wheel of a car, and forget about it! Game over!"

We finally found the Red Cross compound. Most international parties in Kabul tried to be unobtrusive to avoid drawing local ire, but we could identify this one by a couple of signs: the inconspicuous white x on the compound door, and the dozen white Land Cruisers with aid agency logos parked along the road, their Afghan drivers idly chatting. The x on the door may have been a bit too inconspicuous; as we arrived, a group of partygoers who had missed it roused the unamused Afghan family across the street from their dinner. We knocked on the marked door and were admitted to the compound by three impassive guards.

Hip-hop beats rose around us as we strode up to the house. A sign by the entryway mandated a tequila shot for all comers (the three bottles were long empty). The house was packed with aid workers from all over the planet, drinking, dancing, talking shop. A long table held an international array of booze: Australian wine, Latvian vodka, an unpleasant Macedonian ouzo. There was a bonfire in the backyard, and as a surreal complement, someone had set up a projector to shine the "fire" animation from Windows Media Player onto the ten feet of plastic sheeting that topped the rear wall of the compound. The sheeting was refugee camp standard issue, complete with UN logo, set up here to keep anyone from seeing over the wall (and vice versa, to dispel any rumors that the Westerners were spying on the neighbors' women). I wondered if the neighbors were enjoying the light show.

As I chatted with the other guests around the Red Cross bonfire, I realized anew just how out of my depth I was. It seemed that half my fellow partygoers had spent their lives on refugee work in Bosnia or landmine removal in Angola. I had a half-hour conversation with a woman who had distributed emergency food supplies in western Afghanistan throughout the Taliban era. All the reading I'd done on the country suddenly seemed laughable; I didn't know the Afghan authorities she referred to, or the towns she offhandedly mentioned, or how much of the country was still undergoing a food shortage. We left an hour or so later, with our Aussie friend seeking directions on her mobile: "Yeh, we were just at that party, but it's a bit crap. Is the Bearing Point party still going on Flower Street? Is there room to park?"

At three in the morning, Pete caught my shoulder. "Dude, these guys are leaving. You cool with walking home? It's only like fifteen minutes from here." It was the first time I'd walked around Kabul—something our security briefing had strongly advised against—but Pete knew his way around, and I figured that even after a few drinks he wasn't going to put us in danger. We left the compound onto an empty and noiseless street. With the cars gone, the dust had subsided. Stars and a sliver of moon were visible over the hilltop fortress of Kolola Pushta. The two of us kept our voices low as we swayed back to the guesthouse. We didn't see another soul the whole way back.

The next morning we slept in for an hour or two, then went to the office. A seven-day work week was pretty common among expats in Kabul, even when we only got paid for five or six. People went in to the office on Fridays, often because that was where the e-mail was, and stayed to take care of a few odds and ends. Plus, we wanted to get as much paperwork as possible done before the beginning of the holy month of Ramadan, when shorter work days and closed government offices would make negotiating the bureaucracy a nightmare. I offhandedly asked Pete if he was going to honor the Ramadan fast, and he glanced up with a challenge in his grin. "Well, we don't have time for anyone in the office to be all like, 'We're fasting and we can't do shit.' I'd like to be able to say, 'Hell, *I* can fast and still do shit.' You?"

I shrugged. "Sure. I don't want to flaunt my lunch in front of Jahan and the guys, and I figure fasting would be easier than smuggling food into the bathroom. More dignified, definitely."

"Done. Let's fast."

"Plus, it would drive poor Zee crazy if we ate a big dinner in front of her while she's trying to make it to sundown without eating."

"Good point. Let's fast anyway."

Zulaikha was delighted to hear that we were going to join her in the fast. Besides appreciating the companionship, she was plainly pleased that Pete and I were giving ourselves an infinitesimally greater chance of getting into heaven. Our other Afghan friends, who I think tended to consider us beyond redemption, greeted our decision with general incredulity and the sly question, "Ah yes, but what time do you get up for breakfast?" In Pete's case, the answer was generally, "Not at all." I tended to drowse awake around four in the morning, munch a couple McVitie's biscuits, down a liter of water, and fall asleep again. All this was before the dawn call of the muezzin, and we didn't eat or drink again until sundown. Zulaikha initially tried to muster us for a full breakfast, which would have been marginally more meritorious, but then started snoozing through the alarm herself. Our work was so relentless that I usually didn't notice I was hungry until we drove home in the evening. In the cool of the autumn, even going without water was manageable. By the time dusk rolled around, we were all famished and ready to pack away a grand *iftar* fast-breaking dinner.

I spent my second Thursday evening in Kabul taking iftar with our project logistics assistant, Aziz. We had been out late that afternoon, visiting Deh Mazang, the welders' quarter down by Kabul Zoo, with a sheaf of procurement contracts for wheeled water tanks. The metalworkers had sat patiently while we skimmed through the various contractual provisions—no parts from Iran, the price includes a paint job, all work to be completed within two weeks—and by the time we had gotten everything signed, the sun was touching the peaks of the Paghman range in the west. As we drove back through the wreckage of West Kabul, Aziz asked me, "Mr. Joel, why are you not married?"

"Haven't met the right woman," I replied glibly.

Aziz nodded with interest. I knew he was unmarried himself. "Can't your mother and father help?"

"They don't know the right woman either," I said. "I'm going to have to find my own wife. Was this all part of the Wahdat Party area back in the war, by the way?" I gestured at the broken cityscape around us.

"Yes, they fought here. What if your father said no to the woman you found?"

"I would think about what he said very carefully, because I respect him. But in the end, I would make my own choice. Sorry, Aziz . . . Who was based on that mountain during the war?"

"The television mountain? Massoud was there. He fired shells at this area when he fought the Hazaras. Gulbuddin was on that other mountain for a while, before Massoud drove him back to the south. You have a girlfriend?" Aziz queried. Our young driver listened with obvious curiosity.

"Sort of," I said. I had been dating a terrific fellow grad student in Boston, but when I moved to Washington the relationship had subsided into a mostly-friendship. This seemed a difficult thing to explain. "What about all these bullet holes here?"

"It was a Hazara base. They fought against Sayyaf's men from Paghman. Many people died. If you have a girlfriend, maybe you will wait a long time to get married." Aziz grinned nervously.

"No, I'd like to be married," I said with feeling. "You're right, some people in America are happy to live together as boyfriend and girlfriend for many years. But I would rather find the right woman, get married, have a few children . . ."

"How many children?"

"I don't know," I said, laughing. "I'll ask my wife." At this our Tajik driver suddenly chortled and nodded. Aziz gave a puzzled nod and, clearly hoping for more details on the girlfriend-wife distinction, invited me to take iftar at his home. Our young driver was initially reluctant. He probably had his own family meal to attend, but after some hushed but insistent appeals in Dari from Aziz, he agreed to join us.

Aziz lived with his parents and seven siblings in Khair Khana, one of the neighborhoods on the northwestern outskirts of Kabul that had survived the mujahidin war more or less intact. Refugees from West Kabul and the other frontline neighborhoods had poured into Khair Khana and stayed. Today it was a sandy crush of small, square compounds threaded with narrow alleys. Aziz hustled us through his family's tiny courtyard and into a cozy, carpeted room with long floor cushions, the *hujra* or guest room where nonfamily visitors were entertained. After allowing me to give cursory salaams to his flustered sisters, Aziz ducked out and drew a curtain across the doorway. It was the last I saw of his family, with the exception of the brother and six-year-old sister who would periodically bring in food.

We sat cross-legged around a plastic tablecloth, and at the dusk call of the muezzin, we all drank deeply from the bottled mineral water Aziz had produced for the occasion. Then the iftar meal arrived. We tore off chunks of warm, ridged naan and tucked into heaps of mashed potatoes (deliciously heavy on the garlic, coriander, and pepper), fresh curd, and barely fried eggs that rolled liquescent around the plate until we mopped them up with our bread. I ate until I was bursting, then leaned back to savor the pleasure of realizing just how hungry I had been. An austere country like Afghanistan would offer this kind of pleasure often: the banquet after the fast, harvest after hunger, the rain after the drought.

Over our dessert of lightly salted pomegranate seeds, I asked Aziz what he would do when our current project was finished. "I will find some other international NGO to work for. It is the only job, especially for me."

"What do you mean?"

Aziz shrugged. He had taken off his light blue suit coat, and in his rolled-up shirt sleeves and dusty polyester trousers, I realized how thin he was. "My father was in the national army when Dr. Najibullah was president. When we went to our village in the south five years ago, they called us all Communists. It is the same with me. I work with the French and Americans, and they call me a foreigner." He shook his head glumly.

I felt for him. Somewhere between the values of his rural clan and his Western colleagues, there had to be a balance he could justify to himself: cosmopolitan but righteous. The trick was believing in it.

Into the Minefield

Ghorband Valley, Parwan—October 25, 2003

I left Kabul only once on that first assignment, for a morning in the Shamali Plain just north of the capital. The Shamali was about as far as most foreigners ever traveled outside Kabul; it was safe, close, and photogenic—with plenty of war damage to keep journalists happy and aid agencies busy. Our Quick Impact Project's work had been focused there, helping restore the region to its old glory as Kabul's breadbasket. Pete and Zulaikha were heading to the far corner to see what was holding up our last dam-building project on the Ghorband River. I was curious to see what was left of the Afghanistan that older Afghans reminisced about, the prewar paradise of orchards and verdant hillsides.

"There will be too much traffic on the main road today," Basir advised as we crammed into his Land Cruiser shortly after dawn. "We will go through Deh Sabz." We drove north over a low range of hills and into a muted gray wasteland. *Deh Sabz* meant "Green Village" in Dari; I could only imagine that somewhere out there was an oasis that had given its name to the entire desert. Basir flew across the empty flats, unchecked by traffic, slowing only for the occasional bump or trench in the road. Periodically the rusted frames of tanks, artillery, and troop transports appeared along the roadside. "Some of this is from the Russians," Basir commented. "Most is from the fighting between Massoud and the Taliban."

When the Taliban had pushed Ahmad Shah Massoud out of Kabul to the north, the Shamali Plain had become the war's new front line. For three years, the two armies surged back and forth, fighting bitterly for vital assets like the Bagram Air Base. Only in 1999 did the Taliban finally gain control of the region, after carrying out a scorched-earth policy in Shamali villages that favored Massoud, leveling their fruit groves and dynamiting their houses and canals.

We crested another rugged incline at the north end of the Deh Sabz flats, and the desert gave way to walled fields and homes. Large white check marks had been painted on the recently repaired packed-earth walls, and white stones lined the roadside. I remembered an Australian friend explaining the code for travel around Kabul: "White graffiti means the de-miners have been through. If you see red stones, *stay on the road*. If you don't see any colored stones, stay on the road. If you see white stones, ask yourself seriously whether you have a reason to leave the road."

Long famous for its vines and orchards, the Shamali region was now the landmine heartland of Afghanistan. Massoud and the Taliban had both reinforced their ever-shifting front lines with tens of thousands of buried explosives, adding to extensive Soviet minefields. Afghanistan as a whole was one of the most heavily mined countries on earth. The UN guessed it would take a decade just to clear the most dangerous areas. Meanwhile, Afghans were being killed and injured at a rate of about a thousand mine victims per year. As we drove toward Charikar bazaar, we passed a one-legged man on a bicycle pedaling gamely down the road.

I had been looking forward to the Shamali scenery and was disappointed at first to find the foliage almost entirely hidden by walls. Many of the surviving vineyards and orchards were tucked into people's home compounds. The fields and dry, scrubby pastures were often walled off too, to reinforce property boundaries and allow women to work there modestly. The patches of green we did see were visually overwhelmed by the parched brown mountain ridge that towered on the western side of the plain.

We sped through the drab terrain until mid-morning, when the road dropped precipitously away into the valley of the Ghorband River and the landscape was transformed. From this height, we could see over any wall, and the broad river basin running away to the east revealed itself as an unbroken expanse of fields, trees, and vines fed by a silver skein of canals. I had never lived in a desert before, and I was caught off guard by the intense pleasure of being suddenly immersed in green.

We rumbled off the main highway and jounced along a dirt track toward the sharp cut where the river left the mountains. "This road wasn't one of ours," Pete clucked disapprovingly. "That European Union group patched this up last year. Look at it—it's already fallen apart. You can pay hundreds of people to fucking shovel dirt into potholes, but they won't thank you when the road washes out again next year."

As we reached the mountains, barren slopes shot up to either side of us. The cloudy waters of the Ghorband churned at the bottom of the gorge. On the far side, tier after tier of canals had been carved into the steep slope, supported by dry-mason rock walls built all the way up from the valley floor. Most of the downstream greenery depended on these canals, so our Quick Impact Project was installing durable concrete dams at the three highest intakes to keep them from being washed out in the spring floods. As Basir wheeled around a bend, we heard the *whut-whut-whut* of a pump and saw men swarming around a deep pit in the riverbed. A sandbag cofferdam diverted the river from the worksite. This would be the topmost of our three diversion dams. It looked like it had a long way to go.

When we got out of the car, I glanced up and found my eyes held by the skyline. Unlike the Himalayas where I had grown up, the Hindu Kush was not softened by a yearly monsoon. Wind and torrents of snowmelt were the shaping forces here, and they had created a landscape of knives. Staring at the jagged outline of the gorge against the sky, I felt a familiar craving to clamber as high as I could, to perch at the top and see what a whole horizon of these austere Afghan mountains looked like. "Where does this road go?" I asked reverently, gesturing on past our vehicle.

"Bamiyan," said Basir tersely. "Maybe eight hours."

I had heard of Bamiyan, a broad valley at the mountainous heart of Afghanistan, in the middle of the Hazara homeland. The largest Buddha statues in the world had stood there until early in 2001, when the Taliban had blown them up in a fit of iconoclasm. I felt an absurd, barely resistible desire to ask Basir to get back in the car and keep driving. Instead, I looked away and shuffled down the steep trail to the worksite.

Pete was already in action. He had found the supervisory engineer from our Afghan partner agency, a short man wearing a flat white skullcap and a bristling full beard. The supervisor was politely incredulous when Pete reminded him that the project was supposed to end by the beginning of November; the downstream communities had only recently allowed him to divert the water out of the canal. Pete nodded. "I understand, but we won't be able to fund any more work after the project closing date. How long will it take you to finish it?"

"Do not worry, sir; if you give me . . . ," the supervisor glanced vaguely around the site, "fourteen more days, I will have it finished."

"Why fourteen days?" Pete pressed. "Can you break that down for me? Will it take you three days to finish excavation, five days for stonemasonry, and so on?"

"Twelve days. Definitely twelve days."

"No—can you tell me *why* twelve days? What is your work schedule?"

The supervisor looked pained and thought silently for a long moment. "I would say . . . thirteen days, sir. Do not worry; if you just give me thirteen days, we will finish the dam."

I drifted away as the wrangling continued. Fifteen minutes later, Pete walked over to me, disgruntlement and relief warring on his face. "Okay. When you add up the time needed for each activity in each process, it falls within the time we have. Plus, there's some stuff they can work on simultaneously." He shook his head. "It's funny; you meet these guys who could build a dam with their eyes closed out of whatever shit you hand them, but if you ask them to break the job down into tasks and schedule it, they're lost."

The supervisor strode stiffly up to us, and Pete turned to him. "Thank you, Engineer. I know it's hard to work during Ramadan. Your whole crew is pushing hard to get this done, and we really appreciate your effort." He had that grave, formal tone in his voice again, which I'd noticed when he addressed our guards the first evening. The supervisor half-regained his smile and beckoned us after him to see the rest of the site.

• • •

I had wavered for years before going into international development, plagued by the half-conscious assumption that to work usefully abroad I would need to be some kind of technical expert: a doctor, a forester, or an engineer like my father. Working with Pete Siu in 2003, I started to see what a mere manager could offer the Afghan reconstruction. Beyond the dams, roads, chickens, wells, and other concrete benefits of our project, Pete was leaving a personal legacy of management skills and tools.

It wasn't just a matter of helping one undertrained engineer in Ghorband sit down and condense his technical knowledge into a work schedule. Pete had spent long hours at the offices of our four partner Afghan aid organizations, getting them up to speed on accounting and reporting systems that would help them run more efficiently and transparently. On his own initiative, without any funding or suggestion from USAID, he had launched a monthly series of women's leadership seminars. Pete had noticed that a lot of Kabul-based aid organizations had only one junior female employee, and that most of those women had no access to mentors, peers, or a career path. Our own project's young administrative assistant, Hossai, had been a cardinal example.

"Hossai didn't have much to do around the office, and she had no confidence," Pete explained wryly. "She was super resistant at first when I asked her to set up the seminar program, but I basically forced her to. I started the ball rolling, and she had to carry it because I couldn't be involved in the meetings at all. They were safe spaces, for women only, with everyone speaking Dari." To lead the discussions, Hossai and Pete invited some of the most successful female leaders in Kabul: a top lawyer, journalist, and university professor; aid organization directors; civil servants; an Afghan Air Force general; the country's first woman presidential candidate. The junior professional women who attended the seminars were soon enthusiastically networking, sharing problems, and getting an idea of potential career paths. Hossai took over the program, and within a few months, her family was commenting on her steep increase in self-confidence.

"It took like zero resources. Just time, plus a meeting space that we had available anyway," Pete said, sounding unusually somber. "Women get so screwed over here. Especially the young ones, trying to figure out if they can have a career or just fit in with traditional expectations. No one had been doing anything to give them a support network, or just a place they could talk safely about whatever's on their minds. I hope someone else picks it up and keeps it going."

In general, Pete had poured lots of energy into training and mentoring our own project staff. He built up their computer, accounting, and English skills and helped them make the most of previously unimaginable opportunities. I never met Hossai, because Pete and Zulaikha had helped her get a visa to study in Wales. On one of our busiest days in November, Pete set several hours aside for the project's young monitoring officer, Farid, who had similarly applied for a study program in the United States.

Pete personally ran Farid's visa application over to the U.S. Embassy to make sure it got through the gate by the deadline. On his return to the office, he sat Farid down and gave him a ferocious practice interview. He picked on every flaw in Farid's English, criticizing him for using the passive voice, interrogating him mercilessly about his prospects of returning to Afghanistan. When Farid stammered, paused, or smiled nervously, a stone-faced Pete rebuked him for it and pushed him to answer promptly and naturally. Just as I was thinking, *I could never be that relentless to someone*, Pete handed Farid over to me to continue the rehearsal. He leaned down to whisper to me as he left the room.

"Be hard on him. He's good, but he doesn't know what he's in for."

Sounds familiar, I thought apprehensively, after I had finished practicing with Farid. No one had grilled me before I took off to Afghanistan. They checked to see if I was willing to go, and that was about it. I still had no idea what I was in for; I didn't know if I was able to do what Pete did. But my principal qualification, the willingness to come back, had been growing steadily stronger as I formed Afghan friendships and caught the first hints of the country's magnificent natural beauty. I was finally, solidly hooked the day I followed Ray Baum into a minefield.

Sherdarwaza, Kabul—November 7, 2003

Ray Baum, the bluff Alaskan who had been Pete's boss, was still living in our guesthouse. I didn't see much of him for the first couple weeks of my trip. Chemonics' RAMP project was in a start-up frenzy; Ray often got back from the RAMP office at ten o'clock or later, and my jet lag knocked me out around nine if I was lucky. When we eventually got to know each other, though, we discovered that we had an interest in common: hiking the 1,400-year-old boundary wall of Kabul.

Rising squarely in the middle of Kabul are twin mountains: Asmayi (informally known as Television Mountain, for its forest of broadcasting antennae) and the higher, more barren Sherdarwaza. The Kabul River trickles through the steep, narrow ravine between the peaks. The second mountain is the anchor of Old Kabul, which spreads out from its skirts in a tightly packed, mostly treeless maze of small houses. The old city's boundary wall runs far above the last houses of the city along Sherdarwaza's jagged summit ridge, from an imposing if dilapidated castle at one end to the abrupt plunge to the Kabul River at the other. From the minute I first saw the long wall, I'd wanted to walk it from end to end.

Like every bit of high ground in Kabul, Asmayi and Sherdarwaza had been poles in the mujahidin civil war. Ahmad Shah Massoud had set up his artillery on Asmayi; Gulbuddin Hekmetyar had dug in on Sherdarwaza, until Massoud forced him out to the south. Both mountains were still plagued with mines and rumors of mines. I'd heard secondhand accounts of people exploring Sherdarwaza, though, and Ray was enthusiastic. "Been meaning to do that since I got here," he said cheerfully. "Looks like a great hike. Just been too damn busy."

So early one Friday morning, Ray, Basir, and I arrived at the Kabul River side of the mountain. Basir was a former mujahid himself and had spent much of the 1980s up in the Paghman range sniping at Soviet troops. Like most of my Afghan friends, he didn't climb mountains unless he had to and had never been up Sherdarwaza. He seemed entertained at the idea of escorting us, though, and I figured he could get us out of any trouble we were likely to find. Basir suggested that we start with a gentle climb up the western shoulder of the mountain, but Ray and I both wanted to follow the wall as strictly as possible, which meant starting at the foot of the ravine and scrambling straight up. "It's like sheep hunting in Alaska," Ray said confidently. "The cliffs look tricky from a distance, but when you get there, you can always find a way up."

The lower slope of Sherdarwaza was densely inhabited, with sturdy mud houses built on tall stone terraces. The friendly neighborhood headman told Basir that a couple of Westerners had explored around the foot of the old wall, but we were the first he'd seen who wanted to hike all the way up and over. He also assured us, to our relief, that there were no land mines along the wall. As the incline grew steeper, the houses dwindled to a scattering of small stone buildings balanced on rocky outcrops, many still only half-built. Kabul's population boom was driving people ever higher on Asmayi and Sherdarwaza, despite the lack of water and the near certainty of losing everything if an earthquake hit. We soon left the last homes behind. Basir began to cough heavily and drifted away to take a less steep path up. Ray went straight for the wall, scaling its 1,400-year-old parapets wherever he could. I mostly stuck with the craggy precipice just to its left, elated to be rock climbing in fresh air after weeks pent up in the Kabul smog.

Basir rejoined us at the first crest, where the wall leveled out and began a more gradual ascent to the peak. For a couple hundred yards the wall was reduced to a rough mound of earth and stone, toppled a decade earlier by Massoud's artillery. As we approached the summit ridge, the wall rose crookedly up again, pierced with occasional shell holes. Soon we were close to the earth ramparts at the top. At this point, however, we noticed three young men loping up the hill toward us. Ray asked Basir to find out what they wanted and strode briskly toward the summit. I hung back and heard Basir matter-of-factly say, "Mine?" Ray was about to climb into the fortifications at the peak. Running toward him, I yelled, "Ray, I think I heard them say . . ."

"Mine!" one of the young men yelled as he crested the wall below, illustrating his point with an explosive noise and gesture. Basir craned his neck to face us and clarified helpfully: "He says there are mines up there." I froze. Ray looked around doubtfully, then continued at a deliberate pace in the direction he'd been going. This elicited a frantic burst of Dari from the three young men. Ray scowled, and we walked back down together.

Our benefactors informed us that there were mines everywhere up here, and that a shepherd had been killed by one just a few months before. Ray suggested that surely there were only a few mines, and that we should be safe if we stayed to the main trails. The young men persistently disagreed. "Does it seem funny at all to you, these kids just showing up here all of a sudden?" Ray murmured. He was clearly more convinced by the neighborhood headman who declared the wall to be mine-free. "Could be they're hoping to get some money out of us. Be careful."

At length, one of the young men tentatively led us up to the summit fort, a cluster of run-down machine-gun nests littered with shell casings and kite string. Much of Kabul's morning haze had burned off, and we had breathtaking views out to the lofty Paghman range, Basir's homeland. Glancing around, wondering where the mines were, I felt my joy honed by an unusual vertigo. It was like admiring the view from a high cliff: a misstep could literally kill you. We realized we hadn't actually reached the topmost peak of Sherdarwaza, which was a few hundred yards farther along the fortified summit ridge. As we watched, a tiny silhouette walked up to that peak from the far side of the mountain.

This was more than enough to convince Ray that we could go there too. He interrogated the young men by way of Basir, and got them to concede that we probably would be safe on the broad trail that ran a short distance below the wall. Ray headed down to the trail and forged ahead, me and Basir in reluctant train. After a few minutes, though, Ray's eyes began to wander back to the wall; it was clear that the magnetism that had drawn him back on the cliff was still in full effect. "I think we should try to stay closer to the wall," Ray said decisively. "Try not to step on any loose piles of rock." He stepped off the path—behind us, the three young men threw up their hands and stalked away—and began climbing up to the old wall.

Through the shock, my justification mechanisms quickly kicked in. *If he does step on a mine, I'll need to drag him out. And if he gets more than a few steps ahead, I'll lose track of where he's put his feet.* But my feet had already been moving, before I had come up with any conscious reason. "You figure if they mine anyplace, it'll be the area right in front of the wall," Ray commented as we walked gingerly onward. "Once we're on the wall, we should be fine." I concentrated on stepping precisely in his footsteps, and wondered how Ray got his sheep back down those cliffs in Alaska.

After three everlasting minutes, we made it safely back to the wall. Basir and I exhaled windily. At the high peak, a bunch of Afghan soldiers emerged from their dugout to look at us with some curiosity. They had a well-oiled Russian 22mm artillery gun on a tripod, a fence made of old rockets and mortar casings, and a very unfriendly off-white dog. We chatted with them for a while, and they reassured us that all the mines were on the West Kabul side of the mountain. Ray had been right, or lucky; on the Old City side of the wall, we had been safe. We surveyed the hills off to the south, with the soldiers pointing out minefields. The view was amazing, and I idly imagined taking a few guys from the garrison out to mark "Mine-Free" hiking trails for tourists.

Leaving the peak, we ambled down a stretch of the ancient wall that was essentially intact, battlements and all. Here the extraordinary scale of the thing really struck us: at least twelve feet thick, built from a darker, harder stone than any found on the mountain itself, sealed with clay and mortar on a waterless slope. Virtually all the supplies for the wall would have been carried up the mountain. Basir explained that the old wall predated Islam in Afghanistan, built during one of the chaotic times when no single kingdom or empire dominated the region. From a military standpoint, the wall was majestically superfluous. Surely a few summit forts would have been enough to deter enemies from attacking over the mountain, and building a sheer succession of parapets down the ravine of the Kabul River could only have been meant to impress.

Through old arrow slits, we could see the valley to the east: Shuhada-i-Salehin, the largest cemetery in a city full of graves. The graveyard ended at Kabul's widest lake, now an empty basin dried up over the long drought years. On the other side, the sounds of the old city of Kabul reverberated up through the clear, dry air: the laughter of children, the clangor of metal-smiths, chanting from the Shi'a mosque. About halfway down the mountain, the ancient wall collapsed into a mound again, with a crooked pillar of brick and stone rising like a monumental finger from the last rampart. We descended to the remains of the Bala Hissar, the High Citadel, a massive, battered castle crowning the final foothill of Sherdarwaza. Basir warned us not to approach the walls. "There are *many* mines there," he said with an emphasis that brooked no question.

From the Bala Hissar, Ray called for a ride to the office, but Basir's willingness to indulge my tourism was at its height, so I convinced him to spend another hour or two showing me around. We drove to the far end of Kabul, where twin low hills marked the beginning of the road south to Kandahar. Atop one hill was the much-abused concrete and glass frame of the Intercontinental Hotel. The other held a small, domed palace: the Bagh-i-Bala, or High Garden, of Amir Abdurrahman, first ruler of modern Afghanistan.

In the late nineteenth century, Britain and Russia had warily agreed to leave Afghanistan as a buffer zone between their expanding Asian empires. They drew the country's borders without regard to Afghan preferences, excluding Pashtun-majority bits of British India like the cities of Peshawar and Quetta, and including the northeastern "chicken neck" of Afghanistan, the frozen Wakhan corridor, which the amir of Kabul had to be bribed to accept. Ultimately, however, Amir Abdurrahman chose not to fight the foreign imperialists and instead spent his life unifying the territory within his artificial borders. Known as the Iron Amir, he crushed tribal revolts, subjugated the previously free Nuristanis and Hazaras using British guns, and shrewdly resettled restive Pashtun clans in areas where they would be ethnic minorities.

In 1901, Abdurrahman died in the Bagh-i-Bala, his summer palace. His death marked the first time that any ruler inherited effective authority over the whole territory of modern Afghanistan. It was also the country's last peaceful transition of government to date. Every king, president, premier, and amir in the twentieth century was forcibly, often fatally ejected from power.

We found the Bagh-i-Bala closed and shuttered, its plaster gone shabby with age. The Iron Amir's wading pool had been replaced in the 1970s by a swimming pool, now dry and dust-stained. Basir meandered through the grounds with me, hands clasped behind his back, his eyes resting for long seconds on the gnarled conifers and newly raked but lifeless garden beds. "These trees are very old, you know," he said suddenly, nodding at a drought-stricken pine. "When I was a young man, they were old. There were many grapevines here then, and flowers everywhere. And fruit trees. It was very beautiful." He spoke gruffly, with no trace of sentimentalism. He simply wanted me to see the barren plot around us for what it had been—and might be again.

That day in 2003, Afghanistan settled into my marrow. I was already fascinated by its history, and I had been struck by the generosity, kindness, and resilience of my Afghan friends. After hiking the old wall, I fell in love with the stark beauty of the Afghan landscape—and, I had to admit, the frisson of slight but mortal danger. After visiting the Bagh-i-Bala, I began to see the past and future garden in the present wasteland.

Kabul Airport—November 15, 2003

Mullah Omar's Drought was well and truly over, and for the second year in a row, Kabul was getting its rain in season. Unfortunately, the steady drizzle made air travel impossible; Kabul's civilian airport lacked the radar and lights to guide planes safely down in conditions of poor visibility. My first assignment was finished, but I might not be leaving any time soon. I had eased my way to the front of the crowd at check-in, and when the guards briefly parted to admit two passengers through security, I walked briskly in with them. The three of us sat in a deserted aisle, comforted by the idea that if anyone got out of Kabul that day, it would be us.

One of my two companions was a young Afghan-American with a base-ball cap and a Long Island accent whose father owned the Pepsi franchise in Afghanistan. The family had refurbished their old mansion in the Kabul sub-urbs, which now (the Pepsi scion assured me) surpassed its former glory: swimming pool, marble floors, state-of-the-art video and stereo systems. The cheerful, T-shirted young man leaned against a pillar while his retainers flut-tered about, consulting with airport staff and giving us updates on the weather.

My other companion was an Indian engineer named Mukesh. His pale, plump face sagged slightly, as if he had lost weight, and he walked with a stiff-legged limp. "I am going home to England. And about bloody time. A week ago, I was very badly shot."

"I'm sorry?" I said. From his tone of voice he might have been describ-ing a commonplace irritation, but his eyes were abnormally wide and un-blinking.

It turned out that he worked for an Indian engineering company, han-dling a construction project at the U.S. air base in the Shamali Plain. "One week ago, I went up to collect a payment of several hundred thousand U.S. dollars. I was driving back to Kabul from Bagram by the desert road—you know Deh Sabz?—when I saw a Toyota truck full of gunmen in my mirror. Someone had told them I would be there. Of course I sped up, and they chased after me, shooting at my car. First the bastards shot my back tires, and then one of the front ones as well. I was hit here," indicating his shoulder, "and here," his buttock. His piqued expression was slightly comical, as though what really irked him was the indignity of it all.

"My car flew off the road and landed upside down. One of the gunmen, he walked out to me and stuck his gun in my face, told me he knew I had a lot of dollars. I pointed to the bag of money and he took it. When he walked away, I undid my seat belt, and I crawled out the window of the car. I could hear the robbers arguing with their friend, asking why he didn't kill me. They shot a few more times into the car and then drove away. An hour later, an American patrol arrived. I called for help and they found me, out there in the desert. And then they started asking me angry questions about where the money had gone. I had been shot—here, and here!—and they thought I had been part of the robbery!"

I expressed the appropriate sympathy, thinking queasily that only a few days earlier, I had been driving around the streets of Kabul with twenty-seven thousand dollars in my jacket pocket to pay for construction equipment. Afghanistan still had scarcely any banks, so huge cash payments were pretty much unavoidable. Mukesh pursed his lips. "Bloody Afghans. I tell you, they are barbarians here. Barbarians. It will take a thousand years to build anything useful out of this damned country. I am *never* coming back."

"Sir?" It was a valet of the heir to the Kabul Pepsi empire. "There will be no planes today. They cannot land any planes."

We cursed and walked back through the guards and the dissipating crowd. I met Basir in the parking lot where he had waited all day, and we drove back to the office through the drizzle. The next day, I arrived at the airport around six o'clock in the morning. At mid-morning, there was a half-hour break in the rain during which four planes landed in quick succession. We cheered as each one touched down. There was a frenzy in the waiting room as each flight was called—first Herat, then Baku. Once again Mukesh got ushered to the front of the line due to his injury. Unfortunately, as soon as the Dubai flight was called a couple dozen Afghans surged up around him, and I winced as he was crushed, squawking, against the doorway. He managed to extricate himself, and I heard him mutter, "Barbarians!" one last time before he limped through the door.

As we walked across the tarmac to the plane, the clouds parted. For the first time I saw snow on the ring of mountains surrounding Kabul. The white mantle softened the craggy wall into a thing of arresting beauty. I knew I would be back.

Salaam to Helmand

Kart-i-Sakhi, Kabul—November 17, 2004

For half an hour, as we drove between the Park Palace guesthouse and the RAMP office, I leaned up to the dust-flecked Land Cruiser window and did my best to ignore the frantic whirl of tasks in my head. The squatter shacks had crept a little higher on the antenna-crested flank of Television Mountain, I thought; a few more of West Kabul's shelled ruins had been torn down or patched up. It was my third trip to Afghanistan, and the packed streets of Kabul had become satisfyingly familiar. I looked forward to shedding my Western clothes and throwing on the kamiz partoog that Jahan had given me back in June.

A bored-looking police guard waved our driver through the gate of the Afghan Ministry of Agriculture. Chemonics International's RAMP project was based in a cramped constellation of bungalows and trailers; the massive generator and Internet satellite dish unmistakably signaled the presence of well-funded expatriates. On my first Afghanistan trip a year ago, I had visited this office once or twice to drop off some papers. From April to June 2004, Chemonics had sent me back for a second assignment, working mostly with RAMP in Kabul but with plenty of travel around the fertile north and mountainous center of Afghanistan. Now I was back on familiar ground with old friends—but only for about a week. I just hoped that, over the coming year, some of the reference points I'd picked up in Kabul would be useful down in the completely unknown territory of Helmand.

The first person I saw when I strode into the main Chemonics bungalow was my friend Daud Sangarwal, an exceptionally sharp and haughty young Afghan manager. "Daud!" I called happily, extending a hand in his direction.

Daud's smile froze, half-formed, and he arched an incredulous eyebrow at me. Looking down, I realized that thanks to my jet lag and the sheaf of folders clutched under my right arm, I had unthinkingly offered him my left hand. As in many Asian cultures, Afghans eat with their right hand and reserve the other for cleaning themselves after defecation and other polluting tasks. The taboo takes extra force from the example of the Prophet Muhammad, who was reportedly particular in such matters. I abashedly switched my folders and presented Daud with the proper hand.

"You are going to Lashkargah?" Daud said primly, returning my handshake. "You had better not do that there, or you will be dead in the first week."

After apologizing to Daud, I headed off to console myself by finding other familiar faces in the RAMP office. I soon found Jahan, Mumtaz, and the other guys I'd worked with on my previous trips. They were delighted that I was back in Afghanistan, and laughingly taught me the first rudiments of Pashto that I would need to get by in Helmand. *Tsanga ye*—how are you? *Khuday paman*—good-bye. *Manana*—thank you. And the all-important question of whether I wanted *chai sia* or *chai sabz* (black or green tea, in Dari) would in the south be between *toor chai* or *shney chai*.

My Kabuli friends also promised to help me with my most immediate tasks as the field administrator for our Helmand project. My job was going to involve a little bit of everything: opening a bank account, finding us vehicles, buying our equipment, hiring many of our Afghan staff. I was uneasily aware that I was facing a learning curve so steep it was almost vertical. I had never done anything remotely this complex before; managing an $18 million project was clearly going to throw my inexperience into sharp, painful relief.

In particular, I had little sense of what it would take to keep us safe in a place like Helmand. I had gotten some idea of the expected precautions from Dave Guier, the Chemonics director who would be monitoring our project from Washington. Dave was, in a word, intense—a workaholic with a lean face, piercing eyes, and short-cropped hair, who tended to move and speak in short, clipped bursts. Behind his restless exterior, Dave was a deeply gentle man with a wry sense of humor, but during the Helmand proposal, he had been as high-strung and serious as I'd ever seen him. "Okay, Mr. Field Admin, you'll need to have a handle on this. When you get there, you'll need to rent two staff houses for you and the other expats. We're going to budget a few thousand dollars extra for making them habitable and adding on security measures."

"Right. Uh, what kind of security measures?" I had asked, trying to sound brisk.

Dave had rattled off a quick, almost absentminded litany. "Blast film for the windows, razor wire for the walls, a safe room—windowless, lined with sandbags—where you can lock yourselves in if things get ugly, security lighting around the walls, guard huts . . . check out the report from my RAMP visit."

Still, I felt slightly more cheerful after seeing my Kabuli friends and getting the language lesson. My next stop was the project trailer park where I hoped to find Johannes Oosterkamp, Chemonics' advisor on irrigation work. I had gotten to know the brusque, gray-haired Dutch engineer a little during my time on RAMP. He was notorious for always speaking his mind without varnish, and he had a knack for incisively finding the weaknesses in any plan. These traits greatly endeared Johannes to everyone who had not wound up on the wrong end of his more scathing judgments. In conversation, he tended to speak somberly and forcefully, lending his comments extra emphasis with raised eyebrows and pursed lips. This extreme gravity often veiled a joke—but God help the man who laughed when Johannes was in earnest. "So you are going to Helmand?" he greeted me now. "On this poppy project, this emergency jobs business."

"That's the idea," I said ruefully. In the development industry, the kind of jobs we were going to create were called "cash-for-work": simple, large-scale manual labor, aimed at getting money into people's pockets. But the term *emergency jobs* was pretty apt. Everything about this project so far had been carried out in an atmosphere of emergency.

A month ago, Chemonics had confidently assumed it would be a shoe-in for any Afghan poppy projects. After all, the company had won generous praise from USAID for its efforts at weaning farmers off coca in Colombia and Peru. We had heard the rumor that USAID's harried Kabul office was about to announce big cash-for-work projects in Afghanistan's top three poppy-producing provinces, so we had spent the last weeks of October preparing a grand scheme for a three-province project.

Then on November 3, USAID's Kabul officers sent Chemonics a withering e-mail informing us that they were leaning toward awarding all of the cash-for-work projects to other contractors. We had forty-eight hours to write a project proposal, focused exclusively on Helmand, that would change their minds. I remembered Chemonics' shocked senior vice president for Asia, Ron Ivey, urging us on with an emphatic tremor in his voice: "Ladies and gentlemen, we *cannot afford* to lose this project. This Helmand job is the gateway for all the alternative livelihoods contracts that USAID is about to bid out in Afghanistan. Literally hundreds of millions of dollars of contracts. We cannot let this one slip."

Chemonics was nothing if not a proposal-writing machine. The company prided itself on being able to whip up a plan and a team to carry out pretty much anything USAID might want to do: clean up air pollution in Cairo, train Russian judges, help Ugandans export cut flowers. But finding expert consultants who would agree on forty-eight hours' notice to spend a year in southern Afghanistan was impossible. Our only committed long-termer was Yaqub Roshan; we had written him in as government liaison when we thought we would have to coordinate our work in three provinces with the Kabul Ministry of Counter-Narcotics. Now that we were only supposed to work in Helmand, it wasn't even clear what he'd end up doing.

Chemonics' unflappable president, Ashraf Rizk, decided to cobble together a temporary team of the most impressive technical experts and Afghanistan veterans from the Chemonics home office. This "Go Team" would head out immediately for one month to set up the project. If we could sell USAID on the strength of a glowing rapid-response squad, we would win a little more time to recruit staff who would stay for a year. So Ashraf called up Ray Baum and talked him into accepting the position of Go Team leader. Pete Siu agreed to leave his well-feathered nest in the communications department to once again be Ray's deputy. The president made the rounds of the Washington office, relentlessly wheedling three or four of Chemonics' top staff into abandoning their Thanksgiving plans, promising that they'd all be home by Christmas.

Finally, they needed one junior staffer to go out indefinitely, ensuring some continuity between the Go Team and the long-term team. I think I was the only young Chemonics administrator who was actually eager to go to Helmand. At any rate, I was the first to volunteer, so I ended up on the proposal.

"I don't know if you saw the plan we sent to USAID?" I said cautiously to Johannes. "We don't know for sure what kind of jobs we're going to create. But I've heard Ray and Pete talk about getting lots of men to clean out silt from the irrigation ditches."

"Oh, yes, there will be plenty of work for you down there." Johannes nodded to himself. "I think I will fly down with you to have a look at the canals."

"That would be excellent," I said with fervent relief. "I saw one of your reports on the Helmand Valley irrigation system—was it the Boghra canal?" Johannes had worked in Afghanistan and Pakistan for decades, and his encyclopedic knowledge of the region came across in his famously wide-ranging, thorough reports. If our Go Team had one great area of weakness, it was specific knowledge of Helmand province. Ray had been down there a few times when he was fixing canals for RAMP, but we would need more knowledge than his to get this project off the ground.

"Ja, and so far we have only reports," Johannes said dourly. "In Helmand, RAMP has been all assessments, no action. Have I told you what *ramp* means in Dutch? It means disaster."

I wasn't sure whether to laugh or wince. Over the last year, the grand agriculture program had turned from a $130 million jewel in Chemonics' crown to a millstone around the company's neck. RAMP had suffered greatly from having too many cooks in the kitchen—or, as the more graphic Afghan proverb goes, "With too many doctors at the birth, the child's head will be deformed." Both USAID and Chemonics had struggled to inspire their Kabul staff to stay for more than a few months; the constantly changing faces and priorities were a management disaster. Most of the project's actual work was carried out not by Chemonics itself but by dozens of feisty independent subcontractors. The first minister of agriculture under the Karzai regime had been a Hazara warlord, Sayed Hussain Anwari, who by his own admission was better qualified to kill Taliban than to run the Afghan government's largest bureaucracy. On top of it all, the ambassador or the White House jumped in from time to time to demand that USAID carry out some politically essential project at once, treating RAMP as a sort of reconstruction slush fund. Our $18 million Helmand cash-for-work project was a case in point. To Chemonics' dismay, it was coming out of RAMP's budget.

"At least RAMP doesn't mean anything in Dari or Pashto," I offered wryly. "Unlike *our* project name."

The development profession is pathologically addicted to acronyms, and we figured our Helmand project's name should have alternative livelihoods—AL—in it somewhere. Back in Washington, Zulaikha had suggested SALAAM, and after some word-juggling, we had come up with a title to fit the acronym: Supporting Alternative Livelihoods Activities and Assistance Mobilization. "*Salaam* means peace in Arabic," Zee had reminded us. "And it's the most common greeting everywhere in the Muslim world. So it's like we're introducing, you know, peace."

It wasn't until we were en route to Kabul and reviewing reports on the opium economy that we discovered our clever acronym's full range of meanings. Within the Afghan drug trade, "salaam" was slang for the advance payments provided by opium traffickers to farmers as an incentive to plant poppy—in effect, a loan where the interest was claimed later in opium. So along with greetings and peace, our project would be associated with drug-running and exploitative moneylending. We were still debating alternative names two days later when we headed in for our first council of war with USAID.

Macrorayan, Kabul—November 19, 2004

I had been inside the American Embassy a couple of times before, and each visit made me profoundly grateful that I didn't work for the U.S. government—or at least, that I only worked for it at one remove. A grand new Embassy fortress was rising up among cranes and scaffolding on one side of the compound, but while it was under construction, the representatives of the world's mightiest state were crammed together in a ramshackle old edifice and a bunch of trailers. Their movements were limited by a strict curfew; the government security code for civilian employees required advance notice of any trip and forbade visits to any but a handful of "safe" Kabul neighborhoods and restaurants. A daunting cordon of U.S. Marines and Nepali Gurkha guards kept USAID staff insulated from the dangers of Afghanistan.

The claustrophobia and sense of constraint must have been maddening, especially for aid-agency swashbucklers of the Ray Baum model. A year earlier, I had visited a USAID office so densely packed that finding space for everyone's elbows, let alone workstations, was a major logistical triumph. At the end of a long day's work, the USAID staffers had retired to shared trailers a two-minute walk from their stifling office. Things had improved greatly since then. The Embassy had walled off a large field across from the main compound and built a temporary trailer city, big enough for its American staffers to have personal, air-conditioned spaces to work and sleep. Still, I wouldn't have readily surrendered my freedom to hike up Sherdarwaza or wander the bazaars of Kabul. I also didn't envy USAID the responsibility for managing the reconstruction of a country roughly the size of Texas from inside a bunker.

For security reasons, USAID contractors like us generally had to come "inside the wire" to get our marching orders. Today, there were ten of us: the whole Helmand Go Team, plus RAMP's top two managers. We flashed our passports at the heavily guarded gate and walked through the metal detectors. I scraped up the leftovers of my childhood Nepali language skills and chatted with the amused Gurkha sentries. Then we were all ushered in to USAID's office complex, an airtight, fluorescent maze of plastic passageways and trailers, permeated by the faint thrum of unseen generators. Ten more people were waiting for us in the conference room.

The grizzled man with sunken cheeks was mission director Patrick Fine, USAID's top man in Kabul. Seated around him were six other USAID staffers, including Dan Miller, a mustached, Minnesotan technical officer who had brought a much-needed steady hand to RAMP and would also have oversight of our Helmand project. In most countries, only USAID staff would have attended this kind of session. In Kabul, however, President Bush's

National Security Council had created a shadow USAID—a small group of high-powered advisors from the private sector, each monitoring a particular development area like agriculture, electricity, or education. They reported to the State Department but had been recruited by the Defense Department, the Bush administration's favored nation-building and development agency. These advisors were meant to shake up the faltering Afghan reconstruction with "outside-the-box" ideas. Though they had no independent budget, they had the powerful ambassador Zalmay Khalilzad's ear and a backchannel to the White House, which made them more powerful in their way than the agencies they were advising. Three of them had joined us for the meeting.

Patrick Fine introduced everyone, then congratulated us on our speedy arrival with a faintly acid tone that belied his words. "I can not overstate to you the importance Washington currently places on alternative livelihoods," he declared. The three National Security Council consultants nodded avidly. "I had hoped to start this kind of project much earlier. The problem has been choosing contractors to implement it. The problem, frankly, is that they're all a bunch of fucking liars." Fine glanced around balefully to give his expletive extra force.

"Since my arrival in Kabul, I have been trying to get our contractors to give me accurate work schedules. *Not one* has yet been able to stick to the projections they've given me. Believe me, I do not enjoy explaining to Ambassador Khalilzad why RAMP has failed to meet its targets. Again. And again." Fine spoke fervently into a stunned silence; no one had expected him to launch the meeting with such vitriol. "This is Chemonics' last chance to redeem its reputation in this country—to show that it can stick to its deadlines, keep management costs down, and limit its promises to those it can keep."

I glanced over at Ray and Pete, both of whom were impassively taking notes. It had to rankle that their little project in 2003—which had shown all the qualities Fine was asking for—had essentially been forgotten as USAID directors came and went. The two RAMP managers with us also appeared to be biting their tongues. Since their arrival, RAMP seemed to be finally emerging from its early deformity; the project had caught up with nearly all of its targets, and met several other emergency requirements that had come down from USAID. On the other hand, Fine's anger was understandable. Whatever the reasons for his contractors' many missed targets, ultimately Washington would blame his USAID mission—and Afghans from the Karzai cabinet to the Taliban insurgents would blame America.

"So we don't want your team to spend any more time than you have to in Kabul," Patrick Fine continued sharply. "We want you in Helmand as soon as humanly possible. We want to visit and see results within the next two weeks. And we want a realistic workplan, with targets you won't miss. As you can imagine, this project will be taking place under the most intense scrutiny. President Bush has asked the ambassador to keep him regularly informed of progress on the counter-narcotics front."

"That's right," an eager National Security Council consultant said, leaning in. "Condoleezza Rice will be getting weekly updates on this project."

"That's right," Fine repeated caustically. I suddenly wondered how much of this harangue was for Condi's benefit. "So falling short of your targets is not an option. Also, as you may know, USAID and its contractors have been taking a lot of flak for spending too much on management. I want seventy percent of this project's money to go to the people of Helmand. Whatever it costs you to administer the project, keep it below thirty percent, or Chemonics will not work with this USAID mission again." He leaned back in his chair, still glowering.

"Understood," Ray said gruffly. "We'll have you a draft workplan in two days."

"We appreciate that." Dan Miller, the agriculture technical officer, spoke up in a conciliatory tone. "Let's make sure we're all on the same page with the targets. We figure you should aim to employ roughly fifty thousand people for roughly fifty days' labor—that's a total of two and a half million work days by next November. We realize some of the activities will wind up being shorter than fifty days. Just keep your eye on that two and a half million total."

"Besides other aid groups, who do we need to coordinate with in Helmand?" Pete Siu asked briskly.

"Well, there's the PRT." Outside Kabul, the Pentagon and its NATO allies had set up experimental Provincial Reconstruction Teams, or PRTs—small military outposts that tried to win hearts and minds by funding local development projects and helping the provincial government provide security. "The Lashkargah PRT is only a month or two old, and they haven't quite finished setting things up yet. It should be up and running before long, though. You can harmonize your development activities to make the biggest impact. And they might be able to help you with security."

"What about the government of Afghanistan?"

"You'll be working with all the relevant ministries—rural development, agriculture, irrigation, and so on." Dan Miller glanced around, looking suddenly a little uncomfortable. "As for the provincial governor . . . well, USAID doesn't have a relationship with him. Ambassador Khalilzad knows him, of course. The ambassador knows all the governors. Down in Lashkargah, the

PRT commander can fill you in on the governor's background." I thought I recalled hearing that the governor of Helmand had been tied to the poppy trade. If true, I wondered how closely we would be working with him.

We spent another hour hashing out details with USAID and its National Security Council advisors. By the end of the meeting, I had realized just how much we wouldn't know until we arrived in Helmand. We had proposed to spend a little more than 1 percent of the project budget on security, but we really had no idea what it would take to protect ourselves—nor did USAID. For our proposal, Pete Siu had made educated guesses about the costs of the job-creation side of the project; but since we didn't know yet what jobs we would actually be creating, most of the details were clearly going to be improvised on the ground. I just hoped the improvising would be largely done before Christmas, when everyone except me and Yaqub went home.

When the conference was over, we retreated to lick our wounds at Lai Thai, Kabul's first Thai restaurant. "The mission director was not very diplomatic," Yaqub offered, with typical understatement.

Ray looked pained. "I don't think this was the right kind of meeting for making comments like that." Then he shook off his ire and rallied the troops. "But fair enough. Let's take it as a challenge. This is a great chance to exceed their expectations."

Pete glanced up from his Thai green curry. "We could start by picking a name that doesn't make us sound like a bunch of drug traffickers. Supporting Alternative Livelihoods Program—SALP?"

"It's got AL, but it's not a real word," I joked. "How about QUALMS? Quick Alternative Livelihoods . . . um, Mobilization . . . System?"

Ray shook his head. "Forget the AL. We're not really providing a long-term livelihood, just an income for this season. We're an alternative *income* project. And I think that's all we ought to call ourselves—AIP. Keep it simple."

"Ape?" Pete said with a snicker.

"Pronounce it how you like," Ray shrugged.

A Million Dollars a Mile

The Kabul–Kandahar Highway—November 24, 2004

At sunrise, the first cold light fell with rare clarity onto a mostly silent Kabul. The smoke of kerosene and wood and desiccated dung was just beginning to drift up from hundreds of thousands of compounds. The first Corollas coughed their way down streets that would soon be packed with vehicles and carts and pedestrians, all kicking up dust. As we rolled through the nearly deserted lanes of Shahr-i-Nau, I found that I missed the normal hubbub. Kabul's street crowds were something I could engage with; in the dawn emptiness, the high walls and shuttered shopfronts seemed to exclude us completely from the life of the city. The feeling of alienation mingled strangely with my excitement as we approached the rendezvous point for our convoy to Helmand.

Five of us had decided to travel from Kabul to Helmand by road, in a pair of Land Rovers loaded with essential project equipment. It was a slightly foolhardy plan, and I was primarily responsible for it. As part of my logistical duties, Ray had given me responsibility for security planning—a stopgap measure while Chemonics recruited a security manager with real experience.

A few days earlier, I had called Nick Downie, the British chief of the security network that offered free information and security coordination to every aid organization working in Afghanistan. His opinion of our road trip plans was plainly negative without being alarmist. "Bottom line: the Kabul-Kandahar Highway isn't safe. You'll have heard that these days, most convoys drive down and never see any trouble. But some get hit. Zabul and Kandahar provinces are core insurgent territory, and we've seen violence in Ghazni and Wardak as well. You just have to ask yourself: How would you feel if your convoy was the unlucky one?"

Yet I still ended up proposing that the majority of the team drive down to Helmand. Flights were unreliable, I pointed out to our leaders, and with USAID pressing us for early results, we didn't want to get half the team stuck in Kabul waiting for space on a plane. RAMP got its security from an American company, United States Protection & Investigations (USPI), whose Afghan troops ran regular armed convoys along the Kabul-Kandahar Highway. USPI's convoys had occasionally come under fire, but not all that often, considering how often they made the run. If we headed down under escort, the chance of anything going wrong was slim enough to be an acceptable risk. My suggestion fell on friendly ears. Everyone wanted to get down to Helmand reliably and soon, and I wasn't the only one with a tacit interest in seeing the lay of the land between Kabul and Lashkargah.

So in the early morning of November 24, a week after our arrival in Afghanistan, we drove up to USPI headquarters and waited while the convoy formed up around us. We would be driving down with a few vehicles from an Afghan landmine clearance organization. Our convoy was bookended by five battered Land Cruisers full of USPI's hired Afghan "shooters." USPI's bearded young Afghan captain wore wraparound military-issue shades from the bazaars around Bagram Air Base, which sold all sorts of American military paraphernalia (including, it later emerged, flash drives full of classified intelligence data). His men were dressed in a motley array of camouflage fatigues. Most of them carried Kalashnikov automatic rifles, and we glimpsed a rocket launcher on the backseat of one vehicle.

When our escorts gave the order, our ten-car convoy rolled out together, heading south through the increasingly busy streets. The Kandahar road began at a West Kabul roundabout, under a soaring wreckage of concrete, wire, and broken tile that had once been an abstract monument. Below the blasted sculpture, wiry day laborers swathed in rough brown *patu* shawls waited patiently for work. We drove past turbaned bird-sellers standing beside wire-mesh cages of chickens, pigeons, and fighting partridges. Fruit and vegetable vendors hawked mounds of pomegranates, pumpkins, and eggplant, plus carrots in a surprising range of colors: pale yellow, red-tinged pink, a deep purple-black. The carrot had originated in Afghanistan, and there were genetic strains here that hadn't made it out to the rest of the world. My mouth watered as I caught the aroma of *bulani*, deep-fried leek dumplings, Afghanistan's finest street food.

As we rolled through the street market, I could see the giant Russian-built Silo looming off to the north, its shell holes patched up and painted over. It was once again storing grain and milling flour for Kabul's innumerable bakeries—a small victory for development. When we reached the fringes of the city, the markets gave way to giant rock-crushing plants, and the worn, pitted road surface turned to smooth blacktop. We were passing onto the Afghan reconstruction's single most vaunted achievement to date: the 300-mile Kabul-Kandahar Highway.

The original highway had been part of the same Cold War aid competition that had produced the Silo. Starting in the 1950s, the Russians had built highways north from Kabul to the border with Soviet Central Asia, while the Americans had paved the main roads connecting Afghanistan to U.S. allies Pakistan and Iran. The Kabul-Kandahar Highway had been completed in 1966, spurring a trade boom between the cities—though not at first between Afghanistan and Pakistan, which spent much of the 1960s at daggers drawn over Afghanistan's aid to Pakistani Pashtun separatists.

During the long Afghan war, the highway had been blasted, mined, and flooded into a barely traversable wreck. After conquering Kabul, the Taliban had tried to repair the road link to their spiritual capital of Kandahar, but laboring under an international embargo and the continuing costs of combat, they only managed to pave the first twenty-seven miles. In 2002, travel between Kandahar and Kabul took fourteen hours for a robust vehicle under good conditions. During the winter floods, when the fords washed out along dozens of usually dry gullies, it could easily take days.

The highway had been one of Hamid Karzai's top priorities for reconstruction. He understood the importance of bringing a major, visible benefit to Kandahar, the first Afghan city to welcome Taliban rule back in 1994 (and home to Karzai's own Pashtun clan, the Popolzai). Unfortunately, throughout 2002, the Kabul-Kandahar Highway project was handed off and dropped by one group of donors after another. USAID ended up committing $80 million toward the project, with smaller contributions from Japan and Saudi Arabia. By the end of the year, work had started at a normal pace. In early 2003, however, Washington was finally infected with President Karzai's sense of urgency, thanks to American ambassador Khalilzad and U.S. military commanders who wanted to be able to move troops by highway. Louis Berger, the engineering company and government contractor that had won USAID's $665 million "major infrastructure" program for Afghanistan, got the extraordinary order to pave the remainder of the Kabul-Kandahar Highway by the end of 2003—whatever the cost.

Berger accordingly airlifted in equipment and supplies instead of bringing them overland from Pakistani seaports. It sprayed on a single layer of asphalt to meet its paving deadline, planning to come back and apply extra layers later to give the road durability. It expanded its local work crews to three thousand men, with work going on seven days a week all along the course of the highway. The company brought in extra landmine clearance organizations to accelerate the inherently slow job of finding and removing the explosives hidden along the road path. It also needed a small army to protect its operations from bandits and insurgents all along the highway. Berger chose USPI, the cheapest security company on offer, and thereby transformed USPI into a major national force. To get the highway built at triple speed, America ended up paying more than triple price, or $270 million— roughly $1 million for every mile repaired. But the whole highway was paved, if thinly, by the December 2003 deadline.

Berger had spent 2004 going back over the highway with extra blacktop, culverts, and shoulder-widening to bring it all up to spec. Some of its bridges had failed to pass USAID's initial inspection, and as we drove down in November 2004, we had to detour around a handful of bridge repair sites. Other than that it was an excellent, smooth highway, and it cut the travel time between Kabul and Kandahar to seven hours at a reasonable pace (five or six, at the speed of most Afghan drivers). The highway clearly had a few broader drawbacks: a surge in fatal road accidents, too few police to deter bandits, and an unclear future once USAID stopped paying for maintenance. But it remained the Afghan reconstruction's one widely recognized success story, revitalizing trade and travel between north and south Afghanistan. Disillusioned Afghans now commonly said, "What have we got for all those billions of aid dollars . . . besides the Kabul-Kandahar Highway?" Which was something.

• • •

We sped through Wardak, Yaqub's hilly home province, a landscape of dusty promontories overlooking lushly planted valleys. The dark greenery of the valleys spread out like a lake, rising to an almost horizontal line that marked the highest irrigation stream. Above the waterline, the mountains soared bright and barren, with only the occasional hardy pistachio tree breaking their sun-seared monotony.

The road then dropped down a long slope into the valley of Ghazni. Though we were still three hundred miles by road from the Helmand River, we had just entered its vast watershed, which drains 40 percent of Afghanistan. The unassuming foothill town of Ghazni had strong historical links to Helmand. Like a disconcerting number of other Afghan cities and towns, Ghazni had once been the seat of a major regional empire, with a winter capital next door to present-day Lashkargah.

In his conquests from AD 998 to 1030, Sultan Mahmud Ghaznavi had pioneered a simple but enduring Afghan empire-building tactic: invade and pillage India. The same principle was later followed by the Ghorid, Mughal, and Durrani Pashtun dynasties to their great profit. (Invading and pillaging Persia was also tried periodically, but met with more unified resistance.) The fabulously rich Ghaznavids reigned over much of South Asia for a century and a half on the strength of their military prowess and Indian plunder. Every winter the court of Ghazni would travel to their southern capital of Bost, on the Helmand River, to keep their 2,500 war elephants from freezing in the northern snows. Both capitals were sacked by the rival Afghan kingdom of Ghor in 1151. All that has survived of the old empire in Ghazni are the ornate stubs of two ancient minarets, standing unobtrusively at the outskirts of the modern town.

We drove south of Ghazni for monotonous hours, through a barren valley that rose on either distant side to hunched, brown mountains. The dusty hills drew in closer to the road, and at a little after 11:00 a.m., our driver told us that we had passed into Zabul province. There was a taut note in his voice; Zabul was one of the areas where the Karzai government's control was weakest. We were now driving down a corridor within striking distance of insurgent sanctuaries on both sides—Pakistan's unruly tribal zone in the east, and the mountains of Uruzgan, childhood home of Taliban leader Mullah Omar, in the west. On the UN's latest security map, Zabul and Uruzgan were the only provinces that were completely shaded in as "high-risk" areas, without a single district of relative safety.

Self-proclaimed Taliban spokesmen had declared that they controlled most of Zabul, but it was hard to know how much to believe such claims. Violent lawlessness, which Zabul undeniably had, wasn't the same thing as domination by a rebel movement. Across the country, much of the bloodshed attributed to insurgents really stemmed from a variety of thugs united only by their common interest in a weak, ungovernable Afghanistan. Drug traffickers, militia commanders, and corrupt police covered their feuds and murders by blaming the Taliban, and Taliban spokesmen were generally happy to take responsibility for as many disruptions as possible.

In any case, the label "Taliban" was questionably accurate as a nutshell description for the antigovernment insurgents. The Afghan government tended to favor the more general term "enemies of the country." The Taliban had melted away into Pakistan's wild west after the fall of Kabul in 2001, and it wasn't clear how much of their distinctive identity had survived the change from a government into a dispersed insurgency. Over the last couple years of fighting, two general characteristics of the anti-Karzai, anti-NATO guerrillas had become plain: They were predominantly Pashtun, and they were at their strongest in the provinces that bordered on Pakistan's tribal belt (with a few exceptions, like Uruzgan, in Afghanistan's mountain heartland). Those traits were hardly unique to the Taliban. The insurgent commanders included plenty of conservative Pashtuns who answered only to themselves, notably former foe of the Taliban Gulbuddin Hekmetyar.

In November 2004, the insurgency's fortunes seemed to be at a low ebb. Taliban spokesmen had promised terrible violence to derail the presidential elections a month earlier—and had embarrassingly failed to deliver. Throughout the insurgency's heartland, the voters had turned out in droves to make sure that their fellow Pashtun Hamid Karzai didn't lose to his main rivals, a Tajik and an Uzbek. The guerrillas' planned attacks in Kabul had been thwarted by heightened security measures. President Karzai, energized by his new mandate, had renewed an amnesty offer to any insurgents (short of a few top commanders) who laid down their arms, and some well-publicized Taliban were beginning to take him up on it.

On the other hand, while 2004 was ending with humiliation for the Taliban, it had still been a more violent year than 2003. American generals predicted that the Taliban movement was on the road to collapse, but they had made similarly confident pronouncements ever since Mullah Omar fled Kandahar in 2001. The snowy Afghan winter generally forced an end to fighting for the year; we wouldn't know until the spring whether the insurgency was genuinely faltering. Meanwhile, whether or not Zabul was under "Taliban" control, it was certainly out of government control, and the sooner we were through it, the better.

Our convoy leaders soon pulled off into a heavily fortified Louis Berger construction camp, where lofty conveyor belts, mountains of crushed rock, and ranks of steamrollers testified to the scale of the just-completed highway project. We had lunch there and, to my relief, switched to a new set of USPI guards before leaving. One of the squads that had driven down with us had a photo of Tajik martyr Ahmad Shah Massoud displayed prominently on their dashboard—not a good way to make friends as we drove through solidly Pashtun, Taliban-sympathizing Zabul or Kandahar. Our new escorts came from a local Zabul militia and were (I hoped) less likely to start fights.

I wasn't exactly thrilled that we were using USPI in the first place. The small American-run security outfit was able to offer its services so cheaply because it put minimal resources into training, arming, or managing its hundreds of guards. Instead, it subcontracted armed units from Afghan militia commanders across the country, helping those commanders justify and finance their personal armies. USPI's Afghan "shooters" were notorious for their unreliability and lack of discipline, but they also came cheap enough to meet USAID budget requirements. With Berger already paying USPI to maintain a standing army along the Kabul-Kandahar Highway, the security outfit could offer discounts to other USAID contractors, and RAMP had a policy of using USPI escorts for all of its road trips. Still, even though our project was technically part of RAMP, I was determined to review all our security options once we got down to Helmand.

I was mulling over those options when our driver suddenly hit the brakes hard. The USPI convoy leader had slowed sharply to avoid a stone in the road. Our Land Rover screeched to a halt, then leapt forward with a bang, rear-ended by one of the de-mining agency vehicles. We slammed against our seat belts as our vehicle caromed back and forth between our neighbors in the convoy. USPI shooters spilled out of their Land Cruisers, bringing their rocket launcher with them. Some of them formed a loose perimeter, while others milled around the accident site, staring at the crumpled front of the de-miners' pickup and our battered Land Rovers. With no warning, we found ourselves stalled on a gritty plain in the middle of Zabul.

When it became clear that I was shaken and didn't know how to get the situation in hand, Pete took control. "Get on the phone with the USPI base," he ordered me in a no-nonsense voice, and strode over to the drivers. By the time I had gotten reception on our Thuraya satellite phone and reported the accident, Pete had taken down an incident report from the drivers and was assessing the damage. No one was injured, though the landmine agency truck was wrecked beyond repair. Our Land Rover had held up well, given that it had taken punishment from both front and rear. Its radiator was cracked, but our driver Ahmad Khan was already applying his uncanny vehicle surgery skills to get it in working order.

I thanked Pete, trying to shrug off my embarrassment at being unprepared to take the lead in an emergency. We opened the Land Rover's dented back door to make sure our precious cargo was intact. The well-padded computer boxes were fine, as expected, and to our relief, the porcelain toilets were also uncracked. Demand for Western-style "thrones" in Lashkargah was all but nonexistent, and we couldn't count on the local shops having any in stock. Long minutes passed in sun and silence; I let go of my pointless worry that we were going to attract bandits. A truck full of USPI reinforcements showed up to tow the de-miners' vehicle back to the construction camp. Ahmad Khan patched up our radiator, banged the doors back into shape, and cheerfully declared that the Land Rover would keep running if we didn't push the engine too hard.

The sun was low in the sky by the time we arrived in Kandahar. At first glimpse, Afghanistan's second-largest city looked much like Kabul, with high walls everywhere, dilapidated concrete buildings, and dense pedestrian bazaars—but with fewer trees, fewer Indian film star posters on obvious display, and, perhaps most strikingly, fewer war scars. Unlike Kabulis, the citizens of Kandahar had not lived through mass shelling and street fighting. In the post-Communist anarchy of the early 1990s, the Pashtun south had not produced warring blocs strong enough to destroy the city. Rather, Kandahar's nightmare had been one of rape, robbery, torture, and oppression by hundreds of minor commanders and bandits, each heavily armed and untouchable on his own turf. The Taliban had been welcomed as saviors in the Pashtun south when they first poured out of Pakistan in 1994, and their capture of Kandahar had been nearly bloodless.

Kandahar was the historic center of Pashtun power in Afghanistan. Mullah Omar had chosen it as his home and capital. Here in 1996, just before conquering Kabul, the Taliban chief had publicly displayed the Cloak of the Prophet Muhammad—a relic deposited in Kandahar by a Pashtun emperor two centuries earlier—and accepted the title of *Amir al-Momineen*, "commander of the faithful," successor to the Prophet. I wondered how many of the long-bearded men we drove past in the street had attended that great pageant, had cheered and wept at the sight of the one-eyed mullah brandishing the heavy mantle, had dared to believe in his vision of peace through conquest, law, and uncompromising righteousness. I wondered where they placed their hopes for peace today.

By the time we rolled under the boom gate of the high-walled Continental Hotel, we were all restless and thirsty from our extended trip. We cracked open the hotel's complimentary cans of Mecca-Cola (which advertised that a share of every purchase would support the oppressed Palestinians) and paced around the garden, calling down our security list to let the relevant folks in Kabul and Washington know we'd made it to Kandahar safely. When we were done, Pete glanced over the emergency contact list and gave a snort of laughter. "You see anything missing?"

I scanned it, wondering what I had left out. It was based on RAMP's list, and had phone numbers for (among others) the Kabul Fire Brigade, the U.S. Embassy, a twenty-four-hour NATO emergency line in Kabul, and the UN-funded security network's advisor in Kandahar. "What?"

"I like how there's nothing for Lashkargah." Pete grinned. "Hope we don't run into any fucking emergencies after tomorrow."

Lashkargah, Helmand—November 25, 2004

After a few early-morning repairs to our Land Rover, we set out on the Kandahar-Herat Highway, built by Russia to link the biggest cities of south and west Afghanistan to the northern border. The highway was paved with concrete slabs instead of an asphalt surface. Years before the Soviet invasion, Afghans used to joke that the Russians had designed all their roads to bear the weight of a tank column. The road had weathered well over the decades, with only a few large gaps or potholes between the huge slabs.

In the morning light, I got a better sense of the Kandahari landscape: a dusty plain partly ringed to the north and west by high, toothy crags of rock. Our driver gestured toward the most striking hill, a solitary outcrop that rose steeply to a blunted peak. "That is Fil Koh—Elephant Mountain. Mullah Omar had a big house there. Very big. Very rich." There was a note of bitter contempt to his voice, aimed, I thought, at the hypocrisy of a leader who preached asceticism while living in luxury. As we left the city, we passed another grain elevator, the twin of the Kabul Silo. This one didn't have the scattered shell holes I had seen a year earlier in Kabul, but its square tower had been blown apart by a much greater explosion. I pointed at it quizzically, and the driver nodded. "America," he said with the same bitter tone, and mimed a bomb falling from above.

Much of the land around the highway was barren, but for long stretches we drove beside mud-walled fields, most either fallow or newly plowed. I wondered how many would sprout poppies in the next few months. We periodically passed de-mining crews working the highway shoulders, armored and masked like riot police to protect themselves from accidental detonations. Once or twice, to my fascination, we glimpsed clusters of black tents which I took to be Kuchi camps. The Kuchi were Afghanistan's main nomadic group, expert herdsmen who followed the seasons around the country. In the summer, they retreated to mountain pastures fed by snowmelt; as the winter storms approached, they moved into the southern wilderness to graze their herds on sparse, rain-fed greenery. For centuries, their migrations had provided rural Afghans with more livestock than the desert could rightfully sustain.

The drought and war of the 1990s had struck a terrible blow to the Kuchi way of life, wiping out their herds and driving many into towns where they formed a desperately poor underclass. Today, there were still traditional

Kuchi camps on the verge of many Afghan villages, low mud walls and pits that could quickly be transformed when a caravan arrived. Tents would go up in a dusty patchwork of animal hides, thick cloth, and plastic sheeting; the Kuchis' notoriously large and ferocious dogs would appear around the perimeter; and the local villagers would arrive to trade with the nomads, sometimes warily muttering about the Kuchi penchant for theft and their immodest women. The caravans had grown fewer, however, and some agricultural experts feared they would disappear entirely. The surviving nomads often earned more from smuggling than from livestock.

As we drove on, a sandstorm gusted in from the south, and the landscape around us vanished in a grainy, brown haze. I didn't realize we had entered Helmand province until we pulled off the highway at a remote gas station. "This is the road to Lashkargah," our driver called, accelerating gaily into the blowing sand. He peeled off to the right of our convoy leader to avoid the head vehicle's thick white dust cloud. Fearing that we would get lost, I snapped at him not to leave the road. Within a few minutes, I sheepishly realized there was no single road, just a mesh of rutted dirt tracks weaving back and forth across the arid plain. An intermittent aisle of hardy salt cedars, the only trees anywhere within eyeshot, limned an old highway, but its surface had deteriorated so greatly that driving off-road was quicker and easier. The hard-baked desert earth was still far from smooth, and we were soon sore from constant jolts and lurches. Dust filtered invisibly into our car, parching our nostrils, tongues, and eyes.

After an hour, the USPI guard captain waved us to a halt. Three armed guards walked over to our Land Rover and held a sharp, muted conference with the driver. A young Afghan staffer who was accompanying us translated. "They say in this area there have been attacks by robbers. For the next ten kilometers, we should drive fast and not stop for any reason." Moments later, we were jouncing along again at double speed as our anxious driver pressed the pedal down. The web of tracks converged into a single road, and high-walled farm compounds loomed up to our left. As we passed under the shadow of those walls, my dusty throat clenched, trying to swallow. I wondered if our Land Rover would be able to clear the irrigation ditch on our right if the vehicle ahead of us were taken out by a rocket or mine. We had to slow down to cross a deep rut in the road, and I realized how much easier it would be to set up an ambush in a place like this than on the highway.

There was no trap, no explosion, just more bone-jarring desert driving. That morning we had covered our first sixty miles out of Kandahar in roughly one hour; our twenty-eight-mile drive across the plains of Helmand took more than twice as long. The sandstorm subsided, though the sky remained a discolored gray-brown. We began crossing irrigation channels with greater frequency, the dirt around them stained salt-white from waterlogging. Finally we saw a spindly metal archway spanning the road ahead of us, marking the city limits of Lashkargah. The police post by the city gate was empty, and we drove into town unhindered.

Lashkargah's main street was more modern than I'd imagined: an asphalt-paved boulevard with a fenced-off strip of brown grass, shrubs, and flowers in the middle. Single-story shops built of mud bricks and packed earth lined the avenue densely on both sides, and a multistory concrete and glass marketplace was under construction. The bright pictures on the shopfronts advertised barbers, motorcycles, satellite phones, televisions, chic Pakistani women's clothing. Some vendors worked from tiny wooden booths on stilts, selling cigarettes and small plastic sachets of what looked like shampoo and skin creams. We passed a small soccer arena, a small Ferris wheel in dubious repair, and a modern mosque with attractive blue tile work. Not only the main street, but also most of the major streets around town had been paved, which definitely put Lashkargah into the most advanced tier of Afghan provincial cities.

The Chemonics guesthouse was in a residential neighborhood on the quieter western end of the main market street, not far from the Ferris wheel. From the street, it looked like any other walled household in the neighborhood—no barbed wire, no searchlights, no external guard hut. The wall wasn't particularly high, and the guards who came to open the gate were unarmed. (We later learned that one of them, a cheery Afghan Uzbek with a deeply lined face and startling falsetto laugh, was mainly there to do the laundry, but drew a guard salary in his spare time.) The guesthouse was perfect for a project that wanted to keep a low profile and expected to make no serious enemies.

Inside, a five-bedroom bungalow and its outbuildings took up most of the compound space. The guesthouse had garden plots in front and back, and a concrete porch where we could sit outdoors. We headed in and found our beds: folding metal cots with thin cotton mattresses, topped with mounds of heavy blankets to fend off the coming winter chill. There weren't enough beds for all of us, even sleeping two or three to a room. Pete promptly volunteered to sleep Afghan-style on *toshak*s, long floor cushions, in the domed dining room.

We soon met our neighbor, host, and guide to Lashkargah: Haji Habibullah, RAMP's office manager. The Chemonics guesthouse belonged to one of Habibullah's relatives whom we never met, so "the Haji" was in all but name our landlord, too. A small door connected our guesthouse to Habibullah's family compound, where he lived with his wife, six sons, two unmarried daughters (he had found husbands for two others), the sons' six wives (one son was unmarried, but one had two wives), and something like twenty grandchildren. We would never pass through the back door to visit this adjacent multitude; the door opened on an area of Habibullah's compound where the family females roamed freely, insulated from the outside world. The Haji could come through the door to check on us, but whenever we visited him, we would do so through his front gate, to a guest room kept separate from the rest of the household.

The Haji was of middling height, portly and broad-faced, with twinkling eyes and a silver beard of respectable but not fanatical length. Like most Afghans, he looked older than his forty-nine years—partly because of the weathering effects of an arduous desert life, and partly because Afghans respect old age and work less to hide its signs. He had learned his fluent English from American Peace Corps volunteers, and had helped administer USAID projects in Helmand throughout the 1970s. After the Communist takeover, Habibullah had spent three months in jail for owning suspicious English books. He then laid low as a shopkeeper for the better part of two decades, until in 1998, an old USAID friend recommended him as a manager to another U.S.-based aid organization. Haji Habibullah's pride in his acquaintance with American customs came across clearly from our first day in Lashkargah. "I know today is your Thanksgiving holiday," he said jovially. "So I have ordered a special dinner, to welcome you to Helmand."

We all crowded around the guesthouse table that evening, worn out from our long drive. I thought wistfully about the Thanksgiving plans I had canceled to be here—a trip to Edinburgh to celebrate with some American friends and Fiona, my English girlfriend. I accepted a glass teacup of vodka and Coke from Pete, half in mourning, half in celebration. The guards began bringing out our banquet on large platters. First we got the staples: fresh naan, fried rice, hot French fries still dripping oil. Then, in a pattern we would come to recognize over the next few weeks, we got a fried vegetable, something tasty and slimy like eggplant or okra. Finally, we got the main course, which as a Thanksgiving special was fish: deep-fried brown lumps a little longer than my hand, with a profusion of fine, sharp bones. I thought it wasn't bad, but mine was the minority opinion around the table. The guesthouse cook, a tall, clean-shaven Hazara man with a forthright smile, clearly believed that what distinguished a fine meal from a cheap meal was a sea of palm oil. Only the naan was dry, since it was meant to mop up the deep-fried food on our plates.

Haji Habibullah arrived halfway through the dinner and looked slightly crestfallen at our lack of enthusiasm for the Thanksgiving fish. Feeling guilty, I took a hearty third helping. We were going to be relying completely on the Haji in the next few weeks, and I didn't want him to lose face. Besides, we had arrived safely in Helmand, for which I was genuinely thankful. A little extra risk to my arteries was the least of my worries.

The next morning, after a breakfast of deep-fried eggs and tomatoes, we headed to the office and got down to the business of creating a temporary income for roughly one-third of the households in Helmand.

The Place of the Soldiers

Helmand is Afghanistan's largest and longest province, stretching from the country's rugged center to its border with Pakistan. At its parched extremities, the mountains of Baghran and the wilderness of Dasht-i-Margo (literally, the Desert of Death), Helmand is home only to nomadic Kuchi herders and a scattering of villages that subsist largely on the migrant labor of their young men. The densely inhabited, agriculturally rich heart of the province takes its life from the Helmand River. The great river, Afghanistan's longest, spills into the province at the Kajaki reservoir in the northeast and exits in the southwest, heading toward its final dispersal in the Sistan marshes of Iran.

Historically, the Helmand has been an artery of trade, civilization, and conquest since at least the time of the ancient Greeks, who knew it as the Etymandros. Alexander the Great had a friendly encounter in the Helmand region with the "Ariaspans," who impressed the young king with their military achievements and sophisticated government. According to his biographer Arrian, Alexander believed that the Ariaspan system "laid claim to justice equally with the best of the Greeks"—an astonishing admission for a Greek, who regarded his own institutions with the same sense of self-evident superiority that Americans tend to feel for democracy today.

Helmand's well-governed Ariaspans might have been the forebears of the famously independent Pashtuns; the anthropologist Louis Dupree, an often-cited authority on Afghanistan, believed they were. If so, it would be the last time in centuries that the Pashtuns were complimented on their governing institutions. Their Persian neighbors consistently referred to the Pashtun homeland as a barbarian *Yaghestan*, "land of the unruly." Perhaps the Ariaspans lost their exemplary government over the centuries. Or perhaps, as

Dupree suggested, it was some version of the Pashtun system of *jirga*—egalitarian councils that brought together otherwise independent tribes to seek consensus—that struck Alexander as admirable and later Persian emperors as lawless anarchy.

In any case, ancient Helmand benefited not only from Greek-caliber government, but also an elaborate irrigation system that turned it for centuries into one of the most fertile regions of what is today Afghanistan. The Arabs brought Islam to the lower Helmand watershed (known as Sistan) in the late seventh century, conquering up the river as far as the fortified citadel of Bost. The region's high-water mark began in the 860s AD with Yaqub bin Laith al-Saffar, a Sistani coppersmith's apprentice turned military adventurer. Like many Afghan warlords today, al-Saffar built himself a mighty private army based on personal loyalty and reliable, generous pay. Taking the lower Helmand city of Zaranj as his capital, he proceeded to conquer nearly everything between the Indus and Iraq. He set up his royal mint in Bost, and though his kingdom dwindled dramatically after its founder's death, Bost continued to prosper. Eventually, it became the winter capital of the much greater Ghaznavid Empire. For more than a century, the aristocracy of Ghazni whiled away the rainy season in Bost's opulent riverside palaces, while their army stayed in a bazaar just to the north of the capital. The bazaar was called *lashkar gah*, "the place of the soldiers."

As with most Afghan empires, the Helmand region's glory and prosperity were destroyed by outside marauders. The palaces were sacked in 1150 by Alauddin, a prince of Ghor who earned the title of *Jahansuz*, "world-burner," for his obliteration of the Ghaznavid capitals. The mighty citadel at Bost and the Sistani capital of Zaranj were razed by Genghis Khan's Mongols in 1220. The deserts began to encroach on Sistan, and in the late 1300s the wantonly destructive Central Asian armies of Timur-i-Leng ruined the irrigation systems that had kept the sands at bay. For more than five hundred years afterward, the Helmand River ran through a mostly barren wilderness of small villages and massive ruins.

In the 1940s, a newly confident Afghan government resolved to create a modern version of ancient Sistan's legendary canal network. To make it happen, the Afghans hired Morrison-Knudsen, the American engineering company that had built the Hoover Dam and the San Francisco Bay Bridge. The Truman administration eventually chipped in millions of dollars for the project, seeing it as an equivalent to the Tennessee Valley Authority, that key part of Roosevelt's New Deal which had revived the American South through irrigation, hydroelectricity, and linked social programs. The Morrison-Knudsen engineers dammed the Helmand and Arghandab rivers, and excavated irrigation canals that opened up huge tracts of desert in central Helmand for settlement and cultivation. The Americans also built a city for their engineers, next to what remained of the Ghaznavid place of the soldiers. Nicknamed *kichne nowyork*, "little New York," this revived city of Lashkargah eventually became the provincial capital.

Not every foreigner knew the meaning of the city's tongue-twisting name, and I had heard several Americans and Britons mispronounce it "Lashkagar"—I believe in an unconscious rhyme with the neighboring, more famous city of Kandahar. The error was picked up in print by a number of reputable newspapers and magazines. When I asked Haji Habibullah if there was more than one spelling, he shook his head with indulgent annoyance. "There is no 'gar.' It is 'gah' that means 'place.' Saying 'lashkar gar' . . . it is like when some Afghans heard that British money was called 'sterling,' and they thought it was 'shotor-i-leng'—meaning, a camel with three legs. It is a mistake."

For a decade or two after its rebirth, "place of the soldiers" had been an incongruous name for the city. Lashkargah in the 1960s had been a peaceful place of tree-lined streets, Peace Corps high school teachers, and flat-roofed brick bungalows that would have fit into any California suburb. The American-built tract homes had big picture windows overlooking their front lawns, and none of them had walls. Today, Lashkargah's main riverfront avenue was closed with rolls of barbed wire and armed guards at either end. Its bungalows had been taken over and walled off by local power brokers, their picture windows bricked up or refitted with clouded glass. The former bank building was now, thanks to its sturdy defensibility, the provincial governor's office. The grand Bost Hotel, once an exclusive club for government employees, had become the governor's audience hall.

Only one building had kept more or less its same function since the days of Morrison-Knudsen: the sprawling, three-story headquarters of the Helmand-Arghandab Valley Authority (HAVA), the Afghan government agency that regulated Helmand's modern irrigation system. Before the war, the director of HAVA had been arguably the most powerful man in southern Afghanistan, the Emperor of the Two Rivers. He controlled the Kajaki Dam (source of electricity for Kandahar and Lashkargah) and the reservoirs on the Helmand and Arghandab rivers that provided water to most of the area's farmers. By 2004, like many of the Afghan government's devastated and bankrupt institutions, HAVA kept going on a bluff and a shoestring. It kept asserting authority over the grand canal works, while manifestly lacking the money or equipment to keep them in good shape.

Both the power and the poverty of HAVA were evident from a quick scan of its grounds. It had tenaciously hung onto its building, the largest in Lashkargah, ceding only a few rooms to other government ministries. Perhaps more impressive, HAVA had also kept an aisle of towering old pines through years of drought and lawlessness that had seen most of Lashkargah's trees sold to Pakistani timber smugglers. At the same time, the HAVA building's shattered windows, broken doors, and grime-caked yellow paint testified to years of neglect and violence. The yard beneath the grand pines was littered with decrepit trucks and earth-moving machinery, most of which would clearly never run again.

We needed to work with and through this weakened institution; without HAVA's cooperation, our speedy project launch would grind to a halt. The quickest and simplest way for us to employ thousands of laborers in Helmand was clearing silt out of the canals and drains in HAVA's irrigation system. If HAVA withheld its permission, we would have to start work on older, secondary canals (which would employ fewer people over a larger, hard-to-manage area) or roads (which would take longer to plan properly and cost more on materials and equipment). Also, in a province with dismally few real engineers, we hoped to use HAVA's irrigation specialists to design and supervise some of our activities. Finally, we wanted to move into the HAVA building. The director had granted RAMP three rooms on a corner of the top floor, with a view of the river. We wanted to expand that foothold, where we already had satellite Internet, instead of hunting for a new office.

We made our petitions to HAVA's director, Engineer A. K. Dawari, a balding, white-bearded sovereign determined to restore the dignity of his impoverished office. Within the confines of his HAVA building, Dawari was still Emperor of the Two Rivers. The grand, carpeted antechamber where supplicants waited for his attention was dominated by an old framed blueprint of Lashkargah as it had been four decades earlier: a small, tidy city designed by and for Americans. Engineer Dawari (who like many technically educated Afghans proudly adopted the title "Engineer" as part of his name) wore a Western-style business suit and white collar shirt to work, though virtually every other powerful man in Helmand wore kamiz partoog and a turban. Unlike most of his subordinates, he spoke English fluently. He had two deputies, a red-bearded giant and a white-bearded dwarf, both of whom were maneuvering to fill his shoes.

It was clear from our first meeting that our project delighted and alarmed Engineer Dawari in nearly equal measure. Over the last few years, foreign donor projects had become HAVA's lifeblood and its poison. They helped keep the all-important canals in working order, but they also took the credit and (in many cases) decision-making power away from Dawari. Some big aid agencies had mused aloud about devolving responsibility for the canals entirely to local water-user groups, which would be HAVA's *coup de grace*. Our multimillion-dollar project was large enough to either breathe new life into Dawari's atrophying empire or make him irrelevant. He was clearly determined to exert as much influence over our work as possible.

Having us headquartered in the same building was a good way to start. With his two extraordinarily sized deputies in tow, Dawari walked with us around the premises to identify the best rooms for our project headquarters. "You can tell this was built by Americans," Ray said approvingly. "Twenty years without maintenance, but you can still climb the stairways, walk on the roof. A Russian building would be coming down around your ears."

At the engineering and design wing, Dawari introduced us to the aged HAVA archivist, who had struggled to preserve the institution's irreplaceable collection of surveys and blueprints during the civil war. We poked our heads into rooms piled high with reports and maps that had once been filed in some sort of order but were now stacked haphazardly under an inch of dust. The blueprint machine, like virtually every other piece of equipment in the building, was broken; the resourceful old record-keeper developed his blueprint copies using sunlight instead of electricity.

Engineer Dawari gestured around the dusty engineering wing and asked whether we would be interested in renovating it as our headquarters. It was perfect for us. There was only one entrance, so we could control access. It had plenty of offices and a spacious central area (currently filled with huge, grimy drafting tables) that would serve as a great operational hub.

I beckoned Ray and Habibullah off to the side. "I don't think we should take it," I said hesitantly.

"Why not?" Ray asked, surprised.

"Down on the ground floor, there's nothing but pillars under this wing. It's basically a car park. And it's right next to the gate. If a car bomber got under here, he could take out the whole wing."

Ray frowned, looking exasperated. Trying to avoid hypothetical car bombs was exactly the kind of timid contingency planning that could needlessly slow down our project launch. Haji Habibullah shook his head. "I do not think we need to worry about this kind of thing, Mr. Joel. For years, Helmand has not had such problems. There are thieves and drugs, but not bombs. Not here in Lashkargah."

I persisted. "RAMP's existing office faces the river, with the gardens as a buffer. We can get more rooms along that hallway. It'll be just as good for office space, and less exposed to bombs. Why risk it?"

Ray began to say something, then stopped himself and sighed. "I gave you security responsibility, and you're in charge of setting up the office space. I don't think it's the best call, but it's your call. We'll see what Engineer Dawari has to say about it."

Within a few days, we had fleshed out the details of our "capacity-building" agreement with HAVA. We would clean and renovate four rooms on what I thought of as the "safe side" of the building for our project headquarters. We would give the HAVA director a computer and Internet connection. We would renovate the HAVA soil laboratory (a nearby building in a state of general ruin) as one of our cash-for-work projects. We would pay HAVA surveyors to survey our activities and HAVA engineers to supervise some of them. The chief of those supervisory engineers would be Khan Aqa, the massive, imperious, henna-bearded man who served as Dawari's first deputy.

Most importantly, we had HAVA's permission to start cleaning its drainage ditches by hand. Our mass job creation program would begin, fittingly, in the remains of the last American attempt to bring the New Deal to Helmand.

• • •

To help get our first activities off the ground, we hired Dick Scott, a fiery, irrepressible old American adventurer who had been managing cash-for-work projects in Helmand since the year I was born. Dick had first come to Helmand in the early 1970s, studying the province's patchwork of tribes and ethnic groups for USAID, and had found himself periodically drawn back for the rest of his life. Dick was now in his seventies and profoundly deaf; he had misplaced the brush used to clean his tiny hearing aids, which slowly clogged up with dust over his weeks on the project. Dick lost none of his dynamism or his blazing, irascible fervor, though. If he ever felt that we were being too bureaucratic or hurting the farmers of Helmand, he would rebuke us for it, stridently and at length. Perhaps surprisingly for such a tribune of the local people, Dick had never learned more than a few basic phrases in Pashto. He worked instead through a network of Pashtun friends, who were now bony old men, long-toothed and gauze-bearded. Most were from the district of Nad-i-Ali, where we planned to get our first few hundred laborers.

Ray and Pete spent much of their time on daylong field trips with Dick. Meanwhile, I spent my days confined to Lashkargah, flailing and failing under a heavy burden of start-up work. My direct supervisor on the Go Team was the formidable Carol Yee, a short woman with penetrating dark eyes and spiky, cropped black hair. Ray and Pete were in charge of the big picture; Carol was responsible for making sure that the details panned out. She was a trusted advisor and troubleshooter for Ashraf Rizk, Chemonics' president. She was also one of Chemonics' most demanding managers, with a reputation for dealing out incisive, frank, and relentless criticism. I had seen seasoned Chemonics directors come back shattered from a budget review session with Carol. I could count on one hand the number of times I'd seen her smile.

I gave her few reasons to smile in those first weeks. The sheer scale of our assignment didn't just expose my lack of experience—it also showed up all of my worst work habits. Like many inexperienced managers, I tried to do everything myself instead of delegating work. I had always tended to ramble through my daily work and rely on a last-minute push to wrap up anything urgent. Here in Helmand, I was suddenly responsible for dozens of urgent tasks, each far too big to finish with an all-nighter or two. Because of our tight schedule, Carol asked for daily progress reports and had me copy her on all e-mails, which opened my eyes to another weakness: my instinct to dodge accountability by keeping my work (and my potential mistakes) to myself for as long as possible.

To her credit, Carol was unsparing, but never unkind. She didn't let me hide a single mistake, and she didn't hide her dissatisfaction, but she said not a harsh word more than was necessary to tell me what I was doing wrong and how to change it. I felt my mistakes acutely, however.

In particular, I was failing to find us housing that could accommodate seven or eight long-term personnel. We clearly needed to get out of the cramped Chemonics guesthouse as soon as possible. Its hot water boilers were failing under the strain of overpopulation. It offered no escape from cabin fever; when Pete and I suggested climbing up to the roof for a breath of fresh air, the guards delicately warned us that the neighbors might shoot us for sneaking a peek at their women. During the frequent power outages we relied on a deafening generator jerry-rigged from a Toyota engine, which was particularly unfortunate when we were trying to sleep and every pane of window glass was rattling in its frame. To no one's great surprise, the cook turned out to be a carpenter by training, and though he happily accepted culinary advice, his enthusiasm for palm oil proved unconquerable.

I began hunting for staff houses with Yaqub, who was still trying to sort out his job description. By this point, it was clear that our project wouldn't involve huge amounts of government liaison work. Since Yaqub was underemployed and the two of us were the only long-term staff in Lashkargah, Carol asked him to help me find housing. "Don't let Yaqub get carried away," she said privately to me. "Your job is to tell Ray and me what's available, not to negotiate the rentals yourselves. Don't make any offers."

After a day or two of fruitless searching, Yaqub and I discovered a big two-story house on Lashkargah's riverside drive, past the barbed wire and guards that protected the governor's office and mansion. The eager home-owner had expanded it in the hopes of attracting foreign tenants. It had enough rooms to house fourteen people, and a cavernous basement that would stay cool during the blazing summer. Yaqub and I walked around its empty, water-stained concrete halls in delight, imagining how we could fix it up. From a security standpoint, I thought, it was great—we would benefit from the same fortifications as the governor of Helmand. It was practically next door to the HAVA building, minimizing our daily travel exposure.

We settled down on the porch with a cup of tea. Yaqub began talking with the owner about the necessary renovations, which turned into a discussion of the time and cost of the renovations, which turned into a discussion of hypothetical rents. Periodically, Yaqub would translate the conversation for me, clearly happy at our find and feeling slyly useful as a negotiator. While I sensed that we were going beyond what Carol had asked, I was likewise convinced that we had found the best place around, so I did nothing to discourage him. I don't believe Yaqub made an actual offer, but the conversation converged on a figure that obviously made us all happy.

We soon returned to headquarters and proudly declared that we had found an affordable, secure place that could fit us all. When Ray visited the house, he didn't see the same potential. He saw the dinginess, the current dearth of bathrooms, the fact that we would all be living on top of each other. I could sense his indignation building, and it burst as soon as we got back to the office. "I don't know what you're thinking, Joel. God damn it, when we bring people out here, we don't want them to be roughing it. I don't care what the owner says, this would take *months* to fix up. And it *still* wouldn't be a comfortable place to live. You need to be looking for a place that feels like a home, not someplace that makes people feel like they're in a war zone."

"But we can get it for only $2,000 a month," Yaqub said, subdued. "And the owner will bear almost all the costs of renovation."

Carol glanced over, incredulous, and later cornered me. "I explicitly told you not to make any offers, or to let Yaqub make any offers. What happened?" I tried to explain that we hadn't actually *offered* the rent, just discussed possible numbers, while I mentally added another management weakness to my list: exceeding my authority.

The mildly aggrieved Yaqub started heading out to the field with Ray, Pete, and Dick, while I kept up the house search with Haji Habibullah. We eventually settled on two places: a plain four-bedroom house with a large garden, and a fancy four-bedroom house with a conflict of interest. During our discussions with Engineer Dawari about office space, the HAVA director had mentioned that his son had nearly finished building a fancy bungalow that would be perfect for our project. We had kept the idea at arm's length while we worked out our HAVA agreement, and as far as I was concerned, that was where we should have left it. We would be dependent enough on Dawari without also having him as our landlord. But a couple of Go Team members had seen the house, and came back raving about its attractiveness and lavish comfort—precisely the criteria that we were supposed to favor.

So Habibullah and I went over to take a look. The bungalow was next to Lashkargah's radio station, in a low-walled compound rather smaller than the existing Chemonics guesthouse. Most of the yard was covered in concrete, broken by flower beds and an incomplete fountain. The house itself was still under construction, but it was clearly going to be something special—it had two wide porticos, and every door and window was framed with elaborate woodwork of the kind I'd seen in Nepali temples and the houses of the Indian *nouveaux riches*. Two of the four bedrooms had attached bathrooms, a rare and welcome Western design touch. I could see why my teammates had liked it.

"What do you think, Haji-sahib?" I asked. I had started using the basic honorific (roughly, "Haji Sir," where a *haji* is a man who has made pilgrimage to Mecca) after hearing how other Afghans addressed Habibullah.

"I think it will make Mr. Ray Baum happy." The Haji shot me a nonchalant look tinged with mischief. "And I think it will make Engineer Dawari happy. So I think we should rent it. We will be working with Dawari a great deal this year."

Some of my American colleagues compared Haji Habibullah to a biblical patriarch, which I thought was pretty apt. I believe they had in mind his silver beard, ever-present turban, and natural air of authority. To me, the Haji evoked a different side of Abraham or Jacob, the holy rogue: wily, tough, not above tricks or bullying, a born negotiator who could be imagined wheedling with the Almighty Himself. Habibullah knew where the power lay in Helmand, and would cheerfully exploit a conflict of interest to get on the right side of it. Yet I believed we could trust his overall honesty and his judgment; he had a good sense of which rules needed to bend in the face of Afghan realities and which needed to be enforced with all his considerable authority. And he was right: Ray and Dawari were both happy when we decided to rent the bungalow.

• • •

While I floundered, Pete Siu was displaying his usual ridiculous brilliance. He prolifically churned out reports, workplans, strategy papers, and useful forms and templates. He talked strategy with Dick Scott and banking logistics with Habibullah. He held job interviews and helped us fill some key Afghan staff positions. He engaged with our guards and drivers in much the same respectful way that I'd seen him do in Kabul, acknowledging them by name and always giving the impression of taking them seriously. He even taught the guesthouse cook how to make tacos. Through all this, he somehow managed to apply to Harvard Business School, occasionally heading out into the garden for an interview by satellite phone. And he usually had time to watch a pirated DVD from the Kabul bazaar in the evening.

One evening, when I had brought home a folder full of paperwork and was clearly failing to get any of it done, Pete turned to me with no trace of his usual profane good humor. "You have got to pull it together, Joel. Write out a task list. Mark your priorities. Figure out what you can do in a day, and then do it." I'd heard the same harsh tone of voice back in 2003 when Pete was grilling Farid in preparation for his visa interview. I reminded myself that he'd respected Farid. It still hit me hard.

By the end of November, as far as I was concerned, the question of whether I could be a Pete Siu had been answered. I wasn't organized, driven, or knowledgeable enough. My time management skills felt like they were roughly on par with those of the Afghan engineer that Pete had argued with back in the Ghorband Valley. When push came to shove, I was flailing and confused, and I made bad judgment calls.

While I struggled to deal with house rentals, office renovation, and staff hiring, Pete, Ray, and Carol revised the project workplan to reflect some of the realities we'd encountered in Kabul and Helmand. They proposed to keep me on as "public information and reporting specialist"—a post with lots of writing and very few administrative responsibilities. At the same time, they sent urgent appeals to the Chemonics Washington office to recruit a long-term team leader and deputy team leader to overlap for at least a week or two with the Go Team. Pete and Carol would be leaving on December 11, Ray on December 17. The prospect of leaving the project to me, Yaqub, and Dick Scott was unthinkable. In particular, Carol warned, we needed a strong deputy who was thoroughly comfortable with Chemonics management systems to handle the increasingly complex administrative side of the project. "If we do not have a deputy team leader by the time the Go Team leaves, this project simply will not function."

Jack of All Trades

Lashkargah, Helmand—December 1, 2004

We didn't get a deputy team leader. The home office couldn't convince any of Chemonics' administrative experts to spend a year in Lashkargah. Fortunately, we did find a strong candidate for the top job: Jim Graham, an old USAID hand with decades of leadership experience in Latin America's coca-producing regions. Jim hadn't worked with Chemonics before, but he came strongly recommended by both Johannes, RAMP's Dutch engineer, and Bob Kramer, our team's humanitarian aid expert, which counted for a lot.

Like Yaqub, Bob had joined the Go Team to do a job that quickly evaporated. USAID had initially suggested that we hand out small packages of food and other necessities to Helmandis who couldn't do cash-for-work activities. By the time we reached Kabul, however, they had changed their minds and just told us to give $1 million in grants to aid organizations in Helmand that could do the job. "Don't get distracted from the cash-for-work," Dan Miller had exhorted us. So Bob spent his time in Lashkargah meeting with the PRT and the handful of other development agencies, mostly Afghan, that worked there. While the other groups were cautiously friendly, virtually none of them wanted to collaborate with our project. The risk of association with poppy eradication was not worth it.

Bob was a lean man with narrow eyes, hair shaved almost to the skull, and a warm, sandpapery voice. Like many of the veteran humanitarian relief managers I had met, he combined great personal kindness and patience with a mordant, almost angry efficiency on the job—a deep aquifer of compassion whose springs could run bitter. The evening before he left, we both found ourselves in the guesthouse backyard. Bob was drinking tea on the porch; I was pacing around, searching for good satellite phone reception while I tried to contact some finance manager candidates in Kabul. "You certainly keep yourself busy," Bob remarked amiably in between calls.

"Only until the home office finds us a deputy team leader," I replied with unhappy fervor. "Then I'll just do monitoring and reporting."

Bob looked amused. "They haven't even finalized a team leader yet. Don't count on them getting a deputy out here anytime soon."

I winced. "Ah, hell. I hear Yaqub's wondering whether RAMP needs a government liaison up in Kabul. If Chemonics isn't careful, they'll end up with *me* as team leader by default."

"I wouldn't be too surprised," Bob said with unexpected warmth. "They could do worse."

Surprised, I gave a helpless bark of a laugh. Bob and I had worked apart for much of the last couple of weeks. I hadn't known that he had any particular impression of my work, but he clearly hadn't seen enough of it. "Thanks, but I'm not remotely ready for that."

"You're never ready for something like this," Bob replied. "A year back, I got drafted as chief of party for the Peru alternative livelihoods project. Same kind of thing we're seeing here: coca eradication just about to start up, no alternatives in place, USAID in a panic, Chemonics looking bad, and the deadline for everything was 'tomorrow.' Or 'yesterday.' In the first few weeks I had to hire a hundred and fifty staff, set up five offices—some of them in crazy, hostile places you could only reach by boat—and get millions in grant money out to villages that agreed to rip out their own coca. We pulled it off, but it was brutal."

I had heard about the Peru project, of course. One USAID officer had said that Chemonics' accomplishments there were "nothing short of a miracle"—a phrase echoed ever since in the company's proposals and promotional materials. Thanks to that one-year project, Chemonics had won a $100 million follow-on contract.

Bob stared out into the dust-brown evening sky and took a drink. "I've worked with all four of the big USAID counter-narcotics programs now—Bolivia, Colombia, Peru, here—and I hate it. First, we force the host governments to accept a program they don't believe in. Did you ever hear about the Peruvian Congress declaring coca their national plant and planting coca bushes in the atrium of the Congress building? That happened while I was there." I laughed; Bob didn't. "Once the eradication starts, you lose the communities as well. You can get them interested in whatever alternative you're touting, until the government starts taking out their crops. Then nothing works.

"And the whole time, you're dealing with enemies who have huge resources and a tremendous interest in your failure." Bob paused, the lines of his face tightening. "They kept this quiet around the home office at the time, but some of our guys got shot up in Peru. They'd been out in one of those villages you could only reach by river. The locals had warned them to watch their backs. On their way back, they gave a lift in their boat to a traveling family, with a pregnant woman, an infant. They got attacked. Four of our people were very badly injured. The infant was killed." Bob's voice was harsher than usual, his eyes piercing. "You don't *ever* want to wonder what you should have done to prevent something like that. We're not safe here. Don't stop trying to get the security we need."

I sat down myself, taken aback. "I . . . I won't."

"Good," Bob said, leaning back. After a moment's silence, he smiled and spoke again. "You're going to do fine. Hopefully they'll get Jim Graham in as team leader. He's a good guy. Laid-back, great sense of humor. You'll like him."

• • •

When we first moved into HAVA headquarters, our only Afghan employees were Habibullah and two office cleaners. I was ultimately responsible for hiring everyone else. We posted a list of job openings on the ground floor of the HAVA building, and advertised by radio in Lashkargah and Kandahar. In Kabul, RAMP circulated ads for our top positions. The response was both overwhelming and frustratingly meager—we got a deluge of applicants, hardly any of whom we could use.

Few Helmand residents had any experience of office work, and it was the rare applicant who could proudly claim to have completed "twelfth-class" (high school). Most of our office positions required decent spoken and written English, which ruled out most of the candidates who appeared in my doorway. I tried to conduct even brief and obviously fruitless interviews with respect and warmth; I saw the courage and desperation that brought underqualified candidates into our office, and I didn't want to make them feel foolish for trying. On a more pragmatic level, I never knew which powerful family I might antagonize by ending an interview too abruptly.

In private, I had a chuckle at some of the best-qualified candidates. Many Afghan professionals had learned to use the spell-check function in Microsoft Word, which produced résumés with few misspellings but plenty of malapropisms. My favorite was the aid agency office manager who declared that he wanted to work in a "mullet-cultural environment," boasted of his UN "de-meaning" (de-mining) training, and described his marital status as "mired."

Throughout the hiring process, I kept running across echoes of Little America. When we were interviewing cooks, silver-bearded candidates presented their yellowing certificates of culinary hygiene from the American Ladies' Home Association. One of our young drivers proudly introduced me to his grandfather, who had chauffeured USAID engineers around Helmand thirty years ago. To oversee our activities in the villages around Lashkargah, we hired an old black-bearded gossip who had taught Pashto to Peace Corps volunteers and still waxed nostalgic about apple pie.

Most of our eventual hires, however, were energetic young men in their late teens or twenties. They were in that sense "average Afghans," in a country where the median age is around eighteen. Many had grown up as refugees in Pakistan or Iran, though by and large their families were well-off enough to afford housing outside the refugee camps, plus courses for their sons in English and Microsoft Office. The boys returned to Helmand with laminated diplomas, cheap mobile phones, and determination to find development agency jobs. They spoke with solemn sincerity about their duty to rebuild their homeland, and haggled (zealously but in vain) for salary increases every couple of months after we hired them. Theirs were the jobs that made the project move: logistics, translation, office administration, payroll distribution.

In that last category, my recruitment efforts weren't promising—most applicants balked at the combination of carrying lots of money and making periodic trips to the wild fringes of Helmand. When I tried to encourage one quiet young English-speaker named Nazar to consider being a paymaster, he hesitated and finally said, "I would like a job where I will not be killed," with a pleading smile and transparent alarm in his eyes.

"You should know that we will do everything possible to protect our payroll," I insisted. "You will never go out without a strong security escort, and we will never send you anywhere unless we believe we can protect you."

"Mr. Joel, it is on you what job I do." Nazar spread his hands. "How can I say no? You have come here, a long way from your home. You might be killed for Afghanistan. Why should I not do the same thing you do? It is in God's hands if we live or die."

I sighed and hired him as a logistics assistant. Few of the candidates I interviewed expressed a strong fear of insurgents; as Haji Habibullah had said, the problem in Helmand wasn't bombs, but thieves, and the more you traveled, the more likely you were to encounter that problem. All of our applicants would have been happy to take a job that involved sitting in a Lashkargah office. Our first work activities, an hour or two away from the capital, were in areas generally regarded as safe. But we were also sending a survey team to Darweshan, the southernmost of the grand HAVA canals, which petered out in the desert some eight or nine hours' drive from Lashkargah. Sooner or later, we would have to start activities in the upper Helmand hill country, too. Between tribal violence and banditry, those areas made most of our staff intensely nervous.

We were lucky that our best engineer, at least, was happy to travel around the province. As a *sayed*, or descendant of the Prophet Muhammad, the long-bearded Engineer Akbar benefited from inherited influence and a certain distance from Helmand's tribal politics. He had been born in upper Helmand, lived in Lashkargah, and had managed construction projects for powerful local leaders in the south, so he had friends and connections across the whole province. Personally, Akbar was a grave workaholic and introvert who did not flaunt his virtues; his courage, competence, and pride were all as understated as they were substantial. He had just finished a contract with another aid organization, but he felt they had insulted his professional competence, so he rejected their offer of a raise and came to work with us. Ray sensed correctly that Akbar was the strongest engineer we would find, and asked him if he would be willing to manage our southern work along the Darweshan canal. Without hesitation, Akbar went home to get his things in order, and headed south with a HAVA survey team in tow.

It was a fortunate fluke that Akbar was as good as he was. We couldn't be particularly choosy in our engineering hires. There were precious few trained engineers in Helmand (especially after we excluded those who were already working for other aid organizations), and few Kabul professionals were willing to leave their families for a job in a lawless frontier province. For engineering candidates, we didn't care if they spoke next to no English; as long as they knew their work, we would snap them up.

Finding female employees was an even greater challenge. We met with the local head of the Ministry of Women's Affairs—a courageous activist named Fauzia, who ran English and computer education projects for local women in the face of death threats from conservatives—and put the word out that we hoped to hire some female administrators. A few résumés came in. Carol and Pete spent their last week in Lashkargah interviewing the willing candidates, looking for ones who spoke enough English to work directly with our project's expat staff. Finally, Carol introduced me to our new administrative assistants, Rubina and Safeena, two tiny girls who shuffled into the office with faltering smiles and greeted me inaudibly, without meeting my eyes.

Both were swathed in burqas, with the front screen rolled back from their faces. Both looked about fourteen years old. We took their word that they were of age, since it was rare to find a Helmandi family who would send their daughter to work in a mixed-gender office—and without them, we wouldn't be a mixed-gender office.

Since we were still short on office furniture, we set up Rubina and Safeena together on a corner of what would be the team leader's desk, in the same room with Ray and Habibullah—well away from any young men. The girls' only work experience had been registering women voters for the recent presidential elections, and I was too swamped to give them meaningful training now. I set them up on e-mail, explained the purpose of basic office forms, and showed them how to use the photocopier, but for much of the first few weeks, they ended up huddled in their corner, quietly studying English or staring at the floor. Every time I saw them, I miserably wished that I was organized enough to do everything that was important on this project.

Lashkargah, Helmand—December 6, 2004

I met our incoming team leader, Jim Graham, at the Lashkargah airfield on the southern outskirts of town. Thanks to the newly established Provincial Reconstruction Team (PRT), Helmand's small American military base, our project staff could piggyback for free on flights around the country. "PRT Air" was a private outfit, hired by the U.S. government to ferry personnel between every Afghan city with a PRT base. Weather permitting, PRT Air's jaunty South African bush pilots would make request stops in Lashkargah on Saturdays or Mondays.

A little after 11:00 a.m., a tiny Beechcraft plane appeared in the cloudless blue sky. Sergeant Rick Singer of the Iowa National Guard waved his PRT detachment into position and lobbed a smoke canister onto the end of the compacted gravel airstrip. While generally a laid-back, flexible bunch of guys, the PRT Air pilots were intensely security-conscious, and wouldn't land unless they saw Humvees and smoke on the runway. The plane came down in a tight corkscrew to evade any hostile potshots, straightening out just before its wheels hit the dirt. The passengers woozily disembarked, and I hurried over to meet our new boss.

Jim Graham was a tall, weathered Bostonian with silver hair, an ample mustache, and a strong Massachusetts accent. He didn't say much at first. I introduced myself as the project's field administrator—which I would remain until Jim got his deputy—and as soon as we got into the car, I began nervously rattling off a long status report. Our first few hundred laborers had started work in Nad-i-Ali on Saturday, December 4, clearing silt out of drainage ditches under Dick Scott's supervision. We would add more men over the next week in Nad-i-Ali and other nearby districts until we had about 3,500 or so. That was still only about half of what we would need to make serious progress toward our two and a half million work days, but it was a decent start.

Jim nodded absently as I chattered. Then he glanced over at my kamiz partoog. I had gone down with Haji Habibullah to a local tailor shortly after arriving and ordered four sets of flowing Afghan clothes in various shades of beige, pale green, and sky-blue. They were pretty much all I wore these days. "Everyone here dress like that?"

"No," I said. "I mean, the Afghans, and Dick Scott, but not the rest of the expats. I just wear them because they're comfortable."

"Hmmm," Jim grunted. I had the uncomfortable feeling that I was being appraised—a feeling I would get more than once in the next few days.

I tried to demonstrate my limited accomplishments by taking Jim around to see our two future staff houses. Work was slowly progressing at the first one. Two workers had just finished digging a deep septic pit in the backyard. "This will make for some good gardening," Jim said meditatively. He looked around the compound and nodded. "Not a bad place."

"Wait until you see the other house," I said with enthusiasm. "It's our 'luxury' residence—fancy woodwork and a fountain." We drove over to Engineer Dawari's bungalow, which I hadn't seen since my first visit with Habibullah. I knew that Dawari had been paying his builders to work around the clock to get the house habitable. When the workers opened the metal gate for us, we saw the results of their hard labor.

Jim turned to me incredulously. "It looks," he pronounced, "like a Guayaquil whorehouse."

The ornate wooden doors and window frames were now painted orange. Each portico had been fitted with something like a hundred lightbulbs, which when lit up were doubtless visible from orbit. The finished fountain was a concrete ring of stagnant water, which didn't flow unless its loud, droning electric motor was turned on. The interior was painted a light shade of purple, and decorated with elaborate glass and chrome chandeliers. In the bathrooms, our toilets were about to be installed directly under the showerheads.

"A Guayaquil whorehouse," Jim repeated in strident disbelief, while I was still trying to absorb the scale of the disaster. Then he winked at me. "Not that I'd have any way of knowing myself. But those Peace Corps volunteers give pretty detailed descriptions." He guffawed, and I relaxed the slightest bit.

Lashkargah, Helmand—December 11, 2004

The Go Team was vanishing, one or two people at a time—and as they left, they handed their jobs to me. On December 10, Haji Habibullah drove up to Kabul to close out his contract with RAMP, leaving me to do his job for a week. That night, Carol showed me how she'd been keeping accounts for our project and counted out the remaining project cash into my hand. In the morning, she and Pete wished me good luck and flew out on PRT Air. We were still recruiting for the deputy team leader position, so that clearly wasn't my title. But after December 11, I was the project's administrative manager, finance manager, personnel manager, transport coordinator, facilities manager, security officer, procurement agent, recruiter, and (in name only) public information and reporting specialist.

I more or less stopped sleeping. We didn't yet have an office safe, so I carried tens of thousands of dollars in project funds in the inside pockets of my gray waistcoat—U.S. currency in one pocket, afghanis in another, Pakistani rupees in a third. (Many vendors in southern Afghanistan would only take payment in rupees, since their Pakistani suppliers still refused to accept Afghan currency.) Between the bricks of cash, my satellite phone, my mobile phone, and a giant ring of keys, it felt like I was walking around all day with lead weights hanging off my shoulders. On the plus side, my week as a human cash register helped me get a handle on where we were spending our money.

The day after Habibullah left, the owners of our rented Toyota Land Cruisers came by the office to collect their pay. USAID had given our project five Land Rovers, but they were stuck in bureaucratic limbo in Kabul, so we had been renting vehicles here at an extremely generous day-to-day rate. I decided it was time to renegotiate for the long haul. After a quick discussion about the cost of fuel and maintenance with one of my young Afghan colleagues, I sat down with the vehicle owners. Most of them were wealthy local elders; many had doubtless bought their vehicles with earnings from Helmand's main cash crop.

I explained with as much friendly confidence as I could muster that we were now looking for partners who would rent us vehicles for a renewable one-month term—at half the previous rate. The owners bellowed in disbelief and stormed as one out of the HAVA building. I spent a fretful night wondering if I had just lost the project its rental vehicles as well as its Land Rovers. The next morning, a gruff young driver came in and furtively agreed to rent us his Land Cruiser for 60 percent of what we had been paying. Within a couple days, the rest of the vehicle cartel also came in one or two at a time to negotiate cheap contracts.

Encouraged by what felt like my first success, I decided to get an early lead on buying picks and shovels. My friend Graham had bought a thousand shovels for the activity in Nad-i-Ali, but given the scale of our activities, we were clearly going to need a much larger tool stockpile. Nazar, our logistics assistant, came from a family of bazaar shopkeepers. I asked him to take me to every shovel vendor in Lashkargah to get their price quotes.

We parked on the city's main avenue and walked back into its unpaved bazaar alleyways. The colors and smells of the bazaar—bins of aromatic orange spices, shimmering boxes of hammered tin, rainbow bolts of rich Pakistani fabric, the pink splash of soap—were vibrant intrusions against a backdrop of dull mud-brick walls, wooden doors, and dusty lanes. Many shopkeepers worked out of old, rust-red shipping containers, with mud caked along the top to keep them from roasting in the sun. As we walked, a circle of curious Helmandi men soon formed around us. All wore kamiz partoog, most with a broad patu shawl to keep out the cold. Most also wore the conventional Pashtun turban: seven meters of cloth wound around a small, intricately embroidered cap decorated with tiny mirrors and sequins. One end of the turban trailed loose to the waist, and could be wrapped around the face to fend off cold or dust. Boys and some men wore the little flat cap by itself, their heads sparkling in the sunlight.

The bazaar was home to seven ironmongers who could sell us shovels, picks, and axes. With Nazar translating, I explained the scale of our project to the first vendor. We were going to be buying tens of thousands of shovels over the coming year. We'd prefer to buy them from the Lashkargah bazaar instead of ordering them from Kandahar or Pakistan, but we would need a reliable supply and a good price. The merchant shrugged and asked whether we wanted cheap blades or strong blades, handing me what I assumed were an example of each. "The strong, of course," I said. While Nazar and the ironmonger fell into negotiations, I fingered the edge of one blade and tried halfheartedly to bend it, looking thoughtful.

"Boss—do you know how to tell the good shovels from the weak shovels?" Shamim intervened. Shamim was our other logistics assistant, a young man with a long, curly black beard and irreverent grin.

"Er, no, Shamim," I answered, as unabashedly as I could manage. "I trust you and Nazar on that one. But if there's a simple way you could teach me . . ."

Shamim grabbed two shovel blades and clanged them together as hard as he could. I jumped, then laughed. It would as soon have occurred to me to test a hammer by pounding nails into the shop wall. "You see?" Shamim gestured. There was a notch in the edge of the weaker blade. "When that one hits a rock, *tchk*, it will be no good. And there are a lot of rocks in Afghanistan, boss."

"Let me try," I said, grinning. The vendor watched with equanimity as I put another dent in his wares. I handed the blades back to him and looked gratefully at our bearded logistics assistant. "Thanks, Shamim. Without you guys, I'd be lost out here."

Shamim took me aside later, smiling in earnest embarrassment. "You know, Mr. Joel, when you thanked me for this small thing, it made my heart feel good. So good, I cannot tell you."

I was shocked. "Shamim . . . there are like a million things I don't know and you guys do. Please, for heaven's sake, keep on helping me, and I'll keep on thanking you." Feeling a sudden glow of virtue, I resolved never to pretend to know more than I did, and to readily ask my more knowledgeable young Afghan friends for help. It was a resolution honored mostly in the breach.

• • •

In theory I was also responsible for managing our security, but since our security policy was still up in the air, my main job was to get professionals down to help us sort it out. I had contacted several private companies in Kabul to see if they would send a team to Lashkargah for an assessment, and it looked like we might get one around Christmas. Meanwhile, the Chemonics office was hunting for a long-term security manager to oversee our operations. One evening at the RAMP house, Jim Graham brought over the files for the top two security manager candidates with a dismayed grimace. "Joel—tell me the home office isn't seriously considering giving us this joker."

"Which, the American one?" I had shared Jim's reaction. "The guy who spent the past year interrogating prisoners for the U.S. military in Kandahar?"

"Yes!" Jim's mustache bristled with ire. "Hell, this isn't just about having Afghanistan on your CV. It's about attitude. This guy has worked a year in a job where ordinary Afghans are the enemy. If he brings an attitude like that to a project like this, he'll be nothing but a huge goddamn liability. What about this other guy—Watts?"

"Charles Watt. New Zealander." I scanned the CV again. "No obvious torture experience. Looks good, but his references are a little sketchy. As I recall, John at the home office said some of them only speak Russian and are hard to track down by phone."

"Well, he's protected aid agencies before. He understands what we need." Jim poked his finger at the CV. "Rwanda, Chechnya—if he can handle places like that, he can figure out Afghanistan."

"Just so long as we don't get another Todd Rhodes," I sighed. USPI's Kandahar manager was a thickset ex-marine with a black goatee, a hefty sidearm, and a misleading air of efficiency. Thanks only in part to the quality of his troops, Rhodes had presided over a series of monumental screw-ups that put our people at risk—especially our repeatedly overlooked Afghan staff. For example, when the RAMP drivers who had brought us to Lashkargah returned to Kabul in the Land Rovers, USPI left them stranded in the Zabul camp without providing an ongoing escort. The two drivers had eventually driven out alone, so as to not get stuck driving through Zabul by night. Later, when one of my Go Team colleagues was returning from Kandahar with a truck full of furniture, the heavily laden truck dropped out of the convoy with engine problems—and the USPI gunmen didn't even notice, let alone stop. They hadn't thought that they were supposed to be protecting anyone except the American.

Not that Americans were immune to USPI's neglect. When Bob Kramer was leaving via Kandahar, USPI failed to show up at the promised time to escort Bob along the often-bombed Kandahar airport road. "I wouldn't trust Todd Rhodes to protect my pet dog," Bob snapped over the phone. Rhodes's tragicomic Afghanistan career would eventually end in disaster; in September 2005 he shot and killed his Afghan interpreter in a murky dispute, and was whisked hurriedly out of the country by the U.S. Embassy. With nothing resembling a trial, Rhodes soon ended up getting another job with a private security company in Iraq.

In any case, we weren't using USPI's guard services anymore. We weren't using any guard services, in fact. Ray Baum was a firm believer in a minimal security stance: Keep a low profile, behave normally, and show no fear. Most of the aid agencies in Afghanistan adopted some version of this posture, marking their offices and vehicles with the "no guns" logo (a crossed-out Kalashnikov). Ray didn't want our staff houses to look like bunkers, not only for the comfort of the foreign staff, but also because he didn't want to send a message of fear to our neighbors. He didn't want us to use armed guards, because that would make us look more like legitimate targets. When the poppy eradication started, we would be better able to keep our identity as the counter-narcotics "carrot" if we weren't driving around everywhere accompanied by the "stick" (the police or military). Ray believed we could get away with soft security, in part because of Helmand's American-friendly history, and in part because for at least two years, Helmand had been a bubble of relative calm in the turbulent south, with no major insurgency incidents.

Johannes, who had worked in Helmand on and off since the early 1990s, also preferred operating without guards. The Dutch engineer was comfortable hopping into an unescorted Corolla and rattling off into the desert to go examine canals. He lived by the principle that spontaneity and anonymity were the keys to security—if you didn't announce your movements ahead of time, you probably wouldn't get ambushed. Both Johannes and Ray, while working for RAMP, had generally ignored the policy that required USPI escorts for road trips outside Kabul. "I would be much more likely to be shot when traveling in the company of some gunlord's troops than I would be on my own," Johannes said cuttingly.

In Helmand, we would obviously need armed protection for our payroll trips. For that, we would work with local police on the payday. Otherwise, we decided, we would forgo guns—in large part because we didn't have any good options when it came to regular use of armed guards. We didn't think we could trust the local police (often barely reformed bandits and militias) on a long-term, ongoing basis. USPI proved that private security on the cheap was no security at all. On a USAID budget, we couldn't afford (or at any rate justify) the higher-caliber security companies, who had quoted us a multithousand-dollar rate just for a three-day assessment.

Of course, we were practically neighbors to a hundred-odd soldiers from the Iowa National Guard. The Provincial Reconstruction Team base was only a ten-minute drive away from us, in a heavily fortified compound next to Lashkargah's largest graveyard. The PRT was supposed to create a nucleus of security and development in Helmand, but it didn't have the manpower (or mandate) to routinely protect any single aid organization. Colonel Eugene Augustine, the somewhat harried-looking marine in charge, promised to occasionally send a couple of heavily armed Humvees with our payroll trips. We accepted his offer with slight discomfort; though we had nothing against the PRT, we worried about identifying our work too closely with the U.S. military.

Our neutral, minimal-security posture lasted just under a month.

The Babaji Abduction

Bolan, Helmand—December 16, 2004

"Three days!" Ray bellowed. "For three days he hasn't been doing his job. Twice he's been so late, he might as well have not showed up at all. And then he sent his son to do the work for him. No, I don't want to hear an excuse. He's fired. Tell him he's fired."

Our interpreter began reluctantly speaking in Pashto, but Ray's belligerent stare needed no translation. Khan Aqa, the giant, henna-bearded HAVA deputy, gaped down at Ray in disbelief, looking oddly helpless for so massive a man. Ray had been hunting him for a day, and finally caught up to him on the driveway of the HAVA building, along with the seven other HAVA engineers who were managing our newest activities. Now Khan Aqa's subordinates stared on in shock (and some with veiled satisfaction) while Ray publicly sacked their leader. Khan Aqa tried to respond, but Ray was right: Over the last three days, the HAVA deputy director had spent most of his time in Lashkargah, treating his assignment to our project as a sinecure. The giant engineer fell silent, then stalked away into the building, his face flat with humiliation and rage.

Ray gestured at the other HAVA managers. "All the rest should head out as usual. Tell them we'll be out in Bolan today to see what they're up to. We'll get another engineer from Dawari tomorrow."

It was Ray's last day in town, and my first chance (at Jim's invitation) to leave Lashkargah. We were all driving out to see our new worksites in the villages of Bolan and Babaji, just across the Helmand River from the capital. Our activities there were managed by eight HAVA engineers, with overall supervision by Abdul Ghani Gran, the apple-pie-loving former Peace Corps teacher. Gran lived in Bolan himself, and had a good sense of the area. He was highly reluctant to work anywhere but central Helmand ("I am giving my sons English lessons, and don't want to interrupt their learning," he explained feebly), so we figured we would at least start him off close to home.

We left in a pair of Land Cruisers, past the high-walled, riverfront secret police headquarters. Under the Soviets, this had been a KHAD office (and prison, and torture chamber); the post-Communist "intelligence police" had inherited KHAD's property and more than a few of its unsavory techniques. We circled the compound and rolled onto the Lashkargah bridge. The brown Helmand River was shallow and sluggish at this time of year, interrupted by hundreds of sandbars and reed islands. On the far side we entered the bazaar of Bolan, a long string of stalls that literally overflowed with produce from the local farms.

The villages of Bolan and Babaji had existed in the Helmand floodplain since time out of mind, but they had boomed after the new HAVA canals brought reliable water supply and drainage in the 1950s. To the eye of a non–desert dweller, the farmland around Bolan was mostly dry and brown— dirt roads ground to powder, parched grasses and reeds along the canal banks, dusty trees with their lower limbs stripped for fodder or fuel, featureless mud walls around nearly every farmhouse. At this time of year, most of the fields were newly plowed and empty. Still, compared to the real desert, this landscape of orchards and dense brown grass was a paradise. I could imagine what the fields would look like when they were full of golden wheat or flowering poppy.

After twenty minutes of driving down the narrow canal-side tracks, we arrived at what would be our project's emblematic scene: scores of muddy men brandishing shovels along the banks of a deep ditch. The drainage channels of Bolan and Babaji had been neglected during long years of drought and government collapse, and some were now completely silted up or clogged by weeds. Without good drainage, the area's irrigated fields had become water-logged, with salt rising to the surface and blighting the crops. Clearing the drains would improve the soil and, in theory, allow farmers to get good, profitable yields from a legal crop. Of course, it might also let them get a better yield on their poppy. But our job wasn't to force farmers to plant a legal crop; we were just hoping to create the conditions that would make a legal crop feasible in the first place.

Meanwhile, we were succeeding in our primary mission: infusing cash into the rural economy. For our daily wage of 170 afghanis (around $3.50, slightly higher than the average local rate for farm labor), the local farmers were reopening their drains with admirable enthusiasm. Gran pointed out a ditch that had gone in one day from a grassy dimple between salt-encrusted fields to a trench five feet deep and more than one hundred meters long. In another area, the workers were eagerly if controversially excavating a local elder's field to replace the long-blocked drainpipe underneath.

As we walked the line, Ray pointed down into the ditch; a particularly skinny, short worker quickly brought the end of his turban up to cover his beardless face. "I was burned by this on RAMP," Ray said soberly. "Some USAID folks came for a site visit and found some kids working on the canal. Got my head bitten off. And USAID was right—the kids should have been in school."

"Well, get him up here," Jim said with a sigh. Gran yelled for the foreman, who called the underage worker out of the trench. The boy blinked around, looking curious; I wondered if he had any idea that child labor standards existed. Jim squinted at him. "How old is this kid?" he queried in a loud voice.

The boy spoke almost inaudibly. "He says he is eighteen," Gran reported. Apparently he did have an inkling of the problem.

"What?" Jim retorted with a caw of laughter. "Gran, if this kid is eighteen, then I'm twenty-four. Tell them!"

As Gran translated, the boy grinned nervously, and the surrounding men laughed. Gran then spoke in a tone of tentative sympathy. "They say he is an orphan."

"Look, I'm very sorry," Jim said kindly but unrelentingly, still speaking to the whole crowd. "He looks like a good kid. I'd like to help him. But activities like this can't help orphans. There's a law against child labor. If USAID comes here and finds a kid on the line, the project's over and I lose my job. You guys don't want to lose this project. I sure as hell don't want to lose my job. So if I come here and find kids on the line after today, *this* guy," he thrust a finger at the HAVA engineer, "and *this* guy," pointing at the foreman, "are going to lose *their* jobs. Understand?"

"They understand."

"They better," Jim rumbled. "Joel, will you pay the young man for his time?" I claimed the timesheet from the HAVA supervisor, found the boy's name, and counted out four days' wages for him. We played out the same scene at least ten more times along the work line. Age was subjective out here, of course—no one had a driver's license or other government certificate to prove their date of birth. We argued over the hint of a mustache or the deepness of a boy's voice. Jim repeatedly claimed to be twenty-four. I ran out of change by the end, and discovered (to no surprise) that it was all but impossible to break a 500 afghani note in rural Helmand.

We're missionaries, I thought as I paid out the orphans, *spreading the strange gospel of the modern American work ethic. No payments to the HAVA deputy director for work he doesn't do. No kids on the line.* Helmand operated on totally different rules, but we tried to only play by those rules half the time. We would give Dawari a computer and an Internet connection, and rent his bungalow despite the conflict of interest, but we wouldn't give his deputy a sinecure. We would hire two girls who looked fourteen, but not ten boys who might plausibly have been fifteen.

As we walked on toward the next group of workers, Gran sidled up to me. "How many languages do you speak, Joel?"

"Nothing like as many as you," I replied. "English, some Nepali, a little Spanish."

"Besides English, Dari, and Pashto, I also speak radio," Gran said. He grinned whimsically to expose his five remaining decayed teeth—perhaps a legacy of years searching for an apple pie substitute. "Do you know what I mean?"

"You mean like Alpha Bravo Charlie?" I said, smiling back. "A little. From watching old war movies."

"Mmmm." Gran nodded. "Back when I worked for the UN, we used that language sometimes to talk about people who might be listening. For example, we would talk about *Tangos* instead of—you know who. The guys who used to be in charge around here."

It took me a second. "Right. Like maybe you would talk about *Golf*s instead of mentioning Gulbuddin's men by name."

Gran laughed, but his eyes flickered around furtively, even though I had spoken in a low voice. "That's a good one, Joel. Golfs. Yes, that's good." We walked on for several awkward minutes before he spoke again. "I've heard that Tangos have been around here recently."

I'd guessed where he was going, but I still felt my pulse speed up. "Really?"

"Yes. There have always been a lot of Golfs here, but now people talk about Tangos coming. They say they have been asking questions about our project." Gran kept his voice normal, but his brow was deeply furrowed. "Why do we not have any security, Joel?"

"We'll have security for our payrolls, Gran. We thought because the Tangos have been quiet around here, we would only need to worry about thieves. Anyone who doesn't have to carry money has been going to the field without security—Dick, Yaqub, all of us." I met his eyes. "If you think that's a mistake, we need to talk about it with Ray and Jim Graham."

Gran inclined his head. "I do think it is a mistake. We will talk later."

The sun was low by the time we got back into our Land Cruiser to jounce homeward. Gran suddenly spoke up in a plaintive voice. "When I was with the UN, we would have radios in all our vehicles. What happens if we get into trouble out here? Who will know?"

Ray didn't appear to be listening, and Jim looked at me. "We've been using Thurayas for communications," I offered.

Gran laughed hollowly. "Have you tried using a Thuraya in a moving Land Cruiser?" He was right—it was sometimes tricky enough to get satellite phone reception in an open field. "If there is some emergency, they are no good."

"What's got you worried, Gran?" said Jim, frowning.

"Many things could happen," Gran said with a vague gesture. "Many people might not like this project. Maybe they will decide to make some kind of attack."

Ray turned to face us. "There's no good reason to worry about an attack. The people in the villages need this kind of work. They'll protect us. The governor has said we're protected. The mayor, Engineer Dawari, the ministry heads—they all say we should be okay."

"That is good, but *I* don't say we are okay," Gran said doggedly. "Every day I go out to the field and I hear things. People say the Taliban are interested in this new project, this AIP."

"The hell. The Taliban haven't caused trouble here for years," Ray growled.

"What are you suggesting?" Jim asked, sounding unconvinced.

"We need radios on all our cars, for Afghan and expat staff. We need guards for all our cars, Afghan and expat," Gran declared with a sudden, enthusiastic rush. "If we pay the police, they will protect us on all our trips."

"Goddamn it, we are *not* going to pay the local police to hang on us everywhere we go," Ray snapped, his voice rising sharply. "Do you have a cousin in the police? Or what? If I find out you're doing this for a cousin, you won't keep this job long."

Gran sat back as sharply as if cuffed. "I am only doing my job."

"You're spreading rumors, that's what you're doing," Ray glowered. I had rarely seen him so angry. "I don't want to hear it again." We drove back to Lashkargah in leaden silence. *We'll see what the security guys say*, I thought uneasily. I had finally managed to arrange a date for our private security assessment: Christmas Day.

Nad-i-Ali, Helmand—December 19, 2004

Ray left two days before our first payroll was due. On the afternoon of his departure, Dick Scott collected the muddy, weathered timesheets from our five Nad-i-Ali site supervisors and brought them in to me. I worked on payroll calculations into the small hours, wrapped in heavy blankets, running down my laptop batteries in the blackness after the generator finally sputtered to a halt. Our first thousand workers had earned a total of almost 1.6 million afghanis (more than $33,000)—no small amount to be moving around Afghanistan.

The first trick was getting the cash to a city without banks. During our week in Kabul, I had opened an account for our project at the National Bank of Pakistan, which made transferring money from America to Afghanistan fairly straightforward. To bring it down to Lashkargah, though, we relied on *hawaladars*—informal moneychangers who could move cash into the country's wildest corners.

The international *hawala* system ("transfer," in Arabic) is perhaps the only thriving global institution that relies entirely on personal trust. A migrant Afghan worker in England trying to send remittances home can give his money to a London hawaladar, who can then call up a fellow hawaladar in Lashkargah and tell him to give the money to the worker's father or brother. The two moneychangers deduct a small fee, and later settle accounts between themselves. The system wouldn't work if there was any significant worry that the first hawaladar would keep the money for himself. Yet without any outside enforcement or regulation, the system moves tens of billions of dollars around the world every year. A hawaladar who fails to live up to a commitment doesn't get a second chance; no one will work with him again. Many branches of the hawala network come from the same family, caste, or tribe, heightening the spirit of mutual accountability. The result, even in a lawless place like Afghanistan, is that hawaladars manage to transfer cash around the country with near-total reliability.

Of course, because the hawala system operates outside legal scrutiny, it's useful not only for migrant laborers but for smugglers, terrorists, and drug traffickers. When we asked Haji Ansari, the moneychanger who came recommended by the National Bank of Pakistan, whether he could really move a million dollars in cash every month between Kabul and Lashkargah, he just chuckled at our naiveté. We might be the richest aid project in Helmand, but we certainly wouldn't be his richest customers.

Despite our qualms, the hawaladars were our only option for getting money to Lashkargah quickly, affordably, and reliably. We had made our first hawala transfer in early December, and since we didn't have an office safe, we had left a good chunk of cash in the Ansari brothers' care. They had assured us it would be available on a day's notice. On the Friday before our Nad-i-Ali payroll, I requested the necessary cash—not just the Af 1.5 million total, but the exact change required to pay every worker. I didn't want to get stuck again trying to make change in the middle of nowhere.

On Saturday, December 18, Haji Habibullah returned from Kabul, bringing with him two safes for our finance office. I had never been so glad to see anyone in my life; not only could I share the project's administrative burden again, but I could also finally unload the deadweight cash from my waistcoat. The hawaladar's representative showed up at about the same time, nonchalantly carrying a duffel bag full of afghanis. He had brought the right total, but on one day's notice (especially a Friday), the hawala office hadn't found nearly enough Af 20 and Af 50 notes to meet our request for exact change. We locked the door, and the moneychanger emptied out dozens of fat, rubber-band-wrapped bundles of money. It took Habibullah and I forever just to thumb through the notes and confirm that we had the right amount.

We then called in Shamim and Nazar to help us sort out the Af 1.5 million into a thousand individual, paper-clipped pay packets. Nazar sorted money with the outrageous speed of a born shopkeeper, but we soon had to send him out to hit up his friends and family in the bazaar for every small-denomination note they could spare. We temporarily rescued Rubina and Safeena from their corner of Jim's desk and set them to work as well. Unfortunately, when we ran out of the change to make the hundreds of necessary Af 1,530 and Af 1,870 pay packets, we had nothing to do but wait for Nazar to come back from the shops. "You know, boss, this would be much easier if we paid the workers Af 200 a day," Shamim offered with mild exasperation. Nazar finally returned after dusk with a sack full of small change; I sent everyone else home and finished all the pay packets I could. When I got back to the RAMP guesthouse, everyone was in bed but the irate cook, who had stayed up to make sure I was fed. I wanted to hug him, but did my best to look apologetic instead.

The payroll day had an almost festive atmosphere. Jim had declared that the whole office would take part, to be absolutely sure we got the payments made on time. Dick, Yaqub, Jim, the Haji, and I each led one pay squad. I had called up five of the local English-speaking guys who had come in to the office seeking jobs, inviting them to join us for on-the-ground paymaster trials. At our office we were joined by three Humvees, bristling with antennae and gun turrets, full of heavily armed Iowans—a gift from the PRT for our first payroll.

It all went astonishingly well. The PRT handed us over to the Nad-i-Ali police once we reached the payroll sites. I worked with a trainee paymaster named Raz Muhammad, a young man with artfully trimmed stubble and the floppy, well-kempt hair of an Indian film star. Raz's pent-up energy and pride had stood out from our first interview, and I had wanted to give him a try in one position or another. We moved briskly down the line of workers, calling them out of the ditch one at a time, handing them their paper-clipped bundle of afghanis, and getting them to press their muddy thumbs onto an ink pad and then onto our timesheet. Raz proved to be a brisk, competent paymaster. By two or three in the afternoon, our four pay squads had successfully paid all thousand laborers—and we had found enough small-denomination bills in the Nad-i-Ali bazaar to make up the last remaining pay packets.

"Congratulations, Hafvenstein," Jim said with obvious satisfaction. "That went off perfectly." I laughed, thinking of our frantic hunt for change, but Jim shook his head. "It works! And it'll work just as well without us babysitting next time. *Now* we can kick this project into gear."

Lashkargah, Helmand—December 21, 2004

"Mr. Joel—there has been a jacking."

I had no idea what Habibullah was talking about. He had appeared at my desk while I was wrapping up for the evening, and was clearly very upset about something. "Mr. Joel," he repeated urgently, "our engineers have been jacked." When my brow stayed furrowed, the Haji grabbed my shoulder and said, "Jacked! Eh . . . kidnapped, kidnapped is the word!"

We rushed into Jim's office, and Haji hurriedly reported what little he knew. At around 4:30, three of our HAVA engineers and their driver had been heading home from Babaji. Their Land Cruiser had been hijacked by six armed men in a deserted wash. A local farmer had witnessed the kidnapping from a distance and hurried in to tell the engineers' families, who had got word to Habibullah.

"We need to let the authorities know," Jim declared grimly. "Yaqub, see if you can raise anyone at the PRT. Haji, you and Joel go inform the governor. I'll get Kabul and Washington up to speed, and coordinate communications from the office." Habibullah and I hurried over through the growing dusk to the governor's mansion.

In the 1970s, the Bost Hotel had been the most luxurious government club in southern Afghanistan; the former king, Zahir Shah, had stayed here during his frequent shooting and boating expeditions in Helmand. Now bereft of its tennis courts and swimming pool, the Bost served as the seat of Sher Muhammad Akhundzada, the *wali* or governor of Helmand province. Inside, the governor's audience hall was decorated with hyperbolic landscapes of 1980s Afghanistan: every hill was crowned with artillery, tanks rumbled down every road, MiG jets darkened the horizon. Sher Muhammad's family was a product of that decade, not of Little America.

Akhundzada was not really a surname but a title, "son of a religious teacher," that tended to run in families of mullahs. At the time, I knew only a few facts about the governor's family: that his uncle and father had been mullahs from Upper Helmand who led a provincial mujahidin faction; that they had been enemies of the Taliban and friends of the Karzai family; and that they had presided over Helmand's transformation into the opium heartland of Afghanistan.

When we entered the hall, it took me a moment to realize the short, portly man in his mid-thirties listening to the radio was Governor Sher Muhammad. The influential Pashtun men I had met were usually physically imposing, with flowing black or silver beards beneath strong, rugged features. The wali of Helmand had a plump, pale face with slightly protruding eyes and full lips smiling through a shock of reddish-brown beard. He waved us in, jovially accepting the disruption to his evening tea.

"Thank you for seeing us, wali-sahib," I said tersely, sitting down at the governor's left hand. "We have bad news. Four of our men have been kidnapped."

The governor's eyes widened as Haji Habibullah told him what we knew about the abduction. He questioned Habibullah intently, removed his turban, wiped the sweat from his balding head with a handkerchief. Then he summoned his provincial security chief and got on the radio to the districts, putting out an all-points bulletin. Our rented Land Cruiser had been blue, and we had thirdhand reports that the kidnappers had driven a white Corolla— the commonest car in Afghanistan. We quickly had contradictory vehicle sightings rolling in from all corners of the province.

Our host tried to put us at ease by offering us cups of green tea, thick with swirling leafy fragments. Sher Muhammad lacked the gravity I had come to expect from powerful Helmandis; there was something decidedly friendly and informal about him. He sat with a casual slouch, and in conversation he twinkled, beamed, clucked sympathetically through pursed lips. When we did not relax, he shook his head. Habibullah translated his comments: "Up in the mountains there are so many Americans and Filipinos repairing Kajaki Dam. Nothing happens to them. But in Babaji, in our own backyard, this happens? Have you made enemies so quickly? Who would want to do this?"

"We have no idea, sir," I admitted. "Perhaps it is only criminals. Maybe it is Taliban. Maybe it is Gulbuddin." I thought of Gran and his Tangos and Golfs.

When I said Gulbuddin's name, even before Habibullah had time to translate the context, the wali glowed with delight. Many of my Afghan friends were pleased when I could recite bits and pieces of their history, but Governor Sher Muhammad's reaction went beyond normal enthusiasm. He responded at fervid length, hinting darkly that many people in Helmand and Kabul were trying to oust him, and that Gulbuddin Hekmetyar might indeed be behind it all.

No useful information came in over the radio, and the governor's tone became brisk and businesslike. "You should not have been working without police. If there had been police with your men, this would not have happened." He dispatched armed guards to the RAMP guesthouse, and we agreed to arrange police escorts for our field workers in the future. Our project was now under the direct protection of the man widely alleged to be Helmand's most prolific opium trafficker.

Babaji, Helmand—December 22, 2004

I left the house at sunrise the next morning, got into one of our rented Corollas with a policeman, and told the driver to take us to Gran's farm in Bolan. Someone had to warn him not to head straight out to the field today, and I wanted to be the first to see his reaction to the news. A thick mist clung to the ground as we drove across the bridge and off the main road. I huddled in the backseat under an Afghan patu, staring out across the misty farmland and realizing how completely different a familiar bit of territory looks when you're scanning it for an ambush.

At the farm, Gran came out to greet me, his cheer fading as he saw the guard and my face. "What's wrong?"

"You haven't heard?" I asked warily.

"Heard about what?" Gran asked. He sounded genuinely ignorant—surprising for someone with his connections. I told him about the abductions; if his surprise and alarm were feigned, they were well feigned. "What do we do now?"

"We're going to suspend all work in Babaji and Bolan until we know what's going on," I replied. "And we're going to start using police escorts for all our trips."

"That's good, Joel, that's very good," Gran said in a tone that mingled bitterness and approval. "I told you that without better security, this would happen."

"I remember," I said bleakly. *So did Bob Kramer, and I didn't listen to him either.*

When we got back to the office, we heard (to our immense relief) that the engineers and driver had been discovered safe and well, out on the fringes of Nad-i-Ali. It would be hours before they were safely back in Lashkargah. Meanwhile, Jim, Gran, Habibullah, and I headed back to Bolan and Babaji with two government representatives and a Land Cruiser full of armed police. At our four worksites, we met with local council members and brought the same message: Stop work. All our activities are suspended while the police investigate the carjacking. We will pay you all for the days you've already worked, but we can't resume the project without assurances that your whole community will help to keep this from happening again. In particular, we need anyone with any knowledge of the carjackers to share it with the police.

When we drove into Babaji, I saw the village's main drain for the first and only time. It was huge, bigger than anything we were working on elsewhere, the sort of thing that would normally be cleaned by machine rather than by hand—but the men of Babaji had tackled it nonetheless. They stood in ranks along the steep slope of the ravine, passing mud up from shovel to shovel, leaving the heavily silted drain clear and smooth behind them. They were a magnificent swarm, like men shoring up a dyke or building a pyramid. I hated telling them to stop.

As soon as we got back to Lashkargah, we headed to the police station to check on the returned HAVA engineers and driver. They filled us in on the full story of their carjacking. "We were taken by three men, not six," a feisty old HAVA engineer explained via Habibullah. "Only two had Kalashnikovs. I didn't know them, but they sounded like they were from Helmand. They stopped our vehicle, tied our eyes so we could not see, and put us in the back.

"They told us that we had to promise not to work for the Americans anymore. I told him we worked for the government of Afghanistan, not for Americans. So they put us out of the vehicle in the middle of the desert, and then they drove away. We walked for two hours until we found a farm, and spent the night there."

The driver miserably cut in, asking if he would get any compensation for his vehicle. We replied that for now, all our attention would be on *finding* his vehicle. The engineers seemed very stoic about the whole experience. One of them asked how soon they could get back to work. The elderly engineer even offered to rent us his new van to replace the stolen Land Cruiser, which I thought showed remarkable faith that the carjacking was a one-off event.

We sent them home to rest and stopped in on Haji Abdul Rahman Jan, the *Qumandan-i-Amnia*, or commandant of police for Helmand province. "Before the commandant allied with the governor, he and his men used to stop cars on the Kandahar-Herat Highway," one of my young colleagues whispered. "When he is not listening, instead of Haji Abdul Rahman, people call him Robber Abdul Rahman." The commandant, a hollow-cheeked, snappish man wearing a heavy Soviet-era coat, echoed Governor Sher Muhammad's rebuke: We should not have been sending staff to the field without an armed escort. From now on, he said, our engineers should always collect two or three police from the Bolan station, run by the commandant's brother-in-law.

We asked for his thoughts on the carjacking, and he declared that it was probably just a criminal act. "In a case of this sort," he said curtly, "there is a sixty percent chance of recovering the vehicle, but we will probably not catch the thieves." The commandant spoke for a quick-growing consensus that the carjacking hadn't been motivated by anti-American or other political ends. Ray wrote a heated message suggesting that it might have been revenge by a fired employee, or possibly a scam to get us to pay for police escort services. Colonel Augustine of the PRT e-mailed USAID with his diagnosis: "I believe this was a random carjacking, and that the culprits did not realize the four worked with Americans until they asked the driver whose car it was."

That seemed a bit much. We were employing hundreds of men in Babaji on a pretty high-profile project, and the carjackers had been waiting at a very convenient time and place to catch our Land Cruiser going through. In the end, though, it was a moot point. "Whoever jacked the car, it shows we underestimated the risks," Jim stated flatly that evening. "Security took second place to getting men in the canals. That stops now. We use police to protect our guys in Nad-i-Ali and Marja, we freeze Bolan and Babaji, and we put all the other expansion plans on hold until we've got our security straight. We can't do this work unless we can protect our people."

Christmas in Helmand

Lashkargah, Helmand—December 24, 2004

There was a silver lining to the shock of the abduction. For the past five weeks, I had worked between eight and fourteen hours of every day. Over Christmas, we enjoyed a genuine lull in our workload for the first time, courtesy of the Babaji kidnappers. With our expansion plans temporarily on hold, we turned our attention to a new preoccupation: Christmas dinner.

Jim and I couldn't face the prospect of celebrating the holiday with the same oil-drenched meats and vegetables we'd been eating for weeks. The out-of-town guests who would be flying in on Christmas Day gave us an extra excuse to whip up something special. So one day before Christmas, we launched a last-minute quest for three essentials: good ingredients, a good oven, and a good cook.

Given another Western holiday, Haji Habibullah was determined to provide a banquet far more memorable than our Thanksgiving fish dinner. He invited us along to Lashkargah's Friday animal market to collect a live-and-kicking main course. As we loaded ourselves into a Land Cruiser, Habibullah beckoned two of the armed police into his car. "The market is on the same side of the river as Bolan and Babaji," he explained casually. "No one will cause trouble. But just to be safe."

Just below the bridge, the Helmand River curved west, cradling a broad expanse of waterworn stones that was usually occupied by a few gravel-laden tractors. Today, innumerable men and animals swarmed over the gray floodplain, sending a haze of dust and smoke high into the cloudless sky. A steady stream of mule carts, tractors, and camels forded the Helmand to join the multitude, while overloaded Toyota hatchbacks and battered vans sputtered down from the road. Overshadowing the Friday market from the east bank of the river were the ruins of ancient Lashkargah. The palaces of the Ghaznavid nobility were impressive even after a millennium of decay—imposing mud-brick bastions half-crumbled to the ground, weathered towers like an array of melted candles. Even on the banks of Afghanistan's largest river, the air was dry enough that the remnants might last another thousand years.

Our vehicles rumbled down the dusty embankment onto the gravel flats. At the outskirts of the market we drove under bristling towers of dried thorn-brush, stacked four times the height of a man and roped to broad tractor carts. Hundreds of gnarled, thick root-ends tangled darkly together in the middle of each cart, while pale, spiny branches burst out densely from the sides, over-hanging the roadway like the foliage of a huge desiccated tree. The thorn farmers stood in the shade of their wares, wresting clusters free to sell as fuel.

We drove in along impromptu avenues of bazaar stalls. Close-packed tents and tarpaulins blocked our view of the great herds to either side. Some stalls were linked to the market's core purpose. Butchers dispatched and dis-membered animals on the spot; cooks diced the meat fine and fried it up over a gas torch; tea tents provided a place to haggle, socialize, and rinse the dust from one's throat. Then there were dozens of opportunistic vendors with their wares stacked on sacks or dangling from wires: radios, shoes, seasonings, tow-els, bicycles, dried mulberries and pistachios. At one end of the market, men clustered around a brightly painted, kerosene-powered popcorn machine.

Our drivers threaded their lumbering vehicles between two fabric ven-dors, and we disembarked into an enormous herd of camels. We were in-stantly immersed in the musky smell of thousands of animals, tinged with the faint aroma of the frying meat and spices on sale behind us. Dung, blood, and offal were scattered across the river gravel, their strong odors quickly dissi-pating on the dry desert air.

Haji Habibullah vanished into the crowd in search of our dinner. Jim, Dick Scott, and I dodged nips from the camels, moved through a knot of docile-looking donkeys, and climbed a gravelly dune lined with droves of mo-torcycles—the early twenty-first century's favored beast of burden. A cluster of boys ran behind us, calling out their one remembered English phrase: "How are you?" (I remembered hearing that in Kabul, Afghan kids used *hawaryu* as slang for foreigner: "Look, there goes a hawaryu!") Some of the boys produced mesh cages full of pigeons and tried to sell us a bird or two. When the crowd pressed in too close, our police guards pushed back roughly with their automatic rifles. We asked the guards not to be so forceful, and they rolled their eyes. How were they supposed to protect us if we wanted to interact at close quarters with lots of random people?

Passing markets for cows, goats, chickens, and turkeys, we arrived at a huddle of fat-tailed sheep—one of nature's most undignified adaptations. Like camels, these Afghan sheep retained water in a fatty mass, but instead of rising from their backs, their hump hung off their rear. When spurred to move, the sheep fell into a quick but ungainly trot, their broad rolls of fat bobbing and jiggling behind them. The tail fat was a rural Afghan delicacy. We quickly discouraged our cook from preparing it, but when we were guests of honor elsewhere, it was often served glistening and chewy at the side of our plates.

After an hour of wandering, we eventually rejoined the Haji, whose Land Cruiser had two new occupants: a black lamb and an enormous, self-important turkey. As we climbed back into our vehicles, I reflected that among the hundreds of vendors and customers in the animal market, I hadn't seen a single woman. Odd as it seemed from the standpoint of Western gender roles, shopping was a public activity, and conservative Pashtun men kept their wives and daughters out of public as much as possible. The Kuchi nomads who sold many of the animals were reputed to give their women more liberty, but none of them had been in evidence here. The thronged market was beginning to dissipate as we drove away; by early afternoon, the men had to bathe and head to the mosque for Friday community prayers. There would be no women there, either.

We returned to the guesthouse and loosed our future dinner to roam the garden. Dick Scott grew curious about the health of the fat-tailed lamb, and began chasing it around the garden to get a closer look. For a man of seventy-plus years, he was spry if stiff-kneed, and three times got within a yard of the sheep before it outran him. As Dick tiptoed up behind his quarry's wobbling rump for a fourth try, Jim guffawed and called across the garden, "Dick, we know it's hard to get a look at a lady around here, but are you really that desperate?"

Dick threw Jim an angelic grin, and said in his age-hoarsened voice, "They may be a little hairy, but, ah, when they look into your eyes . . ."

In-jokes were one of the things that kept us sane, and Dick's sheep became an immediate and abiding favorite. A month later, when we were at the PRT discussing the health problems of Helmand's livestock with a visiting U.S. congressman, I would nearly cause disaster by whispering to Jim, "They may be a little sick, but, ah, when they look into your eyes . . ."

To roast the lamb and the turkey, we would need a proper oven; so far, the RAMP cook had been working with a gas range, only good for frying and pressure-cooking. Haji Habibullah fretted that we might not be able to find an oven this side of Kandahar, but took me to hunt around the Hazara quarter. In Pashtun-dominated bits of Afghanistan, Hazaras often worked as tinkers and mechanics; in Lashkargah, they included most of the welders and gas-sellers. We drove through muddy back streets between open-air, cluttered bazaar shops, and arrived at a crossroads where the air smelled rank and sulfurous. Along the roadside stood gas canisters of all shapes and sizes; the wooden stalls offered heaters, lanterns, and camp stoves.

Gas ovens, however, were a peculiar luxury. Afghans generally baked bread in earth pits, and roasted their meat over trays of hot coals. The biggest shop had two small Pakistani gas ovens against one cluttered wall; they were currently being used as storage cupboards for spare parts. One of the ovens was missing a door, though the optimistic Hazara vendor assured us he could find it, given a half-hour.

Then there was a large oven that looked just about perfect—big enough for a good-sized roast lamb, with all the obvious parts in place. I looked it over, then glanced hopefully at Habibullah. "You didn't say where this one was from, Haji-sahib."

"That is because it is . . . not from Pakistan," Habibullah replied. Unsure of my reaction, he did his best to look at once conspiratorial and apologetic.

"Mmm. Well, if it weren't Iranian, it would have been great," I finally said. We were buying it with U.S. government money, which also excluded any purchases from Cuba, Syria, Libya, North Korea, or Iraq.

"It is a great shame," the Haji said mournfully. "Look, the only way you would know it is from Iran is this small, small drawing." He gestured at the logo, a stylized lightning bolt with Persian script below it.

"It's a small thing," I agreed. "But I'm afraid it rules it out."

Habibullah explained the problem to the vendors, who nodded regretfully but without surprise. Everyone knew that Iranians and Americans hated each other. We walked down the street to investigate two more stalls, neither of which sold gas ovens at all. Then a boy from the first shop ran after us, calling Habibullah's name. They exchanged a few words, then Haji turned to me with a faint smile. "One of the man's cousins has found an oven that he thinks we will like."

"Really?" We followed the boy back to the cousin's stall, a couple doors down from the first place. Sitting in the middle of the churned-up, muddy street, flanked by cheerful-looking Hazaras, was a large gas oven. The vendor was kneeling next to the oven, attaching a gas canister and checking for leaks in the rubber hose.

I leaned over to Habibullah and murmured, "Strange. It looks quite similar to that other oven we saw. Just without the logo panel. Without any logo panel, for that matter."

"He assures me this one was made in Pakistan," the Haji said solemnly.

"You don't say." I stepped back, considered the broad oven. "Does it work?"

• • •

When we got back to the guesthouse, I found a stranger had invaded and occupied the kitchen, where he was briskly giving orders to our rueful cook. The newcomer didn't speak a word of English, but was clearly comfortable with Western styles; he went around bare-headed, wearing a neatly trimmed black mustache and a Western shirt and slacks. Like the RAMP cook, he was a Hazara in his mid- to late twenties. His name was Ali Asghar. Habibullah had found him through a friend of a friend and invited him to prepare a test luncheon for us.

The meal was delicious—chicken and eggplant, fried lightly with masterful spicing. Ali Asghar poked his head in, and his nonchalant expression cracked into a puckish smile when we gave him a unanimous thumbs-up. Through Yaqub's translation, we discovered that our trial cook had traveled to Istanbul a year ago in search of work and ended up in a restaurant learning the basics of Turkish cuisine. He must have been a quick study; the Turkish immigration police had nabbed him after only a couple months and deported him straight back to Afghanistan. I told him I would be traveling to Istanbul for a few days with my girlfriend in January, and Ali Asghar nodded with cosmopolitan approval. "It's the most beautiful city on earth," he assured me. "My time there was too short. Yours will be much, *much* too short."

We asked him to mastermind our Christmas dinner, with the promise of an immediate hire if he produced something as tasty as lunch. Ali Asghar grinned self-assuredly and agreed. To our surprise and satisfaction, we had found everything we needed to celebrate the holiday. Now all we lacked were the guests of honor.

Lashkargah, Helmand—December 25, 2004

PRT Air nearly canceled its Christmas flight at the last minute when the Lashkargah PRT protested that they couldn't provide a security detail at the airstrip. The troops had been given a day off, and a gospel choir was coming in by helicopter from Kandahar for a morning church service. We pleaded with the PRT to reconsider, given that our all-important security assessment team was due on that flight. After a flurry of e-mails, Colonel Augustine generously agreed to send an escort out when the choir service was done.

I headed out to the airstrip shortly after noon and found the PRT Humvees already in place. Sergeant Rick Singer and his squad were remarkably good-humored for having had their Christmas interrupted. Their Afghan interpreters were less cheery, hurling rocks to keep excited, scampering dogs and children from crossing the invisible security perimeter. The sky was growing hazy with dust or impending rain as the tiny plane dropped down onto the runway in its usual tight spiral.

The first to disembark were Mack and Zoran, our security consultants, wearing understated black flak jackets. Mack was a staid, unblinking, and twitchy American; Zoran was a lanky Slav with an untroubled air and a languid grin. Of the host of private security companies in Kabul, only Mack's had agreed to provide an initial two-day assessment for free—or rather, in exchange for a free flight down to Lashkargah plus room and board. Mack and Zoran shook my hand and went back to the plane to unload their suitcases and automatic weapons.

The last man off the plane was Jeff Yates, a laid-back young American whom I knew well from Kabul. Jeff had been both a sharp, good-humored aid agency manager and a fixture on the raucous expatriate party circuit. He had been popular with our Afghan friends and had picked up a bit of Dari that he threw out occasionally. Jeff had asked if he could stay with us for Christmas in Helmand while he tried to recruit staff for another upcoming project. I'd warned Jeff not to expect to find many of his top staff in Lashkargah. We were still having more luck bringing Afghan professionals down from Kabul than recruiting them in Helmand. But Jeff wanted to cover all the bases and scope out possible office space while he was in town.

"Hey, Mr. Yates," I greeted him. "Good to see you. You bring the necessary?"

"Merry Christmas, dude," Jeff said casually, patting his bag to clink bottle against bottle. "Santa made a trip to Supreme." The Supreme Market next to the British military compound in Kabul was one of the handful of places in Afghanistan to stock Western alcohol. Without Supreme, our liquor options would have been limited to local moonshine or White Lightning, a blisteringly alcoholic concoction produced by a Kabul distillery "for medicinal use only," which tasted like gasoline with a tinge of raisin.

The security consultants rejoined us, with Mack looking around in dismay as the American soldiers piled back into their Humvees and drove away. "They don't escort us back to the compound?"

"No, the PRT's just here to make sure no one targets the plane," I explained. "The city's quiet. And small. It's not like Kandahar. So far, we've driven around Lashkargah without escorts."

Mack nodded, gnawing nervously on his cheek. "No escorts in town. Got it. Well, we've only got two days, so what say we start looking at your operation?"

We drove first to the office, through the flimsy gate and past the local police guards sprawled incuriously on their picnic blanket. Zoran immediately loped off to explore the HAVA compound; Mack inspected the interior floor by floor, while I described the other inhabitants of the building and explained what we hoped to do to limit traffic on our wing. We met up again in our top-floor office, gazing out across the Helmand River to the forest of brush and low trees on the other side.

"Nice view," Zoran said mildly. "Someone could shoot at you from there, and you would never catch them."

"The mujahidin used to shoot at the Russians from the jungle," Habibullah confirmed helpfully from his desk. "It was why the Communists stopped using this building."

"Well, we're pretty much stuck here," I said, scanning the far bank ruefully. Few buildings in Lashkargah could fit a project our size, and with less than a year left to run, we didn't have time to adapt another. "We've just got to secure this one as best we can."

Jeff had already gone in to see Jim. Now I took Mack and Zoran in to meet the boss. "Merry Christmas, gentlemen!" Jim greeted them enthusiastically. "Welcome to Helmand. At this very moment our cook is slaughtering a fatted lamb in your honor. Much to Dick's regret." He shot me a broad wink and chuckled.

"Hey, we really appreciate your hosting us, and we look forward to seeing what you're doing out here," Mack replied, pleasant and businesslike. "We've read about the carjacking, and we wanted to hear the details from you guys. Also, we thought we'd check in with the PRT this afternoon, maybe set up an appointment to talk to their intelligence people."

"Good—that's very good, because the PRT has one absolutely essential resource that we need you to get for us," Jim declared gravely.

"Really?" Mack replied, startled. "What's that? Maps? Razor wire?"

"Ice." Our team leader barked out a laugh. "Our fridge doesn't have the juice to freeze anything, and I'm damned if I'm going to drink any of that fine whiskey Jeff brought down for us without ice. See if you can't get into the PRT mess hall. They've got four freezers, and they keep bottles of Poland Spring in there."

• • •

Later that evening, we sat down to sample the fruits of Ali Asghar's labor. The lamb was stuffed with a succulent mix of herbs and spices, blending the best of Afghan and Turkish cookery. It was without a doubt the best lamb I had ever eaten, and the turkey was nearly as exceptional. Haji Habibullah paid us a visit halfway through the meal, and beamed with satisfaction when we thanked him for masterminding a perfect dinner. Bottles of wine emerged, and then whiskey. We drank from smudgy glass teacups, and dismembered a frozen bottle of spring water to chip away at the rounded ice block inside. Ali Asghar readily joined us in a toast to his own culinary genius.

After dinner four of us struck up a game of poker. I quickly lost my shirt to Zoran and Jeff. I was coming back from a bathroom break when Jeff met me in the hallway, looking casually furtive. "Listen, I've got something else to celebrate with. Is there anywhere around here where we won't get interrupted?"

I laughed doubtfully. The RAMP house had been cramped even before we acquired four extra guests. Right now I was sharing a bedroom with Jim, which was pretty much the only place Jeff and I might avoid notice. "No guarantees, but Jim's likely to be enjoying his Jameson for a while."

We headed discreetly to the room and opened a couple of windows. Jeff produced a lighter and a wad of brown cannabis resin, expertly punched a couple of holes in a Pepsi can, and soon had fragrant smoke wafting from the lip. "You sure the boss'll be cool with this?"

"No idea." I'd been wondering the same thing myself. "He's had a cold, so he might not even smell it. I think he'd let us know if it bothered him. I can't see him getting upset."

"Yeah, you're right," Jeff grinned placidly as he took a long drag. "I'll bet Jim's cool, dude. I bet he sparked up all the time back in the sixties." He held out the can.

I'd turned down cannabis plenty of times in my life, and accepted once or twice. It would have been easy to turn down Jeff's offer now—especially given the *prima facie* hypocrisy of smoking hash while working for a drug eradication program. But the absurdity of the whole thing suddenly struck me. In Afghanistan, where all drugs were officially illegal, there was no question about the relative gravity of drug use. Hashish smoking was a widespread peccadillo, opium smoking (as distinct from heroin) only moderately more serious. Down here in Pashtun country, alcohol was the truly wicked drug, the addictive life-destroyer explicitly condemned by God. People indulged in it, certainly, but almost always in bad conscience. And the alcohol trade was a Western hypocrisy which the farmers of Helmand felt very acutely. "Why can American farmers grow wine and send it here, but we are bad men if we grow poppy and send it back?" I heard on a trip to Nad-i-Ali.

We had smuggled down our sinful wine and Jameson whiskey from Kabul at considerable effort for our private, recreational consumption. If that made us hypocrites, so be it—my conscience was comfortable with the difference between whiskey and opium. I put my mouth to the can, got nothing but air. "No, man, you're doing it wrong. Cover that hole with your finger and inhale through the lip." Jeff demonstrated with a tolerant smile. "Yeah, there you go."

I blew smoke out the window. *No hiding it from the guards and cooks.* I tried not to worry about what they'd think. It occurred to me that most of the Afghans I'd actually known to smoke hashish were militia gunmen—not exactly objects of emulation. Jeff saw my unease and grinned. "Dude, if the Afghans smell it they'll be in here with us. Just chill." He lounged back in his chair. "So how's it going? I mean in general. Hell, I'll bet you're wishing you'd never set foot in this place."

"It hasn't been easy." Suddenly I wanted to tell him everything—to have him tell me how to do everything. "I'm supposed to be doing public info and reporting. But there's no one here to do the rest of it . . . recruiting and hiring staff, negotiating for our office space, planning how many damn shovels we're going to need. We don't even have a finance manager, and we're making payrolls with tens of thousands of dollars. I've had to do all that stuff."

"Yeah, that's how it is." Jeff nodded soberly. "Always more work than you can fit in a day, or a week. I remember that shit."

"Monitoring, reporting . . . I just don't have time!" I rubbed my fore-head. "I was supposed to send a report to USAID in Kabul every couple of weeks. I just sent in my first one this morning, a week late, and most of what I had to say was 'Our men got kidnapped and we've stopped work. Merry Christmas.'"

"You gotta do what you can, dude. At a certain point, you learn that you've got to say fuck it sometimes—you can only do so much." Jeff got up and walked over to the window, where he exhaled gustily. "The most impor-tant thing to remember? People are gonna tell you whatever they think they need to in order to get shit from you. They've seen all of these donor funds pouring into Kabul, seen the economy skyrocket in the last couple of years, and everyone's desperate to get a part of it. They're trying to survive, man."

Outside, it had started to rain. "Does it get easier?" I asked pathetically. I couldn't tell if my lassitude was from the hashish or the whiskey.

"Did for me," Jeff said, gazing out the window. "Probably will for you. Just don't try to do everything. Understand your role, do your job . . ." He glanced back at me with a wry expression that was not quite a smile. "And give up on the idea that you can save this place. Hopefully we'll help some people along the way, but politics are fucking driving this machine. Just do what you can, and try to find a little time to relax."

"Time to relax? Fuck, by the end of the day, we've barely got time to knock ourselves out." I shook my head. "I know you're right. Still, the week's supply of booze is much appreciated."

"No problem, dude. This place makes alcoholics of us all."

Lashkargah, Helmand—December 26, 2004

Jim spent the next day in Nad-i-Ali and Marja with the security consultants, reviewing our field operations. I would have liked to go along, but I was too busy setting up our first Marja payroll with Raz and the other paymasters. Mack came back pensive and gave us an evening debrief. "On the one hand, you guys have great rapport with people at the sites and with your Afghan staff. But friendly faces can give you a false sense of security. You can't let your local staff know everything. Odds are, your office has already been infiltrated by the bad guys." He suggested we hire two foreign security experts, one to manage the house and office guards, and another for our mobile units. He also recommended heavily armed convoys for our field travel—a couple mo-torbike scouts in front, and in the rear, a pickup truck with a machine-gun mount and outward-facing benches for gunmen. Zoran later added privately that of course they were recommending a maximum level of safety, and we shouldn't be put off if we wanted to go for something less extreme.

The rains continued all day, turning the air damp and cold. The fine layer of dust covering everything turned into a fine layer of pudding covering everything. Despite the weather, PRT Air told us they still planned to fly out as scheduled on Tuesday morning. I was skeptical, but when I suggested traveling overland to Kabul, Mack shook his head adamantly. "We don't drive the Kandahar Highway. That's a good way to get yourself killed."

Jeff and Zoran both looked dubious at this. After supper, their nightly poker game involved a good deal of scheming in low voices. Jeff took breaks to smoke with me in Jim's room. "Forget that, dude. I'm not spending the next week in Lash Kar Fuckin' Gah just because Mack's scared of driving. He and Zoran have got guns. We'd be safer driving up with them than with any of those redneck USPI fuckers."

He took another drag. "Hey, you sure Jim's cool with this?"

I shrugged, hoping that I hadn't misread Jim's general mood. "He didn't say anything yesterday."

"Yeah. That dude's got to be cool." Jeff nodded to himself.

The next day, the rain was coming down in sheets. There would obviously be no plane, and Zoran and Jeff browbeat Mack into leaving by road. Just before their departure, Jeff came into my room, chuckling. "I knew it, man. I knew he was cool." While passing in the hallway he had handed Jim Graham half his remaining stash, saying nonchalantly, "Hey, Jim, here's something to keep the party going when the whiskey runs out." Jim had squinted at the resinous wafer, nodded slightly, and put it in his pocket without saying a word. Jeff gave the rest to me, clapping me on the shoulder. I held onto it for a week or two before admitting that I was never going to smoke it on my own. In the end I flushed it, feeling churlish and mildly guilty.

Jeff's generosity had an unexpected postscript. In late January, just before leaving for a well-deserved vacation in the States, Jim came up to me with a perplexed expression on his face. "Joel. Back at Christmas, Jeff gave me this little chunk of brown stuff. I'd thought it was, I dunno, chocolate or something. I had forgotten all about it until just now, when I was packing and happened to find it in a shirt pocket." He fixed me with a quizzical eye.

I blinked, tried to keep a straight face. "Yeah?"

"Well, I still don't know what the hell it is. But I smelled it, and whatever it is, I don't think it's chocolate."

At that, my composure disintegrated; I couldn't stop laughing for a solid minute. "No. No, I don't think it is, either. Thank God you found it before you got on a plane." Chemonics had already had one chief of party arrested for smuggling guns. All it needed was to have the head of its alternative livelihoods project caught drug-running.

Jim shook his head bemusedly. "What the hell. You know, Joel, I was in the Peace Corps from 1964 to 1966. When I left, America was one country. When I came back, it was—hell, it was a whole different planet. I never quite got what had happened to the place. I'm still basically a bourbon guy."

"Not a thing wrong with that."

"Yeah, well, anyway. You want to have this?" He proffered Jeff's hash.

"Nah," I said. "Come to think of it, bourbon's my drug of choice too."

The Warlords' Vendetta

The rains continued well after Christmas, to the elation of our friends and neighbors. In Helmand, unlike Kabul and the north, Mullah Omar's drought had not ended with the fall of the Taliban; Haji Habibullah assured us that there were seven-year-old children in Lashkargah who had never before seen rain fall for more than ten or twenty minutes. Now it fell for hours, days, and the constant gray drizzle brought a damp chill that seeped unhindered through clothes and skin. Our current generators couldn't handle more than a couple of electric heaters, so we bought kerosene stoves that left us woozy and prone to headaches. Outside, the parched earth sucked in the water and long-solid roads turned to sludge. Dick Scott and Yaqub returned early from the field one morning to report that the mud had made large sections of Nad-i-Ali and Marja impassable. We suspended work and postponed our second payroll.

Further north, the downpours were blizzards. We found out that Jeff, Mack, and Zoran had made it as far as snowbound Ghazni in our project's Land Cruiser, but our driver had balked at making the long climb to Wardak on an icy road. "Toyota Corollas and those little van things were whizzing past," Jeff wrote to us in mild exasperation. "So I declared my authority and said we were going to Kabul. I decided I'd rather take my chances on the road than take them trying to find a place to stay in Ghazni." The three expats had switched to a Corolla taxi equipped with snow chains, and arrived in Kabul just before midnight.

Our project remained frozen by Jim's order until Mack and Zoran sent us their written security assessment and, more importantly, until our own security manager arrived. The Chemonics home office had settled on Charles

Watt for the post, and was working on justifying his salary to USAID in Kabul. Meanwhile, we were pursuing our own tentative investigation into the Babaji carjacking. It carried us into territory that we had naively tried to evade: Helmand's convoluted political underworld.

We hadn't altogether ignored provincial politics, but we had hoped to skim along its surface. The governor had assured us of his support, and we had initially gambled on the goodwill or tolerance of all the other political players—even the drug lords. Our project was hardly a challenge to the opium economy, after all. USAID had told us not to make any of our activities conditional on poppy eradication; it was too late for us to change anyone's planting decisions for the 2004–2005 season, and we didn't have any illusions that poppy farmers would now agree to plow up their crop in exchange for a couple months' paid manual labor.

Some State Department analysts hoped our cash-for-work activities would drain the labor supply during the poppy harvest. But over the last couple of years, poppy harvesters around Afghanistan had made on average $6 a day for their work, almost double our daily wage (which we had based on the pay rate for harvesting wheat). If we tried to raise our rates and compete for labor, we would lose; the traffickers could outspend us, or (more likely) turn the price war into a more straightforward kind of war. So we didn't seriously expect to lure labor away from the poppy harvest. Ultimately, a cash-for-work project like ours made sense only as a temporary safety net, a salve for the coming eradication program, not as a serious challenge or alternative to opium.

But of course, even if the drug mafia *did* decide to leave us alone, we were still going to have an impact on local politics. We were putting at least $10 million directly into the pockets of laborers around Helmand. That was bound to attract the interest of all the provincial politicians—or, to give them their other common label, warlords.

• • •

Back before the Communist revolution, the power brokers of Helmand had been large landowning khans who benefited from generations of patronage, tribal leadership, and control of the most fertile terrain. These local chiefs were the first target of the new Communist government; in the early years of the Soviet War, most of Helmand's influential khans were wiped out or fled the country. The survivors soon found themselves competing with a new generation of strongmen whose clout was based not in land and tradition but in guns and cash. The old tribal leaders lost to the warlords because they were slow to grasp a new axiom of power: He who controls the poppy, controls the province.

Helmand had been a minor opium producer throughout the 1970s, with modest poppy cultivation in its dry, northern mountain valleys. The opium gum had been trafficked through small district centers like Musa Qala and Sangin, a respectable distance from the main highway. The Kabul government had periodically cracked down on the trade, but spent most of its energy on upholding agreements with the communities of central Helmand to keep poppy out of the province's fertile heart. The farmers of Nad-i-Ali and Marja had grown cotton as their main cash crop instead, selling it to the government cotton mill in Lashkargah.

The man who eventually brought opium down from the mountains was Nasim Akhundzada, a mullah and mujahidin leader from Musa Qala district. In 1981, Mullah Nasim issued a *fitwa* (religious ruling) declaring that poppy cultivation was permissible for poor farmers who needed to feed their families. Nasim and his brothers set poppy quotas for farmers in areas they controlled, used the *salaam* system to buy opium cheaply at the time of planting, and started taking over Helmand's main trafficking routes. "They killed a lot of people in Musa Qala at that time," one Helmandi recalled furtively, "especially the tribal elders. Mullah Nasim could not rule the area while those people were alive; they were popular people, and always standing against him. Ten to fifteen khans, the Akhundzadas killed. And so he became the emperor."

For most of the 1980s, the Akhundzada brothers' strongest adversaries were a surviving family of khans from neighboring Kajaki district. The khans of Kajaki saw their fellow tribal leaders falling to the Akhundzadas' opium-fueled expansion, and in desperation allied themselves with Hizb-i-Islami ("the party of Islam"), Gulbuddin Hekmetyar's mujahidin faction. Gulbuddin had plenty of American and Saudi money to offer his client warlords, and had already built up a strong base of minor Hizb-i-Islami commanders throughout Helmand. Despite their new source of funding, however, the khans of Kajaki failed to capitalize on the vacuum of power when the battered Communist forces retreated to Lashkargah. Mullah Nasim moved aggressively into central and southern Helmand and ordered the farmers of Little America to cultivate poppy on half their lands. By the end of the decade, the Akhundzadas' multimillion-dollar opium fief funded their conquest of upper Helmand as well. The khans of Kajaki retreated south to the Hizb-i-Islami stronghold of Girishk, the strategic town where the Kandahar-Herat Highway crosses the Helmand River.

Having won most of a province by leveraging drug money, Mullah Nasim took an improbable step in late 1989: He offered to slash Helmand's opium cultivation in exchange for American development aid. The U.S. Embassy in Islamabad offered him $2 million if he actually reduced poppy, and to widespread surprise, the Akhundzadas responded with a rather effective ban. For Gulbuddin, this was a far more serious threat than any turf war in Helmand. His Hizb-i-Islami faction operated many of the heroin laboratories along the Pakistan border, and some of his allies in the Pakistani intelligence services were deeply implicated in the international drug trade. With the end of the Afghan-Soviet War (and thus of vast sums of American money) in sight, none of them could afford a supply disruption. In March 1990, while Mullah Nasim was in Pakistan haggling over his promised aid money, he was gunned down with five of his bodyguards, allegedly on Gulbuddin's orders.

The assassination cemented an increasingly personal vendetta between the Akhundzada family and Gulbuddin Hekmetyar. Mullah Rasul Akhundzada, Nasim's brother, carried out bitter reprisals against Hizb-i-Islami, and stormed Girishk. Though he expelled the last khans of Kajaki, Mullah Rasul eventually left the strategically important town in control of Mir Wali, a burly Islamist with elephantiasis who had agreed to acknowledge Akhundzada rule. Mir Wali had been a major Hizb-i-Islami commander throughout the 1980s, but his first priority was preserving his base of power in Girishk. The Akhundzadas accepted Mir Wali's dubious fealty in order to turn their attention fully to Lashkargah.

• • •

By 1993, Mullah Rasul had forced the last Communist militias out of the capital and declared himself governor of Helmand. The remaining regional warlords accepted his supremacy, while reinforcing their own strongholds. Mir Wali held the Girishk area, with its many remaining Hizb-i-Islami sympathizers. Abdul Wahid, the mujahidin commander known as Rais-i-Baghran (chief of Baghran district), ruled unchallenged in Helmand's mountainous tip, the most defensible and least fruitful terrain in the province. The drug baron of Sangin district, Dad Muhammad Khan, or "Amir Dado," continued to preside over the largest opium bazaar in south Afghanistan, while also taking over from the Communist KHAD at the head of Helmand's intelligence police.

From the perspective of ordinary Helmandis, it should be said, the picture wasn't nearly that tidy. Though Helmand had only a handful of major warlords, it was plagued by dozens of small-time commanders, clients of one warlord or another, who extorted, murdered, and raped at will. The symbol of the early 1990s was the militia checkpoint, set up by entrepreneurial gunmen to collect money and goods from passing vehicles. The Kandahar-Herat Highway literally had hundreds of them. Only with the rise of the Taliban did Helmand finally see a force strong enough to disarm the commanders, clear out the private checkpoints, and thrash or coax the local warlords into a more orderly regime.

If the Akhundzadas hadn't been so determined to cling to their preeminence, they might have gotten along well with the new conquerors. As conservative mullahs, they were ideological bedfellows; the late Mullah Nasim had armed a brigade of Pashtun religious students who were functionally indistinguishable from the Taliban. Mullah Omar of the Taliban would soon issue a fitwa permitting opium cultivation, and, also like Nasim, would later try to ban poppy in exchange for foreign support. But Rasul Akhundzada refused to disarm and acknowledge Taliban rule, though he piously declared that he would not fight against a movement of fellow religious students. He retreated to Pakistan, and the Taliban entered Lashkargah bloodlessly. Mir Wali, Amir Dado, and the Rais-i-Baghran all smoothly switched their allegiance to the new movement.

For six years, the Akhundzadas languished in exile. Mullah Rasul died of cancer; the third Akhundzada brother fell victim to alleged Taliban assassins; and Sher Muhammad, Rasul's eldest son, took over as head of the clan. He strengthened the family's bonds of friendship and intermarriage with the Karzai brothers, whose father had also been murdered by the Taliban. That friendship served the Akhundzadas very well in December 2001, when Mullah Omar's government fell and Hamid Karzai appointed Sher Muhammad as the new governor of Helmand.

In Helmand as throughout the south, the fall of the Taliban took place not through military conquest but through negotiation and bribes to local warlords, which left all the familiar faces in place. Amir Dado continued as head of the intelligence police. Mir Wali immediately declared that he would cooperate with the Karzai regime, which like its predecessors decided not to try uprooting him from Girishk. The Rais-i-Baghran initially gave sanctuary to Mullah Omar, who had fled from Kandahar into northern Helmand, but after a flurry of American bombs and a parley with Governor Sher Muhammad, the Rais declared that Mullah Omar had vanished again and his trail gone cold. Sher Muhammad returned to Lashkargah and began working to restore his family's full authority.

We had been only tangentially aware of this *Godfather*-style history of murder, drugs, and betrayal. As a result, we had walked blithely into the middle of the long-standing struggle between the Akhundzadas and Gulbuddin. Mir Wali had kept the old Hizb-i-Islami patronage networks strong, spreading his power south from Girishk into other areas that had been loyal to Gulbuddin. The Babaji region, just north of Lashkargah, was where Mir Wali's clients became intertwined with Governor Sher Muhammad's. Neither warlord actually controlled Babaji, and (unbeknownst to us before the abduction) armed feuding between their loyalists had claimed several lives that year.

We soon heard rumors that the thieves who had stolen our Land Cruiser were close to one of the warlords, and had impunity. We even heard that we had been targeted because we had inadvertently hired too many people in Babaji from one "side," though the rumors varied on whether it was the governor's side or Mir Wali's. I understood now why Governor Sher Muhammad had been so delighted when I had suggested that Gulbuddin might have been involved in the abduction.

We didn't trust any of the rumors, which smacked of each side trying to discredit the other. Still, we had no desire to return to work in the middle of an active vendetta. Even if our vehicle had been stolen by ordinary criminals, Babaji was clearly an area where we would never get reliable information about—or protection against—a crime. The driver of the stolen Land Cruiser was terrified at the thought of pursuing the thieves. "If I ask questions in Babaji, someone will kill me," he whispered. We paid him what modest compensation Chemonics policy allowed for a rental vehicle, and offered to help him buy a new pickup as part of a long-term contract with our project. He declined and stopped coming to our office.

Haji Habibullah, by contrast, was anything but afraid. He was enraged at the disrespect implied by the theft and by the community's failure to protect us. "Something like this does not happen in a village without someone knowing who did it," he insisted heatedly. "But they say nothing; they do nothing to punish the thieves. You can never trust these people. We should never go back to work there." Jim and I were inclined to agree. Eventually the police commandant reported that he was closing the carjacking investigation, having received no cooperation from the people of Babaji or neighboring Bolan. We paid those labor crews for their week of work and indefinitely suspended our activities there.

• • •

Meanwhile, I had to design a field payroll system that wouldn't get us robbed again. We would of course be using police escorts, but that wasn't necessarily enough to deter a bold bandit. The drive between our office and the work-site was the window of greatest risk; once we were at the site, a thousand eager workers would guarantee our safety. We could have paid local hawal-adars to bring us cash on-site, but we worried that if they couldn't find enough Af 50 notes in Lashkargah, they'd surely not be able to find enough in a remote district bazaar—and we didn't want to discredit the project by not being able to give every worker the right amount on payday.

So we decided to make our payrolls by surprise whenever possible, travel-ing out on an unspecified date every two or three weeks to pay the workers at their worksites. I worked out a confidential payday schedule that would give us enough time to request money from the hawaladars and put together all the pay packets in our Lashkargah office a few days before our unannounced trips. I showed Raz Muhammad and the other paymasters how to use the timesheet processing system I had hashed out. They rapidly improved on it.

I hoped we would soon find an Afghan finance manager to take over my other accounting duties. Chemonics was sending out David Holmes, an American field accountant, to recruit a qualified candidate in Kabul. Other than that, we were finally close to having all the Afghan staff we needed. We had even found a computer manager—a tricky post to fill. Several young Hel-mandis knew Microsoft software better than I did, but none of them had ex-perience managing a network or satellite Internet, so we'd had to bring down someone from Kabul. As we might have expected, the only computer wizard willing to relocate to Helmand was dazzlingly eccentric.

Khaliq Yar was a gaunt Hazara youth who slept rarely and appeared to sub-sist almost entirely on tea and Bollywood music videos. He spoke in a fierce, im-perious chirp, which, combined with his hollow cheeks and deep-set eyes, gave him an unsettling air of fanaticism. Initially, Khaliq regarded Pashtun-majority Helmand as a death trap for Hazaras. He stridently demanded a bedroom in the RAMP house and a personal rental car in which he could flee in an emergency. He also wanted a completely isolated server room in the HAVA building, and a salary that was nearly double what we were paying Habibullah. I explained some of the realities of our vehicle policy, office space, and budget to him, and he grudgingly accepted more modest terms of employment. One day when I was out in the field, however, Khaliq had a large wooden partition installed in the office he shared with me and Habibullah—claiming half the room for his servers and giving me a door of perfect skull-cracking height. We needed him to keep our computers alive, so I stifled my curses every time I hit my head.

On New Year's Day we also hired the one man who would still be working with me if I ever transitioned to my reporting job: Mian Khair Muhammad,

monitoring and evaluation officer. Khair was a brilliant young Pashtun agriculturalist, originally from eastern Afghanistan's Paktia province, but raised and
educated in Pakistan, with a wife and two young kids living there now. He had
spent the last year in Helmand, working for a respected aid organization. Pete
Siu had found Khair and interviewed him for the post. "He's a sharp guy," Pete
had told me afterward. "Comes up with good ideas on the fly. He won't be
available for three weeks, but he's worth waiting for."

When Khair finally arrived to start work, I tore myself away from my administrative work to introduce him to the job. Our young monitoring officer
had a shock of black hair and a scraggly beard; his swagger and nervous smirk
suggested a strong but still uncertain pride. I explained with some reluctance
that I had a lot of administrative duties at the moment, but I was looking forward to the day when Khair and I could work together more closely. "Your
job is absolutely essential," I said fervently. "The information you get us will
go in reports to USAID. Those reports will go to President Bush's office, or
so they tell us. I wish I'd been able to give more time to monitoring so far,
but now that you're here, we'll catch up together."

Khair leaned forward with a challenging, intense glint in his eye. "Mr.
Joel. How will we know if this project is really helping the people who need
help the most?" I was reaching for an answer when he swept on. "We must
ask them. We must be always among the people, and hearing their ideas for
what we must do. No project will have any good effect unless it is according
to the will of the people." Khair was warming to his topic. "So we must begin
with assessments. We will interview the people in each district. Then we will
know which activities we can do . . ."

"Khair," I cut in gingerly. "Yaqub Roshan and Dick Scott are taking care of
the assessment stage. We need to measure the actual effects of the project. How
much agricultural land we've improved, how many poor families have benefited, things like that. And then we need to tell people about those benefits."

"Yes!" Khair had looked slightly lost when I cut off his previous train of
thought, but he rallied now with equal confidence and ambition. "I will talk
to the *walaswal*s and *mirab*s," the district administrators and village watermasters, "to find out how much land is on each drain and how much is owned by
the very poor people. Then we will make radio programs for all the province.
We will make television programs. We will have big meetings in the villages
where we explain what we are doing and get the people's ideas."

"Absolutely," I agreed. "When I get back from Kabul. For now, as well as
talking to the mirabs . . . can you try to find out how many meters of drain
we've already cleared? Our engineers have been collecting that information,

but I need you to get it in one central place. And can you check a few field sites to make sure their measurements are more or less correct?"

"You are going to Kabul?" Khair sounded disappointed, both at my impending absence and at the tedious prospect of measuring drain lengths. He had clearly expected higher-level responsibilities.

"The day after tomorrow, for two weeks," I said wearily. "We need generators for the office and staff houses, and our own project vehicles, and a lot of other things I can only get done up there." *And I need a weekend in Istanbul.* "But when I get back, we'll get on top of the monitoring job. It's very important."

Lashkargah, Helmand—January 1, 2005

That evening, Jim came out to the domed dining room where I was working. "What have you got there, Hafvenstein?"

"Finance stuff." My eyes were swimming, and my head was light from kerosene fumes. "Got to get everything in order before Holmes shows up. Make sure the receipts match what we've got on the books. We've bought a lot of shovels in the last week or two. You probably noticed."

Jim laughed. "Notice? I was just outside. They're piled almost as high as the goddamn house. How many thousand did you order? Right before we stopped work?"

"Next time we have to freeze the project, let me know in advance and I'll cancel delivery," I said defensively. We didn't have a warehouse, so we were storing our tools and wheelbarrows along the guesthouse driveway. "Apparently we won't be able to get any more for a week or so, anyway. Wood's scarce, and the bazaar guys say we've bought every shovel handle between here and Pakistan. What were you doing out there?"

"Trying to put the fear of God into our guards." In Jim's Boston accent, *guard* and *God* were almost indistinguishable. He shrugged in disgust, mustache bristling. "I had to wake 'em up. Again. A lot of good they'll do us if none of them are awake."

"At least they're alive," I offered. Two nights ago, the police had fallen asleep in the small gatehouse with the kerosene heater still burning. Our watchmen found them in the morning, gassed half to death. We had woken to the sounds of one vomiting enthusiastically onto the muddy driveway.

Jim shook his head dismissively. "Ah, enough of that. Put the computer away. I've got the champagne Jeff brought down from Kabul. Let's have a little celebration."

"New Year's Eve was yesterday, Jim." I had been the only one awake at midnight, working on a procurement report. Around 11:30 p.m. I had taken the satellite phone outside and tried calling a bunch of friends in the States. I couldn't reach any of them, and had gone back to work feeling embarrassingly forlorn.

"Was it?" Jim shrugged, his face crinkling into a grin. "We'll just have to celebrate a little late. Now put the computer away, or I swear, you're going to get hit with one of your ten thousand damn shovels."

We popped the champagne in Jim's room, sat down on the creaking cots, and drank a toast to 2005. Jim vented for a while about the difficulty of getting a systematic workplan out of Dick Scott—who, like me, tended to be of the "start work and just keep going until it's done" school. Dick's fierce loyalty to Nad-i-Ali district had become ever clearer over the weeks, as he refused to oversee work in other areas, and harangued us and the PRT to bring more benefits to the district. "But we have no clue how much work Nad-i-Ali needs," Jim growled. "We might finish all the drains there in a month or two, or they might take us until the end of the project."

"Which makes it tricky to send USAID a realistic set of labor day projections," I said. "And God forbid we should send Patrick Fine projections and fail to meet them."

Jim shook his head. "What do you think, Joel? Does Chemonics understand what we're up against out here?" He sounded impossibly weary. "Say USAID starts asking why we haven't already got a million work days in the bag—or why we've stopped expanding the project. Will the Washington gang stick up for us?"

"I'm not sure," I said slowly. "They're proud of us. But I don't know how many of them really understand what we're facing here."

My friends in the Chemonics home office had written to me about the Go Team's warm reception back in Washington. The Chemonics president had hailed our extraordinary start-up work, and organized a Go Team debriefing conference open to all of Chemonics' staff. The session filled one of the home office's big conference rooms to standing room only. Ray, Pete, and Carol talked about the Go Team's accomplishments—the lightning deployment to the field, the draft workplan submitted within seventy-two hours, the quick office setup, bringing on a couple hundred workers within two and a half weeks, the flexible adaptation to USAID's changing demands. Despite the recent carjacking, security barely featured in the discussion.

Only Bob Kramer briefly punctured the congratulatory atmosphere. "On the security front, I can sum up the Go Team experience in three words: *We were lucky.*"

Qala-i-Bost, Helmand—January 2, 2005

On the last day before I left for Kabul, six of us took the morning off to visit one of the great relics of ancient Afghanistan: the arch of Bost. It was roughly a millennium old, built by the Ghaznavid emperors at the foot of a huge citadel that was centuries older. The citadel, or *qala*, had been sacked by the Ghorids and Genghis, but somehow the graceful, ornate arch had been spared. I saw it every time we made a payroll; it was pictured on the back of the 100 afghani note.

As our little Toyota lurched along the rutted track south of Lashkargah, Jim leaned back from the front seat with an unexpected announcement. "So—USAID still wants us to give a million dollars in grants to local humanitarian organizations. You and I are sure as hell not going to get that job done in our spare time. So I'm going to call up Washington and tell them that we need a second field assistant out here to manage the grant side of the project." He turned and fixed me with a sharp stare. "I'm also going to tell them that if they can't find a deputy team leader in Washington, they ought to give you the job. And a salary to match."

The warm, proud swell in my chest was almost instantly choked off by terror. "Jim, I really appreciate it, but . . ." I searched for words. "I don't think I can do it. Deputy team leader is the kind of title they give someone who's been working at the company for ten years and knows USAID systems inside and out. And we *need* someone like that out here. I'm honestly not up to the job."

Jim grunted in response. I could tell he was disappointed and a little piqued. "Well, they'd goddamn well better send us something soon."

"I mean . . . you know I'll do whatever I can."

"Whatever. Just make sure you take a break when you're in Istanbul." Jim turned a baleful eye on me. "If your girlfriend tells me you were even thinking about work, there'll be a shovel to the head waiting for you when you get back."

Qala-i-Bost towered above the convergence of the Helmand and Arghandab rivers. The area around the ruins was well watered, with farmland, orchards, and a grove of weathered cedars planted decades ago as a picnic park. Just beyond the cedars, the road crossed a dry moat and ran over the crumbled outer walls of ancient Bost. Inside, a wide, barren enclosure ringed a massive hill of scree, sand, and broken brick. The weather-beaten, bulbous remains of towers and battlements jutted out from the top of the mound.

At the base of the ruined citadel stood a soaring brick arch some sixty feet tall, flanked by decorated pillars and bending to a gentle point. Along the pillars and span, the jutting bricks had been worked into intricate curlicue designs and Persian script. Much of the fine brickwork had been broken or eroded over the centuries, but the surviving detail was striking, especially contrasted with the featureless, disintegrating mounds all around us. The elderly warden of the arch showed us some of the Ghaznavid coins that he had found in the ruins, weathered away to scraps of rust.

Khaliq Yar, our emaciated young computer manager, responded to our tour with unexpected delight and adventurous energy. He and I raced our Kalashnikov-toting guards up to the top of the ruined citadel, to a circle of small archways that I had taken for the base of an ancient tower. When Khaliq and I climbed to the top, with a heave of vertigo I realized that the tower was actually below us—a great shaft plunging down farther than we could see. Ringing the shaft were brick-walled chambers and balconies, connected by halls and stairs cut into the rock.

We descended by half-buried, eroding steps, brandishing the tiny green flashlights at the ends of our mobile phones. In the impenetrable darkness toward the bottom, the stairs abruptly turned into a rough chute, and I slid the last ten feet with a startled yelp. Forewarned, Khaliq and the police made it to the bottom with more dignity. We stood atop the earth-brick rubble of the ancient citadel and admired the small circle of sunlight six stories above us. I breathed in the damp, cool air and wondered whether this had been the well of the fortress, or perhaps the end of a tunnel to the nearby Helmand River.

When we emerged, Yaqub asked me to take a picture of him on the battlements of the old citadel, looking down over the arch. "Is it not amazing, Joel?" he said with undisguised emotion. He gestured at the ancient wreckage and the park of cedars, the desert stretched out around us like a rumpled brown bedspread, the sweep of hard-won farmland along the converging rivers. "This is my home, my Afghanistan. It has a great history. And *inshallah*, it will again be great." He clapped me on the shoulders with a sudden playful grin. "We are making it great again, buddy."

Perched in the ruins of Helmand's past grandeur, I felt Yaqub's enthusiasm infuse me too. Sure, our project was small, and our activities currently paralyzed. The hapless police guards clambering around Bost with us—nervous, smiling boys with assault rifles—wouldn't be much protection if the Taliban ever came calling. But I was sure we would find a way to get back on track. We would help tens of thousands of farmers; we would reinforce the shaky order that prevailed in Helmand province. We would, in our small way, be part of rebuilding this great and beautiful country.

PART TWO: FLOWERING

Guns and Poppies

The first time I ever saw opium poppy in flower, I was in the company of a handful of ambitious Americans and a motley gang of Afghan gunmen. It wasn't in Helmand. In fact, it was just about on the opposite end of the country, in the northern province of Balkh. But many things were the same.

At the time, I was simply exhilarated by the adventure of getting to drive around northern Afghanistan for three days. I didn't realize that on that trip, I was seeing sketched out in comic form some of the key ways that we well-meaning Americans were actually undermining the reconstruction of Afghanistan.

A year later in Helmand, I would see them illustrated much more starkly.

Kunduz, Afghanistan—May 11, 2004

Most of the time, the departure lounge at Kabul Airport was a microcosm of Kabul itself: a noisy, dusty free-for-all, with hundreds of people pushing forward in disregard of queues or rules until they were physically turned back by men with guns. But by early afternoon, with all the big commercial flights gone, only a few bored guards were left in the tiled, antiseptic-smelling hall. Our six-man team walked briskly up to the security checkpoint, which displayed a perplexing list of items that were forbidden in a passenger's "handbag":

1. *The handbag.*
2. *Explosives and military matters.*
3. *Gases and passions.*

We successfully concealed our passions, passed through security unchallenged, and met the AirServ charter pilots who would be taking us north to the city of Kunduz. Chemonics had brought in two adventurous almond growers from Modesto, California, to assess the needs of Afghan nut farmers. A few of us were accompanying the "Modesto Boys" on a three-day junket around Afghanistan's almond and pistachio heartland. I was in Afghanistan that spring to temporarily fill in for another administrator; going on trips like this was one of his more pleasant duties.

We squeezed ourselves and our luggage into the tiny two-prop charter plane. Our pilots elbowed their way down the aisle, buckled up, and craned their heads back for a conversational safety lecture. I had braced myself for a bumpy flight, but the skies were friendly as we spiraled up over Kabul, and the view so mesmerizing I probably wouldn't have noticed if we'd dropped an engine. The mountains of Panjsher closed ranks in a magnificent white wall to our north. In the west towered the central massif of Afghanistan, with crest after snowcapped crest rippling out to the horizon. We flew over areas I'd seen from the ground before: the wasteland of Deh Sabz, the rich greenery of Shamali. I stared up the long, shadowy crease of the Ghorband Valley toward Bamiyan, and promised myself that I'd find a way to get up there one day.

From the north edge of the Shamali Plain, we passed into *terra incognita*. I gazed down at a long succession of mountain ridges, broken first by snowy valleys that threw back the sun in blinding glints, then by steep, dust-colored furrows veined with dark green. After half an hour, we flew over a final belt of hills and the ground flattened out into a verdant floodplain flanked by barren, crumpled desert. We had entered the northern Afghan plains, the last corner of the great steppes of Central Asia. As our plane veered down toward Kunduz, in the distance I thought I glimpsed Afghanistan's northern border: the muddy, meandering line of the Amu Darya River.

I stepped out of the plane onto the sweltering concrete and sucked in a lungful of clean, warm air. The gritty, grassy hillocks around the Kunduz airstrip were littered with wrecked airplanes, helicopters, and buses, most looking as though they'd died of natural causes and been dismembered for scrap. A handful of local guards regarded us with interest. They wore faded T-shirts and voluminous Afghan pantaloons, and appeared to be sharing one AK-47 rifle. Otherwise, somewhat to our dismay, we were alone.

After ten minutes spent trying to raise our drivers by satellite phone, we spotted them speeding frenetically down the sandy road to the airfield. It wasn't their fault they were late; they had driven up the day before and spent the night in the Kunduz bazaar, a few miles from here. Unfortunately, this afternoon they had been held up by our "protection." Per Chemonics' cautious new policy, we had to take an armed USPI escort with us on all road trips outside Kabul. The American security company's Afghan gunmen had still been mustering up sluggishly in the bazaar when our frustrated drivers finally left to meet us.

At length, two USPI Land Cruisers also pulled up to the airfield and spilled forth a crew of skinny, scruffy, shabbily clad Afghan irregulars, chain-smoking and casually brandishing their Kalashnikovs. My Afghan colleague Samiullah immediately began berating them in Dari for leaving us stranded. The militia captain replied with an impenitent smirk. "Why were they late?" I asked Samiullah, letting some of my irritation seep into my voice. None of us really felt that we needed USPI protection, and they were delaying our field visits. Samiullah rolled his eyes and said, "Because the sky is so high"—a wonderful Afghan phrase that I would hear him use a lot on our trip.

To be fair, over the next three days, we would more than match our guards' unreasonable delays with our unreasonable demands. USPI's pistol-packing American bosses back in Kabul did not operate on the principle that spontaneity equals security. Quite the opposite: They had wanted to know our itinerary days in advance, so they could check intelligence on every district and village on our path. If we went "off the map," we might be heading into danger—or into the territory of some commander who was implacably hostile to the militias that worked with USPI. To control costs, USPI also paid its shooters in advance for exactly the amount of gasoline, food, and shelter they would need to travel along the preapproved itinerary.

Chemonics had just started working with USPI at the time, and none of us knew about those policies. We had given the security company's Kabul office an itinerary along the lines of, "Tuesday: Kunduz. Wednesday: Pul-i-Khumri, Samangan. Thursday: Back to Kabul." When we now told our gunmen that we planned to spend Tuesday afternoon driving around the local farm country, they objected that they weren't supposed to take us outside of Kunduz city. If we were going to head out into the countryside, we would need to pay them more for the extra gasoline. We mistook this for extortion, and snappishly told the gunmen that if they weren't going to do their job, they could get lost until tomorrow.

The sullen USPI shooters left again. We picked up a local agriculturalist and drove out unprotected into the sun-drenched Kunduz farm country. It was paradisiacal at this time of year, with broad expanses of golden wheat and brilliant green rice, densely planted stands of leafy poplar, and gnarled mulberry trees shading the fields. The Kunduz River, our guide explained, was one of the few rivers in northern Afghanistan that wasn't simply swallowed up by the desert. It made it all the way to the Amu Darya, and along the way turned Kunduz province into one of the country's great breadbaskets. "Just like California," enthused Ken Swanberg, Chemonics' silver-maned, endlessly imaginative agriculture director. "Lots of sun, lots of water. Irrigate a desert like this, and it'll grow pretty much anything."

"Kunduz could be one of the best places in Afghanistan," the local farm expert agreed. He pointed out a procession of electrical pylons; on the left side were a trio of new-looking power lines, while on the right, long strands of wire dangled from the steel arms. "In the war, the commanders sold to Pakistan any metal they could find. They got a very good price for copper. So we had no *barq*, no electricity." He smiled proudly. "Now there is a new line from Tajikistan to Kunduz. The city has electricity for two, three hours every day. And the Chinese are paving the roads."

We stopped in on several farmer associations that afternoon, as part of our whirlwind preliminary tour. The Afghan farmers rolled out carpets and cushions in the shade of their almond groves and sat us down to discuss their growing techniques and pest problems. Ken and the Modesto Boys asked lots of questions and offered a few bits of agronomical wisdom. I took notes. We sipped on juice boxes imported from Pakistan, and judiciously ignored the opium poppy three fields over. When the sun was getting low in the sky, we started driving back toward Kunduz.

I rode with Samiullah and Teshome, an easygoing Ethiopian agriculture consultant. Our driver flew along the rutted dirt track at breakneck pace, not wanting to be caught in the countryside after dark. There were few other cars on the road, but dozens of cart-horses bedecked in northern Afghan style— jangling bells, great bouquets of plastic roses, shiny baubles, puffy red tassels. An accident here would be as disastrous as it would be garish. I leaned forward and said, "Hey, Zabi, I think we could go a little slower."

Samiullah laughed and pointed through the ceiling. "It is in God's hands what happens to us."

"Sure," I said, a little testily, "but I'd rather trust Him to protect us from thieves than from our own driving."

Samiullah stroked his short black beard curiously. "My friends, what is your religion?" When Teshome and I both said we were Christians, he beamed his approval. "We are brothers. I believe that Jew, Christian, Muslim, we are all going to the same place."

"God willing," I replied. "Right now, I'm just hoping to get to Kunduz. Zabi *jan*, a little slower, please." In the end, we made it safely back to the high-walled Lapis Lazuli guesthouse by nightfall. Enjoying the warm, starry evening at an outdoor table, we ordered a round of Heinekens while we waited for dinner.

Our cheery German host brought out enough bottles for all of us. Samiullah looked at the last one with an obvious mix of fascination and intense moral discomfort. "I'm happy to take that one, too," I murmured discreetly, leaning toward him. "I mean, if you don't want it. You don't need to drink."

Samiullah gave a gusty sigh and shook his head. "We are all going to the same place," he repeated dolefully, and downed the beer.

• • •

Over our Heinekens, we debated what Chemonics could do to boost agriculture in Kunduz. Before the war, the province had been a thriving center of cotton production, with a big mill in the middle of town named Spinzar, or "white gold." Unfortunately, thanks to the lobbying power of America's cotton farmers, USAID was banned from helping other countries grow cotton. The same was true for a host of other heavily subsidized American cash crops; indeed, the almond farmers of Modesto, California, probably could have derailed our project if they had felt threatened by Afghan nut exports. We could ask the USAID mission in Kabul to apply for a cotton exemption, but if it came down to the farmers of Alabama versus the farmers of Kunduz, we all knew who would win.

"What Afghanistan *really* needs are tree bonds," declared Chemonics' agriculture director, Ken Swanberg.

"Bonds—like investments?" one of the Modesto nut experts asked skeptically.

"Yep," Ken replied, undeterred. "Worked wonders in Bolivia. Take those poplars we saw today. Say they take ten years to grow from saplings to the point when you can cut the whole stand down for timber and make big bucks. The farmer can sell that ten-year income stream now, to an investor. Just like any bond: You raise money today by guaranteeing your investor a future return. The farmer puts the extra cash into his farm and breaks out of poverty."

"Okay, but what's the guarantee for the investor?" the Modesto farmer queried. "What happens to that ten-year return if a drought kills the saplings, or goats eat them?"

"Or if some warlord comes along in year nine and wants to build a gazebo?" I chimed in.

"Look, all that was basically true in Bolivia, too," Ken countered. "It'd work differently here, but you could figure out enough of a guarantee to make it work."

I was still dubious. "How much of the stuff we passed today has been around for a decade? You'd need investors with a heck of an appetite for risk."

Ken's smile grew pained, and he waved a finger in our collective faces. "Guys, I've worked in international development for forty long years, and I tell you: This business is one failure after another. You get an idea, you take a swing at it, you hope it'll work . . . and it almost never does. But tree bonds are different. I've seen this idea work. This is my home run."

There wasn't much we could reply to that. I wondered uncomfortably if Ken had meant to utter such a sweeping indictment of everything we were doing here. *Tree bonds.* Maybe I'd be saying the same thing in another four decades.

• • •

In the morning, Ken decided that we were going to Mazar-i-Sharif. We had originally planned to spend Wednesday touring the hilly almond and pistachio country between Kunduz and Kabul, and spend the night in one of the major provincial towns. But Ken had decided that he wanted to see more of the northern plains, to personally get a sense of the area's agricultural potential. Plus, he knew we'd find more comfortable, air-conditioned accommodations in Mazar, the largest city in north Afghanistan. It would only add another 150 miles or so to our trip. We initially hid the new plan from our mileage-conscious USPI gunmen, figuring that we'd hang on to them a little longer.

As it turned out, our Mazar excursion violated two USPI policies: no changes in itinerary, and no driving faster than sixty miles an hour. Twenty minutes out of Kunduz, Ken pulled abreast of us, rolled down his window, and yelled, "We'll never make Mazar at this rate! You guys take the lead!" Glad to oblige, our driver floored it past the surprised-looking shooters, who soon dropped out of sight behind us.

The terrain south of Kunduz was a broad tableland of pasture and rain-fed wheat fields. The snowy mountains of Badakhshan drifted sky-blue to the east, and on the southern horizon stood a wall of pale green hills, soft with centuries of accumulated dust blown in from the steppes. As we drove closer to the hills, we could see that they were speckled with hundreds of wild pistachio trees.

"The pistachios belong to all the people," Samiullah explained. "Right now, there are Afghan Army soldiers living in the hills, to keep the people from taking the nuts before they are ripe. When they are ripe, in maybe two more weeks, the soldiers will let everyone come and pick as many as they can carry away."

"I'm beginning to see some ways to make the Afghan pistachio trade more profitable," one of the Modesto consultants joked.

Samiullah didn't seem to hear him. "I used to guard the pistachios myself," he said fondly. "When I was in the army, thirty years ago. We would spend weeks in the hills, walking everywhere, sleeping in tents, cooking all our own meals on a wood fire." I tried to imagine a time, before the Soviet invasion, when that sort of thing was normal duty for Afghan soldiers.

Our shooters caught up with us when we stopped for breakfast (a roadside picnic of lamb kebab, warm naan, and yogurt). Ken confessed to them that we were heading to Mazar that evening, and that if they did accompany us, we would pay for the extra gasoline. The gunmen pushed back their sunglasses to stare at us disbelievingly, conferred with each other, and came back to discuss the price of their extended services. Lacking automatic weapons, we were negotiating from a decidedly weaker position. We ended up agreeing to give them another $100, as long as they matched our speed.

With that source of discord resolved, the previously dour shooters became quite friendly. One of them, a pale young man with heavy stubble and light gray eyes, handed me a cluster of crimson flowers. "Baba," he said shyly, pointing to his chest, which was largely exposed by a camouflage T-shirt four sizes too large for him.

"Joel," I said, repeating the gesture. "*Ta shakor*—thank you."

Baba beamed and withdrew to the rest of the gunmen, who clapped him on his spindly shoulders, guffawed, and nodded knowingly in my direction. I knew that Afghan men appreciated the beauty of flowers (and poetry) with a charming, very un-Western lack of self-consciousness; my male Kabuli friends had handed me many a platonic nosegay. Somehow I felt there was an additional level of meaning to Baba's gift. It was comical but slightly disconcerting, coming from a man with a Kalashnikov slung around his neck.

We hit the road again, this time all driving at the same reckless speed. The southern sections of the Russian-paved Kunduz highway had held together well over the years, and we were able to make good time. By late morning we had reached the main Afghan "ring road" highway at Pul-i-Khumri, a major riverside town with plenty of factories and modern glass-and-concrete market buildings. To my surprise, I saw some familiar beverage cans openly stacked up for sale at the roadside truck stops: Tuborg, Heineken, Baltika, and several others I didn't recognize with Cyrillic logos. We would never have seen beer on the street in Kabul, let alone further south. I glanced at Samiullah, who grinned awkwardly and said, "The Russians were here a long time."

We joined the ring road and headed northwest toward Mazar, driving for hours through grassy, treeless hills littered with the wreckage of old Soviet tanks and trucks. The spring landscapes around us had been beautiful all morning, but I was unprepared for the grandeur we encountered as we approached the town of Tashqurgan. The wheat fields yielded to a range of desert crags, which crept in on either side of us until we were driving through a narrow defile. Ahead of us, the highway seemed to dead-end in an array of weathered, russet stone columns hundreds of feet high.

Just before the cliff, the road veered right, and I gaped in amazement. We were about to drive into one of the most dizzyingly sheer gorges I had ever seen—a soaring fissure in the rock, barely wide enough for the muddy little river at its base, with a thousand-foot precipice on each side. The road-builders had chipped an overhang into the cliff face to make enough room for the highway. This was the Tashqurgan Gap, gateway to the plains around Mazar.

We halted the convoy, opened our Land Cruiser doors, and saw the line of red-painted stones at the edge of the asphalt. It was the first time I had seen an uncleared minefield. This one was about five feet wide, running along the road shoulder below the vertiginous cliff. Not ten yards from the danger line, a half-dozen entrepreneurial Afghans had set up fruit stands catering to passing sightseers like us. Ten yards was plenty of room.

We stood between the minefield and the traffic, gazed up in admiration at the chasm walls, and munched on the juiciest, most flavorful apricots I had ever eaten. "You sure can tell these ones weren't grown to look fat and pretty on a supermarket shelf," declared one of the Modesto Boys ruefully. "We should bring them back to California."

On the far side of the Tashqurgan Gap, the towering cliffs quickly descended to low clay outcrops, with a scattering of walled homes and scenic orchards along the river. The local farmers claimed that before Genghis Khan came through here, the fertile plains of northern Afghanistan had been so populous that you could travel the forty miles between Tashqurgan and Mazar-i-Sharif by jumping from rooftop to rooftop. I would later hear exactly the same story about the Helmand River valley between Bost and Zaranj.

As in Helmand, the combination of climate shifts and demolished or abandoned irrigation systems turned the northern plains into a sterile wasteland. Now the only sign of life was a thick ribbon of trees and walled farms along the Tashqurgan River, which dried up long before reaching the Amu Darya. The desert beyond was flat and oppressively featureless. It was a palpable shock to drive out of the dramatic crags of the Tashqurgan Gap and suddenly face a completely empty horizon. The minute we drove down into the arid plains, locusts began hitting our windshield with heavy, wet splats.

• • •

We had lunch at a lonely house in the desert with representatives from a local farmers' association. On the far side of the highway, we could see a few dozen tanks. This was hardly an uncommon sight in northern Afghanistan, where the Russians had lost thousands of armored vehicles. I was getting used to the unremarked-upon place of tank parts in rural Afghan life: tank wheels put to use as planters or wall foundations, tank treads unrolled across the highway as speed bumps, long gun barrels used for irrigation piping—even wrecked tanks wedged into ravines for use as bridges. These tanks, though, looked to be in pretty good shape. Our hosts informed us that we were looking at a depot for the national disarmament program.

Managed by the UN and funded by Japan, the disarmament campaign was probably the single most important task for turning Afghanistan into something resembling a normal nation. It was also one of the most daunting tasks, after decades when American, Russian, and Saudi money had basically provided an automatic rifle to any Afghan who wanted one. Prudently, the disarmament campaign had not started by trying to collect all the privately held small arms in the country. The UN had instead divided Afghanistan's armed groups into two categories: official militias and illegal militias. The officially recognized ones were led by major Afghan warlords, and held most of the country's tanks, artillery, and other heavy weapons. They were the first priority for disarmament.

In the wake of the Taliban's defeat, the slightly nervous major warlords had grudgingly agreed to cooperate with the program. Their "official" militiamen were being paid a Defense Ministry salary until they could be completely disarmed, given job training, and sent back into civilian life. Meanwhile, the American Defense Department was training a new, professional, and multiethnic Afghan National Army. Once the major warlords' forces were decommissioned and the new army was standing strong, the Afghan government would turn to disarming the hundreds of small, illegal militias with their Kalashnikovs and rocket launchers.

There were many hitches and loopholes in this process, but the single biggest one was the Afghan police. No one was seriously trying to phase out militias in the police and build up a new, professional, and multiethnic force.

Warlords could keep their private armies largely intact, as long as they found a way to label them as police or legitimate security forces. And though we didn't know it at the time, we were helping a particularly nasty warlord do just that. USPI hired most of its Kabul-area troops from Din Muhammad Jurat, a militia commander with an unlovely reputation for torture, kidnapping, and black-market commercial interests. Jurat hung on to his troops because they were on the USPI payroll, but because USPI didn't challenge the troops' existing command structure, they remained very much Jurat's private militia—loyal to him, not to the Afghan state.

Tashqurgan, Balkh Province—May 12, 2004

After lunch, we drove back to the town of Tashqurgan with the local farmers' association to check out their almonds. We rumbled slowly through town, hemmed in by sixteen-foot walls of packed earth. The labyrinthine streets were barely wide enough for our Land Cruisers. Other than the walls, all we could see of Tashqurgan were its windowless, domed clay roofs, with the occasional vacant ruin or mosque open to the street. The compounds' outhouses and sewers drained directly into the road. Several hard-faced farmers turned us away from their gates, and our shooters began to look a little jumpy. "*Taryak*," I thought I heard one of them mutter.

When we were finally welcomed inside a farmer's compound, we saw the garden behind the town's forbidding facade. Little canals burbled under the lofty walls to irrigate broad vegetable plots and expansive groves of almond, pomegranate, and apricot trees. The graceful whitewashed farmhouse, fragrant flower beds, and grape trellises were a striking contrast to the compound's spare, dusty exterior. A stranger in the street would hardly have guessed that there was a single tree in Tashqurgan; inside the walls, we realized that the whole town was an orchard.

We also realized why the other farmers had turned us away. In between the well-watered fruit and nut trees, the compound we had entered was full of opium poppy—*taryak*, in Dari and Pashto. The flowers were tall and gangly, with long, bending stems rising to our waists. They had a very faint sweet scent, which I had to lean close to catch. Some were still in pale pink bloom; most had already reached full ripeness, when the petals fell off and the pod could be scraped for opium gum. Many of these pods already had parallel scratch lines, showing that the harvesting had begun. In the next compound we visited, the farmer had diversified his crop, growing a leafy row of cannabis around the poppies.

We couldn't help chuckling at the farmers' shamelessness. Ken told them gravely that while it wasn't our job to enforce Afghan law, Chemonics could only help them with their other crops if they promised to cease poppy cultivation. The farmers told us that they understood, and would take that into consideration when deciding whether they wanted our project's help. Ken and the Modesto consultants went to have a look at the almond trees. Baba offered me a plucked poppy, and bashfully questioned me about my family.

We all sat down on a big red carpet under a shade tree, and the farmers brought out refreshments: a tray of succulent white mulberries, and six glasses of *shorombe*, sour yogurt blended with salt, pepper, mint, and cucumber. Samiullah jokingly called it "the Afghan beer," perhaps because it was believed to cause drowsiness. The Taliban had been famously devoted to shorombe. I thought of my friend Rahimi back in Kabul, an affable, round-faced wit who had once warned the Taliban minister of rural development that their drinking was a security risk. "I told him that Massoud could take Kabul without firing a shot, if he only attacks after two o'clock in the afternoon, when for an hour all the government is asleep from drinking shorombe!"

We drained our glasses and got down to business. The Modesto consultants noted that a number of the almond trees had been infested by bugs, and asked what pesticides the farmers were using. The Tashqurgan farmers broke out a couple of bottles covered in cheery pictures of worms, beetles, and flies on tomatoes, corn, and wheat. Our expert read the label: "Methyl parathion. Huh. You know, the EPA took that away from us in the States a few years ago. Highly, highly toxic. Are you guys wearing any sort of protective covering when you spray this?" No, they had never heard that protection was necessary. The expert put down the bottle gingerly and looked for someplace to wipe his fingers. "Yeah, in California after we sprayed this stuff, we had to post a sign telling everyone to keep out of the field for a week or so. Don't suppose you do that here?" No, they definitely didn't do that. The expert looked around, a little anxious. "You use it on the almonds. Anything else?" Well, yes. Pretty much everything else. Including the produce, like the cucumbers that had gone into our shorombe. We stopped eating the mulberries.

After a few more questions about how many people had dropped dead with poisoning symptoms in Tashqurgan in recent months, we queasily guessed that the bottle was probably full of a different or diluted solution. Samiullah called up the pesticide vendor on his satellite phone, and scolded him for his misleading bottle illustrations that had suggested that the pesticide went well with tomatoes. We chatted a little longer with the farmers, and suggested less drastic pest control methods. The Modesto consultants talked about how they could bring in machines to help the farmer cooperative process their nuts more effectively. As I watched the farmers nod impassively, I wondered how many short meetings like this they had had with aid agencies, and how our promises, warnings, and snippets of advice compared to the attention, money, and agricultural information they got from poppy traffickers.

We headed out late that afternoon into the blasted, locust ridden land scape between Tashqurgan and Mazar. A wall of cliffs to the south marked the edge of the Hindu Kush; the north was flat and empty, as far as the eye could see. "Just like California," Ken repeated thoughtfully. "This place could be as much of a breadbasket as Kunduz, if we got the water here."

It was dusk when the tight-packed brick houses and Soviet-style concrete apartment buildings of Mazar-i-Sharif began rising around us. By the time we had located the World Food Program guesthouse and checked into an air-conditioned room, I was too tired to venture out and see the famous shrine (or *mazar*) from which the city takes its name—the blue-tiled tomb of Ali, son-in-law of the Prophet Muhammad, with its thousands of white pigeons. I thought maybe I'd get a chance in the morning.

Instead, in the morning, Ken made another on-the-spot decision: We were going to go see the Amu Darya.

New California

Hairatan, Balkh—May 13, 2004

Two portraits adorned the brittle-looking metal archway at the Hairatan city limits. The first showed a rather meek Hamid Karzai, wearing his northern *karakul* woolen cap. The second showed a beefy, bare-headed man in military fatigues, with a shaven chin and bristling mustache. This was Abdul Rashid Dostum, Afghanistan's paramount Uzbek warlord and one of the country's most notable brutes.

Though famed as a hard drinker and flamboyant fighter, Dostum was probably best known for his betrayals. During the last two decades, he had fought with the Communists against the mujahidin, with Massoud against the Communists, with Massoud against Gulbuddin, with Gulbuddin against Massoud, and with Massoud's "Northern Alliance" against the Taliban. He was now struggling with most of the other groups in the one-time Northern Alliance for control of the north. Unfortunately, these rival groups included the militia that USPI used for their guards.

We didn't think about that at first as we rumbled into Hairatan, a border truck stop with a stretch of bazaar shops among large, decaying concrete warehouses. This gritty little outpost was more distinguished than it looked, home not only to Afghanistan's only rail depot but also to the country's most Orwellian monument: the Friendship Bridge. The Soviet Union had built it in a fit of friendliness in 1982, when it became clear that they were going to be sending soldiers back and forth across the border for a few years longer than they'd planned. Its nine long trapezoidal steel spans were now the only land connection between Afghanistan and its richest Central Asian neighbor,

Uzbekistan. Underneath the bridge the Amu Darya swirled sluggishly, an impressively wide, impenetrably brown expanse.

"There's more than enough water in there to turn this whole desert into a farm!" Ken crowed with delight. I realized that Ken hadn't just wanted to inspect one of Afghanistan's key border crossings for agricultural exports. We were here because the Amu Darya was key to his vision of transforming northern Afghanistan into California.

The Modesto Boys nodded sagely. "You could pipe it out like the Colorado River," one said.

"Why are we messing around with the small stuff? Let's take our $100 million and build the Amu Darya Canal." Ken had a defiant gleam in his eye, a vision of selling USAID on this new megaproject. He knew it was a crazy idea; I wasn't sure if he knew just *how* crazy.

"You know about the Aral Sea problem?" I asked hesitantly.

"Remind me," Ken said, grinning.

"This river ends in a giant lake in the middle of Uzbekistan, right? Well, the Soviets sucked so much water out of the Amu Darya for their cotton plantations that it doesn't reach the Aral Sea anymore. The sea started shrinking. All the fish died. The farmland around it turned into salt flats." I didn't go into all the grim details, but the generous application of fertilizers and pesticides in the upstream cotton fields had made the problem especially grotesque. The chemicals had flowed to the Aral Sea, dried up, and blown back into Uzbekistan as toxic dust storms. Mothers in the contaminated regions had been advised not to breastfeed their children. As a final, particularly Soviet twist, the largest island in the Aral Sea had for decades been an open-air test site and storage ground for experimental biological weapons, including bubonic plague and anthrax. In 2002, the shrinking sea turned the island into a peninsula. "The whole place is a contender for the world's nastiest environmental disaster area. We couldn't take more water out of the Amu Darya without making it even worse."

"Well . . . you'll get the environmentalists complaining about any canal or dam project," Ken said grudgingly. The Modesto Boys nodded, sympathetic.

"The government of Uzbekistan would hate it, too," I insisted. "And they could put serious pressure on Karzai." I gestured around us. We were standing at a riverside oil depot, with tanker trucks filling up for the long drive through the mountains to Kabul. Afghanistan got much of its fuel from Uzbekistan.

Ken sighed in disgust and shook his head. "Politics."

"Also, Uzbekistan could close the port," Samiullah offered, pointing up the river.

"There's a *port* here?" Ken's whole face lit up again. "This country's supposed to be landlocked! We can send goods out by water?"

"To another landlocked country," I reminded him, but with undiminished excitement Ken corralled us back into the Land Cruisers. We drove down the sunbaked main street of Hairatan. Here, as in Mazar, I spotted a few adult women wearing headscarves instead of burqas. This certainly looked like Dostum's territory. The beefy warlord advocated female education and didn't enforce veiling—though given his men's penchant for abducting attractive girls, most women in his domain hid their faces for safety. Still, Dostum was refreshingly un-ideological as Afghan warlords went, and only moderately predatory toward his fellow Uzbeks. His problems came with every other ethnic group in the country.

I should have foreseen the tensions when we arrived at the gate of the port and our pack of Tajik militia escorts jumped out of their vehicles, all sunglasses and Kalashnikovs and imperious questions. Even Baba managed to look threatening. Five or six gun-toting Uzbek guards spilled from the gatehouse, outnumbered on their own turf, looking dangerously alarmed. Ken and I hurried up to them with Samiullah, who explained our interest in the port. After some failed attempts to raise their boss on a satellite phone, the wary guards let us in but ordered our shooters to wait outside. The gunmen glowered grimly at each other while we civilians scurried through the gate. "The man who runs this port, Abdullah, he is a big commander under Dostum," our driver whispered to me.

The port itself was underwhelming, containing no barges, a bunch of empty shipping containers, and an out-of-commission crane. Samiullah explained that it had been built fifty years ago, long before there was any bridge across the Amu Darya. Commander Abdullah soon showed up—a hefty, smiling gentleman with a denim jacket, a well-groomed mustache, and a sizable, mostly unarmed entourage. He told us (through Samiullah's translation) how glad he was that we had come to see his port, and that he was sure we would provide the resources to get it running at full capacity again.

Ken eagerly asked how far the river was navigable downstream of Hairatan. "As far as Termez, in Uzbekistan," Samiullah translated.

"That's about five kilometers away," I whispered to Ken.

"And when you get your goods to Termez, what do you do with them?" Ken asked, slightly disappointed.

"They will put them on a train," Abdullah explained. "From there, they will go to Tashkent or Moscow, and the whole world."

By chance, while we were carrying on this conversation, a small train had begun to rumble across the Friendship Bridge. Ken pointed up at it. "Where is that train coming from?"

"Termez," replied Abdullah cheerfully, and repeated how very glad he was that we were going to be investing in his port.

To be fair, the Friendship Bridge railway hadn't made the riverport completely obsolete; the port remained an important upstream link to another port in the Kunduz area, which didn't have any train connections. Still, as far as we could see, the main advantage the port had over the railhead was the greater ease of smuggling and avoiding border tariffs along a river. We handed Commander Abdullah our business cards, made some diplomatic comments about the port, and left before the glaring match between our militias deteriorated into anything more serious.

I stared into the desert as we drove south. The pale brown landscape was even more desolate than the flats around Tashqurgan; there were no locusts here, and the plains were broken by huge, road-swallowing sand dunes. I couldn't imagine turning this into farmland, and said so. "No, Ken's right," one of the Modesto Boys corrected me. "This really is what a lot of California looked like before we irrigated it."

"I didn't know that," I admitted sheepishly. Still, whatever the agricultural possibilities for Afghanistan, I figured the downstream impact would keep the plains of the Amu Darya a desert for the foreseeable future.

• • •

At the time, I thought of Ken's Amu Darya plan as a wild but harmless overstretch by a man who produced ideas impetuously and pursued them a little ways to test their quality. I assumed that reality would quickly winnow out the bad ideas. In particular, I assumed no one would give the green light to a massive canal project without studying the consequences and discovering at least the most obvious drawbacks. Ken soon moved on from Afghanistan, and as far as I was aware, the Amu canal idea left with him.

I had no idea that America had already done more or less the same thing down in Helmand. Nad-i-Ali and Marja districts, whose tidy canal grid was the heart of "Little America," had also often been compared to California. Their deep drains, where we would eventually put thousands of men to work shoveling silt, were a poignant reminder of both the ambitious achievements and the grand blunders of American aid.

Two of the grand American-dug canals, Shamalan and Darweshan, had modestly channeled extra water to the narrow Helmand River floodplain. The canal to Nad-i-Ali and Marja had irrigated a previously uninhabitable tract of wilderness, which jutted west of the river like a huge, outstretched wing. This was Afghanistan's contribution to a pervasive modern quest to turn deserts green, or perhaps white with cotton. Starting around the 1850s, European colonial governments and their successors had fed desert rivers like the Indus, the Nile, the Euphrates, and the Amu Darya into extensive new canal systems. These masterpieces of bulldozer and backhoe allowed settlers to move into previously sterile zones and grow cotton, a key industrial crop which thrived in irrigated desert conditions. Yet all these ambitious schemes fell victim to similar drawbacks, most importantly that they tended to water-log the land, drawing salts to the surface.

The Helmand Valley project was launched with an optimistic haste that ignored both the checkered history of grand canal systems and some particularly disastrous local geology. The shallow, salty soils of Nad-i-Ali and Marja turned out to cover an impermeable layer of boulders. The Afghan government and the American engineers had both been vaguely aware of this, but hadn't carried out the necessary soil tests to gauge the extent of the problem. They assumed that it couldn't possibly outweigh the benefits of bringing water to the wilderness.

Their work turned the desert white, but not with cotton. In 1956, as the British adventurer Eric Newby drove through Helmand, he recorded the lament of an old man in Girishk: "It is all salt, the land below the American Dam. They did not trouble to find out and now the people will eat *namak* (salt) for ever and ever."

Fortunately, the embarrassed American and Afghan governments were able to salvage their sinking oasis at great expense. USAID engineers carved deep drains into the rocky soil of Nad-i-Ali and Marja, which reduced the amount of farmland by 10 percent but also reduced the waterlogging and salinity. The new lands would never be as fertile as originally conceived, but with the generous application of artificial fertilizer, they still ended up as a breadbasket region in a desert country. The land proved particularly well suited for opium poppy. In 2000, the year before the Taliban's brief ban on poppy cultivation, Nad-i-Ali and Marja alone produced 10 percent of the *world's* illegal opium—more than the combined output of Laos, Colombia, and Mexico.

I didn't find out about the full, embarrassing history of Helmand's Little America until much later. When I did, I saw Ken's impetuous Amu Darya canal idea in a new and more alarming light. Hard though it was to believe, sometimes mistakes of that ambitious magnitude did get approved. Sometimes foreign donors and the Afghan government charged straight into projects that seemed superficially like a good idea, and didn't spot the most disastrous flaws until the damage was already done.

• • •

My trip around Kunduz and Balkh left me especially impressed with the uselessness of our USPI escorts. "They did nothing but hold us back, hit on me, and almost get in a fight with another gang," I complained with irate amusement to a coworker. "We'd have been safer without them."

"I don't see why you'd take them around the north anyway," my colleague agreed cavalierly. "It's not like you were going to Kandahar." Though the north had its share of violence, it was a comfortable distance from the smoldering insurgency in the southeast and seemed fairly safe for development agencies.

On June 2, 2004, three weeks after my northern tour, that illusion of safety was broken. Five workers from the esteemed humanitarian agency, Médecins sans Frontières (MSF, or Doctors Without Borders), were killed in a roadside ambush in northwestern Badghis province. The killers were swift and professional, disabling the Land Cruiser with a rocket-propelled grenade and shooting the two Afghans in the front seats before moving to the three expatriates in the back. They stole only the vehicle's radio, leaving the victims with all their valuables. This was assassination, not highway robbery. It sent a shock wave through the international community—especially after a Taliban spokesman claimed responsibility.

Two days after the attacks, I met up with Jon Griswold, a lanky, thoughtful American I knew from college. We had scarcely seen each other since we were both freshmen reading Dante's *Purgatory*; now, somewhat incongruously, we both found ourselves working in Afghanistan. Jon worked out west in Herat, and had been friends with one of the five murdered MSF workers: Hélène de Beir, a twenty-nine-year-old Belgian clinic director. When we picked him up at his staff house, he was visibly pushing back grief.

Jon and I were meeting up to drive to Bamiyan, the famously beautiful Hazara homeland in the heart of the Hindu Kush. We had been planning this expedition with great enthusiasm, and despite our shock, we didn't cancel it after the murders. They were a harsh reminder that nowhere in the country was safe; but if we changed our plans based on that principle, we'd never leave the house. Still, though Jon threw himself into our explorations with gusto, the drawn look never entirely left his face.

"I'm sorry about your friend," I said inadequately one evening. "How are you holding up?"

Jon shook his head with an uneven smile. "It's funny how people ask that—how am *I* doing. Feels self-indulgent at a time like this." He looked around the tranquil garden of the aid agency guesthouse where we were staying in Bamiyan. "When I tell friends back home about the murders, about Hélène, I get the sense they aren't really thinking about her at all. They seem to be mistakenly thinking that those of us with the dumb luck to survive out here must be brave."

"They know you; you're the one they're worried about," I offered gently. Unsure whether he wanted to talk, I was silent for a while before venturing, "When did you see her last?"

"Two weeks ago. We had dinner at an Indian restaurant in Shahr-i-Nau." Jon's voice grew slightly warmer. "We talked about carpets, complained about colleagues, swapped rumors. And serious topics—Hélène was never afraid of those. I got an e-mail from her . . . oh, four days ago now. We were joking about how 'compromised' I was for having friends among the diplomats and soldiers at the Herat PRT base."

I nodded, grinned wryly. "Yeah, MSF's had a lot to say about that." Médecins sans Frontières had been one of the most vehement opponents of the Provincial Reconstruction Team model. They argued that it was a colossal mistake to have American soldiers distribute aid and carry out development projects—that it eroded the neutral "humanitarian space" that allowed civilian development workers to operate in a war zone. You wouldn't see MSF cars driving around escorted by USPI police—or by any armed men, for that matter. For MSF, strict impartiality was the foundation of security.

"Hélène was especially frank on the subject." Jon's lips quirked at the uncomfortable memory. "I remember meeting her over dinner at my house in Herat—this new European guest excoriating the U.S. military's attempts to build roads, bridges, and hospitals. I'm not an ardent supporter of the military, but I found myself arguing with her. Not very well. She was the kind of person who could see through your words to what you really meant to say." Jon glanced over at me. "After we became friends, I saw it was all part of the rules she lived by: hold the powerful accountable, help the weak. She seemed drawn to impossible tasks. Helping at births with dangerous complications, keeping clinics going out in the wild, brandishing human rights papers in the faces of Afghan warlords and American soldiers. It wasn't for the faint of heart."

I sat there silently with him for a while. "I wish I thought there would be some justice at the end of this," I said at last.

Jon shrugged bitterly. "The security report says 'a police investigation is under way.' Sound familiar?" We'd read the phrase at the end of dozens of reports. As Jon later said, it came with the echo of a folder closing, a call to the site of another crime.

• • •

Shortly after Jon and I got back to Kabul, a Taliban spokesman issued a further statement on the Badghis murders. The somewhat defensive Talib declared that so-called neutral organizations like MSF were actually working for American interests, and were therefore legitimate targets. For many angry expatriates, this confirmed the point that Hélène de Beir had made so passionately: The American military's attempts to win hearts and minds were lethally blurring the distinction between civilian aid organizations and U.S. military forces.

Yet few people took the Taliban claim of responsibility at face value. The insurgents liked to give the impression that they could strike anywhere in the country, but the prime suspect in the MSF murders was a recently sacked Badghis provincial police chief and patron of the local opium trade. When he lost his job, he allegedly set up the bloody attack to demonstrate that without him, the province would be ungovernable. There were other theories, too, about what MSF might inadvertently have done to annoy some criminal group by being seen to help its rivals. In a lawless environment like Afghanistan, "humanitarian space" could be violated for dozens of criminal or parochial reasons. The blurring of the lines between the military and aid agencies was less relevant than the weakness and corruption of the Afghan police.

By late July, it was clear that neither the Kabul government, the provincial government, nor any foreign force in Afghanistan was going to seriously investigate the crime. Médecins sans Frontières accordingly declared that it was closing all its activities in the country. Several MSF staffers took the opportunity to issue a final broadside against America for its line-blurring. The agency's main reason for leaving was simple, though: If the Afghan authorities could not or would not investigate this crime, there was no reason it couldn't happen again. MSF had no way of protecting its staff against those kinds of attacks. So it left.

On a smaller scale, that was the problem our Helmand project faced in December after the Babaji carjacking. There clearly wasn't going to be a real investigation, given the powerful feuding parties involved. We didn't want to send our guys into an area where they could be attacked with impunity.

But we knew we were going to have to head into even more dicey bits of Helmand—up to the northern mountains, down into the desert plains toward the Pakistan border. We knew we would be starting work in areas that, while now quiet, had never lost their affinity with the Taliban. We didn't have much of a fig leaf of impartiality; our project was funded by the U.S. government, with the explicit intent of shoring up the Afghan government.

So we would need to find a way to protect our staff. And the provincial police provided the closest thing to legitimate protectors we would find in Helmand.

Traveling Difficulties

Lashkargah, Helmand—January 2, 2005

"Well, it looks like so far, we've managed to rack up a whopping fifty thousand labor days." I handed the printout to Jim with a grimace. My mind flashed to the sites I had visited in Nad-i-Ali and Marja. I could see the thousands of wiry laborers, their turbans masking their faces against the dust, their sneakers and sandals barely visible under clots of gray sludge, their kamiz partoog streaked with mud that dried almost instantly in the scorching sun. I could hear the wet slurp of shovels falling into the silt, then rising again arrhythmically, giving the line of workers the look of a vast centipede rolled onto its back. It seemed hardly fair that all that effort should add up to so unsatisfactory a number. "That's, uh, two percent of the way to our target."

"And I say it's damn good progress," Jim declared bracingly. "Between the rains and the Babaji incident, we've done the best we can. By the time you get back from Istanbul, we'll have this Charlie Watt guy here to whip our security into shape. And then we'll have ten months to make up the difference."

"Fair enough," I sighed. I could see the crunch that was coming. The early months of 2005 were going to be wholly preoccupied with boosting our worker numbers and racing to get some kind of security plan in place. But for now, my mind was on a more personal priority.

As soon as I got back from making my report to Jim, I called Kabul and confirmed my great fear. "Sorry, mate," PRT Air's ever-friendly British coordinator said ruefully. "We won't be able to stop in Lashkargah tomorrow. We were stuck in Kabul under the weather all last week, and we've got a full slate of priority flights that we need to make up. Can't get to Lash before next Saturday."

"Thanks anyway." I hung up, slightly wild-eyed. Saturday would be too late. I would have to gamble that spontaneity really was the best security. "Haji-sahib, can we spare a driver and an interpreter to take me up to Kabul by road in the morning?"

"Yes, of course. I will tell Sharif to pack a bag. We must get you to Istanbul on time to meet your . . . I may call her your wife?" Haji Habibullah looked mildly embarrassed at the indelicacy. *Girlfriend* was not a respectable term in Afghanistan.

I grinned with relief. "Of course you can, Haji-sahib." I'd had some thoughts along those lines myself.

The Kandahar–Kabul Highway—January 3, 2005

Around 6:30 a.m., I left Lashkargah in the company of Sharif the interpreter and Saber the rental driver. We didn't take any security escorts; I wasn't about to trust USPI's Kandahar crew after their repeated foul-ups, and the local police were no good outside the province. Taking a squad of armed Helmandi Pashtuns all the way to Kabul would be considerably more likely to spark a fight than bringing Tajik gunmen deep into Dostum-land. So we drove out alone, as anonymous as we could be in Saber's battered Toyota Land Cruiser. I wrapped myself in my brown patu shawl and stuck out my two months' growth of shaggy beard, an Afghan disguise that wouldn't fool anyone who looked twice. With us flying by at highway speeds, though, hopefully no one would have time to look twice.

We jounced out of Lashkargah along the desert "road" to the Kandahar-Herat Highway. As my teeth jarred against each other, I thought ruefully, *We should have paved this thing already.* It was the first request we heard from pretty much every community in central Helmand. "By God, we grow very good fruits and vegetables," I had heard from an irritable Bolan farmer. "But watermelons, tomatoes, all these things we cannot sell outside Lashkargah, because by the time they get to the highway, half of them will be broken and worthless." Opium gum, of course, traveled just fine over bumpy terrain. USAID had been promising to pave the Lashkargah road for a couple years, but at first the funds had been redirected to a military priority highway in insurgency-ridden Uruzgan province. Later, the project was held up in a convoluted subcontractor dispute. We had been told not to worry about it, though—work would definitely start in the spring or summer of 2005.

After two bone-shaking hours, we reached the ring road highway and turned east. This unremarkable stretch of desert between Helmand and

Kandahar had seen the British Empire's worst battlefield defeat in Asia—nearly a thousand soldiers lost to a much larger army of aggrieved Pashtuns. As part of its rivalries with Persia and Russia in the 1800s, Britain had twice sent massive armies into Afghanistan to prop up a useful pro-British client king. On their first attempt in 1839, the British set up a fortified cantonment in Kabul, not far from the location of today's bunker-like American Embassy. Their Afghan puppet king held on for two and a half years before facing a general rebellion.

That first adventure had ended in one of the great disasters of Britain's imperial history. With the 4,500 British soldiers and roughly 12,000 civilians in the Kabul cantonment besieged and outnumbered by hostile insurgents, the British officers foolishly negotiated a retreat in January 1842 through the snowy passes east of Kabul. The hostile Afghan tribesmen knew the passes intimately, and destroyed the foreign army in a relentless string of ambushes. Only a scattering of Indian and pro-British Afghan troops passed alive through the gauntlet of Afghan rifle fire, along with a single Englishman, Dr. William Brydon.

Remarkably, the British tried again less than forty years later, propping up another Afghan puppet ruler with an invading army. That effort had ended here, in 1880, with a British army wiped out in the battle of Maiwand. While the British army was able to make brutal reprisals, the echoes of the first Anglo-Afghan war were painfully clear. When a fierce royal cousin named Abdurrahman declared himself amir in 1880, Britain was quick to welcome him and withdraw from the country.

Maiwand was one of the places that had gained Afghanistan its reputation as the graveyard of empires; it had been the defining point at which the British decided to try controlling Afghanistan from outside instead of sending any more armies in. The battle had also produced one of the few female heroes and martyrs of Pashtun lore, Malalai, a young woman who was said to have taken off her veil and used it as a flag to rally the faltering Afghan warriors. Maiwand was remembered throughout Helmand and Kandahar with fierce pride and greatly embellished detail. The Taliban were now promising to give the American occupiers "another Maiwand," though definitely not another Malalai.

We stopped on the outskirts of Kandahar for a quick breakfast, picking up oranges and naan from roadside stands. Then we were off along the gleaming asphalt highway, flying north into the deserts of Zabul. We chatted about my Istanbul plans, Sharif's family history, and the lamentable fact that Saber had only slept for three hours last night. (He consoled us by explaining that he had previously worked as a truck driver on the Kandahar-Herat High-way, and had gotten used to driving for days without sleep.) After about an hour, as we rounded a stony hillside, the car began to judder strangely and Saber hit the brakes. I felt a dismaying sense of déjà vu. "What's wrong?"

"Puncture," Sharif replied, with none of his customary sparkle.

We got out of the car and began hurriedly changing the tire. At first I tried to help, but Saber and Sharif declined with a smiling nervousness that went beyond politesse. I guessed that they would be more comfortable if I got back in the car and made myself inconspicuous, so I did. Every few weeks, we heard reports of Taliban and police fighting along this arid stretch of high-way. I wondered again how many of those attacks were gestures in a com-pletely different game.

I remembered a story we had heard about Mir Wali, the governor of Hel-mand's main rival warlord, that illustrated the many uses of Taliban assaults. Back in September, the Kabul government had sent a police platoon to re-lieve Mir Wali of responsibility for security along the Helmand section of the national ring road. The commander of Girishk had graciously complied, withdrawing his militia from the potentially lucrative highway checkpoints. Days after the national police takeover, the checkpoints had been hit by co-ordinated "Taliban" attacks for the first time in months. Fifteen policemen had been killed, and Mir Wali had immediately reclaimed control of the road, berating the Kabul government and Governor Sher Muhammad for their in-ability to keep order. There had been no further assaults on the checkpoints.

Still, I wasn't going to hang around in so-called Taliban country any longer than I had to. Having thrown on a new tire with record speed, Saber and Sharif hopped back into the car and we started off again. "Saber says we have one spare tire left," Sharif informed me. "He wonders if we should stop in Qalat and buy another to replace the one we just used."

"I'd like to spend as little time as possible in Zabul," I said pensively. "Do you think we can make it to Ghazni before we pick up a second spare? I'd rather stop there than here."

"Good idea." Sharif and Saber both gave an emphatic nod.

We trundled onward through the arid, forbidding landscape. After a while, I glanced over at Saber. "Aren't we going a little slowly?"

Saber said something in worried Pashto. "The engine is giving trouble," Sharif explained. "He cannot go faster than fifty-five or sixty kilometers per hour."

"Great," I laughed helplessly. So much for flying through Zabul at high-way speeds. At this pace, we might be able to outrun the Taliban if they showed up mounted on buffalos. I buried myself in my patu and leaned back in my seat. The sun-drenched, brown monotony of the wilderness around us quickly lulled me to sleep.

When I drowsed awake, for a bewildered moment I felt like we had driven into an Ansel Adams photograph: flat, monochrome, exquisite. I remembered this section of highway from our drive south in November, the broad, seemingly endless corridor between two mountain ridgelines. Back then, the dun colored crags in the west had loomed sullenly over a dusty, wind-furrowed plain. With the coming of winter, the plain had become a field of deep, unbroken snow, ending at a line of tiny trees that suggested a river, and the gouged surface of the mountains was now a canvas of bold, bluish-white sweeps and shadowy whorls. The haze in the air was gone, giving everything a feel of crisp, crystalline abstraction. The peaks no longer loomed; rather, they seemed immeasurably distant, like a movie backdrop, with the thin line of trees marking a leap from pure horizontal to pure vertical. It was like driving along a panoramic frieze that just kept going and going.

Our Land Cruiser also kept going, but grudgingly, with noticeably more noise and fumes than when we had started. We paused a few times in the magnificent snowy landscape for Saber to tinker with the engine. "It is a turbo-drive problem," Sharif diagnosed mournfully. "We will need a new part to fix it." By the late afternoon, when we reached the outskirts of Ghazni, the sluggish car gave off a distinct smell of burning oil. "Should we stop here for a mechanic?" I asked Saber with concern.

Sharif translated Saber's reply. "He says that if we stop here, we will probably stay all night. But he thinks the Land Cruiser can get to Kabul."

"All right," I acquiesced. Ghazni was out of the main danger zone, but I didn't really want to go hotel-hunting there. "Let's keep going."

Driving south from Kabul in November, I hadn't realized just how long the slope between Ghazni and Wardak provinces was. I understood why the driver we sent with Jeff, Mack, and Zoran hadn't wanted to tackle it with fresh snow and ice on the road. It wasn't actually steep in more than a few places, but the long upward grade took a toll on Saber's beleaguered vehicle. By the time the snow-blanketed incline leveled out into the hilly Wardak farm country, our smoke-spewing Land Cruiser could just about gasp along at forty kilometers per hour. The sun disappeared over the peaks to our west, and we drove on through a long mountain dusk.

Forty minutes later, the last light was gone, and we were still creeping through Wardak with a handful of other cars. For the most part, the blackness around us was unbroken; any lanterns were hidden in people's houses, behind high mud walls. Saber spoke up conversationally, and Sharif leaned forward. "He says, last time he went to Kabul, he only got one puncture."

"Well, it's a good thing we'll only have one this time, too," I said blithely. "I don't think any mechanics will be available at this time of night if we need another tire." Less than a minute later we had our second puncture. Saber and Sharif bolted on our last spare in the dark; I prayed that our remaining tires would survive as far as Kabul.

They did, but by the time we reached the outskirts of the capital, our vehicle was belching foul black smoke in such quantities that Saber refused to go any further. "He says the police will arrest him if he drives into Shahr-i-Nau like this," Sharif declared. Instead, Saber dropped us off at the first available taxi stand. Remarkably, he still looked wide awake. I thanked him wearily but warmly for getting us to Kabul in one piece. Saber grinned, said in Pashto, "So hire me as a project driver," and drove off to find a mechanic.

We had been on the road for more than thirteen hours by the time Sharif and I pulled up to Kabul's cozy Le Monde guesthouse. Gary, the friendly proprietor, had blessedly kept some dinner leftovers warm for us, and I was able to have a beer and a hot shower before hitting the sack.

Kart-i-Sakhi, Kabul—January 4, 2005

My time in Kabul was mostly a whirlwind of long-overdue shopping. I ordered generators for our staff houses and picked up two cash-counting machines that could tally a stack of afghanis faster even than Nazar—though just barely. I also found out why the registration for our Land Rovers was taking so long.

"These applications are always slow, Mr. Joel," explained Farooq, Chemonics' vehicle coordinator, with a strained smile. "First, we applied to USAID for one recommendation letter to give the Ministry of Foreign Affairs. Then the Ministry gave their approval to General Custom Department of the Ministry of Finance. Today, we were in General Custom Department all day," he paused for breath, "but they told us that tomorrow, they will issue the order for Kabul Traffic Department. Then we will make application there for the registration."

Appalled, I told him to prise the Land Rovers out of the bureaucracy and send them down, whatever their legal status. We needed them now—and down in Helmand, no one would care about registration. Farooq gave a resigned, slightly relieved shrug of assent.

I also met up with David Holmes, Chemonics' recently arrived field accountant. Holmes was a towering, heavily built, bespectacled man whose features were usually folded into some combination of patience and amused skepticism. He would be taking Saturday's PRT Air flight down to Lashkargah, where (to my indescribable joy) he would take over our project's finances and train our still-hypothetical Afghan finance manager. Holmes gave his tentative stamp of approval to my improvised payroll system, but seemed less happy as I explained our cash transfer practices.

"Let me get this straight," Holmes finally rumbled, looking politely aghast. "You send an e-mail to the National Bank of Pakistan, authorizing them to transfer $400,000 to Haji Ansari's personal bank account. In exchange, we get the good Haji's promise that his hawala cousin in Lashkargah will give us $400,000 in cash."

"Right." I thought he was putting undue emphasis on the word *promise*. "These guys don't stay in business if they don't keep every promise, every time."

"From a liability perspective, you do realize this is crazy talk."

I laughed. "Yes."

Holmes shook his head in disbelief. "How often do these hawala guys get robbed? If our money is sitting in Haji Ansari's Lashkargah office and someone comes in and cleans the place out, do we still get paid?"

"Good question," I said thoughtfully. Haji Habibullah had reassured us that he had never heard of a hawaladar being robbed. "They seem to be pretty confident in their own untouchability. Everyone uses their services, including all the big traffickers, Taliban, whatever. But no one's too powerful to get hit, I guess."

"See, we have theft insurance for money we give to a bank. I'm pretty sure our insurance won't cover money we give to Haji Ansari."

I shrugged helplessly. "Dave, as far as I can see, Haji Ansari is all we've got. We can't ensure anything down there."

I was soon reminded that there were few sure things in Kabul, either. On Thursday, as we were driving back from a long day of equipment shopping, our invaluable young logistics guy Masoud called up Ariana Airlines to confirm my Friday flight to Istanbul. His voice took on a dismaying note of urgency, and when he hung up, his normally imperturbable brow was creased. "Joel, they have changed your flight."

"I'm sorry?" I had expected this from PRT Air, but not from the national airline.

"To Mecca. To take more people on haj." It was the annual pilgrimage season approaching the feast of Eid-ul-Adha, the most meritorious time for Muslims to make their obligatory once-in-a-lifetime visit to Mecca. The government was responsible for helping would-be Afghan hajis make the trip, and was now commandeering extra airplanes to avoid scenes of outraged, stranded old men rioting at the airport.

"Masoud, I can't go to Mecca." I felt a frantic laugh bubbling up somewhere in my throat. "Are there any other flights to Istanbul?"

"No—they say that all of Ariana's flights are full of hajis."

"What about Kam Air?" Some people said the fledgling private airline wasn't safe, but I was willing to take my chances. "If I can just get out of the country, I should be able to find another flight to Istanbul. Does Kam Air fly to Dubai tomorrow?"

"I will call them now," Masoud said, recovering his poise. "My cousin works for Kam Air," he added hopefully while his phone rang.

At this worst possible moment, the Chemonics Washington office called me on my mobile phone, wanting to catch up on the status of our generator-buying and other plans. I lay down in the backseat of the car, trying to keep the despondency out of my voice as I made my report. At the end of the call, Dave Guier, the project director, asked if there was anything we needed from the home office. "Dave, you've got to get a deputy team leader out here," I said wretchedly. "I'm keeping things together, but frankly, it's more than I can handle."

"I know, Joel," came the apologetic voice down the line. "We're going to find someone. We're doing our best."

"Joel?" Massoud's face was bright. "There is one Kam Air business class seat left to Dubai."

• • •

I'd known Fiona Mackay since we were both kids in Nepal, where our engineer fathers worked on some of the same hydroelectric dams. In 1990, both our families left, hers to England, mine to Minnesota. Fiona and I met up again unexpectedly in Nepal ten years later, sheltering in the same guesthouse during a surge of Maoist rebel violence. As we became friends, I quickly found that we didn't just share a common childhood home, but a set of core passions: travel, adventure, family, God. Fiona was studying for a career in international development; she was also a talented artist, with a mischievous sense of humor and an inexhaustible capacity for fun. Ever since we started dating across the Atlantic in the spring of 2004, we had found ourselves circling the incandescent prospect of marriage like light-drunk moths.

Four blessedly tranquil days in Istanbul after months of exhaustion, uncertainty, and anxiety on both our parts was all Fiona and I needed to push us into a decision. I e-mailed Jim and our Washington office that I was getting engaged and gave them my notice, telling them I'd need to be gone by the end of May. This wasn't the right time for Fiona and me to spend a full year apart—especially with me in a place where she was understandably worried for my life. To my relief and regret, my days in Helmand were now numbered.

I wondered how Jim would take my desertion. When I got back to Lashkargah on January 15, he greeted me with his typical boisterous cheer. "Joel! Welcome back, and congratulations! We'll have to break out John Jameson's best to celebrate your good news."

"Fiona's sent me back with a bottle of Glenmorangie for just that purpose," I said, grinning with relief.

"She's got taste in whiskey, at least," Jim retorted. "Ha! Joel, meet Charlie Watt."

Charles was a New Zealander of medium height and muscular build, with bluntly chiseled, clean-shaven features and short black hair. I relaxed a little as soon as I saw him; I later decided it was because he wasn't trying to look like a marine. Many of the private security guys I'd met (especially, it must be said, the Americans) kept their hair shorn in a military cut, wore fatigues, and constantly carried a sidearm. Though I knew Charles had begun his career as a tank commander in the New Zealand military, he didn't seem to be trying to live into any particular stereotype. We shook hands and exchanged pleasantries as our Istanbul-trained cook brought in dinner.

Jim, Yaqub, Charles, and Haji Habibullah had spent the day in upper Helmand—our project's first cautious excursion north of the Kandahar-Herat Highway. The four of them had left at dawn under police escort for Kajaki and Musa Qala districts, to figure out what kind of mass employment projects we could start up in the north, far from any grand irrigation canals. They had returned to the guesthouse after dusk, travel-sore and hungry. Over dinner, I questioned them jealously about the rugged upper reaches of the province.

As the whiskey came out, the reminiscences took a more confessional turn. "Funny thing this afternoon," Charles said bemusedly, pouring more Jameson into his glass teacup. "We stop for a break, and I'm feeling the need for a piss. So I head a few paces into the desert, stand with my back to the breeze, and go about my business, right? I hear the Afghan guards start laughing, and I look around, thinking, *Are you bastards laughing at me?* They are. 'Cause they've all squatted to piss. These hard-arsed mujahidin fuckers are all squatting down, dainty as a bunch of ladies, to piss in the dirt, and they're laughing 'cause I'm standing up and taking a piss like a man."

"They think you're splashing yourself," Dick Scott offered with a grin. "It's unclean."

"Look, my mother taught me how to piss without splashing myself," Charles insisted. "If they laugh at me, I'll fucking well laugh back at them. Anyway, I told them to pull their trousers up and go establish a perimeter."

"Did the police ever look nervous, while you were driving around up there?" I asked.

"No, they knew things were more or less under control." Charles's smile hardened. "I'll tell you something I've noticed, though, driving around this province. The police tell me they don't have radios, and the whole local government gets by with sat-phones. But there were ultra-high-frequency base-station antennas popping up every two or three kilometers along the Darweshan Canal when I was there last week, and today I saw the same thing in all the pretty marble mansions around Sangin. *Somebody* sure as hell has radios."

Sangin was the biggest opium bazaar in south Afghanistan; the Darweshan Canal ran along one of the major smuggling routes down to Pakistan. It was obvious who had set up those radio networks. "They're not afraid of advertising their location," I said wryly.

"More to the point, they can track any movement along those roads, quickly and without any monitoring by the police." Charles finished his whiskey. "We've got to get our Land Rover radios working. Until we've bought high-frequency base stations and set them up here in Lashkargah, those big black antennas we've got on there are just a bluff. And I don't like the idea of some drug lord in Sangin having a better idea of where our people are than we do."

Lashkargah, Helmand—January 16, 2005

The next morning, Charles and I met up in his largely empty office to discuss security. I began by mentioning Mack and Zoran's report, but Charles shook his head. "Scrap it. It's bullshit. Completely fails to understand what's appropriate for a project like this. Those guys wanted you out there in technicals with mounted machine guns."

"Sorry, Charles—I don't know what a 'technical' is."

"Proves the point," Charles said, not unkindly. "It's a pickup truck with outward-facing benches in the back for shooters. Handy enough for military operations, but this is a development project. The culture's totally different. You guys don't want to be out there bringing jobs at gunpoint, right? One carjacking doesn't change that."

Charles had us pegged. We wanted to be able to defend our staff against a handful of armed thugs like the Babaji highwaymen, but we were highly reluctant to drive around looking like a branch of the U.S. or Afghan military—both because we worried that we might draw attacks, and because we worried that it would distance us from the people we were working with. We wanted our security to be discreet and controllable, a few armed policemen in a pickup or Land Cruiser.

"So we aren't going to build an army," Charles averred. "But we do need to tighten up our operations—guards, vehicles, communications, houses, and office. First off, we've got an obvious problem controlling access to this building."

"Dawari offered us the engineering wing, with only one way in," I confessed, "but I kept us on this side of the HAVA building to cut down on car bomb risk."

Charles shook his head. "Mate, we shouldn't be in this building at all. It's not *our* building. Any bastard could walk in off the street carrying a bomb in a box and no one would ask him what he was doing. HAVA's guards are about as useful as tits on a fucking bull."

That judgment was, if anything, too kind. Governor Sher Muhammad had assigned HAVA a small squad of gunmen who spent six days a week lounging malevolently on a blanket in the dusty front yard, underneath a rusted climbing frame that presumably had once entertained the children of American and Afghan engineers. The guards' eyes were thickly lined with kohl to reduce eye infections, which left them looking at once predatory and camp. They were the terror of our staff. Our young Hazara computer manager, Khaliq, told me that the office guards had questioned him in menacing tones about where he was living and how long he planned to stay in Helmand. After my frequent late-night work sessions, the cleaning guys implored me to hang around while they closed up the office, so they wouldn't have to walk out alone past the guards after dark. One cleaner reported that they had tried to steal his bicycle. Habibullah had gone on the warpath and got a guard sacked for making inappropriate comments about Rubina and Safeena, our female office assistants.

"We'll see if we can get the whole guard troop replaced with a squad that answers to us," Charles said resolutely. "Meanwhile, we need to put up a boom at the main gate, set up a checkpoint down on the ground floor, wall off two of the stairwells to our office, and get a receptionist to block anybody who doesn't have a photo ID signed by Jim Graham."

I wasn't looking forward to getting HAVA's permission for the structural changes. "Well, Engineer Dawari is spending Eid in Mecca. We'll see what we can get his deputy to agree to. Maybe give him some juice from the new generator."

"Whatever it takes," Charles shrugged. "Then there's the house guards. We've got to start treating them like a guard force, mate. We can't have guards doing the laundry; we can't have them running errands. They need to respect themselves and think of themselves as guards, not as errand boys."

"Good point," I said, somewhat abashed. "And the police?"

"We treat them like they belong to us," Charles said crisply. "We feed them; we give them uniforms; we make sure they've got all the weapons and equipment they need; we barrack them if we can. We take them out and drill them, give them some proper training. We try to build their loyalty and discipline so there's some chance that when the bullets start flying, they'll return fire long enough for you to get away . . . instead of bolting and leaving you ten different kinds of fucked."

• • •

Later, over a nighttime whiskey, I found out that Charles had held together a squad of troops through a fighting retreat far more brutal than anything we would encounter in Afghanistan. Back in the early 1990s, he had been left disastrously stranded deep in Angola after leading a raid on a guerrilla camp. He and his troops had run for a week through the jungle to their backup extraction point, pursued by vengeful guerrillas. Charles spoke bleakly of men vaporized by rockets, or abruptly losing most of their heads to gunfire in mid-conversation. "At night, we'd hear the bastards torturing any of our men they'd caught. After that, when anyone got wounded so bad that he couldn't run, we'd put a bullet in his brain."

At the time, Charles had been working for one of the many private military companies—mercenaries, to their detractors—in the employ of the apartheid government of South Africa. The guerrillas were part of the African National Congress, the liberation movement whose friendliest face was Nelson Mandela. Even while the beleaguered South African government had been dismantling itself in negotiations with Mandela, it had stepped up attacks against the Congress's camps in Angola in the hopes of weakening Mandela's less peaceable comrades. Charles refused to apply moral categories to his work for the dying regime. "Apartheid, bullshit. My men were black, and the guys we were fighting were no fucking Gandhis."

After the Angola bloodbath, Charles had quit the mercenary company and taken a job protecting aid agencies in post-genocide Rwanda. Then he went to London, got a master's degree in business, and moved to the former Soviet republic of Georgia. He had worked in Georgia and Chechnya for years in an eclectic blend of jobs: generator salesman, security consultant, rescuer of kidnapped expatriates. Eventually, Charles wooed and wed a Georgian Russian woman, settling in Tbilisi. They had just had their first son.

Charles's stories from the Caucasus were by and large more amusing than horrific: run-ins with the local mafia, hard-drinking business meetings (usually also with the mafia). One of his Russian colleagues was an ex-Spetsnaz captain, who had spent the late 1980s leading Soviet commando missions in the mountains of Panjsher. "He was their top man in Afghanistan. Over five years, this guy's unit only lost two men," Charles said proudly. "These days, he spends part of his time on ransom operations with me, and the rest doing mercenary work for Putin in Chechnya."

Calling Charles amoral was accurate in a limited sense. He was a soldier who rejected the usual soldierly justifications for killing—no patriotism, no just causes, no good guys and bad guys. I remember him laughing scornfully one evening when Yaqub and I described Gulbuddin as more monstrous than the other Afghan warlords. "Fucking hell, Joel, they're *all* a bunch of monsters." At the same time, Charles displayed in abundance the best military virtues: courage, generosity, ardent loyalty, and fierce protectiveness toward his comrades. He didn't make a virtue out of cruelty, and he didn't despise our innocence. I believed that on a deep level, his moral temperament was better suited to the role of guardian and rescuer than soldier-for-hire.

In any case, we needed Charles's experience, his toughness, and his suspicion—a survival skill honed by years in African warfare and post-Soviet business. Charles restlessly probed the world around him for threats, and tested his theories by passionately, angrily inhabiting them, asserting them with conviction to see how far they would go. If new information came up that contradicted his working theory, he would adjust or shed it without embarrassment and jump into a new one. But he never stopped scanning for signs of, as he put it, the crocs in the water. "When a croc goes for you, it's all over in a second. You don't see anything in the pond before it happens, then suddenly it's up on the bank with its teeth around your leg, and you're in over your head before you know what's happened to you."

"What can you do about it?"

"Once they've decided to go for you, you can't stop them," Charles said harshly. "For a project like this, you've just got to know where the crocs are, and stay out of their way."

• • •

There was no question about which of Charles's new security provisions I felt most acutely. For weeks, Jim had been haranguing me to get out of the office at six o'clock like a normal human being, but with no Internet in the guesthouse, I often ended up coming home late. Every day, I had a constant flow of staff bringing urgent problems to my attention; only when they'd all gone home for the night could I actually make headway on my e-mail backlog.

Charles was having none of it. We had to be home before dark, which meant the office closed at six—no excuses, no extensions. I managed to follow the new rule for a couple of weeks, but finally the day came when I'd spent all afternoon revising the project budget, and still needed to compose an e-mail of questions to the Washington office. I asked Sharif to wait for me with a car, and shrugged off Habibullah's reminder. Back at the guesthouse, Jim greeted me with a raised eyebrow and a scowl. "What took you so long, Hafvenstein? It's been dark out there for an hour."

"I needed to stay online long enough to finish a few things," I answered, braced for one of Charles's outbursts.

Charles looked grim, but spoke quietly, sounding almost hurt. "It's not my job to play nursemaid. You know the policy. I'm not going to hang over your shoulder and carry you out of the building at dark. But I tell you, Joel, it's a fucking stupid reason to get killed, and I don't fancy having to call up your Fiona and tell her that you got shot up because you hadn't finished your e-mail."

It was funny, how easy it was to prioritize work above security, especially when everything seemed relatively quiet. Charles's mention of Fiona had the intended effect: I stopped staying late.

The Way of Love

By late January, for the first time since I had arrived in Helmand, I found myself able to catch my breath. Field accountant David Holmes had taken over the books. Charles was handling everything security-related. I passed as much of the day-to-day administration as I could on to Haji Habibullah and our project's promising whiz kids. The slightly saner workload didn't just do wonders for my own happiness; it also gave me a chance to talk with my young Afghan colleagues about things other than work.

Sadly, I was usually still too busy to join them for the local entertainments. Sharif invited me to go fishing with him in the Helmand; when I asked whether he planned on using a rod or net, he smiled, grasped imaginary wires in his hands, and said, "Generator." Other friends invited me to go see a dog-fighting match in the Mukhtar refugee camp. The beloved pastime of Lashkargah's militia commanders had been banned by the Taliban as Communist depravity and an incitement to gambling, but was now being revived with gusto. I queasily declined. My less-fastidious American colleagues came back describing a surprisingly gentle blood sport: huge mastiffs snarling at each other in a ring, then being pulled back quickly by their owners with little more than scratches to determine the victor.

Given the pace of the project, I had to make my friendships on the job, through conversations on our long road trips out to the districts or in the rare moments of calm at the office. Most of my young colleagues were eager to share their stories and thoughts, and wanted to know more about me. Our discussions held plenty of froth, but also dipped into deeper waters: attitudes toward family, marriage, God.

I couldn't help comparing the attitudes and values I encountered in Lashkargah to those I had seen in Kabul. Down here, the traditional Afghan modesty code was plainly more robust, shored up by conservative religious passion; the flood of libertine foreign pop culture was breaking against it with less obvious effect. You could certainly find Hindi music, Bollywood films, pinup posters of Indian starlets, and form-fitting Western clothing for sale without hunting too hard. Southerners tended to use them behind their high walls, however, not on the street as in Kabul.

That discretion was partly nervousness about physical punishment by vigilante remnants of the Taliban, but social pressure was also far more intense. My more conservative Pashtun friends, who also tended to have the most domineering personalities, expressed firm resistance to even the smaller inroads. Mian Khair Muhammad, our proud young monitoring officer, made a point of only wearing kamiz partoog and complimented me for following suit. "Only once in my life have I worn the pant-shirt," Khair boasted, using a common South Asian expression for Western clothes. "Afghan dress is the best for our culture and religion."

Southern Pashtuns were keenly aware of how different things were in the cosmopolitan north. Our floppy-haired lead paymaster Raz Muhammad offered a blunt summary of the division. "The people of Kabul, every time, most of the time, they want the regime of democracy. They need to be so free, whatever they do. Right now in Kabul, you will see hundreds of women on the street without any burqa. In these areas, Kandahar and Helmand, you will see one woman in a thousand. And she will be a bad woman."

To Western eyes, Kabul hardly seemed a warren of immodesty, but there was no doubt in the minds of most of the southern Pashtun males I met. We knew that by employing two young women in our office, even in junior roles, we were ruffling some feathers. Still, our own male staff treated Rubina and Safeena with at least overt respect, and our female employees were as modest as they could be without actually being invisible. They wrapped their dark headscarves tightly around their small watchful faces, doing their best to conceal every lock of hair. Often they wore their burqas as cloaks even while they were at their desk.

Our Helmand project's most socially provocative moment was probably a celebration later that spring in honor of International Women's Day. We gathered all our office staff for cake and brief speeches of praise to the hotly embarrassed Rubina and Safeena. Many of the tributes to "our sisters" were delivered by our young Hazara staff, who tended to be more laid-back than the Pashtuns. The crucial accolade, however, was delivered by the incontestably Pashtun Haji Habibullah, who had taken the two teenagers under his wing as honorary daughters. His authority and gravitas put their presence in our office beyond overt reproach. Under the Haji's chaperoning eye, his brilliant assistant Jawed taught Rubina and Safeena the ropes. The two young women adjusted quickly to the alien, masculine hubbub around them and mastered one office task after another. While they still answered most of my requests with a demure nod and smile, their smiles no longer looked timid so much as gracious.

Sophisticated young Pashtuns like Raz took great pains to distinguish the clear and immutable rules of Islam from mere customs or habits that denigrated women. Once I made the mistake of suggesting that Afghan women are expected to have lots of children, and Raz objected reproachfully. "Not every Afghan thinks like that, Joel. Only the uneducated villagers, only maybe four or five percent of the population, think that women are supposed to have too many children."

"Sorry, Raz. For educated people in the cities, how many children?" I asked, chastened.

"The average is only about five or six," Raz estimated.

I couldn't hold back a laugh. "By Western standards, that's a lot."

"Oho, a lot?" Raz returned my laughter. "By Afghan standards, twenty-two is a lot. I know a man with three wives. The third one had twenty-two children, so you tell me how many children that man has."

Children were the one joy of private life that all my male friends were happy to boast about. Khair Muhammad was passionate about his offspring, a seven-year-old son and two-year-old daughter. "She is named Shabnam," Khair told me fondly, the usual proud tension draining from his face as he showed me the faded snapshots. "It means dew. And my son is Ubaidullah. He is already very intelligent." He took every opportunity to make family visits, which unfortunately meant that when I needed him he was often in the mountains of Pakistan, a good three days' journey from Lashkargah. Unlike most of our employees, who never used their vacation days, Khair drained them as they built up and requested one or two in advance.

In good Pashtun fashion, Khair didn't say much about his wife, a maternal cousin he had wed when he was still a fifteen-year-old student. It was dishonorable to speak too much of such things with another man; my young Helmandi friends smiled uneasily at my happy blatherings about marrying Fiona. Unlike in Kabul, down here there was no cosmopolitan culture to mask the widespread distrust of romantic love. Falling in love, in the Pashtun folk tales I heard and read, was generally linked to the great dishonor of adultery. There were recurring stories of two men (a king and his captain; a scholar and his friend) who discover that their wives have taken lovers, behead the treacherous couples, swear never to marry again, and embark upon a lifetime of platonic male friendship. "Mr. Joel, do you know the meaning of love?" Khair said to me once with an expression of sly solemnity. "It is L, land of sorrow, O, ocean of tears, V, valley of death, E, end of life."

I got much the same reaction from Raz Muhammad. On one of our payroll trips to Nad-i-Ali, he asked with some concern whether Fiona was in love with me. I told him I surely hoped so. Raz shook his head gravely. "Most Pashtuns would not want their wives to be in love with them. If a woman falls in love once, she can fall in love again."

It wasn't that Raz didn't appreciate the power of love or beauty. He was a passionate aesthete and artist as well as a devout moralist. Raz prided himself on his intricate hand embroidery skills; for a while, he had worked as a women's tailor in the Pakistani city of Quetta. He loved Pashto popular music and poetry, and had founded a very sharp-looking online literary magazine for aspiring poets like himself. "Sometimes I write poems about Country. Sometimes about Romance. Sometimes about Nature."

After we had become friends, I asked him what kind of romantic poems he wrote. "There are two meanings of Romance," Raz clarified matter-of-factly. "One is false and one is the actual, true type. In my understanding, the false kind of romance is when you just want to sing or say something for only one person. With the true type, you write about the beauty of hair, eyes, lips, anything else, but you don't say who they belong to. Then you are not only writing about the beauty of the human beings; you are really talking about the Creator of this beauty."

• • •

For many of my friends, exceptional devotion to the Creator was a core part of their family identity. Mian Khair Muhammad was descended from a Sufi saint (that was what the title *Mian* indicated) whose son had migrated to the Paktia valley to preach to the local Shi'a. In keeping with his missionary ancestry, Khair had been the *imam* or prayer leader of his hostel mosque during his years at Faisalabad University in Pakistan. Khair's disapproval of un-Islamic behavior was exacting, and he had little sympathy for poverty-based justifications—whether they came from farmers growing poppy or his own younger brother trying to smuggle himself into Britain. "I believe it is every

Muslim's job to call the people to good deeds and request them not to indulge in evil," he told me earnestly, quoting the Qur'an. I recognized the verse; the Taliban had used it as the motto for their infamous vice and virtue police.

Raz Muhammad inherited his devoutness from his father, a skilled HAVA civil engineer, who during the initial frenzy of Afghan Communist rule had been imprisoned and beaten with bricks for praying in his government workplace. Raz had been born on December 31, 1979, six days after the Soviet invasion, while his father was working in a distant punishment post. His uncles briefly named him Jangyalai, warrior, before his father arrived to insist on Raz Muhammad, the secret of the Prophet.

As Helmand was devoured by militia fighting, Raz's father fled with his family to the Pakistani city of Quetta. They were on the verge of getting a refugee resettlement visa to New Jersey when an anonymous thief paid a bribe to assume Raz's father's identity. "But you know, I am too happy with that," Raz confided, as I imagined this brash, poetic, devout young Afghan growing up in Hoboken. "Because in New Jersey, I could not get such a modern Islamic school as I attended in Quetta." Raz had attended a Saudi-funded school that provided Afghan refugees with free textbooks and a well-rounded education, with a quarter of the classes focused on Islam.

It would be easy for anyone familiar with Raz's background, passionate religiosity, and illiberal convictions to assume that he backed the Taliban. In fact, he loathed them—and I thought his hostility offered one insight into why the Taliban remained unloved even in the conservative south.

Raz had studied medicine at the all-male Kandahar University during Mullah Omar's regime. Five years after the Taliban takeover, life in Kandahar wasn't a reign of terror for young Pashtun men; most punishments were limited to humiliating slaps, beatings, or short incarcerations. Still, Raz and his friends found the mullahs' strictures deadening. "We could not even go for a picnic without being searched two or three times on the way for any cassette," Raz recalled irritably. "And my long hair was the reason for me to be in trouble every time. It was not long like ladies; only maybe one centimeter longer than now." The university appointed three monitors to regularly gauge the students' hair and beard lengths and check their attendance at prayers.

Raz finally left the university in humiliated rage after the director cuffed him in public. He had worn his shoes into the dining hall, which was part of a mosque. "I was not angry that he slapped me because I went into the mosque with my footwear. It is wrong. He must slap me." Raz struggled to express the source of his indignation. "But I would have taken off my shoes too if I didn't see a hundred other students' footwear inside the dining hall. I was a hundred and one. He could give me a warning; he could teach me with love."

I asked him once where he thought the Taliban had departed from Islam. Raz immediately answered that most of the Taliban wear their turbans too long, preventing them from touching their heads to the ground properly during prayer. Something deeper seemed to be bothering him, though. After a moment, he offered another answer. "If you catch someone who has very long hair, Islam doesn't tell you to beat him, or abuse him, or put him in a metal container in the summer heat for ten days. Islam tells you to follow the way of love. You should tell him, Please, do not do that. This thing is not good for you."

I thought that neatly expressed the key difference between the Taliban and a host of conservative Pashtuns like Raz or Khair: They accepted the same stark, demanding law, but disagreed on whether it should be enforced mercifully or severely. Neither Raz nor Khair would accept the least watering down of the divine rules, but they didn't want a government that monitored and punished every infraction.

With that in mind, I understood Raz's disdainful comments about Kabulis' love of freedom and democracy in a new light. Raz had actually been delighted when the new Karzai government began in 2002. "Everywhere there was happiness, everyone's face was shining," he recalled warmly. "Everyone was too happy that we have got freedom from a strict government again." It all came down to different ideas of freedom. Raz wanted a society as free as possible from violent coercion, but not a society where everyone did whatever they desired.

So Raz kept trying to convince people to voluntarily embrace the way of the Prophet, and meanwhile tried to keep his floppy hair to an Islamic length. "You comb it to the back with a part in the middle, and cut it between two ears from the back side—not longer than that," he explained gravely. "The Prophet himself, peace be upon him, had hair like that for some time, though not for fashion, as we do."

• • •

Even in a region so fixated on public righteousness, I found myself bumping up against the signs and effects of private vice. Alcohol was the great taboo, though its force varied greatly in different parts of the country. In the Afghan north, as suggested by the six brands of beer openly for sale in Pul-i-Khumri, attitudes tended to be more relaxed. Once on a remote road in the north, my Tajik driver refused to help a stranded trucker because he had vodka on his breath. As we rolled on, my driver inquired if I ever drank vodka, and chuckled at my slightly uneasy assent. "*Vodka, arusi, khub,*" he said decisively, in the pidgin Persian he knew I would understand. "*Vodka, sarak, khub neyst.*" At a wedding, it's good. On the road, it's not good.

In the south, that sort of relaxed ethic was unthinkable. I was struck by the depths of self-excoriation I saw in one soft-spoken Afghan employee who openly and miserably disclosed his alcoholism to me. "It is not easy to get a bottle in Afghanistan." His complete lack of guile lent his wretchedness an unexpected dignity. "I do not get one often. But when I do, I can't drink a little. I must drink the whole bottle. Even though I know it will make me sick." I wondered if he would have developed similar habits in the West, or if he bolted down his liquor to avoid the shame and potential violence of being caught with it. "I always tell myself I must stop. I tell myself this is far from God. But I do not listen to myself."

As I watched the guilty circlings of Afghan friends around alcohol, I wondered why it seemed so familiar. I had grown up in an evangelical Christian culture that censured drinking and drug use, but had never seen drinkers with the same depths of shame. Then it struck me: These young Afghans who broke the taboo against alcohol reminded me of devout young American evangelicals breaking the taboo against sex. I saw the same fascination and bad conscience; the reluctance to justify a sin that so clearly ran in the face of a divine text; the dread of discovery; the rationalization (half indulgence, half despair) that having once crossed the line, there wasn't much point going back. Of course, this spoke volumes about how seriously devout southern Afghans took both alcohol and sex relative to Westerners.

Sex, in southern Afghanistan, was all but invisible. Given a culture that so relentlessly tried to prevent extramarital eye contact between men and women, it was perhaps unsurprising that certain substitute vices were widespread. Kandahar, the most socially conservative city in Afghanistan, had a long-standing reputation for pederasty. The mostly Kandahari leaders of the Taliban, struggling to live down this image, eventually released a rule book which included the decree: "Warriors of the jihad are not allowed to take young boys with no facial hair onto the battlefield or into their private quarters." Under their regime, men convicted of homosexual acts had been killed by having walls toppled onto them by bulldozers.

No one in our office admitted to seeking such brotherly comforts, of course, but a few of my young friends were noticeably more tactile and tittering with each other—and effusive in expressing their attachment to me. "Mr. Joel," one of them said to me ardently, "I *like* the way you walk."

I didn't seek out conversations about my own religion. The Taliban accused America of having a secret Christianizing agenda, and labeled the Karzai government a Crusader tool to convert Afghans; the last thing I wanted was to confirm their propaganda. But it was impossible that it wouldn't come up in so God-haunted a country.

Many of my friends were satisfied once they learned that I too believed in God and prayed on a regular basis. I grew used to the rhythm of their own prayers around me, early afternoon, late afternoon, dusk. The quieter corners of our office were often occupied by young men kneeling on their thin cotton shawls. I had to postpone many an urgent discussion when I burst into an office to find the person I was looking for prostrate and beyond distraction, focused entirely on his murmured litany.

The Afghans I met generally went out of their way to show respect for Christianity—though I had no illusions about the degree of toleration that any Afghan Christian could expect. Afghans were proud that their country had never been colonized by the Christian West. That anticolonial fervor, combined with the stark shari'ah laws on apostasy, meant that the treatment of converts would surely be grim. But we foreigners were guests, and those of us who followed the prophet Isa were more than tolerated.

At a meeting in May with the PRT, Engineer Dawari, and some tribal elders, the elders raised the fact that "your religious leader," Pope John Paul, had just died. They wondered how they could pay respects. Somewhat taken aback, the PRT captain proposed a moment of silence. We sat wordlessly together in the dusty, plastic-paneled military trailer, until Dawari intoned, "Ameen," and the elders passed their hands ceremoniously over their faces.

With another Pashtun friend, I was discussing my marriage plans, and mentioned that Fi and I would have a Christian wedding. "You follow Isa Masih?" my friend interrupted—Arabic for Jesus Christ. "I knew it! I told my father there was a good American man in the office who grew a very long beard, so he must follow Isa Masih. My father said no, in America men grow long beards even if they are not Christian or Muslim. But I knew you were a man of religion."

I laughed. "Your father was right. I don't grow my beard for religious reasons. I grow it because I am lazy. When I am in America, I cut it short." My Muslim friend proceeded to describe the DVDs about the life of the prophet Isa that he had found in the Kandahar bazaar. The cheery enthusiasm in his face left me doubtful that he was referring to *The Passion of the Christ*, but I didn't press too hard into what he had found.

From time to time, my friends and I would find unexpected points of common ground. One spring afternoon, I took weary refuge in my guitar following a late lunch. Sharif and Saber poked their heads in the door and gestured that it was time to head back to the office. I nodded at them but kept singing until I'd finished the poignant last verse of Leonard Cohen's "Hallelujah."

As I put the guitar down, Sharif clucked his tongue appreciatively. He had given up English lessons to work with our project, and tried to compensate by figuring out pop song lyrics on long car rides. The two of us had spent hours deciphering and discussing Maroon 5's *Songs About Jane*. "What does it mean, hallelujah?"

"It means praise God, thanks be to God. In Hebrew. The language of the *Tawrat*, of the Jewish prophets, which Christians also sometimes use," I over-explained. Sharif looked a bit puzzled, and translated to Saber, who stared impassively at me. Perhaps they were wondering whether I was a Jew, or a Christian, or something in between. I struggled for a parallel. "Its meaning is something like *Allahu akbar*, and something like *Alhamdulillah*."

Both drivers immediately nodded, and Saber broke into a sudden smile. We had all learned from childhood to praise God in a language not our own, the tongue of the prophets.

• • •

The friend with whom I felt the strongest spiritual affinity was Muhammad Ehsan, a twenty-eight-year-old Hazara whose round face, deeply lined forehead, and fuzzy beard gave him the look of a pensive teddy bear. Like most Hazaras, he was from the minority Shi'a sect of Islam. He was introspective rather than assertive, morally serious but deeply kind, with a generosity and humility that drew me to him from the moment we met.

Before we ever spoke about faith, I had come to trust Ehsan as one of my right-hand men at work. Haji Habibullah and I hired him to take care of the staff houses and office after finally admitting that we were too busy to keep on top of the melting wires, clogging pipes, and peeling paint. Ehsan had previously overseen the renovation of Lashkargah's Italian-funded Emergency Hospital and came with the hospital's highest recommendation.

During our months working together, I only saw the meticulous, workaholic Ehsan make two mistakes. The small one was to issue a formal request on Chemonics letterhead for fine Iranian windowpanes. It was the best-quality glass available in Lashkargah, and Ehsan didn't want the vendors to fob off a cheap substitute on us. Luckily, we caught it in time to retract the request and to remind our facilities manager of U.S. government policy toward Tehran.

The greater mistake, which almost lost Ehsan his job, was to directly disobey an order from Jim Graham. At the time, the soft-spoken young Hazara had only been working with us for two days, and he was trying to fix the hot water pressure in our staff house—an issue close to Jim's heart. For the previous week, a clumsy local plumber had been trying to increase the wheezing dribble, but managed only to cut off the water supply completely at inconvenient moments. Jim finally ordered them to quit disconnecting the pipes, saying he'd rather get a trickle of water than get the whole system screwed up. When he returned from lunch that day, Jim was livid. "Damned if they didn't have the tank completely off its blocks, and not a drop of water in the place. I want you to go over there and fire the guy, Joel. I want him gone."

It ended up also being the one time I directly disobeyed Jim's orders. Ehsan was probably the gentlest of our employees, too unassuming to explain himself to our fuming Bostonian boss. When I got to the house and saw the apparent shambles of the plumbing—all the pipes unscrewed, the tank empty to one side, bricks and mortar strewn everywhere—I understood why Jim had been appalled. But Ehsan promised me in a pained, pleading voice that he knew what he was doing. I went back and told Jim I still thought he was the guy for the job. The hot water was flowing that night at the staff house, with strong pressure at last. "See, sometimes you've got to yell a little to get things done," Jim concluded gruffly. I nodded with a grin of irrepressible relief.

It was a small incident, but it was the foundation for a fast-growing, unreserved trust between Ehsan and me. He worked even longer hours than I did, and I would often find him patching up the staff house when I got home in the evenings. We talked about his family in Kabul—how they were nervous to have him staying deep in Pashtun country, even though he had relatives in Lashkargah's Hazara community. "But they trust in God that I will be safe." Before long, Ehsan began sounding me out on religion. "You remind me of an Italian man I used to work with at Emergency," he told me with a small chuckle. "He was a Catholic, but he prayed almost as much as a Muslim."

We spoke often about prayer—why we prayed, what sort of words and thoughts we used when addressing the Almighty. I soon found out my Shi'a friend was plagued with an acute conscience. Talking to Ehsan reminded me of Saint Augustine, Martin Luther, and the other great guilty minds of the Christian tradition, searching for reassurance that God would listen to them in spite of their offenses. Ehsan was mournfully convinced that his own constant prayers were unlikely to carry much weight. His grandmother was a saintly woman who prayed daily for him, but while he took some hope in the power of her piety, it also made him feel all the more undeserving.

I did my infidel best to encourage him. We talked about the idea that God might forgive us in proportion to the amount we forgive other people, which Ehsan mulled over with a slight lightening of his creased brow. He was a man inclined by nature to forgiveness. Once I mentioned the importance in Christianity of forgiving enemies, then faltered with sudden embarrassment. The Hazara had been a much-exploited underclass in Afghanistan for centuries. Only a few years ago, the Taliban had declared Ehsan's people to be non-Muslims and slaughtered them by the thousand. I had no idea whether any of my friend's family had been caught up in those horrors; no idea what I might be suggesting that he forgive.

Ehsan waved my hesitation away. "No, it is a good idea," he said soberly. "I do not want to think of any man as my enemy."

Good Cop, Bad Cop

Without the passion of Yaqub Roshan, our project would probably have rumbled cautiously along, close to Lashkargah, with a few token activities in upper Helmand. After Charles took over our security systems, Jim had ended the project freeze, but he didn't want us to run into another Babaji by expanding too quickly. Yaqub, by contrast, was possessed by an almost missionary determination to spread USAID's largesse to every district in the province.

Far more than me, Yaqub had found himself shoehorned into unfamiliar duties when his original job fell through. After our house-hunting misadventure, Yaqub had started going out to the field every day, and wound up managing all our activities in Marja district. The Babaji abduction left him briefly but profoundly shaken; what if he had been in that car, and the kidnappers had found out that they had an Afghan-American hostage? But the people of Marja swore up and down that nothing like that could happen in their territory. Yaqub soon rediscovered his passion for the job, and asked me to adjust his title to Senior Government *and Community* Liaison. Once he'd found his feet, it was inevitable that he'd soon start looking outside Marja.

Yaqub had picked up the basics of his new job from watching Dick Scott at work in Nad-i-Ali, but he elaborated on Dick's model with a confidence that came in part from being Afghan himself. Where Dick relied entirely on the local shuras (governing councils) to choose qualified worksite supervisors, Yaqub came up with transparent testing and hiring procedures. Where Dick preferred to add work crews gradually, Yaqub saw no reason why we couldn't bring workers on by the thousand. And where Dick argued for a focus on central Helmand—especially his beloved Nad-i-Ali—Yaqub increasingly saw himself as an advocate for the people of the whole province, and beyond. Like his father, King Zahir's itinerant provincial governor, Yaqub traveled all over Helmand to wrangle with the local power brokers on our behalf. He would spend a weekend in a district with the walaswal and district shura, and come back proclaiming that we could have a new full-scale activity within a week or two.

Jim and Charles responded warily (and sometimes wearily) to Yaqub's enthusiasms, but I knew that without him as its engine, our project wouldn't make its targets. Moreover, like Yaqub, I was a politician at heart. I didn't want us just to create two and a half million work days in easy, forgettable activities within a couple hours of Lashkargah. I wanted the far corners of the province to associate the Karzai government with jobs, cash, and lasting benefits. To be honest, I also wanted to see the farthest corners of the province—which fueled my unspoken motivation for supporting Yaqub's attempts to get us working in the northernmost corner of Helmand. Baghran district was as rugged and remote as anywhere in Afghanistan, and every time I looked at the map I wanted to be there.

Jim, who was neither a politician nor a tourist, countered stubbornly with his mantra: "Let's not get ahead of ourselves." He recognized the opportunity to regain some of the ground we'd lost during the security freeze, but he threw on the brakes whenever it looked like we were heading outside our logistical or security comfort zone. "If we can find good, safe projects in upper Helmand, great. But if we have to meet USAID's targets by paying our neighbors to dig holes in the ground and fill them in again, that's fine too," Jim growled. "We just don't want to get our guys killed. That's got to be top priority."

• • •

The elders of Babaji and Bolan kept sending delegations imploring us to resume work in their area. At first, all of our project's top staff met with them; later, Habibullah and I ended up fielding a meeting or two alone. I tried to be compassionate but firm, while the Haji scolded and glowered—a good cop–bad cop routine we ended up using a fair amount. We maintained the same message: We couldn't go back unless we felt safe, and in the wake of the carjacking, we gravely doubted the community's willingness to protect us.

Since Babaji was part of Lashkargah district, our discussions regularly included the capital's *sharwal* (literally, city-governor, or mayor), Abdul Munaf, a portly man with a tubular gray beard jutting out fifteen inches from his chin. I had a lot of respect for the cheery and competent sharwal. He was the reason that Lashkargah had asphalt streets; without any help from Western development agencies, he had gotten the bazaar merchants to fund the paving with a one-time tax. Abdul Munaf was also, as Jim liked to point out, "the only elected politician in Helmand." Other district heads were appointed by the governor, but the sharwal of Lashkargah was chosen in a municipal vote. He championed the interests of his constituents with the wheedling vigor of a successful local politician. Unfortunately, this put us on opposite sides of the Babaji issue.

Besides the sharwal, the delegations were dominated by two Babaji elders. Though I learned their names from Habibullah, I mentally nicknamed them Priam and Odysseus (I had just finished watching a pirated copy of *Troy*). Like Homer's aged king of Troy, the vocal Elder Priam wept heart-wrenchingly and appealed to his gray hairs. Like the famously cunning Greek hero, Elder Odysseus seemed the shrewdest and most strategic member of the Babaji delegation. He generally sat in watchful silence, but when he spoke, his normally raucous fellow elders fell silent to listen, and he knew just which arguments would hit us hardest.

Elder Priam, whose face was a sun-blasted maze of wrinkles, declared that for three long years he had tried to talk HAVA into fixing Babaji's deep drains. He had planted his fields this year, in the expectation that the drains would clear the land of salt. Now his crops would wither. He was related to the driver whose vehicle had been stolen. "Do you think we would steal from ourselves?" Tears spilled from his rheumy eyes. At one of the meetings with only me and Habibullah, he tottered up to me and pressed his strong, cracked hands imploringly to my beard—a gesture of desperation which (in the local culture) created a strong obligation on me to do whatever I could. He said that he would personally pay for the vehicle and give us his land as a guarantee that no future incidents would take place, just as long as we came back. Telling him we couldn't make any promises was miserable work.

"You should not have quit work just because of one theft," Elder Odysseus declared at the end of our first meeting. "Now any time our enemies want to take some benefit away from us, they know they only have to steal one thing from you, and you will leave."

"There are people in your community who know who stole our vehicle," Haji Habibullah retorted hotly. The shura members looked uncomfortably askance, and Elder Odysseus gave a small, resigned nod. "It is on you to protect us from these enemies. You must help the police find our vehicle. When we get our vehicle back, only then we will think of starting work again." It was a strong, unreasonable condition, but it might focus minds on cooperating with the police investigation.

On the other hand, our Western vision of civilians cooperating with a police investigation didn't fit here. Our demand presumed that the police were impartial representatives of the state, protectors of the peace and enforcers of the law, when in fact the Afghan police were a balkanized, tribal, predatory mess. In a feuding region like Babaji, the governor's police were anything but a neutral party.

• • •

Afghans had just over a century's experience with a national police force. In the 1880s, as part of his brutal unification campaign, Amir Abdurrahman ensured that each provincial city had a Kabul-appointed police chief (*kotwal*) and officers. The main mission of Abdurrahman's police was not to serve and protect, but to monitor and control; their duties included enforcing curfews and travel restrictions, breaking up large assemblies, and recording births, deaths, and epidemics in their neighborhoods. Separately, Abdurrahman established an impressive internal spy network, which would later evolve through the secret police of Prime Minister Daud, to the Soviet KHAD, to the Amniyat or intelligence police of today.

Outside the cities, the Iron Amir didn't try to create the same degree of control. Rather, Abdurrahman made tribal khans largely responsible for securing their own areas. "If a traveler is killed, or his property is stolen in the vicinity of a town or village," he explained in his autobiography, "the people of that village are either to find the wrongdoer or answer for the injury themselves." The rural administrators of the central government focused on sending information and taxes to Kabul, while relying on tribal militias to keep order. In any serious turmoil, the king would send in the army.

For about a century, the Afghan police evolved in this odd compromise: a mostly urban force dedicated to reinforcing central control, and rural forces which were barely domesticated tribal militias. Then the Afghan-Soviet War gutted all of Afghanistan's central government institutions, leaving the police fragmented and unrestrained. In Helmand after the 1989 Russian withdrawal, the desperate Communist governor had decreed that he would recognize as "police" any group of ten or more men who were willing to fight the mujahidin. This policy created hundreds of official militias on top of the multitude of antigovernment militias—a nightmare for Helmand's civilians.

"When I was ten years old, I remember two police betting on the shooting of another ten-year-old boy," Raz Muhammad told me once. "One said, 'Can you shoot him?' The other said, 'Sure,' and he shot the boy. Nobody asked the man why." Raz's voice was bleak. "In the half time of my school, they used to come inside the compound and use bad words to girls and female teachers. They could use hard drinks and hashish very free. That was the reason for most of the public to leave Lashkargah. Normal people couldn't use it because of police."

The Taliban had imposed a welcome peace across the south, but after their collapse, influential Afghan warlords once again began declaring hundreds of their men to be provincial and highway police. Today Governor Sher Muhammad presided over a motley array of small, tribalized forces who generally loathed and distrusted each other. We couldn't bring our eighteen Bolan escorts into our office compound, lest they start a fight with the kohl-eyed HAVA guard squad. Indeed, the Bolan police flatly refused to accompany our survey trips into the northern half of Helmand province. They were from the Noorzai tribe of Pashtuns; Sangin was dominated by the rival Alokozais, and the areas further north by the governor's Alizai tribe. Sher Muhammad was of course determined to get us working in Alizai territory, so he had to give us a second escort force of twenty Kajaki-born police.

Both of our guard cadres were led by brutal, charismatic commanders who held their men's loyalty through a combination of personal credibility, ruthlessness toward enemies, and reliable provision of food, shelter, and cash. Our new upper Helmand police followed a short, whip-thin captain named Hayat Khan—or "the little Taliban-killer," as Charles called him. During the war, Hayat Khan informed Charles, his village had been attacked by the Taliban; fifteen members of his family were killed, and he was beaten to within an inch of his life. "The next day he got up, washed his face, said his prayers, and walked out with his knife," Charles related. "Spent a year hunting every man involved in the attack. Knifed 'em all. Scary little man." This spectacular act of revenge had recommended him to his patron Sher Muhammad, who sent Hayat Khan south to control the remote desert district of Khanishin.

Once during a (slightly nerve-wracking) payment dispute, I asked Hayat Khan how much he had been paid by the governor during his stint as police chief of Khanishin. "He gave us no salary," the red-eyed little commander snapped. "The people gave us money. To thank us for solving their problems."

Though they would have preferred receiving a lump-sum payment, both of our captains tolerated our curious and irksome Western convention of paying their men individually. In a fortnightly payroll ritual, we got each guard to put his thumbprint on our timesheet, gave him his per-diem money, and watched him walk out and hand the pay packet to his commander.

Charles took on the monumental task of training, coordinating, barracking, and equipping this shambolic guard force. As I worked with him, my sympathies for USPI increased tenfold. Our police shared all the shortcomings of the USPI gunmen we had rejected. Their sole advantage was that we could address their indiscipline directly, instead of relying on an overstretched subcontractor.

The governor had given his police no formal training and few resources, just a handful of old guns and shoddy blue uniforms. (Our guards usually wore their kamiz partoog underneath the foreign garb; with their long tunics and baggy pantaloons bunched up thickly inside their blue trousers, they looked like incontinents.) The Kajaki police also had no barracks in Lashkargah. Charles saw this as an invaluable opportunity for us to replace the vicious, lazy pack of HAVA guards with a permanently resident guard force that answered to us. The governor thankfully agreed to the switch. Hayat Khan's twenty men began sleeping in the dank ground floor of the HAVA building; we started building them a long-term barracks in the corner of the compound with the fretful acquiescence of Dawari's short deputy, the acting HAVA director.

Charles did an arms inventory early on and summed up the results for me with a hollow laugh. "Our twenty Kajaki boys have thirteen Kalashnikovs. Nine of them actually work. The newest one was made in 1959. They also have one machine gun and two rocket launchers. That's twelve working weapons, with shit for ammunition. Only five rockets! That'll make a nice loud noise at the start of a fight."

Needless to say, as a USAID agriculture contractor, we weren't allowed to buy assault rifles or rocket-propelled grenades for the local police. So, along with Farid, Charles's cheerful but hard-nosed young Afghan aide, we began visiting the governor's office to haggle for Kalashnikovs.

• • •

One day, Charles beckoned me past the carpenters into his small security office. "Here's an interesting fact. You know who else spent the Eid holiday in Mecca, besides Dawari? Governor Sher Muhammad; Helmand's chief of police and head of intelligence police; and, I hear, half of Afghanistan's known opium kingpins."

"Huh. Mecca seems like an irreverent place to network." But it made sense. The haj was the least-conspicuous way for the big traffickers of north, east, and south Afghanistan to meet up and prepare for the 2005 harvest. They all had an interest in talking with the Helmand police. Helmand wasn't just the country's biggest poppy producer, but also one of the main conduits for opium gum smuggled from all over Afghanistan into Pakistan and Iran.

Of course, Governor Sher Muhammad insisted fervently that he had no direct involvement with the drug trade—unlike his father Rasul and uncle Nasim, who had had nothing to lose by admitting their opium connections. Like them, Sher Muhammad had repeatedly declared his willingness to plow up the cursed crop if paid appropriately. "Let the government or America give me compensation for my people," he assured us winsomely, "and I will eradicate every field with my own hands!" Back in the autumn of 2002, less than a year after his installation as governor, Sher Muhammad had indeed slashed Helmand's opium cultivation by nearly half. The northern valleys remained full of poppy, but in Nad-i-Ali and Marja, the governor had successfully driven an 85 percent cut in production.

Unfortunately, Helmand didn't immediately get the compensation or attention that Sher Muhammad had been expecting. Dick Scott ran a small cash-for-work program in Nad-i-Ali. The British government promised to pay Afghan farmers for any poppy hectares they eradicated, but this created a perverse incentive for the farmers to plant more, and the ill-conceived compensation program collapsed under the weight of fraud and underfunding. In the 2003 planting season, Sher Muhammad forlornly declared that he "did not have the resources" to carry out eradication. The farmers of central Helmand got the message and turned their rich agricultural lands into one huge poppy field by the spring 2004 harvest.

Our project was the governor's payoff. Accordingly, in this opium season, he was once again sending police out into central Helmand with tractors to plow up newly sown plots of poppies. We had seen the eradication tractors by the roadside in Bolan, and Yaqub said he had spotted them rolling around Marja several times. Most of the farmers of central Helmand appeared to be planting wheat this year. Sher Muhammad and his walaswals (district administrators) repeatedly stated that only our cash-for-work compensation to the farmers made these counter-narcotics measures possible. Yaqub liked to quote the walaswal of Nad-i-Ali: "Your project has sharpened our blades of eradication."

• • •

Meanwhile, the winter rains continued, and the general rejoicing at the end of the seven-year drought was tempered by tragedy. Johannes, RAMP's Dutch irrigation engineer, had once told me an apt Afghan proverb: "It is better to be foolish with fire than to be foolish with water. Fire leaves ashes; water takes everything." The Helmand River surged greedily, swallowing the reedy sandbars and the gravel plain of the Friday animal market, sweeping away houses and fields too close to its banks. Dick Scott told us that this was nothing; the spring snowmelt was when we could expect some real water. "During the worst flood year, the river was lapping at the underside of the Lashkargah Bridge," he said gravely.

"Isn't that like thirty feet high?" I queried, aghast.

"Oh, more," Dick assured me.

For now, the chilly downpour was itself a destroyer. Most of Helmand's houses and walls were made of sun-dried earth—a material which was friendlier than concrete in both the blazing summer heat and the normal winter damp, but which now began to succumb in a host of little mudslides. Just across from Lashkargah's small American military outpost, a compound wall collapsed to expose a sizable field of poppy. I'd never seen a wall go back up so fast.

In northern Afghanistan, things were much worse. Kabul had not had so bitter a winter in living memory; all over the capital, roofs were collapsing from the weight of the snow and people were perishing in the cold. Hundreds more died on the highways, victims of ice patches, or drifting snow, or engine failure on a freezing mountainside. Our computer wizard, Khaliq Yar, had tried to make it back to Lashkargah on January 25 from celebrating Eid with his family in Kabul. His taxi skidded off the road, and though no one was hurt, Khaliq was stranded in Ghazni. Khair Muhammad was trapped in the mountains of Pakistan with his family.

Of course it was during these weeks, with half of Afghanistan shut down by snow, that we wanted to get a half-dozen staff into and out of Lashkargah. USAID had authorized short sanity breaks in the States for American staff every three months or so; Jim, Yaqub, and I were all scheduled to fly out of Kabul in quick succession. Meanwhile, we needed to get some key staff down to Helmand. Our project director, Dave Guier, was flying in from Washington to take over in Jim's absence. Johannes Oosterkamp had completed his assignment as Chemonics' irrigation advisor in Kabul, and Jim had invited him to come work with us.

Our transportation tragicomedy began on Saturday, January 29. Jim's PRT Air flight was axed at the last minute, so he hopped into a Land Rover to travel overland. His e-mail Sunday morning was eloquent:

Joel/Charles—

We arrived at 9:00 p.m. The road conditions are the worst I have experienced. From an hour out of Kandahar through to Kabul, snow is blowing in two- to three-foot drifts onto the road, and with the wind, there are white-out conditions. The road itself is covered with ice and snow and reduced to one lane at best. If we had broken down we would have had it. Cars, trucks, and buses were either stuck in drifts on the road or had slid off. By Ghazni our snow chains had broken.

Jim ordered us to stop all nonemergency road travel between Kabul and Lashkargah for the winter, and then closed his e-mail:

David and Johannes should stay in Kabul until either spring arrives or a PRT flight is available.

Regards, Jim

PS: We just found out the PRT flight has been canceled for tomorrow and are checking for the next one available. At 7:00 a.m. it was minus 15° C!!

Monday's canceled PRT flight was rescheduled for the next day, but even though the skies were temporarily clear, the Tuesday flight was also called off at the last minute. "The Salang Pass and the roads in from Pakistan have been closed by heavy snows," the PRT Air guy apologized over the phone. "It's played hell with our supply of aviation fuel, so we've had to ground some planes. But we should be able to fly the southern loop tomorrow."

Understandably disgruntled, Dave Guier didn't want to risk a third cancellation and booked himself on a commercial Kabul-Kandahar flight. The flight didn't have room for Johannes, so the Dutch engineer stayed on the PRT Air roster. On Wednesday morning, PRT Air defied expectations by delivering Johannes smoothly to Lashkargah. Meanwhile, Dave's flight ran into a massive dust storm in Kandahar. "The pilot made three passes at the airport but couldn't line the plane up for the runway," Dave e-mailed us resignedly, "and we therefore returned to Kabul." It started snowing that evening in the capital, defeating our hopes that the road might become passable anytime soon.

The snowstorm soon had a much more grievous impact. On Thursday, February 3, a Kam Air passenger flight from Herat was unable to land in Kabul due to zero visibility. While trying to make it to Pakistan, the pilot flew into a mountain. One of the hundred-odd passengers was my friend Cristi. I had met up with her in Kabul only a month earlier, just before I flew out to meet Fiona. She had waxed poetic about Istanbul, and absorbed my stories of Fi with a vicarious, sisterly delight.

The painful news of the Kam Air crash crystallized my half-formed intentions: I wasn't going to Kabul. I had already been dreading the prospect of flight cancellations. I was due to meet Fiona's parents in England on the evening of February 9, then fly back with Fi to America to see my family. I had a ring to buy, an engagement to announce. If I got trapped in Lashkargah or Kabul, we'd have to cancel all those plans and plane tickets. There was one other airport I could reach that was unlikely to be closed by snow.

On Friday I cornered Charles in his office. "You know our emergency action plan says that if we can't get out by air in a major crisis, we head out overland to Quetta?"

"Dude," Charles replied in his exaggerated American accent, "in a major crisis, our plan is to knock on the gate of the PRT and say, 'We're Americans; don't let them shoot us.' Things would have to be pretty fucking disastrous before we actually ran a convoy to Pakistan."

"Fair enough. But it's still an alternative way out, and I think I ought to test the route now, while things are quiet." Charles just looked at me, and I shrugged uncomfortably. "Obviously, I know there's some risk." The Pakistani provincial capital of Quetta was widely held to be the unofficial headquarters of the Taliban resurgence. "But plenty of expats travel around there all the time with no problem. In weather like this, it's just as risky to fly out of Kabul. If I can even get to Kabul."

Charles was quiet for a second, then nodded briskly. "Okay. Talk to Johannes—he used to work over there, so he'll be able to tell you what to do from the border. Your boy Raz knows Quetta. You should take him along, too, for as far as he can go."

I called up Dave Guier, who was understandably unhappy at the prospect of arriving in Lashkargah to start running the project with no overlap with me or Jim. "And I want to talk with you about this large petty cash supply you've left here in Kabul for Masoud's use," he said testily.

Oh Lord. I suddenly felt that there were a million decisions I had made that would require elaborate justification—and David would be here for two and a half weeks, dissecting them all in my absence. "I'll write a report that explains everything," I promised in despair. "And I'll be available by phone from the States."

Raz Muhammad and I drove to Kandahar the next day, where I paid an outrageous sum for a same-day visa application at the Pakistani consulate. We lunched on smoky lamb kebabs before heading out of town to the border. The road traversed an arid landscape in bleached shades of brown and orange, with low hills and rocky outcrops offering variation but no shade. Ahead of us, without warning, a bulbous gray smoke plume shot up to a startling height in the cloudless sky. Long seconds later, as the top of the pillar was broadening into a mushroom shape, a deep boom rippled across the wilderness. "The de-miners," Raz said, seeing my surprise. "They bring the bombs here and explode them all at once."

Around 2:30 p.m., we reached the border town of Spin Boldak. We drove down a long muddy strip of mechanics' shops past hundreds of trucks—luridly painted Indian Tatas, dour but indestructible Russian Kamaz, others with so many decorations and alien parts bolted onto their chassis that it was hard to tell what they had originally been. It was no accident that this grand truck stop was where the Taliban conquest had begun, back in October 1994. The Pakistani trucking trade was dominated by Pashtuns, who in the 1990s had grown sick of losing cargo to impromptu militia checkpoints all across Afghanistan. They decided to sponsor a band of law-and-order vigilantes, led by a one-eyed mullah and his religious students, who had reportedly punished a few minor commanders for kidnapping and rape. With money and arms from the "trucker mafia," Mullah Omar's militia liberated the Spin Boldak border crossing from Gulbuddin's men. It was the first Afghan territory to fall under Taliban control.

The Afghan immigration office in Spin Boldak was nowhere near the actual border, and we drove around for some time before getting the exit stamp in my passport. Then we headed back to the border crossing, where crowds of pedestrians ambled through a metal turnstile. I was the only Westerner anywhere in sight. I discreetly tipped the two guards, and thanked Raz for his help. Then I walked through the turnstile and headed to the Government of Pakistan checkpost.

"What have you been doing in Afghanistan?" the Pakistani official said with sociable contempt as he eyed my freshly minted visa. "Those people are animals."

Politics as Usual

The relationship between Afghanistan and Pakistan had never been cordial, thanks in large part to the border I had just crossed. To Afghans, it was the infamous "Durand Line," forced on Amir Abdurrahman in 1893 by the Foreign Secretary of British India. Sir Mortimer Durand drew the boundary a comfortable distance west of the precious Indus valley, through the middle of wild mountain districts that neither government actually ruled. Abdurrahman protested, correctly but futilely, that this unenforceable border would make it permanently impossible for any government to control those Pashtun tribal areas.

In 1947, India became independent from Britain and was bloodily partitioned to create Pakistan, "land of the pure," as a homeland for Indian Muslims. Unlike Afghanistan, from the outset Pakistan was plagued by ethnic separatist movements and uncertain boundaries. Along the western border, Pakistan's impoverished, unruly Baluch and Pashtun tribes repeatedly tried to break away in bloody insurrections.

The Afghan government couldn't resist the chance to reverse the colonial division of the Pashtuns. When the British left, the regents of young King Zahir declared the Durand agreement null and void, and called for negotiations on a new border. The very idea gave the founding fathers of Pakistan cold sweats. The Pashtuns represented a relatively small share of Pakistan's huge population, but if their territory became part of Afghanistan, Pakistan would be reduced to a narrow belt of densely inhabited plains between the Afghan mountains and the Indian army. Fortunately, the Afghan demand could largely be ignored, as Pakistan's population, economy, and military strength were all many times greater than its neighbor's.

Still, this "Pashtunistan" issue permanently poisoned relations between the countries. Though Afghanistan had no hope of adjusting the border by force, its nationalist government under Prime Minister Daud sponsored and funded Pakistani ethnic insurgents (in an ironic mirror of Pakistan's later policy in both Kashmir and Afghanistan). In retaliation, Pakistan repeatedly shut off Afghanistan's main routes to the sea. It also gave training and sanctuary to Islamist insurgents against Daud, like the young Gulbuddin Hekmetyar and Ahmad Shah Massoud.

The Pakistani government had profoundly mixed feelings about the Afghan-Soviet War and its aftermath. On one hand, the war made Pakistan indispensable to rich anti-Communist powers like America and Saudi Arabia. The Pakistani military (especially its clandestine branch, the Inter-Services Intelligence) controlled the floodgates for guns and weapons going to the Afghan mujahidin; this not only provided plenty of skimming opportunities, but also allowed Pakistan to bolster the Afghan warlords of its choice. Pakistan's generals saw a chance to gain "strategic depth" against India by establishing a client government in Afghanistan.

On the other hand, many Pakistanis bitterly concluded, "America used us like a condom"—put coarsely, to screw the Russians while protecting themselves from the Afghans. The Russian bombing campaign sent somewhere between three and five million Afghan refugees into Pakistan. The refugee tide not only created the usual anxiety about jobs and crime in the host country; it also heightened Pakistan's insecurity over the border issue. Suddenly there were millions more poor, tribal Pashtuns in the Northwest Frontier Province, who considered themselves Afghans but didn't want to go back. To Pakistanis' added ire, as the war began to wind down, few Afghans seemed grateful for the shelter and succor they had found in Pakistan. Instead, they accused Islamabad of trying to control their country. This was true, some Pakistanis would concede, but what did the Afghans expect when they perversely refused to accept the internationally recognized border?

The upshot was widespread and passionate dislike between Afghans and Pakistanis, especially non-Pashtun Pakistanis. Both sides, with justice, accused the other of malign interference in their affairs. A dismaying number on both sides had come to see the other as an existential threat. "I believe that in another ten or twenty years, we will either have Afghanistan or Pakistan, but not both," Yaqub prophesied to me once.

The Taliban were a product of this neighborly conflict. Mullah Omar's early conquests succeeded for many reasons—warlord-weariness in the south, Pashtun tribal loyalties, funding from the trucker mafia—but when the Taliban began fighting Afghanistan's non-Pashtun ethnic groups, they would have failed without their overwhelming support from Pakistani military intelligence. Pakistan welcomed the Taliban as an Afghan government preoccupied with internal purification rather than redrawing borders, and quietly provided Mullah Omar with cash, weapons, tank and airplane repair, logistical support, and strategic advisors. The beleaguered Ahmad Shah Massoud regularly protested that he wasn't losing ground to a bunch of Afghan mullahs, but to a Saudi-funded, Pakistan-equipped proxy army.

When the Taliban's guest and ally Osama bin Laden drew down the wrath of America in 2001, Pakistan was presented with a painful choice. General Pervez Musharraf, the Pakistani president, chose to back America and appeared to abandon his Afghan clients, with only a few face-saving measures. He quietly sent planes (with American acquiescence) to airlift Pakistan's military advisors from the siege of Kunduz, the last pocket of Taliban resistance in northern Afghanistan. In the south, Mullah Omar's government fell apart mostly through negotiation rather than combat, and many of the remnants fled unhindered into Pakistan.

The Taliban enjoyed sanctuary in the anarchic Pashtun tribal districts east of the Durand Line, where Pakistan had never exercised much control and American and Afghan troops couldn't legally follow. Pakistani generals snippily suggested that if the Afghans seriously wanted them to stop infiltration across the rugged border, they'd be happy to fence the whole thing off and lay down land mines. Of course, this tacit recognition of the Durand Line would be anathema to most Afghan Pashtuns. Hamid Karzai had no intention of squandering his political legitimacy; whenever asked, he repeated that the border was a question for the Pashtun people, to be decided by a *jirga* (assembly) of both sides.

In 2004, however, following two al-Qaeda attempts on his life, General Musharraf ordered 80,000 Pakistani troops to pacify the tribal agencies of North and South Waziristan, where many Taliban remnants (and not a few al-Qaeda fighters) had holed up. This was a remarkable break with Pakistan's earlier policy in the Pashtun tribal areas, which had essentially continued the hands-off British system. Musharraf frequently held up his Waziristan offensives as evidence of Pakistan's costly willingness to support America and Afghanistan against the Taliban. The new policy sat oddly with the fact that known Taliban commanders were strolling unmolested around Quetta—a city which unlike the tribal agencies was solidly under the control of the Pakistani government.

Still, given that Pakistan continued to regularly hand over major al-Qaeda terrorists and the Taliban insurgency was showing signs of faltering, America wasn't about to press Musharraf too hard to clean up Quetta. There was, after all, a world of difference between Pakistan's former full-throated support of the Taliban and its current selective blind eye.

Chaman, Pakistan—February 5, 2005

As I strode out of the Pakistani border office with my suitcase, several taxi drivers perked up and began trying to catch my eye. This was going to be the dicey part. None of my Afghan friends had been able to cross the border with me, and I had at least a two-hour drive ahead of me through territory where the Taliban reportedly roamed free. There was a small but non-negligible chance that some of the taxi drivers here at the border might be interested in collecting a Taliban bounty on foreign travelers.

So I walked up to a driver who clearly hadn't noticed me. "Quetta?" I said hopefully. "Serena Hotel?"

He glanced up, shrugged, and popped open the trunk of his weathered little Corolla. "Urdu?" he asked hopefully.

"Nay," I said. I didn't speak Pakistan's main language, though from my travels in Muslim bits of India, I figured that my Nepali vocabulary would be intelligible to Urdu speakers about 10 percent of the time. "English?"

The driver gave a jaded laugh and gestured for me to get in. We didn't speak ten words in a common language, which left neither of us quite sure of how many rupees I had agreed to pay (he seemed to be worried that I had confused the word for "thousand" with the word for "hundred"). Still, I figured arbitrary choice was my best defense in a situation like this.

We began our trip in the Pakistani border town of Chaman, a hectic trading outpost overshadowed by a craggy range of hills. Most of the goods our project bought in Lashkargah had passed through here, from shovel handles to car parts. When Charles tried to rent us newer-model Land Cruisers (hoping for vehicles that were less likely to fall apart or catch on fire), he soon discovered that in Helmand, a "new" car meant any car that the owner had recently bought in Chaman. Unfortunately, the Toyotas that made it to Chaman were whatever wouldn't sell in the secondhand markets of Dubai; the Arabs tuned them up and shipped them to Pashtun country to die. The newest vehicle for rent in Lashkargah bazaar dated back to 1996. Most of them were closer to twelve years old.

As we drove up into the hills, I got to admire the century-old Chaman railway. It was a masterpiece of British imperial engineering, bridging precipitous ravines, boring through the stony crags, easing itself by gradual loops up the steep gradient. It culminated in what, when it was first built, had been the longest tunnel in Asia. Amir Abdurrahman had seen it differently: "Having cut a tunnel through the Khojak Hill, they were pushing the railway line into my country just like pushing a knife into my vitals." He was determined to preserve his country's greatest defense: its impassibility. One reason Abdurrahman invited Durand to settle the border issue was to stop the railway getting any closer to Kandahar.

Today, the highway to Quetta followed more or less the same path. As we ascended, the hills around us revealed a maze of pillbox bunkers and gun emplacements, at once formidable and incongruous. Whether or not these fortifications had ever deterred a conventional invasion, against Pashtun tribesmen they were an obvious Maginot Line. The sky above the hills was a bruise of purplish-gray thunderheads, and at the height of the Khojak Pass there was fresh snow. But it was shallow, fast-melting stuff, and we soon descended into irrigated farm country, leaving any trace of winter far behind.

After three hours on the road, the sun sank behind the border hills. I willed the driver to go faster, hoping to get to Quetta before we lost the final light. Instead, he stopped next to a single-room brick mosque in the middle of a wheat-covered plain. "Namaz," he explained tersely, *prayer*, and headed out to prostrate himself beside three other travelers in the dusty courtyard.

Raz would have approved. More than once, he had halted our pay convoys (on our way home, empty of cash) so as not to miss the dusk prayer, carrying out his ritual ablutions with bottled water and kneeling at the roadside. I got out of the car, leaned against the door, and admired the last reddish traces of an unseen sunset on the clouds and ridgelines for a moment. *I will lift up my eyes unto the hills, from whence comes my help.* This landscape, so akin to the rugged deserts of Palestine, seemed particularly appropriate for psalms. *The Lord is your keeper; the Lord is the shade upon your right hand. The sun shall not smite you by day, nor the moon by night.* My nervousness yielded to exhilaration— for the first time, I let myself believe I was going to make it out on time for my rendezvous with Fi—and I offered up my own prayer of thanks.

When I opened my eyes, the driver was back and looking curiously at me. "Namaz?"

"Isawi namaz," I ventured: the Christian version.

He shrugged tolerantly, apparently unimpressed at a style of prayer that could be mistaken for a nap. The shadows deepened as we drove onward, and it was fully night by the time we reached the light-speckled valley of Quetta.

• • •

The next day, with the help of some convivial Pakistan Airlines staff, I was able to squeeze myself onto a last-minute flight to London. Fiona and I had dinner with her family, then headed on to Minneapolis for some time with mine, by way of the Chemonics office in Washington, D.C. For two weeks, I was able to relax and put Helmand out of my mind.

Reality descended when I got back to Washington on February 24 and checked my e-mail. Chemonics had just won the bid for the four-year, $119 million Alternative Livelihoods Project in southern Afghanistan. This was the real deal, the sort of stuff that was intended to wean Afghans away from poppy long-term—loans to farmers, high-value crops, electricity for the villages, support for would-be legal entrepreneurs. The new program would be centered in Helmand, with likely work in Kandahar and other southern provices. It would include plenty of cash-for-work; the kind of jobs our project had been creating were politically popular, and could continue to serve as a short-term safety net for farmers switching to a new crop.

A lot was going to change, though. Ray Baum and Carol Yee were on their way to Kabul, once again leading a start-up team. When they had set everything up and handed USAID a detailed workplan for the next four years, Jim Graham would become the big new project's chief, and Carol would take over our Alternative Income Project for its remaining eight months. That was for me a chilling prospect. Jim had always expressed happiness with the results of my frantically ad hoc management, but I'd assumed that was because he was laid-back, not because my work was really much good. I imagined that Dave Guier was dissecting it right now; after he was gone, my old supervisor Carol would surely find the holes in whatever was left.

Braced for humiliation, I said my good-byes to Fiona for another three months—we'd have no weekend break together, this time—and headed back to Afghanistan.

Lashkargah, Helmand—February 28, 2005

"Welcome back to Helmand, sir." Nazar showed his teeth in a shy smile. "How are you? And how is your wife, Piano?"

I hugged him, returned his grin. "Glad to be back, Nazar. Fiona's well. She's not my wife yet, though. We're still just engaged. Until January 2006."

"Oh," Nazar said with surprise and a hint of reproach. "Haji-sahib said you had gone for your wedding."

"Did he?" I laughed. Habibullah always did his best to make me respectable. "I must have said something to give him the wrong idea."

I was still greeting the boys and trying to settle in at my desk when a brief, bass reverberation hit the HAVA building—a muffled swell of sound, a shiver in the windowpanes, a thrum in the concrete underfoot. Our conversation and cheer evaporated in its wake. In the stillness, all heads tilted involuntarily toward the source of the tremor. Every Helmandi recognized the sound, and even an ingenuous American could guess at it. Something had exploded within a few blocks of our headquarters.

When the silence remained unbroken by gunfire or further blasts, the conversation rose up again, soft and distracted. Explosions weren't common in Lashkargah, but nor were they cause for panic. Habibullah caught my eye, and together we hurried over to our security center. Charles was up in Kabul at the moment, consulting with Ray and Carol about defense measures for Chemonics' grand new project; he had left our security to his unflappable assistant, Farid. We eventually found Farid outside speaking with the Kajaki guard captain. Several of our police were ambling over in the direction of the blast, looking alert but not particularly alarmed.

"What was the noise?" I asked, scanning the empty horizon for smoke.

"There has been a bomb somewhere near the police station," Farid reported crisply. "We have sent some guards to find out what is happening." He had a quick exchange in Pashto with Haji Habibullah, then shot a wry grin in my direction. "I have not said yet: Welcome back to Lashkargah, Mr. Joel."

I couldn't help chuckling. "I've missed you guys too, Farid." I suppressed the urge to grab a couple of guards to go and indulge my own curiosity. Farid clearly had things under control. "Let me know when you find out what's going on."

Twenty minutes later, Habibullah descended on my desk, huffing through his silver beard. "We have a problem, Mr. Joel."

I scanned his face, worried, but he looked more exasperated than alarmed. "You've found out more about the bomb?"

"It was a car bomb," the Haji explained. "At the Ministry of Culture. Three police guards are hurt. But that is not the problem. The problem is that one of our men has been arrested."

"What?"

"Homayoon," Haji said, his face twisting in a half-smile. Homayoon was RAMP's agriculture expert in Helmand. "He went to the Ministry to see what had happened, and started taking pictures of the car. The police did not know who he was."

"Oh, for . . ." I almost laughed with relief. We headed to the police station to rescue the feckless Homayoon. As our Land Cruiser rolled past the Ministry of Culture and Information, Habibullah inclined his head discreetly at the blast site. The previously anonymous wall of the ministry compound was half-toppled. Outside, armed men in kamiz partoog hovered watchfully around a splintered wooden cart and the wreckage of a pickup truck.

"Why on earth hit the local branch of the culture ministry?" I wondered aloud. As far as I was aware, it was a conservative outfit with a microscopic budget. It seemed an unlikely target for insurgents.

Habibullah wagged his head noncommittally. "We will see what they say."

At the jailhouse, Habibullah's conversation with the police captain lasted rather longer than necessary to get Homayoon out of the clink. The captain finally dispatched his men to fetch the prisoner, and Habibullah rejoined me, looking pensive. "He says the bomb was in a fruit cart, pushed up next to the police car. The police don't think this was Taliban. They think it was something personal, an attack by some enemy of the deputy director of the culture ministry."

"Just politics as usual, then?" It seemed that almost all the violence in Helmand could be explained away as either skirmishing opium gangs or the latest blow in a generations-long tribal feud. Those were worrisome, but much less so than a serious antigovernment strike. Still, I felt newly glad that we hadn't taken the engineering wing of the HAVA building—on the side that was most vulnerable to car bombs.

• • •

Contrary to my fretful delusions, acting team leader Dave Guier didn't greet me with a list of things I'd done wrong that needed fixing—quite the opposite. I had a lot of respect for Dave as a resourceful, seasoned manager, and when he welcomed me back with the wild-eyed fervor of a drowning man, it gave me new perspective on the difficulty of the work we'd all been doing for three months. Dave had been valiantly filling in for both Jim and me, and was more than relieved to hand me back my mishmash of responsibilities. To my surprise, I felt adequate to them.

Dave was grappling with two major conflicts: First, our relations with HAVA were at a nadir. Engineer Dawari was back from Mecca and ranting about what we had done to his headquarters; he was especially incensed to discover a squad of Kajaki gunmen camping out on the ground floor twenty-four hours a day. With what must have seemed like pure impudence, we broke the news that Chemonics was going to be working in Helmand for four more years, and asked if we could exchange a little more general repair work on the building for two more top-floor offices. Dawari was flabbergasted. "No, no, I cannot give you any more rooms. It is out of the question. This is a government building!"

Across the country, the struggling institutions of the Afghan government complained that they were being crowded out by richer international development organizations. Our relationship with HAVA was a particularly vivid example. We were colonizing Dawari's building from top to bottom, and had replaced a gang of guards answering in theory to him with guards who answered to us. Engineer Dawari had wanted to use us as a source of patronage, but his operations wound up suffering because literally *every* HAVA staffer, not just the engineers, was fighting to have a turn working for our project. (We protested and imposed stricter standards when we found out that a semiliterate office cleaner had finagled a position advising one of our field activities.)

Dawari's red-bearded deputy, Khan Aqa, who greatly resented his public sacking on the driveway, nearly managed to supplant his boss by filing a complaint in Kabul: "Dawari is giving everything to the Americans." Needless to say, we didn't intend to ride roughshod over Dawari. We consulted him in our work planning, managed our activities with the help of HAVA advisors, and vocally shared credit for our projects with Dawari and the provincial government. Yet precisely by carrying out so many of HAVA's priority projects with so many of its best staff while swallowing its building, we were threatening to become HAVA.

We were also drawing criticism from an unexpected new source: Colonel Eugene Augustine of the Provincial Reconstruction Team, America's small military garrison on the edge of town. The PRT had a significant budget to carry out development projects, and was building schools, wells, and bridges throughout Helmand. Even more important, however, was its mission to help the Afghan police secure areas around Lashkargah, so that timid civilian development organizations like us could be coaxed into working there. Colonel Augustine did not appreciate our implication that this wasn't succeeding in neighboring Babaji.

Two weeks before my return, the colonel had invited Dave Guier to a PRT meeting with the Babaji shura. The purpose of the meeting, it emerged, was to browbeat Dave into restarting our activities across the river. Before the meeting, Dave and Habibullah had privately shared with Colonel Augustine our concerns about the violent feuding in the region. At the meeting, the colonel explicitly brought up the list of incidents and asked the Babaji elders what they thought of it. The elders denied that there was any feud under way, and accused us of propagandizing. A shura member who sounded rather like Elder Odysseus berated Dave, "Why didn't you send guards with your engineers from the beginning, like we warned you to? If you come back now, of course, we will help and cooperate with your security." Wizened Elder Priam was there, and wept again for his barren fields and stolen car.

"On balance, the shura painted a pretty convincing picture, those six men sitting there in their turbans, probably four hundred years on this good earth between them," Dave admitted to us. "And I was no match for the crying old man." But Dave held the line with admirable resilience. "I told them our project couldn't afford security disruptions like this one." He concluded that while we would consider working in Babaji eventually, security issues and the community's non-cooperation had sent it to the bottom of our priority list.

"It was at this point that Colonel Augustine had heard enough," Dave recalled bitterly. "He told the interpreter not to translate what he was about to say, and proceeded to read me the riot act." Augustine was sure that Babaji was basically a secure area where we could win hearts and minds. He had no patience for our argument that the community was in some sense responsible for the theft, or that in the absence of a reliable police force, the only way we could keep ourselves safe was staying out of demonstrably unsafe areas. "The colonel said it doesn't matter if someone in the village knows who the thieves are. People there need help. It's time to move on."

• • •

Ironically, the one trait above all that distinguished the PRT from us was its overriding concern for "force protection." Most of the hundred-odd Iowa National Guard troops spent their time behind their formidable walls and barbed-wire moat on the outskirts of Lashkargah, protected by dozens of police commander Abdul Rahman's Afghan gunmen. Unlike the British PRT in north Afghanistan, which made regular foot patrols kitted out like police rather than soldiers, when American troops left their base it was in full body armor, riding in Humvees with gun turrets. Their convoys required security clearance several days in advance. They would never go to most of Babaji, because the rural roads were too narrow or rugged to safely admit their broad vehicles.

This defensive, militarized security posture made it difficult for the PRT to make frequent monitoring visits to the reconstruction projects they funded; if we had taken a similar stance, we would surely have lost tens if not hundreds of thousands of dollars to fraud. It also isolated the American soldiers from the communities they were supposed to help. I remembered Bob Kramer's stories about meeting with the PRT back when we were starting up the project. He had first headed over to meet the colonel with Ray and Pete on Thanksgiving Day. "We arrived at the gate and waited," Bob had told me, "and waited, and finally after about an hour in the sun, someone came to let us in. They hadn't been expecting us, so we got the same treatment we would have if we had been community representatives."

To be fair, the PRT regularly brought local leaders inside its compound for consultation. In early December, Sergeant Reggie Truss had invited Bob Kramer to observe the PRT's introductory meeting with elders from all over Helmand province. "The idea was to present the U.S. government's strategic plan for Afghanistan," Bob had reported to us afterward, sounding a little bemused. "It was a PowerPoint. Reggie wasn't the one who came up with it—the Department of Defense and USAID gave it to him, and he clearly understood some of its problems."

Nonetheless, Sergeant Truss had gamely tried to present the grand strategy to the local elders with the help of his Afghan interpreter. The purpose of the meeting was getting the elders to decide which of them would be "accountable" for achieving various goals in Helmand. "The interpreter had a terrible time translating goals like building a four-star hotel," Bob said dryly. "Or freedom of speech. Or setting up competing newspapers. But Reggie did his best to explain the ideas behind the goals. When one leader asked him to explain what 'a free media' meant, Reggie basically said, 'Well, suppose someone wanted to complain about some official act. Where would they go?'" I couldn't help chuckling. Even in Kabul with its freewheeling new papers and radio stations, the answer would rarely be, "to a journalist." In Helmand, people would take their complaints to their elders, who would appeal to the governor or other powerful commanders.

In a funny way, the PRT's weaknesses complemented our own. Chemonics had plenty of experience running development projects, but was reduced to frantic improvisation when it came to protecting itself from theft or attack. The U.S. military was more than capable of protecting itself, but its defensive culture and lack of expertise weakened its development efforts. All of us had parachuted into Helmand, basically ignorant of the local culture and politics, and were learning as we went along. From what I'd learned so far, I was willing to bet that heading back to Babaji was a bad idea. But Colonel Augustine made his case to our superiors at USAID, and they too began pressing us to go back.

When Jim Graham returned, he conceded that we should head back into Bolan, though not Babaji. "I don't give a damn what Augustine wants," Jim said gruffly. "On the day that the Babaji shura comes in with any concrete proposal for how they'll help protect our staff from an attack, we'll go back in. Until then, forget it."

We met with the elders of Bolan on March 15, and explained that since their village wasn't the actual site of the attack, we were relaxing the condition of cooperation with the police—it was too late for anything to come of that. But we requested some concrete commitment to our security, like having an elder accompany our engineers to and from the worksite, or some equivalent. The Bolan shura declared themselves totally helpless and cast themselves on our mercy.

For a moment, it sounded like we were going to get a guarantee from Abdul Munaf, the portly mayor of Lashkargah; then he finished his sentence. "We promise you that this time if you come work with us," the sharwal declared, "you should bring guards."

The Royal Bungalow

On the morning of March 18, Jim, Habibullah, and I found ourselves sipping green tea with the governor on a riverside terrace of the Bost Hotel. The morning sun cast hard shadows from the riverbank cedars onto the silt-solid brown torrent below us. The Helmand had swallowed the last of its stony shoals, and now yawned unbroken between our balcony and the sparsely forested far bank. Back in the 1970s, this had been King Zahir's hunting terrace; he would sit here with a rifle close to hand, ready to take shots at the wild pigs that snuffled cautiously through the underbrush across the river. The king had reportedly loved Helmand province, visiting often for shooting expeditions or boating on the Kajaki reservoir.

Now Governor Sher Muhammad was offering us King Zahir's old cliff-top bungalow in Kajaki as our northern headquarters. "I will not ask you to do anything else for me all year," the chubby, roguish wali pledged fervently. "Only this one thing: start your activities in as much of upper Helmand as you can, as quickly as possible."

There was an edge of desperation to the young governor's usual twinkling affability. After what we presumed was a productive Eid in Mecca, Sher Muhammad had headed to a drug-fighting conference in Kabul with President Karzai, the American and British ambassadors, and fellow provincial governors. In a fit of job-retaining enthusiasm, he had promised to slash poppy cultivation by 80 percent in Helmand. It wasn't completely unthinkable; two years earlier, Sher Muhammad had brought poppy down by 50 percent just by clearing out Nad-i-Ali and Marja. To beat that now, his early eradication in central Helmand wouldn't be enough. He would have to clear large swathes of upper Helmand as well—the mountainous heartland of his own Alizai tribe.

"Karzai's poppy inspectors will be here soon," Sher Muhammad informed us tersely. "Yesterday evening I came from Kabul. Today I have sent my police to destroy poppy in Sangin, Kajaki, and Musa Qala. But if I send the eradication tractors without sending jobs, by God, there will be trouble." In 2002, two thousand Helmandi farmers had marched on Lashkargah to protest poppy eradication, leaving eight men killed and thirty-five wounded. This year, though Helmand had been quiet, we had heard reports from other provinces of eradication police shot by snipers or blown up by land mines in the fields.

I shared a wary glance with Jim. I'd planned to go up and oversee our first Kajaki payroll next week, and we both knew that Yaqub was champing at the bit to expand our work in upper Helmand, but we hadn't expected to do it at the same time as a major poppy eradication push. "Wali-sahib," I replied, "as you know, we do not have all the weapons and ammunition we need for our Kajaki guard force. We want to help you, but we have barely enough security for our existing activity in upper Helmand."

As usual, Sher Muhammad rolled his eyes in disgruntlement. "I only have fifteen guns and two rocket launchers left! Tell Karzai to give me back my rockets and I will arm your police."

The increasingly successful national disarmament program had reached Helmand, reducing the officially recognized militias of both the governor and Mir Wali to personal bodyguards. The burly Islamist Mir Wali, who had so successfully seen off the national highway police in September, was this time genuinely weakened. The district police of Girishk continued to answer to him, along with some small unofficial militias, but he had clearly lost a good share of his arsenal. The UN gave Mir Wali a consolation trip to Japan for his exemplary cooperation with his own disarmament. When he got back, he began gearing up to run for parliament.

Sher Muhammad, on the other hand, could keep on exploiting the greatest loophole in the disarmament process: the police. With no real central control over Afghanistan's police force and no coherent effort to reform it, governor-warlords like Sher Muhammad simply packed the provincial police with as many of their own men as they could get away with. I believed the wali was feeling the pinch of disarmament, but I didn't believe he was as hard up for weapons as he pretended. "We can't ask Karzai for guns, wali-sahib," I said, with diplomatic regret. "Karzai listens to you, not to us."

Sher Muhammad shook his head in disgust. "So be it. If you go to the north, by God, somehow I will find you guns."

"We'll send a group up north to have a look around on Sunday," Jim promised.

Sangin, Helmand—March 20, 2005

Our mission to Kajaki rolled out through a landscape subtly but unmistakably in the grip of spring. Thousands of tiny plants had appeared in the folds and creases of the desert terrain; in the shimmer of noon they all but vanished, then reappeared to stipple the slopes green when the dusk light hit them soft and slantwise. The Kuchi around Lashkargah had decamped for the Registan deserts between Helmand and Kandahar to graze their herds on the fleeting greenery. The strong winter rains had been a godsend for the nomads, who had no houses or fields to lose and whose sheep and goats had died in droves during the long drought.

For many of upper Helmand's farmers, the downpour had been less welcome. Not only were their homes collapsing, but their poppies were getting waterlogged, which would dilute the precious opium resin. Almost as soon as we crossed the highway, we found ourselves driving through broad, blatant fields of poppy. At this stage it looked like an exotic salad plant, with long, crinkle-edged leaves springing up in bunches. The leaves were a vibrant green, far brighter and more striking than any other color in eyeshot. Soon each plant would sprout a gangling stem with a plump pod at the end, and flower in varying shades of pink, white, maroon, and cherry-red. Then the petals would fall, and the harvest would begin.

Our road north led through Sangin, one of Helmand's traditional opium hubs. As we approached the district center, we began passing multihued, concrete narco-palaces, bristling with radio antennas and satellite dishes. Sangin's lively and prosperous bazaar teemed with pickups, coughing Kamaz trucks, and rattletrap Corollas. Off a side road, under a broad cloth awning, I saw a corral of motorcycles, the preferred vehicle for petty drug traffickers collecting their wares from high mountain ravines. We didn't seek out Sangin's hundreds of opium shops, but I was told that in the harvest season, they were all but impossible to miss. This was southern Afghanistan's largest drug bazaar, where small buyers from all over the country sold their wares and large buyers organized convoys to Pakistan or Iran.

The walaswal of Sangin met us in his cavernous concrete headquarters. Despite being brother to intelligence police chief Dad Muhammad (known as Dado), one of Helmand's most feared warlords, the walaswal was a courteous, heavy-browed man who looked more melancholy than fierce. He welcomed the prospect of a jobs project, and suggested repairing the broad dirt road we had just driven up on. "The people are very unhappy with eradication," he said bleakly. "Maybe this will give them reason to believe in the government."

We saw the source of the walaswal's gloom an hour and a half later, when we abruptly ran into Sher Muhammad's eradication team. The first sign was the motley rank of tractors parked along the roadside, roughly a dozen of different makes and colors. Then we rounded a bend and saw the swarm of nervous, blue-uniformed police, AK-47s at the ready. This was clearly one place the governor had chosen to invest his guns. At the base of the steep road embankment, three tractors churned up the bright green fields with their many-tined harrows. In fields the tractors couldn't easily reach, the police led crews of mutinous-looking villagers to lash the poppy to death with mulberry switches.

From that point on, all the poppy fields visible from the road were plowed over or trampled. We passed farmers squatting in their fields, weeding out the dead plants and salvaging whatever they could. Some had reopened irrigation channels to flood their land, hoping that the tattered poppy would revive. Their eyes invariably snapped up at the sound of our engines, and followed us intensely but without expression until we were out of sight. I decided against taking any photographs.

We left our cars to visit one of our project's worksites in lower Kajaki district, and walked for five minutes through deep green wheat fields, earth-walled compounds, and whispering poplars. Then we passed out of sight of the road, and the real crop reappeared all around us. Our laborers were heaving gray-black mud up from a drainage ditch onto the fringes of a broad poppy field. An old man rolled out his patu shawl in the middle of the crinkly green plants and performed his midday prayers without embarrassment.

"We destroyed the bridge over our own canal, so no police tractor can reach these fields," a villager told me defiantly. "The police still came with sticks, one month ago." Many poppy plants showed the scars; they had grown sparse and small, and would probably not yield much opium. The villagers weren't giving up on their investment, though. We walked past several who were casting handfuls of fertilizer, fine as sand, from pouches at their hips. After the repeated decimation of their crop, a whole season's work and money was bound up in the plants they'd managed to save. By harvest time, they would clearly be prepared to do just about anything to defer eradication for a crucial week or two.

One hawk-nosed local elder gestured without apology at the fields around us. "All of us have too much debt," he declared. "If we had jobs, no one would grow taryak. But there are no factories here, no place to work. And now the government *kampeyn*," tractor or combine, "will take away our only income, unless we pay the police to spare our fields."

"We are not bringing the kampeyn," I assured him. "Our purpose is to help you with jobs. And a project is coming that will bring more than just jobs."

The elder inclined his head politely, but with a certain skepticism; we hadn't yet made our first payments in Kajaki. "Your project is the only support here. Other agencies bring food, but the wealthy take it away from the needy. The government has done nothing for us." His eyes suddenly smoldered. "We know that taryak is far from Islam. But our children need to live. Any human being would do it. Give us jobs, and it will be the end for taryak."

• • •

Without an eradication campaign, I'd heard people argue, the Afghan government's struggle against poppy would lose all credibility. Antonio Maria Costa, Italian director of the UN Office of Drugs and Crime, often declared that laws were meaningless without a plausible risk of punishment. "Last year and the year before, three to four percent, possibly five percent, of the land cultivated with opium was eradicated. This is the equivalent of having a three to four percent chance of being caught robbing a bank." Who wouldn't rob a bank, or plant poppy, if the risks were so low?

Yet the risks of eradication fell on the Afghans who had the least choice: sharecroppers and small farmers. If these petty poppy growers lost their crops, they would have to repay the landowners and traffickers in cash, land, livestock, or—not infrequently—a daughter. For most Afghan subsistence farmers, opium didn't hold out any serious prospect of getting rich; it was simply the only way to escape destitution and shame. Poppy eradication just pushed them deeper into the poverty that had led to their growing opium in the first place.

Meanwhile, the powerful landowners and traffickers were insulated from eradication by the system of debt, and by their ability to buy off the enthusiastically corruptible police. Indeed, far from enhancing the credibility of the Afghan government, poppy eradication showed up its worst weaknesses. In a province like Helmand, where virtually every government institution was led by a trafficker, the hypocrisy of the campaign was breathtaking. "The police do not bring the tractors to their relatives' fields, or the fields of people who pay them," one of my colleagues said quietly. "And the commanders' own poppy is never hurt."

I shook my head disgustedly. "How did the Taliban ever manage to get zero opium in Helmand?" In 2000, after six years of profitably taxing the drug trade, Mullah Omar had declared a total ban on poppy cultivation (though not on buying and selling opium). He claimed it was motivated by religious concerns, while other Taliban hinted that they hoped to win international recognition or aid. Skeptics suggested that the Taliban were just trying to boost the price of opium, which had declined after the record 1999 harvest.

My friend laughed. "The Taliban did not have to eradicate fields. They did not even have to punish many people. Everyone was so afraid of them—even the commanders. Mullah Omar only had to speak, and no one planted poppy."

The ban's success had been a testament to the Taliban's authority. Across their domain, poppy cultivation plunged by 98 percent; only in northeastern Badakhshan, the last province under Ahmad Shah Massoud's control, did large-scale planting continue. The world supply of opium collapsed, sending prices soaring. Anyone with stockpiled opium (including many Taliban commanders) made windfall profits.

However, the Taliban ban also testified to the disastrous results of eliminating poppy without introducing any alternatives for farmers or laborers. Most rural Afghan households couldn't feed themselves from their own small plots of land; they relied on a cash crop or other jobs to buy bread. The poppy ban thus worsened a nationwide famine, and sent a surge of illegal laborers into Pakistan and Iran. Meanwhile, many farmers still owed opium gum to the traffickers. Since they couldn't grow poppy, their debts were converted into cash—but at the new opium price, five to ten times higher than the rate at which they had borrowed. Under the weight of hunger, poverty, and debt, farmers all across the Pashtun belt began grumbling against the Taliban. As opium stockpiles ran out and the traffickers also started complaining, observers wondered whether even Mullah Omar would be able to enforce the ban for a second year.

The question would remain moot; America invaded Afghanistan just before the 2001 planting season. Soon afterward, a Taliban spokesman reversed course, declaring that cultivating opium "for medicinal use" was permissible. The insurgents didn't want to be shut out of the poppy revival, spurred by sky-high prices, that was going on all over Afghanistan. Many of them, like Gulbuddin, had been tied into the opium economy for decades, and reports soon confirmed that the insurgency was skimming money from the drug trade.

This provided another common justification for poppy eradication. No one could reliably guess how much drug money went to the insurgents, or how it compared to other sources of funding like the Pashtun trucker mafia and "taxes" on hawaladars. Still, by 2004, I heard highly placed U.S. government staffers claim that eradication "is really a terrorism issue. This is just like Colombia. We won't really beat the Taliban unless we cut off the opium money that feeds them."

To me, this seemed to ignore the first principle of counterinsurgency: You win by winning over the people. No matter how many insurgents you kill, no matter how much of their money you intercept, if you hurt lots of local people in the process, the insurgents will come out on top. If we succeeded in impoverishing the Taliban by impoverishing millions of Afghan farmers and laborers, we would wind up with a poorer but fiercer rebellion. On the other hand, successful development projects in rural Afghanistan would both weaken the insurgency and give farmers an alternative to poppy.

The Afghan government couldn't win by just playing nice, of course, but for the next few years the place to get tough was with traffickers, not farmers—jailing big opium kingpins, breaking up heroin labs and convoys, and above all, punishing drug-related corruption in government. It would admittedly be much harder to enforce the law against the rich and powerful rather than the poor and desperate. It would require far-reaching and time-consuming reforms of the justice system. It would, if successful, be an unparalleled boost to President Karzai's legitimacy.

Yet America remained fixated on poppy eradication. The U.S. government recognized that the current program was failing due to police corruption—but instead of putting serious resources behind police reform, the White House was pushing a reluctant Hamid Karzai to start spraying herbicides from the air.

Kajaki, Helmand—March 20, 2005

All morning, the blunt brown hills had been encroaching on us from the east, looming steadily higher and closer to the road. The town of Kajaki sat at the crux where the hills finally leapt out across the Helmand River, severing the deep green belt of canal-watered farmland along the east riverbank. North and west of this point stretched the dry, rugged highlands known as Zamindawar, where farmers eked most of their water from narrow *karez* tunnels—underground channels linked to far-off mountain springs.

This point where the hills crossed the river had been a natural point for a dam. The 320-foot-high Kajaki Dam itself was tucked away invisibly in a well-protected ravine, but the spray from its spillway created a lustrous white aurora at the head of the valley. On the west bank of the flooded Helmand, the dust-brown buildings and scattered trees of the town sprawled beneath a gravelly hill. The east bank was far steeper, a giant's staircase of stone cliffs. Yaqub pointed to the top of one bluff and cheerfully said, "That is the King's House." Squinting upward, I saw a dozen towering pine trees and what looked like Romanesque pillars. Then the road dropped away to the foot of the cliff, where the swollen river sucked unnervingly at the mud three feet from our tires.

We reached the district headquarters in time for a late lunch—fatty lamb chunks hidden in mounds of rice, with yogurt and radishes. The silver-bearded walaswal of Kajaki looked very relieved to see us. "There has been some rumor that the Americans are not going to pay after all," Yaqub explained. Considering the challenges of our impending payroll, I was worried we might end up confirming the rumor.

In two days, Raz and the boys would arrive with all our remaining Kajaki guards and over $140,000 in small bills. We had to pay two thousand workers, half in lower Kajaki and half fixing karez tunnels up in the Zamindawar highlands. We couldn't just meet them at their worksites as usual; the lower Kajaki crews had already finished the job, and our karez crews were scattered too widely. So we had to identify relatively secure payroll locations, get the word out to our workers in advance, and head out under heavy security. Paying everyone would take at least two days—our first overnight payroll trip. At the royal bungalow, we hoped to set up a secure headquarters where our paymasters could spend the night with bags of money.

King Zahir's cliff-top resort turned out to be a cluster of six flat-roofed stone cottages in varying states of disrepair. On two sides, it was flanked by steep bluffs, and on a third by the high fence of the Kajaki Dam compound. Living on the other side of that fence, protected by locally hired USPI guards, were engineers from Louis Berger (the company that had paved the Kabul-Kandahar Highway). They were trying to repair the Kajaki Dam, which was currently generating only a fraction of its potential electricity; one of its valves was stuck open, and its turbines were in bad shape.

Yaqub scowled at the fence. He had stayed in Berger's cozy, Internet-equipped guesthouse on his first Kajaki visit, but on his second visit had been bluntly turned away by USPI's American security boss. Flustered and offended, Yaqub had had to fall back on the walaswal for accommodation. "They have hurt our project's reputation," he told me bitterly. "To stay one time with the foreign engineers, and then to be shut out, made us lose much face." I later saw an e-mail from the local Berger manager, explaining the decision to a colleague: "We thought their previous stay was a one-time thing. We feel that the risk is too high to have any association with this other program, as it is really a poppy eradication program, with a nice name."

The royal bungalows, however, weren't under Berger's authority. They were occupied by the district police commander, a small, bony man with a feline gait and a massive, bristly mustache. We handed him a letter from his cousin Sher Muhammad, evicting him from the "Queen's House," the only bungalow with electricity and functional plumbing. The commander accepted this in relatively good humor, embracing us and rubbing his mustache in our ears. "He does not look it, but he is a very brutal man," Yaqub murmured to me. "Everyone here is terrified of him."

The police immediately began moving their carpets, cots, and kohl-eyed catamites down to the "King's House," the cottage on the edge of the bluff. Once they had moved out, Ehsan took charge of unloading our furniture truck and making the Queen's House as habitable as possible. I found a closet where we could put the safe, and we moved the cots and *toshak* floor mattresses into the rooms where we would be spending the next four nights. Yaqub gestured at a smoke-stained patch low on the wall. "Hashish. Can you smell it?"

When we came back out, we found the commander eyeing our couches. "This is very nice furniture," he blandly commented in Pashto. "Maybe I will steal some of it."

Yaqub gave a strained chuckle. "What is the world coming to, if police began stealing?"

"You are right," our new neighbor agreed, smiling. "You know what the Taliban said when people accused them of theft? We are not stealing. We are just taking." We all had a good laugh over that one.

I walked down to the King's House to admire the view of the Helmand River. Behind the bungalow were several lovely pines and a faux Roman garden, with an arbor of fluted stone columns. I wondered if we could convince Sher Muhammad's mustachioed cousin to accept one of the less scenic bungalows. "How did Berger not grab these houses?" I asked our chief engineer, Sayed Akbar, who on a former job had managed the renovation of the Berger compound.

"We wanted to," Akbar said gravely. "But the commander said that if he had to leave these houses, at night he would fire rockets at us from across the river."

"Ah," I said. "So we'll let him keep the King's House, then."

"It is a good idea."

The next day, I was hit by stomach trouble and what felt like the flu, so I rested in the Queen's House, watching Ehsan manage the repairs with his typical verve. Yaqub and Akbar headed off to see about adding more workers to our successful karez cleaning activities. I was sitting under a mulberry tree, enjoying the sunshine and a cup of tea, when Yaqub returned. "We will get one thousand more workers in Zamindawar by the end of the week, to replace the ones who have finished in lower Kajaki," he declared jubilantly. "I think we can get just as many workers in Musa Qala district. I will ask the police commander to contact Musa Qala by radio to arrange a meeting."

A few moments later, Yaqub was back from the King's House, looking slightly bemused. "He is . . . beating up someone right now. I will talk to him later."

· · ·

On Tuesday morning, we headed out into the highlands of Zamindawar to spread the word about the coming payroll. Zamindawar was like the imprint of a vast, outstretched hand, whose palm had pressed out a broad hub of undulating plains while its fingers squeezed up mountain ridgelines. The winter deluge had been kind to the area's rain-fed fields but a disaster for its underground karez irrigation system, which carried vital water from the rugged "fingers" down to the "palm." Many tunnels had caved in or been filled with silt and gravel, especially those that had previously dried up and been abandoned during the long drought.

Karezes were one of the most impressive and perilous achievements of Afghan agriculture. They could run for miles, and some were literally hundreds of feet deep. From the surface, they looked like a line of human-sized molehills, marking the shafts by which men descended to clear silt or reopen collapsed tunnels. I tried to imagine the work that had gone into the longest and deepest karez systems—the decades of grueling yet precise labor in cold, narrow caves, at constant risk of a cave-in. That was what water was worth, up here in the highlands.

Our first Zamindawar worksite was a karez called Haki Jehannum, "little hell." A chilly draft gusted up from the twenty-foot vertical shaft, which ended at a dark stream three or four feet across. Up in the sun, two workers manned a wooden windlass and cable, hauling up rubber buckets full of silt and dumping them off the back of the molehill. The man at the bottom waved his hammer, chisel, and flashlight cheerfully at us before crouching and wading back into the dank tunnel.

"Can I go down there?" I asked, more out of curiosity than desire.

"It is dangerous," Yaqub said with distaste, "and you will be covered in mud. Also, it will be hard for the men to pull you back up, because you are so much heavier than the average Afghan."

"Thanks, Yaqub," I said sourly. "It's kind of invisible work, isn't it? How do we track progress if we can't see it?"

"We know how long it should take to clear a section of tunnel," Engineer Akbar explained. "If they go too slowly, we will find out whether there is some problem or if they are just working slowly to get more money."

I looked along the chain of molehills, counting the other men and their windlasses. Most of our thousand workers in Zamindawar were divided into these tiny karez crews of three or four men. "And all these small groups—their supervisors will inform them all of the payroll, and they'll all be able to make it to the pay sites tomorrow?" We hadn't wanted to put the word out earlier, for fear of attracting bandits, but I was worried that some workers might miss the news and not get paid.

Yaqub nodded blithely. "Believe me, Joel, news can travel very fast in a place like this. Everyone hears about everything."

• • •

Raz Muhammad and the other paymasters were waiting for us back at the King's House. At around one o'clock we headed down to lower Kajaki to start the payroll. In the first sunbaked village square, the workers trickled in slowly until almost six hundred turbaned men were squatting expectantly in the dust. Raz bellowed bracingly at the villagers to arrange themselves by work crew; he made an incongruous sergeant-major in his elegant gray kamiz partoog, sunglasses, and baseball cap. As our paymasters began handing out paper-clipped wads of afghanis in exchange for thumbprints, I interviewed some villagers and found the mood guardedly cheerful. The Americans were paying up after all.

When I asked about flood damage, a farmer with a long black beard and turban invited me to come see his inundated fields by the river. I told Yaqub where I was going and hopped on the back of the man's motorbike. A couple of our police commandeered rides from other farmers, and we sped off in a little convoy along the bumpy, two-foot-wide farm tracks. The countryside around us was stunning—pink flowering trees behind thorn-topped orchard walls; poplar-edged canals tracing long curves across the landscape; the ever-present, vivid green of opium poppy.

After ten minutes, we reached the Helmand. On the far bank, the desert hills plunged to the river in rippling, water-worn cliffs; our side was obviously the floodway. Nonetheless, the farmer and his neighbors had planted poppy at the top of the bank, and the distinctive leaves were now sticking up staunchly from six silt-heavy inches of water. I snapped pictures and hemmed sympathetically, wishing I'd brought along an interpreter. When I turned back, I saw that a cluster of sullen villagers had formed along the trail. I offered my hand to one black-turbaned young man and greeted him in sketchy Pashto, but he just glared. It seemed a good time to leave. I swapped grins with a few nearby kids who didn't share their elders' caution or hostility, and asked the farmer to take me back to our pay site.

On my return, our drivers invited me to join them in the shade of a high earth wall, where they were drinking sweet green tea. Our police guards lounged nearby with a rocket launcher and machine gun. They teased a smile out of a somber-looking young villager with a bulky white turban by calling him "Talib jan," *my dear Talib*. (Many Taliban had worn white rather than black turbans, considering both to be appropriately devout colors. The unifying factor had not been the color, but the thin, plain fabric, called *paj*.) At one point, the savage-looking village mastiff, almost four feet high at the shoulder, ran up to us and started barking; a guard cursed and swung his long rocket-propelled grenade as if to whack it. This disconcerted me rather more than the dog. A skinny boy barely taller than the beast ran up, dug his hands into the folds of its neck, and dragged it away.

By around 4:30 in the afternoon, we had paid just about everyone at our first two sites. Then Yaqub came over, looking a bit concerned. "Joel, there is bad news. Our last two hundred men have not heard about the payroll."

"What?"

"Their supervisor resigned yesterday," Yaqub scowled. "Some political problem, an issue of tribe. I did not hear about it until just now. Some of them heard that the payment was going on here, and asked when they would get their money."

We sped over to the final pay site, a dishearteningly empty stretch of rocky slope on the outskirts of a village. The local elders welcomed us warmly and insisted that it wasn't too late to muster the people. Our white-bearded Kajaki office manager got on the loudspeaker of the village mosque and bellowed in Pashto that anyone who wanted to get paid should show up in the next half-hour. We settled in on the roof of a nearby house with tea and naan, watching the sun sink as our workers filtered in. The local mullah gave the dusk call to prayer shortly after we started handing out money. We paid the last forty men by moonlight.

Luckily, we were only ten minutes' ride from our guesthouse. Yaqub sighed in satisfaction as we rolled out and said, "You know, I think half the people we paid today were Taliban."

I tried not to sound shocked. "Really? So many?"

"Well, supporters. They were very popular up here, you know. Mullah Omar is a neighbor." The Taliban leader's childhood home, Deh Rawud, was in Uruzgan province just across the Kajaki reservoir.

"What does that mean for our security?" I asked, thinking queasily about my impromptu motorbike ride.

"Our best security is if the people support us," Yaqub declared. "I think these Taliban will see things a little differently after today."

Engineer Akbar nodded meditatively. "Today I spoke with a village elder in Zamindawar. I asked him if anyone had talked about attacking the American project. He said no."

"Well, that's nice."

"Then I asked him what he would do if anyone started talking about an attack. He said," and here Akbar raised his voice with considerable conviction, "'I will *kill* them. What has anyone else done for us? The Americans can stay.'"

The Indispensable Warlords

Musa Qala, Helmand—March 23, 2005

In the morning, Raz and the paymasters left to pay the highland karez workers while the rest of our team headed to the town of Musa Qala (Fort Moses, as I mentally translated it). We crossed the Helmand River together at the Kajaki bridge, a derelict wooden structure paved thickly with dirt. Many of its timbers were buckling, and in several places its eroded surface had been patched with flimsy-looking sheets of corrugated metal. The bridge flexed palpably beneath our Land Rovers, sending little cascades of dust down to the torrential river. Then we were across, and rolling up into Zamindawar; the paymasters turned north while we continued to the west.

The highland landscape around us was waterless but testified to the violence of past floods. We detoured down into deep gullies whose bridges had not survived the winter rains and passed karezes that had been washed out in the widening of nearby canyons. "This is Konjak," Yaqub informed me with a meaningful glance—the region of the Zamindawar highlands that was home to the Akhundzada family. The dry vale straddled the border between Kajaki and the district of Musa Qala, where today Governor Sher Muhammad's younger brother was the walaswal. I was sure the governor would be delighted to have us create jobs here, adding to his prestige in his tribal home turf. His family was still contending with major rivals from the Alizai Pashtun tribe—not least the Rais-i-Baghran, warlord of the isolated northern mountains, who had never recanted his allegiance to the Taliban.

A little over an hour into our trip, we rumbled down a broad, vacant riverbed of smooth stones and saw the town of Musa Qala rising to the south. It was a prosperous bazaar by rural Afghan standards, with its long aisle of busy, boxy concrete and mud-brick shops. As in Sangin, opium trading was the mainstay of the town's success. One civic-minded local drug trafficker had even brought electricity from the Kajaki Dam, by vigorously collecting donations from local merchants to pay for the wooden pylons and power cables.

We headed to the walled district headquarters and found Amir Muhammad Akhundzada in a carpeted and cushioned office. The stocky, red-bearded walaswal of Musa Qala moved stiffly and walked with a cane, the legacy of a wound taken fighting against rival militia leaders. Though he welcomed us with enthusiasm, he lacked his brother Sher Muhammad's roguish charm. There was something strained and fierce about him—the manner of a chieftain, not a politician.

The elders of the district filtered in, and Yaqub talked about the sorts of jobs we wanted to bring to Musa Qala. "It is a shame you have come too late for the canal maintenance," the walaswal growled reprovingly. "We have already done it by *hashar*." Hashar was the voluntary social system by which everyone who benefited from an irrigation ditch (or road, or building) contributed a few days a year to its upkeep.

"We don't really want to do activities that can be handled by hashar," I countered. Our project's brusque Cassandra, the Dutch engineer Johannes Oosterkamp, had been cautioning us since his arrival in February that cash-for-work could kill voluntary social institutions. Instead of keeping their canals in top condition, villagers might let them fall into disrepair, waiting to get paid for cleaning them.

"Yes, but if the canals have flood damage from the heavy rains this year . . ." Yaqub shrugged artlessly. Against Johannes's warnings, Yaqub was an expert at finding reasons that our project was, in fact, addressing exceptional, one-time problems that the local farmers couldn't possibly be expected to fix themselves. We all appreciated his skill in articulating what we hoped was true.

"Our hashar workers are the best in Helmand," the red-bearded walaswal boasted. "There is no weakness in our hashar. You should see them at work!"

At Amir Muhammad's strong invitation, we drove out again to see what he was talking about. I couldn't help noticing that in the fertile heart of Musa Qala, there was far less visible poppy than in lower Kajaki or Sangin. We could glimpse a few bright, crinkly leaves inside adobe-walled farm compounds, but the open fields around us were almost uniformly the dense, dark green of rising wheat. Governor Sher Muhammad would have no trouble convincing Karzai's poppy inspectors of his achievement in Musa Qala. Here, his family had enough power to control appearances.

At one point, we rolled past a white-walled enclosure roughly the size of a soccer field. Each corner bore a small tower, and at one end was an open-air, arched building. One of my Afghan colleagues saw the question in my eyes and explained, "It is the shrine of Mullah Nasim and Mullah Rasul Akhundzada—the uncle and the father of the governor. When the Taliban government was in power, this place was broken by many bombs and rockets."

"By the Taliban?"

"By people from Musa Qala," my friend said with a bitter, lingering smile. "They remembered how, during the jihad, Mullah Nasim took power. They remembered how he invited the other elders of the mujahidin to make peace and then shot them when they had no guns." He sighed. "Now his tomb is looking very clean. Mullah Sher Muhammad fixed it when he became governor."

A short distance past the whitewashed shrine, Amir Muhammad stopped our convoy at one of Musa Qala's last canal maintenance sites. Minutes later, the voluntary hashar workers appeared around a curve in the wheat-lined stream. There were at least a hundred of them, all marching in a nearly military formation, shovels clasped to their bodies. The watermasters trooped alongside them, baying out terse commands, while Amir Muhammad beamed crookedly at us.

The scene was comical, a little uncanny, and undeniably impressive. I couldn't help recalling how much effort it had taken to get our Kajaki workers into a queue to get paid. This whole side trip was one more chance for the Akhundzadas to advertise their great selling point: order. Or, at least, orderliness.

• • •

Our fatigued team of paymasters met us on the road that afternoon as we drove back to Kajaki. They had managed to pay virtually all the karez workers, though with enough chaos and delays that none of us would be going back to Lashkargah today. The sun was hanging low over the hills when we got back to the Queen's House. Raz approached me after a restorative round of green tea, excitement smoldering through his weariness. "Sir, do you think we can go down to the Kajaki Dam? My father helped to build it. I would like to see his work."

"I don't see why not," I replied, my own spirits reviving. I remembered the incredulous pride I had felt when I stood on the dam my own father had helped to construct in Nepal. "I'll vouch for you to the guards. Come on."

Rather unsociably, I had imagined the two of us walking down alone and talking our way through the gate. Instead, Raz rallied the troops: The paymasters jumped back into their Land Rovers, Ehsan took a break from patching together our guesthouse, and by the time we finally rolled up to the chain-link fence of the dam compound, there were probably a good dozen of us. The grizzled American who ran USPI's security detachment at the dam responded predictably to this attempted invasion. "We don't let any Afghans inside the compound. Can't make exceptions."

"Well, rules are rules," I said stiffly. "I realize you're not really comfortable having us opium folks around anyway."

"No, no, don't worry about that," the USPI guy chuckled. "Listen, you should come over sometime and have a beer. The view over the dam is great."

"Thanks anyway." I walked back to where Raz was standing. "Sorry, man. They won't let us in."

Raz tossed his head dismissively, trying not to look crestfallen. We rejoined the rest of the disgruntled crowd, who fell to talking in Pashto. Moments later, Raz glanced up with a defiant grin. "We will drive around to the other side of the hill. From there, maybe we can see the dam." Caught up in the spirit of exploration, I ignored my watch and the darkening sky.

The disk of the moon grew crisper and whiter overhead as our cars grumbled up the steep slope. We were driving through a virtual moonscape ourselves, between stark, stony outcrops and hills of grit. Then we crested the ridge and saw the striking splash of cobalt below the pale mountains: the thirty-two-mile-long Kajaki reservoir. Spilling out of our Land Rovers, we ran exuberantly along the slope, trying to reach a pinnacle from which we could see Raz's father's handiwork.

Unfortunately, the Kajaki Dam was tucked too deeply away in a cleft in the hills to be seen. We didn't want to head too close to the well-guarded peak immediately above the dam, lest the police take a shot at us in the gathering dusk. Raz resignedly lit up a cigarette. I wheezed, realizing how much the lack of exercise and diet of fatty lamb had taken out of me.

While I recovered, I pointed to the deserted eastern bank. The mountains were darkening faster than the moonlit sky and lake, leaving the craggy shoreline a mass of shadows. "So that's Deh Rawud?" I wasn't sure if the wild province of Uruzgan was actually visible from this corner of the lake.

Our paymaster Ahmed laughed. "Why? Are you going to go get Mullah Omar and collect ten million dollars?" The U.S. government's bounty on the Taliban leader was reasonably well known around the south.

"Cash for work," I shrugged.

Ahmed hooted appreciatively. "Mr. Joel, that is cash for death. No one will ever get that cash."

We wandered back to the Land Rovers at a leisurely pace. My friends peeled off a few at a time to find a scrap of mountainside where they could kneel for dusk prayers. Then my Thuraya satellite phone bleeped musically in my waistcoat pocket. I pulled it out, taken aback. I could count on one hand the number of times someone had successfully reached me on a Thuraya. "Hello?"

"Hey, mate." Charles's voice had a grim edge to it. "Are your guys all safe in Kajaki?"

I glanced guiltily around the twilit, empty hills. "Uh . . . yes, we're all in Kajaki."

"A squad of Afghan intelligence police just got ambushed and slaughtered in northern Sangin," Charles reported flatly. "They stopped for a police checkpoint—but the police weren't police."

My throat went dust-dry. The attack would have been scarcely an hour away from where we were standing. "What do we know about it?"

"There was some fighting up there yesterday, probably over eradication. The intelligence boys got called up to investigate by the regular police. We don't know whether the call was part of the trap. This could be a fight over drugs, it could be Taliban, it could be personal."

I started striding for the Land Rovers, waving the drivers over. "Do we stay up here until we know more?"

"No, mate. Get out of there tomorrow, as planned. But come through the desert below Musa Qala, not on any of the main roads. And have Yaqub tell your guards to watch out for men wearing police uniforms. Stay safe."

"Who was that?" Ehsan asked curiously when I hung up.

"Charles," I said tersely. "Reminding us it's time to get back to the guest-house." We waited until the last of my friends had made his last prostration toward Mecca. I offered up a prayer or two myself. I knew it was unlikely that the assassins would pass this way, but I still found myself holding my breath as we drove back through the moonlit hills to Kajaki.

• • •

Our northern expedition had been a clear success. We returned to Lashkar-gah with firm plans to add a thousand workers in the highlands of Kajaki and another thousand in Musa Qala, cleaning flood-damaged karez tunnels. Governor Sher Muhammad was delighted. Our labor-day projections immediately looked much healthier.

In the wake of the Amniyat murders, we held back from starting any road repairs in Sangin district, despite the obvious needs created by the ongoing poppy eradication. That attack remained almost ineffably murky. It looked like a blow against the chief of Helmand's intelligence police, Amir Dado of Sangin—but since Dado was a drug kingpin, was loathed by the Taliban, and had allegedly tortured a host of prisoners, that hardly narrowed down the list of suspects. Five days after the attack, Charles got a warning "from a credible source" that a Taliban squad working with a crooked Sangin cop was planning to lay improvised explosive devices (IEDs) along the very road we were talking about repairing. According to the rumor, the insurgents were targeting Afghan and international military forces, not development workers, but we figured they'd count us as a bonus. "This is the first real threat which, if verified, would halt proceedings," Charles stated unequivocally. "IEDs don't care how many escort vehicles you have. In fact, in a larger convoy there's more chance of blowing something up. The Taliban are not amateurs, and police assistance means institutional shelter."

On the other hand, the tribal elders of Sangin kept sending assurances that they would protect our project if we brought them jobs. Yaqub added his assurances to theirs, determined to see our project in every district of Helmand before the year was out. For my part, I was hoping we could move out of canal work—with all of its untidy questions about disrupting voluntary social systems—and start more road projects. Sangin offered us an ideal opportunity. Fixing the dirt road from Kajaki through Sangin would make a meaningful difference for at least a couple of years. The USAID team at the Kajaki Dam needed a good road before they could bring in a new turbine— and we could get another thousand-odd workers in Sangin. So I kept hunting through the vast HAVA scrap yard for functional road compaction equipment, in case the bomb threat proved unconvincing.

If the Taliban were trying to reopen a front in Helmand, their efforts took an apparent blow on March 30. The obstreperous old Rais-i-Baghran showed up with two thousand of his men in Lashkargah, embraced the beaming Sher Muhammad Akhundzada, and declared that he was forsaking the Taliban and joining the national reconciliation program. Abdul Wahid Baghrani was not an insignificant loss for the militants. He had been one of the Taliban's more effective generals in their battle for Kabul. When the mullahs' regime collapsed in 2001, Mullah Omar had reportedly headed to Baghran on a motorbike to take shelter with one of the few commanders he still trusted. The Rais-i-Baghran had helped Omar get away, and then lain low in Helmand's north-ernmost tip for three years. Now, it seemed, his young rival Sher Muhammad had convinced him that he stood to gain by joining the new order.

I read the news with a mix of trepidation, excitement, and grudging admiration. The Afghan government would surely be calling on development agencies to provide employment for those two thousand men who had pointedly shown up with the Rais-i-Baghran. Sher Muhammad had been hinting for months about how quiet Baghran district was, how much it needed development. Now, I thought, it was only a matter of time until we headed all the way north—a prospect both alarming and exhilarating.

I had to hand it to Governor Sher Muhammad. Since our first meeting, I had come to appreciate that the young wali's unimposing facade concealed a dexterous political acrobat. Karzai had shuffled or sacked most of his provincial governors at least once, especially the heads of major poppy zones like Kandahar or Nangarhar. Yet despite Governor Sher Muhammad's suspected entanglements with the opium trade, he remained in power.

Some international observers explained this in terms of personal or even criminal links between the Karzai clan and the Akhundzada clan. The Akhundzadas had been friends with Hamid Karzai for decades, and their families had intermarried. The president's younger brother, Ahmad Wali Karzai, was reported to be a major figure in the Kandahari drug economy—though these allegations were hotly denied by the whole Karzai family.

I thought those explanations underestimated the extent to which Sher Muhammad had succeeded in making himself look indispensable. His potentially volatile province was calmer than any of its neighbors. He managed to keep inter-warlord feuding to a low boil, without the bloodcurdling public confrontations that had brought down many a northern governor and police chief. Back in 2002, he had shown an ability to reduce poppy, if only for one season. Now he was facilitating the surrender and amnesty of Taliban commanders. All of these achievements also hinted at the disruptions the Akhundzadas could arrange if removed from office.

There was an important flip side to the story, however: If Karzai depended on the Akhundzadas for much of the order in Helmand, the Akhundzadas also depended on Karzai for much of their clout. Much of the Western media had bought into the canard that Hamid Karzai was only "mayor of Kabul," largely powerless outside the capital. It was true that the president couldn't deprive local warlords like the Akhundzadas of all their power and arms at a stroke. But the Kabul government commanded resources and authority that could decide local rivalries and severely hamper even the mightiest provincial power brokers—let alone a tightrope-walker like Sher Muhammad, who was first among his opium-rich rivals in Helmand only because of his resources as governor.

Darweshan Canal, Helmand—March 29, 2005

"Ja, the river is diverting itself into the new channel," Johannes Oosterkamp said, gesturing meditatively at the surging brown Helmand. The river had chewed away at the cracked earth of its eastern bank until it ran within a few fragile yards of the Darweshan Canal, the irrigation lifeline of lower Helmand. Before this year's rainy season, another aid agency had built a high barrage of gabions—masses of river rock bound together with handwoven nets of wire—to push the Helmand west and prevent a canal breach. Johannes and I had come down to check on the finger of metal mesh and stone and see if it was holding up through all the floods.

Our craggy-faced Dutch irrigation expert scanned the riverbank and nodded curtly. "We will not need to start an emergency program here. The gabion dam is doing its work." He then glanced down at a fraying section with matter-of-fact disapproval. "You can see, though, that the villagers have come to steal the wire. And already it is rusty. They should have used properly coated wires."

I grinned to myself. The plainspoken Johannes always noticed the flaws and shortcomings of any plan. Since formally joining our Helmand project in February, he had torpedoed a number of planned activities, and added severe qualifications to others—and I was sure our work was the better for it. I got along well with the gruff Dutch engineer, though his unsentimental candor could be shocking to a maudlin young American. Once, over dinner, we were discussing our older drivers who couldn't quite see the road anymore, and Johannes informed us dryly that his father used to drive well into his nineties. "We were afraid he would kill someone." He paused to chew a slice of cucumber. "But now he is dead, so that worry is over."

Though Johannes didn't wear his emotions on his sleeve, his bluff and critical manner covered a deep kindness. Once when I was looking downhearted after a long phone call with my fiancée, he advised me to buy a tailor's measuring tape. "When I was a young man, just married, and on three-month jobs in the Middle East, I would buy a tape when I arrived. Cut a centimeter off every day. You will see the time shrinking until you are with your Fiona again."

Johannes's wife, Rensje van Neck, had joined us in mid-March. The short, motherly Rensje was as sunny as her husband was austere, but her amiability hid real steel. She had been a UN volunteer in Somalia during the "Black Hawk Down" incident in 1993, and had to take over management of the UN volunteer program in the wake of the chaos. Rensje and Johannes had rambled all over the world during their long marriage, sometimes working on distant continents, sometimes finding ways to get into the same country, or even the same development project. Looking at them, I often wondered if that was what the future held for Fi and me.

After Johannes and I left the gabion dam, he headed back up to Lashkargah to produce a typically meticulous report. I jumped out of his Land Rover when we saw our chief engineer's car arriving, and joined Engineer Akbar to visit some of our labor crews along the Darweshan Canal.

Our grand expansion plans weren't likely to send us farther south anytime soon. Lower Helmand was mostly smuggler territory, not farmland. Most of the area between Darweshan and Pakistan was uninhabited wilderness; the few permanent settlements closely hugged the curve of the Helmand River as it bent west toward Iran. The region's Brahui and Baluch nomads had long made a living by including contraband in their caravans, turning the otherwise obscure Brahui language into the clandestine *lingua franca* of smugglers.

The explosion in opium trading, however, had brought in a wave of new professionals. Narcotics from all over Afghanistan traveled through lower Helmand to the largely unguarded desert borders with Iran and Pakistan. The transit routes were managed by various Helmandi militias, many of whom wore police blue, others of whom declared allegiance to the Taliban. Their clashes were too frequent and dangerous for us to start work down there.

We were employing some fifteen hundred men along the Darweshan Canal, the southernmost of the grand, American-excavated irrigation systems. We also had a few dozen women involved in weaving wire into gabion baskets—one of the few cash-for-work activities that could be carried out inside the home. Though this blazingly sunny belt of farmland was a good distance from the Pakistan border, it was still part of the conduit for traffickers and insurgents. We picked up fairly regular rumors of Taliban passing through this district on their way to cause trouble elsewhere. The Darweshan area itself stayed quiet enough, though, and our engineers declared themselves comfortable working there.

Akbar and I drove south along the high, dusty bank of the canal. The floodplain stretched out to the east, a dense checkerboard of wheat fields and reedy swamps. We saw a few poppy fields, most of which had clearly been plowed over or beaten to death. Akbar pointed up to the eastern edge of the plain, where a low brown escarpment ran south as far as we could see. "Above there is the desert. A very famous person once had an airport there, you know. He brought his friends in there sometimes for parties."

I squinted at the edge of the plateau. It seemed an odd place for a social gathering. Then I caught the twinkle in Akbar's eye. "Who was that?"

"Osama bin Laden." Our chief engineer chuckled. "I worked down here during the Taliban time. I built a house for one of these rich men, one of these opium traders. We saw many, many strange people come here." I could see the trace of tire ruts all along the bluff, the start of the web of desert roads that led to Baramcha, the infamous traffickers' camp on the Pakistan border.

An hour south of the district center, we crossed an invisible line and suddenly found every second field planted with poppy. In these sun-seared, water-rich lowlands, the plants had already pushed up their long stems and the first pale petals were emerging. The simple adobe farmhouses were also abruptly interspersed with extravagant concrete layer cakes, their wrought-iron gates painted in brilliant geometric designs of electric pink, lilac, and chartreuse. I wondered which if any of these mansions Akbar had built.

We stopped at the farthest worksite we could reach that would still allow us to get back to Lashkargah before dark. Our work crews were clearing out drainage ditches among the poppy fields with their usual muddy, photogenic zest. Shortly after our arrival, the paymasters' Land Rover pulled up, followed by a pickup filled with Bolan police. The workers scrambled out of the ditches and hung expectantly around the car. They were getting an unexpected bonus today; in honor of the Persian new year, Nawroz, we had raised our pay rate to Af 200, or around four dollars.

Raz Muhammad walked over to me and greeted me with a grin and a hug. Then his face clouded over. "Mr. Joel, we have a serious problem. Today, the PRT escort left as soon as we got to Darweshan."

"Sure. The PRT has to get back inside their base by a certain time in the afternoon," I reminded him. "They're just there to provide protection while you're driving through the desert." We had continued to accept the sporadic PRT escorts on the theory that they would keep bandits on their toes, never knowing when a payroll convoy might be accompanied by a Humvee full of heavily armed Iowans. "Did you not get a big-enough district police escort when you got to Darweshan?"

Raz tossed his head unhappily. "That is not the problem, Joel. Whenever the PRT is going with us someplace, it just shows to the people that we are under military control. Then they turn back and leave us there alone with the people."

I nodded, troubled. I had never been entirely happy with our close association with the military myself. Part of the reason we were using the PRT escorts was simple ass-covering; if we got attacked again, we didn't want anyone to complain that we turned down their protection. But we had also assumed that no hostile forces would consider us to be particularly impartial anyway. "Do you really think people don't already know that this is a U.S. government program?" I said doubtfully. "Do people really make a distinction between the American USAID people and the American soldiers?"

Raz laughed. "I hope so. I think if you sent the PRT with us all the time, it would bring us attacks. You would have to hire protection for your protectors."

Back on Track

During those months when the poppy was blooming, I was preoccupied with pouring cash into the districts where Sher Muhammad had sent his eradication teams. At the same time, I was aware of a much larger campaign coming to life around us, putting our little project in its shadow. Chemonics was gearing up for its $121 million program to provide alternatives to poppy in southern Afghanistan. Ray and Carol were planning it with USAID in Kabul, while Jim and Charles prepared to make it work in Helmand. After work, I listened to them deliberate about what was coming: the Lashkargah industrial park, the rural hydroelectric plants, the new crops and jobs and credit that USAID would offer in the name of the American people.

Around the same time, a small European think tank turned heads with a radically different proposal: legalize Afghan opium.

The Senlis Council was a drug policy advocacy group, though it was often described by newspapers as an "international security and development" think tank. Before taking on the Afghan cause, it had been obscure. In March 2005, it won headlines around the world by proposing that Afghanistan follow the path of Turkey and India. Both countries had once been major illegal poppy producers; today, they were the world's main exporters of legal opiates for medicines like codeine and morphine. Instead of punishing Afghan farmers for growing poppy, Senlis suggested, why not license and monitor them, and use their crop to make painkillers for cancer and AIDS sufferers around the world?

The Senlis proposal caught the Afghan government off guard; the minister of counter-narcotics stammered about the need for proper research and getting UN permission. The usual suspects responded predictably—praise from European and Canadian parliamentarians, vitriol from the American drug eradication lobby (the "narco-nuts," as a colleague in Washington memorably labeled them). Personally, while I was no champion of America's international drug policies, I thought the Senlis plan was plainly flawed. It reminded me of other anti-poppy plans that centered on promoting a single "silver bullet" high-value crop, like saffron—except in this case, the alternative crop was legal poppy, a particularly tarnished silver bullet.

To start with, legal poppy didn't pay as well as saffron, let alone black market poppy. Most opium farmers in India earned around $20 per legal kilogram, with prices rising as high as $50. If even half of Afghanistan's massive opium harvest entered the legal market, those prices would plunge. By comparison, in 2004 Afghan drug traffickers had offered farmers an average of $142 for a kilogram of dry opium gum. They had paid much more in previous years, when the supply was lower. The traffickers also consistently provided poor Afghan sharecroppers with loans, land, and agricultural services. Legal poppy wouldn't automatically come with those advantages, any more than saffron would.

The international market for legal opiates was also more complex and unreliable than Senlis suggested. The only reason India and Turkey continued to succeed against Australia's industrial poppy farms was an American law requiring U.S. pharmaceutical makers to buy 80 percent of their opiates from those two "traditional" countries (to keep their poppy farmers from reverting to the black market). Even with the benefit of that quota, India had recently been producing more legal opium than it could sell, and its stockpiles were growing as world demand sagged.

This might seem surprising, since as Senlis correctly pointed out, millions of chronic pain sufferers around the world could benefit from opiates. In 2005, 80 percent of the world's population consumed just 6 percent of its morphine. But just as famines don't happen because the world lacks food, the tragic dearth of pain medications doesn't stem from lack of opiates. Plenty of poor countries lack the medical systems to effectively distribute vaccines and antibiotics, let alone addictive painkillers. Many people simply can't afford pain medicine—and fixing that inequality on a global scale would surely bring down the price of legal opium to an even less profitable level.

Afghanistan was already showing signs of "Dutch disease," an economic ailment that hits countries whose exports are dominated by a single commodity (in the original Dutch case, natural gas). When one commodity attracts a tidal wave of foreign currency, the country's exchange rates tend to go up and cripple its other exporters. The Afghan economy was already vastly more dependent on poppy exports than India or Turkey had ever been. If that single-crop focus continued, it would hurt farmers who wanted to export other crops.

Instead of taking Turkey and India as models, I thought it would be better to take Thailand, which had also been a significant opium producer back in the 1960s. The Thai government never legalized poppy, but nor did it aggressively enforce the law against farmers before they had real alternatives to opium. By 1990, Thailand's opium crop dropped to negligible levels, thanks to a long-term development program. This Thai program didn't just offer profitable alternative crops; it also addressed the real roots of the problem—the lack of land, assets, education, and citizenship rights among Thai highland tribes.

As I read a little more about what had worked in Thailand, I came across a few unsettling references to the importance of *empowerment*. Education and citizenship rights weren't just important because they helped Thai highlanders earn a higher income; they also helped the highlanders stand up politically to the powerful forces that were driving the opium trade.

In Helmand, by contrast, we were just focusing on the economic forces that pushed people to grow poppy. USAID's goal was to create ways for Helmandi farmers and workers to earn money legally. It was a worthy objective, but I had to wonder whether any number of new jobs and crops would change the fact that in Helmand, the power was on the side of the poppy traffickers.

• • •

From time to time, I was reminded again just how thoroughly our own project was entangled with Helmand's opium lords. One day in March, Habibullah approached my desk with a half-conspiratorial look I knew well. "Mr. Joel," he began, "you know how Mr. Ray asked if we know any good staff houses for the new project?"

I nodded with a certain skepticism. "I'm sure they'd prefer one where the wiring won't melt in the walls when they plug in their generator." It had taken months to make our own staff houses habitable, thanks to a host of such petty disasters.

"There is a new house I think they will like," the Haji averred. "The man who is building it has brought everything from Pakistan—materials, workers, everything. The wires will not burn in this one. And it is big enough to fit fifteen people."

I was intrigued. Charles was vetting all new properties for security, so I brought him along for an initial visit. The three-story house belonged to Haji Homayoon Khan, who lived in Quetta and was reportedly in the import-export business. From the minute we walked into the towering wood and marble atrium, with its tall glass windows and views to a fountain courtyard, I realized that this was in a completely different category even from Dawari's flamboyant bungalow. Every room had elaborate crystal light fixtures; a whirlpool bath was being installed just off the master bedroom. The enormous house would fit a large project staff with rooms to spare.

Charles nodded approvingly. "Well, that's a stroke of luck. It should be comfortable enough to satisfy Jim. And it'll get everyone in one place, which means less travel and fewer sites to protect."

I shook my head, slightly stunned by the blatancy of the place. "But does it pass the laugh test?"

"Eh, mate?"

"Could you stand up and say with a straight face that this house doesn't belong to a drug trafficker?" I was already proving that I couldn't. "I don't think rent counts as an alternative to poppy."

Charles shrugged. "Mate, just about any house big enough to fit the new team is going to belong to some kind of trafficker. You find me a place that's as big and secure, and we'll jump at it. Until then, we'll go with the narco-palace."

• • •

Khair Muhammad, our ambitious young monitoring officer, was delighted that Chemonics' long-term project was finally on its way. When he wasn't off in Pakistan visiting his family, Khair had badgered me with questions about what we were trying to accomplish. "Who is this project supposed to benefit, Mr. Joel? The poorest people of Helmand, who are poppy laborers, or the farmers who plant the poppy on their land? What is the impact on poppy supposed to be? How are such short-term jobs like this supposed to change Helmand?"

My answers, fairly consistently, had been, "We don't have time to worry about that, Khair. We're just pouring cash in to plug any damage from eradication. The real strategy will have to wait for the long-term project."

Of course, this non-answer drove Khair up the wall. My restless friend had clearly been the smartest kid around since his primary school days in Pakistan. He loved debate, and argued with the aggressive confidence of a man who had usually found himself to be right. University-educated and passionately intellectual, Khair asked me once if I had memorized any favorite sayings. "I collect the sayings of great people," he said modestly. "Someday I hope to write my own."

Khair's searching mind and ambition turned him into our project gadfly. He challenged our engineers' measurements in the field, taking more exact ones himself from global positioning satellites. He inspected timesheets on his field visits, and interrogated the foremen if a worker seemed to be missing. He asked the community leaders why they had given us more workers from certain villages than others. And he grilled me constantly about the project's first principles.

I was consumed with the mechanics of adding several thousand laborers and lacked patience for Khair's questions. In the rare moments when I wrote reports, I focused on sending USAID a few basic numbers: labor days, cash paid, meters of canal cleaned, how much land was irrigated by each canal. I sent Khair out to make maps of what we'd accomplished, not to follow up in depth with the workers and communities.

Feeling a little guilty for under-using an obviously bright and determined guy, I arranged for him to head to Kabul for a course in computer mapping. When he returned, I hired two assistants for him to record data points in the field with a global positioning satellite reader. Khair would be able to take their readings and draw exquisite maps of the areas we'd affected—just the kind of thing USAID liked to see in a report. The three of them shared an office with Rensje and Johannes, who could offer Khair gruff advice on his map-making.

When hiring Khair's assistants, I picked gadflies like him: two young men who had kept coming back again and again to pester me for jobs, despite the fact that English was virtually their sole qualification. If we decided to make them more than just data hounds, I thought wryly, their aggressiveness would serve us in good stead.

The first, Muhammad Nabi, had struck me at first as extraordinarily arrogant and demanding, even for a Pashtun. Visually, the young Kandahari was unmistakable: His beardless face was scarred as if he had been held too close to a fire, and the melted skin pulled his smile into a disconcerting grimace. He came at least five times to look for work at our office, each time a little louder and a little more forceful. Irritated by his persistence, I shunted Nabi off to Kandahar to see if Chemonics' newly opened office there was hiring. When they didn't have a job for him, he came back a sixth time with a keenly aggrieved expression on his seared face. "Sir, you promised me a job, and you are not giving me a job. You send me to Kandahar, it costs money, but they also are not giving me a job. What am I to think?"

"Nabi," I snapped, "I never promised you a job. If we don't have a job, then we don't have a job. Don't push it."

When he saw anger in my eyes, Nabi's face collapsed. I realized with a sudden surge of self-contempt that much of what I had read in his expression—arrogance, ingratiation, belligerence—was his scar giving false stridency to nuances of his smile. His misery and humiliation came through perfectly, though. So did his heartfelt desperation for a job. After I'd hired him as Khair's assistant, I asked awkwardly, "How did you get the scar on your face?"

"It is called leishmaniasis, sir," Nabi said, pronouncing the word with precision and bitter rue. I looked it up afterward; it was a rare skin infection spread by sand flies. "My family spent too much money on medicine in Pakistan. It was no good."

Khair's second assistant had less pathos but was no less pushy. Abdul Qader Khan Zaki was an English teacher in the bazaar; he wore large round sunglasses and had a dramatic tangle of black beard that made him look much older than his twenty-seven years. "You have my students working for you," Zaki pointed out vociferously, each time he came in to ask for a job. "Nazar and ten other young men on your project, they learned their English from me. Is it right that you should have the students, but not the teacher?"

Oddly, as soon as I told Zaki we had a position for him, his confident bluster evaporated into nervousness. He had never worked in an office before, and was especially flustered at having to work in the same room as a non-related woman—even a married Dutch grandmother. Rensje noticed with wry affection that he seemed robbed of speech whenever she was in the room. Nabi, with his cosmopolitan Kandahari background and aid agency experience, was more comfortable.

Khair was delighted to finally get the leadership role he knew he deserved, and threw Nabi and Zaki into a brisk crash course in satellite mapping. Khair never stopped asking me annoying questions, though—and I never lost the sense that he would rather have been doing a serious investigation of our project's impact, not just cartography.

• • •

But we were giving USAID what it wanted, and that was what mattered.

By early April, it was clear that we were back on track to hit our target. We had racked up about 450,000 labor days, and expected to reach our first million by the end of May. We had handed over roughly $1.7 million at our payrolls. We had twelve thousand active workers all over Helmand, and Yaqub was confidently eyeing new districts for expansion. Our security-related hiccup after the Babaji carjacking was a distant memory.

The Kabul powers-that-be were apparently delighted by my hurried monthly reports, which on top of those glowing, simple numbers had plenty of photos and some cheerful verbiage. Apparently Condoleezza Rice hadn't been on the phone demanding more detailed updates after all. The only negative comment we got was from USAID's Kabul contracting officer, who complained, "Chemonics' expatriate salaries are too high. Try hiring more young people—they come cheaper."

Ron Ivey, the Chemonics senior vice president, sent us an e-mail of voluble praise for our hard work, which had boosted the company's image with "the client" to new heights. With typical gruffness, Jim wrote back thanking Ron but severely noting that we were still overworked and understaffed. He called me in to show me the e-mail before he sent it out. "Do you think it's plain enough?"

I couldn't help laughing. "Yeah, I think it gets the point across."

Jim threw up his hands. "Well, I sure as hell hope someone gets it. How long have we been asking for this? We need to get someone out here for the monitoring and reporting job so you can concentrate on doing every other damned thing in this place. You can't have the deputy team leader doing PR for the project. They're both full-time jobs—especially when USAID is asking us to step up the PR side."

I shot him a grateful grin. Over the months of working with Jim Graham, I'd seen him build an intensely loyal team twice: first with our little Helmand project, and now again with the staff who were slowly arriving for the grand four-year program. With Jim, you always knew where you stood. He was fiercely protective of the people he worked with, trying to shield us not only from the dangers of Helmand but also from the unreasonable demands of the job. For our loyalty, he gave us his confidence and total support. Now, I realized with a pang, Jim would likely be spending weeks in Kabul and Kandahar; when he was here, he'd be staying in the new project's narco-palace. I was going to miss the cantankerous, profane, warm-hearted old Bostonian—his bristling white mustache, his full-bodied yell of a laugh.

On April 10, the formidable Carol Yee arrived in Lashkargah to take over from Jim. I still felt a twinge of dread, remembering her penetrating and unsparing diagnosis of my flaws back in November. But when she clambered off the little Beechcraft plane, her headscarf loosely flapping around her spiky black hair, and shot a smile in my direction, my nervousness evaporated. "I hear you've been doing really good work out here," she said with genuine warmth when we got back to the office.

I smiled, a little rueful. "Well, I hope I've learned a few lessons since last time you were here."

Carol shook her head. "Sounds like you've got a solid team, and you're managing them well. So—what do I need to know?" She went to look at the map of Helmand on one wall.

"You want the best news first?" I fished out a copy of my budget projections with barely restrained enthusiasm. "We've kept to USAID's budget demands—we'll easily spend seventy percent of the budget on Helmand and only thirty percent on administration. In fact, on current trends we're set to come in about a *million dollars* under budget. And that means we can start planning some more ambitious projects—fixing bridges, culverts on the roads, things that will cost more money but will actually still be around in a few years."

"Where'd the money come from?" Carol asked cautiously, scanning the figures with a well-practiced eye.

"Pete and Dave built plenty of slack into our cost estimates." I gave a wry grin. "And if there's one area where our understaffing has helped, this is really it." *Young people come cheap.*

Gunfire in the Backyard

Lashkargah, Helmand—April 13, 2005

"Haji-sahib—is that gunfire?"

When I'd first arrived in Afghanistan, I had half-expected to hear automatic weapons going off all the time, from jubilant Afghans firing their guns in the air if nothing more serious. I had read about the July 2002 bloodbath in Uruzgan when an American helicopter came under "hostile antiaircraft" fire and called in air strikes—only to find, once the dust had cleared, that they had just bombed a wedding party. Celebrating with Kalashnikovs turned out to be a rural custom, though. In my mostly urban assignments I had yet to hear a single shot.

So when I heard the unmistakable chatter of an automatic rifle one Wednesday morning in April, it immediately registered as out of place. This wasn't wedding season—that came in the months leading up to the Ramadan fast. I glanced around the office to confirm that others were listening too. A few seconds later, I heard another staccato burst. It sounded strangely . . . adjacent.

"Haji-sahib," I said with dawning dismay, "is that gunfire coming from our backyard?"

Habibullah was already striding toward the door. I scrambled out of my chair and fell in behind him. "Tell everyone to close their curtains," I ordered a wide-eyed logistics assistant in the hallway, trying not to sound shrill. "And then stay away from the windows."

On the ground floor, a gang of our Kajaki guards had jumped up from their mid-morning tea, which still steamed, green and murky, in small glass cups on the floor. The guards now had their Kalashnikovs out, ready for anything that might come through the flimsy glass double doors. One unkempt

youth was laughing as though he had just heard the world's finest joke. Outside, armed men were running toward the firefight in an awkward half-
crouch, trampling HAVA's yellowish lawn and muddy flower beds. Farid
stood against the doorframe, peering out dispassionately.

"Farid," I gasped, joining him, "what the hell is going on?"

"Commandant Abdul Rahman's police are fighting with Khano," Farid
replied, sounding only a little breathless. He was in charge here; Charles was
in Tbilisi, taking a couple of weeks' leave with his wife and son.

"On our lawn?" I asked incredulously.

"All over. Khano's house is not far. Our guards say the police tried to disarm him." Farid gestured southward, where rival bursts of gunfire echoed just
out of sight. "He does not want to be disarmed."

I ducked back into the gloomy atrium. For the first time, its relative lack
of windows struck me as an excellent design feature. "Haji-sahib—who's
Khano?" The name sounded familiar, but I was drawing a blank.

"A local commander," Habibullah replied distractedly. "He was with the
Russians before the mujahidin took over."

That was right. Khan Muhammad, or "Khano," had led one of Lashkargah's most powerful Communist militias as a young man in the 1980s. Among
many dubious achievements, he and his men had reportedly introduced dog-
fighting to Helmand. Khano was a born street fighter who knew the city inside out; he had bloodily thrown back the Akhundzadas and Gulbuddin's
commanders in battle after battle, holding out until 1993, a year longer than
the Communist government in Kabul. Then his luck went spectacularly sour.
Not only did the Akhundzadas form a grand coalition to expel him from
Lashkargah, but he also fell into the hands of a Baluch tribe that had a grudge
against him and got him locked up in Pakistan for several years. Khano escaped and returned to Lashkargah after the fall of the Taliban, investing his
remaining wealth in a cluster of shops and a sizable bodyguard.

It sounded like Khano's unsavory drama wasn't going to have a third act.
As the din of combat drifted away to the south, Habibullah and I climbed the
stairs and made our report to Carol. "Farid seems to have things in hand
down there," I offered with a slightly strained hopefulness. "We're not on the
front line; almost all of the shooting is going on around Khano's house. As
long as we keep everyone inside the building, we should be all right."

For about half an hour, we worked with the sporadic rattle of Kalashnikovs in the background. Sometimes it ebbed into the distance; then it
would burst out again on what sounded like the southern fringes of the
HAVA garden. Our curtains stayed closed, but since the office windows faced

west, people slowly drifted back to the empty desks. Then Carol came in and exclaimed, "What are you doing next to the windows?" and we all sheepishly scrambled back into the safe half of the room again.

Finally, after a continuous stretch of silence, Farid arrived and beckoned me out into the hall. His face was grim, but there was relief in his voice. "It is over, Joel. The police say that three of Khano's men are dead. Khano is now in the Emergency Hospital. He was shot, but he is still alive. They have taken the cache of weapons from his house."

"So this was all part of the disarmament campaign?" I asked, exhaling gustily. Paradoxically, this firefight behind our office might be a sign of growing stability, not instability, in Lashkargah. Taking guns away from illegal militias was a messy process, but any skirmish that ended in a decisive victory for the provincial government seemed like a step in the right direction.

"The police came to disarm Khano for a reason." Farid leaned closer. "He has friends in high authority in Kabul—people who were in Najibullah's government and are now in Karzai's. There was a rumor that Khano was going to be the new police chief of Helmand."

I shook my head. "I guess *Qumandan* Abdul Rahman Jan let him know what he thought of that idea." A bandit like Abdul Rahman disarming his personal rival was a pretty poor victory for the government, even though the conquering strongman wore a police uniform. True, today's fight left the province with one fewer militia group, but it also entrenched the power of an alleged drug trafficker who ran his police with brutal disregard for the welfare of ordinary Afghans. Maybe that was the best stability we could hope for in Helmand.

• • •

Our own police commander was growing more erratic. One evening, our post-dinner episode of *The Sopranos* was interrupted by a clatter and raised voices from the staff house dining room. Charles got up and glanced through the door, then sighed windily, stepped out, and shut it behind him.

When he came back half an hour later, I paused the DVD and looked up with furrowed brow. "What's up? Sounded like quite a party out there."

Charles gave a haggard chuckle. "Hell, mate. You know the Kajaki guard chief—our little Taliban killer?"

"Sure," I said. I often saw Hayat Khan hanging around our headquarters, talking unsmilingly with his men. "What's he up to now?"

"He's off his face. Totally stoned on hashish, shouting, running around. You should have seen our guards—they were bloody shitting themselves."

Charles began pacing, venting a half-hour's built-up tension. "The only person out there who spoke even a little English was the cook, and you know him, he's got about three words. So our commander is gibbering away in Pashto, and me in English, and the cook is trying to get a word in. And I don't know what was on that stoned little man's mind, but it was pretty bloody serious. The shit he's done and seen, mate."

"What did you do?"

"Let him talk himself out. Eventually he realized I wasn't going to invite him to eat or have a cup of tea or anything. So he laughed, got in his pickup, and drove off." Charles peeled the dusty plastic seal off a bottle of Pakistani mineral water. "I hadn't seen him this bad before. But a couple of times at work, he's been off his nut and his lieutenants have had to cover for him."

"What a mess." I sat back, wide-eyed. "I tell you, this province needs alternative cops more than alternative crops."

I would have been happier with the catastrophic state of Helmand's police if there was any prospect of police reform sweeping through at some point as the disarmament campaign had done. Unfortunately, police reform was a nonstarter in Afghanistan, thanks to a well-meaning but disastrous initial division of labor.

At an April 2002 conference in Switzerland, the rich countries had agreed to split the complex task of fixing Afghanistan's security between five "lead donors." America was in charge of forming the new Afghan army; Japan ran the disarmament program; Britain claimed responsibility for counternarcotics; Germany got police reform; and Italy took the lead on reforming the Afghan judicial system.

This occasioned many snickers. "Stop, stop, I've heard this one before," an Australian acquaintance groaned. "In heaven, the Brits are the police, the French are the cooks, the Italians are the lovers, et cetera—and in hell the Brits are the cooks, the Germans are the police, and the Italians run the bloody courts." Still, the principle behind the carve-up was fairly clear. If each country applied itself diligently to its specific task, nothing would fall through the cracks. The system would also in theory help give the occupation a multinational face, not just an American one.

Three years on, the lead donor system had produced wildly mixed results. After a rough start, the disarmament campaign and the building of the Afghan army—closely related programs backed by the world's two richest countries—were making modest but tangible progress. Britain and Italy had thrown their more limited resources at even more challenging pillars and largely failed. As for the Afghan police, Germany had set its sights low; its only direct involvement was reviving the Kabul police academy to train a few thousand top officers. For two and a half years, that was the extent of police reform in Afghanistan. The Germans denied ever volunteering to transform the whole Afghan police force, though they offered to coordinate other countries' efforts.

The aggrieved American government had finally started pouring money into the flagging sectors, but USAID's programs weren't achieving much more than the original British, Italian, and German efforts. In particular, police reform kept getting shortchanged. Neither the Germans nor the Americans were willing to take responsibility for the sweeping, long-term, expensive changes that were really needed. The U.S. security contractor DynCorp had provided two to four weeks of classroom training to thousands of Afghan police, but couldn't offer the field-based operational training that had a serious chance of affecting police behavior. The retired American cops who worked with DynCorp weren't exactly queuing up to become embedded mentors for Afghan police units.

On a structural level, no one had come up with a plan to transform the current jumble of ethnic militias into a professional, accountable police force—unlike the new Afghan army, which the Americans were trying to build from the ground up. The Afghan Ministry of the Interior, which ran the police and Amniyat (intelligence police), was a warren of bribe-taking and ethnic nepotism. It still lacked a functioning "internal affairs" investigative unit, or any remedy for civilians who were abused by police.

So our police remained militias, undisciplined and unruly for all of Charles's efforts. After a long day of locking horns with Hayat Khan, Charles would stalk away his wrath in tight circles around the staff house porch, a cigarette glowing in his fist. "He's caused me so much aggravation. I've spent so many hours dealing with his demands and his shit. He gives no respect to anybody, and his only allegiance is to himself. But I'm not giving him up, because the one thing I'm sure about with him"—Charles exhaled smoke savagely —"is that he hates the Taliban.

"If anyone interferes with us here, Joel, odds are it'll be Taliban. We need guards who we know won't give us up to them. And we need someone who won't do a runner when the shots start flying." Charles looked over at me with bleak conviction. "If they come for us, *he* won't fuck off. He won't walk away from a fight with the Taliban. And his lieutenants will stay and fight with him. And that means we won't be slaughtered at our bloody desks, or whatever." He flicked his cigarette out over the wall.

I ruefully remembered a much earlier conversation, when Charles had talked about training our guards and building loyalty and discipline as a way of making sure that they didn't break under fire. Having started, we now had a better idea of just what an intractable, long-term task that was. While we inched toward professionalizing our police escorts, it made sense to stick with the ones whose visceral loyalties pointed in the direction we wanted. It sat uneasily with me, however, to put our trust in the right hatreds rather than the right kind of police.

• • •

Meanwhile, Yaqub went back to Sangin district to negotiate the terms of our road project there. Almost three weeks had gone by since the murders of the intelligence police, and two weeks since the rumor about Taliban bombers; there had been no further signs of trouble. We decided that if we could get a written, detailed security commitment from the local authorities, we would go ahead with the road repair.

The walaswal of Sangin and his brother, Amir Dado, the brutal chief of Helmand's intelligence police, were happy to sign Yaqub's statement. They assured us that they would use all the means at their command to safeguard our project. "As a practical measure," Yaqub informed us happily, "they will provide twenty local militia to guard our staff. Some will guard our field engineers, and some will provide mobile surveillance along the road. I believe these precautions will give us some room to feel safer with our work in Sangin."

"Now *that's* a security commitment," I said dryly. "Why can't we get anything that concrete from Babaji?" Elders Priam, Odysseus, and company continued to try to talk us back into their district, but offered nothing concrete to back up their assurances—certainly no promise of escorts, either armed or unarmed.

We responded by hiring thirteen hundred workers to repair the road in Sangin and Kajaki districts. Each day, on each of five different road sections, a brightly painted tanker truck would rumble back and forth, sprinkling water from a long perforated bar on its rear. Dozens of our men would chase after the tankers, scooping water into their gritty mouths, then fall in to break up the newly softened road surface with their picks and shovels. After the workers laid down roughly the right mix of dirt and gravel, a tractor would grumble through, towing a ponderous metal cylinder to compact the mix into a hard crust. We hoped the compaction would keep the road smooth through at least a few seasons. I thought back with mild nervousness to Pete Siu's acerbic comment in the Ghorband valley: "You can pay hundreds of people to fucking shovel dirt into potholes, but they won't thank you when the road washes out again next year." We were looking to hire a road expert who knew how to do quality work with manual labor.

The security situation seemed to calm down in Helmand after the fight with Khano. In late April, Governor Sher Muhammad staged another feat of national reconciliation, bringing in the former Taliban governor of Zabul and the one-time Taliban police chief of Farah province to join the new government. It wasn't at all clear that either of these men had been much involved with the post-2001 insurgency. Still, their surrender in Helmand burnished the Akhundzada governor's reputation as a peacemaker, and added to the impression that the militants were on the wane.

Lieutenant General David Barno, the American commander in Afghanistan, triumphantly declared on April 17 that the Taliban insurgency was in the process of falling apart. Its moderate members would make their peace with the new Afghan government, while its more radical members would become increasingly irrelevant. He cautioned, however, that as the insurgency collapsed, "the hard-core fanatics will grow more and more desperate to try and do something to change the course of events in Afghanistan." We shouldn't expect a revived war in spring 2005, Barno suggested, but we could expect some sort of spectacular terrorist event.

Nad-i-Ali, Helmand—April 19, 2005

For the first week after Carol's arrival, much of my time was spent preparing for our project's first celebrity field visit. John Walters, the White House drug czar, was coming to Helmand—and his people insisted that he actually intended to travel outside Lashkargah and see some of what we'd accomplished.

We'd already had a couple of high-profile visitors, and both had likewise insisted that they wanted to get out and see our workers in action. First, a visiting congressman from Illinois had wanted to see our canal repair in Bolan back in December. His security detail vetoed that plan shortly before his arrival, though, and he had to console himself with a PowerPoint presentation inside the PRT base.

In mid-March, we had a less timid guest: Zalmay Khalilzad, the powerful Afghan-American U.S. ambassador. Khalilzad had been the power behind the throne for much of Karzai's tenure, deftly dealing out American rewards and retribution to keep as many Afghan warlords as possible cooperating with the new order. He was an enthusiastic proponent of the idea of Provincial Reconstruction Teams, and came down to Lashkargah to ceremonially inaugurate the PRT here. After the inauguration, he had planned to catch a helicopter out to our worksite in Nad-i-Ali.

Unfortunately, heavy rains for two days before his visit made it impossible for any helicopter to land out in the fields. We got a call from Khalilzad's staff at the last minute, asking if we could grab some workers out of the canal and bring them in to the PRT for a photo opportunity with the ambassador, looking as authentic as possible. Jim took tart amusement in the request, and declared that he would grab the nine most representative workers. To Yaqub's abiding mortification, they included a boy who might have been sixteen, but was probably a bit younger. "The ambassador's going to see the same dog-and-pony show he would have seen if he'd come out here," Jim declared obstinately. When Ambassador Khalilzad walked down the line of our silt-caked, shovel-wielding laborers and paused to ask the boy his age and strike up a conversation, I knew that somewhere nearby, Yaqub was squirming with horror.

Now we had John Walters showing up, along with his Afghan counterpart, Habibullah Qaderi, and while they weren't going to see child labor, they were certainly going to see poppy fields. We were taking them to a grape farm in Nad-i-Ali, run by another USAID contractor, that happened to be near some good-looking drains our project had cleaned. It also happened to be near a scenic pink-petaled expanse of opium poppy. I jokingly suggested the poppy field as the helicopter landing site; it seemed a good, dramatic way to kick off a joint visit of the Afghan Minister of Counter-Narcotics and the American drug control czar.

Instead, Haji Habibullah and I found the closest fallow field, a sunbaked stretch of stubble. It was perhaps a ten-minute walk from the grape farm, along a broad road densely lined with wheat. The PRT security team that came out the day before the visit seemed unimpressed. "Kind of a long way out, isn't it?" said one National Guardsman in a slight Texan accent. The previous PRT garrison had finally wrapped up their tour of Helmand and headed home to Iowa.

"Well, kind of," I admitted, "but it's the closest empty field. Surely we can protect the visitors somehow between here and the farm?"

The PRT guys half-heartedly radioed the coordinates of the site back to the base, but as we were walking back to the farm, they detoured into wheat fields on both sides of the road and nonchalantly called the base again. *Wheat eradication*, I thought with mild irritation. *Good call, guys.*

On April 19, a few of our staff hurried out early in the morning to set up a broad blue plastic awning, folding chairs, and buckets of chilled refreshments for our celebrity visitors. Our elderly Nad-i-Ali engineer, who clearly thought the whole thing was a ridiculous distraction, initially refused to delegate any of his drain workers to our young logistics guy, Nazar. When Haji Habibullah and I arrived, we found the canopy poles still lying on the ground, and Nazar gamely trying to set one up himself.

"This is the problem with Afghanistan," Habibullah complained mildly. "No one respects a young man, even if he is qualified. So we elders have to do everything ourselves." Within minutes, we had a crew of sinewy local farmers pulled out of the drainage ditches to relieve Nazar. We did a couple of quick drills, setting up the blue canopy and then taking it down again so it wouldn't blow away when the helicopters arrived.

We heard the drone of the rotors before the two dark Chinooks appeared over the horizon, slow and strident, blasting dust from the road and churning up a tempest in the fields. One after the other, they landed in the middle of the deep green wheat and flattened the unripe seed heads to the ground. "Find out who owns that field," Carol said resignedly as the passengers jumped out and began wading toward the road, leaving a narrow, dark swathe of trampled stalks.

Both John Walters and Habibullah Qaderi were heavyset men; the former was clean-shaven with a mat of gray hair, while the latter was bald as an egg with a mat of gray beard. Their smiles and nods spoke of long practice in looking at once understanding and tough. In their wake streamed journalists and USAID officers, cameramen and bearded American gunmen. We met them on the road and walked together along the ditch where the local farmers were scooping up muck. The visitors discovered the poppy with much camera-flashing and jaded murmurs, walked back to inspect the USAID-funded farm, and finally gathered under the blue awning for drinks and questions. Then the helicopters reappeared on the horizon, crushed some more wheat, and our visitors departed as abruptly as they had come.

One of the Afghan managers of the grape farm came up to us, looking fretful. "Some of the American soldiers broke into a house behind the farm to search it for weapons. There were women inside. They were not searched, but the local men are a little upset."

I shook my head bemusedly. How much popular alienation could you justify in the name of a little extra security? I remembered Raz's comment when I had asked him whether Helmandis distinguished us from the American military. I found myself vainly hoping so as well.

Lashkargah, Helmand—April 24, 2005

"The thief is the enemy of God," declared the solemn sharwal of Lashkargah, his beard projecting triumphantly into the air. Elder Odysseus nodded earnestly; Elder Priam sat looking desolate and glassy-eyed as ever. I wondered if anyone had told him we were finally coming back to fix his fields. "God willing, there will be no more stealing now that you are coming back with good security. We are all willing to do anything that we can to help."

Carol nodded sternly. "We expect there will be no more problems." She looked on, impassive, as one by one the Babaji shura and mayor of Lashkargah lined up to put their signatures on a security commitment. The paper stated that they would do what they could to protect our project if we came back. Unlike the Sangin equivalent, though, there was no clause establishing protection by a local militia. Given the feuding in Babaji, I thought moodily, it was probably just as well.

Soon after taking over from Jim Graham, Carol had called a meeting of all the top staff to discuss the Babaji issue. "Frankly, we've been taking flak over this from USAID and the PRT long enough." Colonel Augustine was on his way out with the Iowa guardsmen, but we didn't imagine his successor would be much more sympathetic with our refusal to return to the site of the carjacking. Several USAID officials, from Kabul to Washington, had heard about the issue and questioned our "collective punishment" policy in Babaji. "We've come a long way since December," Carol pointed out, "in our security and in the breadth of our project. I don't think it's worth the criticism we're taking. We've stayed out for months now. Let's go back in, finish the job, and get out with our commitment complete."

Yaqub nodded with deepest agreement. "We have punished these people long enough. They do not know who stole our car. And it was only a car. Why should a whole region be hurt for that?"

"Fine, but this is a region where people have been shooting at each other," I argued. "We've told the shura for the last two months that we would resume work if they agreed to take *active* steps in helping our security. They haven't given us a single active measure. Nothing."

"What do you want them to do, Joel?" Yaqub demanded disapprovingly. "They are poor. They do not have the power to protect us."

"Well," I said hesitantly, "a shura member could escort our engineers to and from the field. We talked about that. We even suggested it to them."

Yaqub shook his head. "Joel, why would they do that? What good would that do? These are old men. We must bring our own protection."

He had a point. We had been working in dangerous areas for months under police protection. It did seem a bit absurd for us to work along major drug smuggling routes and within shouting distance of Mullah Omar's hometown, but not to return to an area next door to Lashkargah because of feuds and a carjacking.

"The Bolan police commander doesn't like the area," Charles threw in darkly. "He's said he recommends sending a pickup full of police with each engineer—not just one or two guards."

"We'll send as many as we need to," Carol said flatly, "and we'll send a letter to the governor, USAID, and the PRT, putting it formally on record that the shura has made no good-faith effort to protect us. But we're going back because of the poverty of the people of Babaji—the women and children."

Now Charles stared flint-faced as the last of the Babaji shura pushed their blue-stained thumbs against the paper, a few of them picking up a pen to overlay their thumbprints with Pashto loops and swirls. At the beginning of today's meeting, Charles had given a ferocious speech telling the elders of Babaji it was their own fault we had stayed out so long. "Nowhere else in Helmand have we had this kind of problem," he had barked. "Only in your territory—in the areas for which you are responsible."

"No one wanted this to happen," Elder Odysseus had snapped back. "You did not have security with you before. Now you will bring security, and the thieves will stay away."

I glanced over at the stiff, resigned-looking Haji Habibullah. Our project patriarch had been opposed to backing down, but knew better than to pick a fight he wasn't going to win. I wondered how much of the Haji's opposition was based on evenhanded security analysis of the Babaji situation and how much was based on vengeance—this tribe hit someone from my tribe and must now be made to pay. I wondered the same thing about myself.

PART THREE: HARVEST

Valley of Death

Helmand's opium harvest began in the south, in the river-fed ribbon of Khanishin and the rich farmland along the Darweshan Canal, where the furious sun drew the poppies into full flower by the end of March. By mid-April, the fields were full of crouched silhouettes, men, women, and children working through the day to extract the precious gum. The harvest rolled north into the triangle of old canals around Babaji, where the villagers suspended their feuding and moved into the fields. Then, above the highway where the land rose and water was scarce, there was a pause. The poppy bulbs were still flowering there in early May, not quite ready to be lanced. We saw and felt the harvest as it moved past us—saw the changes in the landscape, and felt the impact on our work.

The fields were no longer a patchwork of red and pink. The poppy petals fell away, and the green bulbs underneath turned brownish-black, stained by drying opium gum along dozens of narrow, parallel scratch-lines. In the Lashkargah bazaar, for a handful of afghanis you could buy the tools of poppy harvesting: two *neshtar*s (lancing sticks), the first with a row of inset metal teeth protruding barely enough to scratch, the other with teeth perhaps a millimeter longer; and a *rambey* (scoop), a curved bit of scrap metal with a wooden grip.

Our cook, Ali Asghar, demonstrated their use for us on an imaginary poppy bulb. First, you squeezed the bulb delicately to make sure it was ripe. You scraped the pale green skin as shallowly as possible with the neshtar, let the opium gum ooze out—cloudy-white at first, but turning brown as it hit the air. The next day you returned and scooped the tar-like latex off with the rambey, collecting it in a bag at your waist. It was a painstaking job; if you moved forward too quickly through the densely planted field, you'd wind up with the opium paste on your clothes instead of in your bag. After scooping off the day's gum, you scraped each bulb again, a little deeper this time. You repeated the process up to five or six times, eventually switching to the longer-toothed neshtar, until you drained the poppy of all its sap. You had to be careful not to cut too deep too early, or the bulb would bleed itself dry. Ali Asghar assured us with a wink that he'd never actually harvested the taryak. "Everyone just knows how to do it."

The resulting opium gum was the rich, mellow brown of date paste (which fraudsters occasionally added to trick buyers). The farmers packed it into clear plastic bags and sold it raw, or, if they had time and felt secure, spread it out in the sun to dry first. Dry opium was less bulky, and could be sold for more. Even the farmers who dried their own opium were unlikely to get much of a cash boost, though. Many, if not a majority, had already sold their crop in November under the "salaam" system for half the expected price. Helmand's police also frequently came calling after the harvest, collecting opium gum in exchange for having left poppy fields untouched.

The real profits were made by the traders, who bought the opium at the farm gate and sold it on to smugglers for transport to the border. Many of the small to medium traffickers were bazaar merchants, who spent most of the year selling fabric, construction goods, motorcycles, satellite phones, and so on. One of my Afghan friends confided in me that he had been an accountant for an opium trader during one desperately poor summer in the Taliban years. He had spent his days in a back-alley bazaar shop that was permanently saturated with glutinous opium paste. "I would come from the house in the morning wearing very clean clothes. After one hour, you wouldn't see my clothes. Ceiling, wall, floor, glasses, water jug, spoon, cooking pot—everything was touched with opium. If you drink a glass of tea, you will use opium. When we ran the fan, it blew up dust full of opium." He laughed sheepishly. "It was a very bad life, but a very good salary."

"Unfortunately, their previous accountant came back. And by then I had started doing some personal business, buying and selling small pieces of opium. The shop owner got angry with me and said, 'You aren't a businessman, you are an accountant!'" My wayward friend gave a self-conscious shrug. "He was right. One time I bought two and a half kilograms of opium from a farmer and dried it in the sun, to sell it for a high price in late afternoon. I bought it around 25 or 26 *lakhs*, and sold for 22 *lakhs*." A *lakh* meant 100,000 of something—in this case, Pakistani rupees. My entrepreneurial friend had lost several thousand dollars on the deal.

The jumps and plunges in price were the greatest risk for any trader in opium. The traffickers did also have occasional problems with the police, who demanded protection money and sometimes confiscated drug stockpiles. In most cases, we were told, the police sold this contraband on to Helmand's most powerful kingpins. Only rarely, generally under close scrutiny from Western donors, did interdiction in Helmand actually lead to a hill of opium being ceremonially burned.

The traffickers refined most of their opium into morphine or heroin in clandestine laboratories. Those processing labs had once been across the border in Pakistan, but during the 1990s they had gradually moved into Afghanistan's main poppy-growing provinces. Today, the UN estimated, some 72 percent of the country's opium was turned into heroin before being smuggled across a border. It was an ironic reflection of what we were trying to do with legal agriculture: set up more crop-processing factories in Afghanistan, so Afghan farmers could export higher-value products. Here as usual, the traffickers were a few steps ahead of us.

• • •

We had braced ourselves for riots during the harvest, with farmers trying to postpone eradication long enough to bring in their crop. I remembered the flat, angry eyes of the villagers in lower Kajaki when they spoke about the expected return of the kampeyn tractors. But in Helmand, that late round of eradication never materialized. Governor Sher Muhammad had done enough to satisfy Karzai's poppy inspectors—even if, in the north, his efforts had been mostly cosmetic. Now the pressure was off, and he relaxed the ban for the rest of the harvest season.

By contrast, there were riots in neighboring Kandahar on April 12, when the Afghan Special Narcotics Force tried to plow up the flourishing poppy fields of Maiwand district. The governor of Kandahar had failed to prevent a boom in cultivation, so the exasperated Kabul government sent down its elite, American-trained eradication squad. The men of Maiwand blocked the highway with burning tires, patrolled their fields with AK-47s, and set the government tractors on fire. Two protesters were killed and four narcotics police wounded before they retreated in disarray to Kandahar city. It was a very minor echo of Britain's fabled defeat on the plains of Maiwand in 1880, where one thousand British soldiers had died; but Helmandis were quick to draw the parallel.

With the highway closed, we lost our best land route out of Lashkargah. For several nervous days, we waited to see if the violence would spread up the road. In the end, Maiwand's tribal elders agreed to allow the governor to destroy one-third of their poppy fields. The negotiations dragged on so long, however, that most of the opium was harvested before the provincial police made their token rounds.

Even though we were spared any serious violence, we felt the effects of the harvest on our worksites. Opium created a huge demand for labor; it took a lot of hands to milk millions of poppies during the week or two when the bulbs were full of gum. The average daily rate for poppy labor was about seven dollars, plus three meals a day. We had local reports of skilled harvesters making the equivalent of ten dollars a day. With our wage set at four dollars, it wasn't hard to do the math.

The labor shortage hit us hardest down south, along the Darweshan Canal. We had hoped to expand there by another five hundred workers; instead, our chief engineer Sayed Akbar reported, we lost two hundred absentees during the harvest weeks. By the time the harvest reached central Helmand, however, our engineers reported no major drop in attendance. We began to hear rumors that the wages for harvesting opium had gone down since last year, making our jobs more attractive. In particular, we heard about workers migrating from other provinces where there had been major drops in poppy, desperate to find work in the fields of Helmand and Kandahar.

Nonetheless, we began to feel the pinch of the poppy harvest in the place where we could least afford it: our police escorts. Our third Kajaki payroll took place on May 4, 2005. I hadn't expected to have any trouble getting guards; after all, our escorts were from Kajaki, and had family there. Unfortunately, it turned out that most of them were already at home, or so Commander Hayat Khan's nephew told us with an apathetic grin. It wasn't hard to imagine what urgent task had called them back to the family fields. He could only give us four guards—to protect a payroll exceeding $170,000 (although of course we didn't tell him the numbers).

Charles was in Kabul, so Farid, Habibullah, and I took it in turns to bellow at the commander's nephew until he found another three young, scruffy policemen somewhere. This was still direly inadequate, but the paymasters declared that they wanted to get on the road. As the vulnerable convoy pulled out of HAVA, I turned to Farid with sudden, sharp concern. "Will we have enough police for our trip to Nawzad tomorrow morning? We'd asked for twelve guards."

Farid conferred with Hayat Khan's sullen nephew, who tossed his head fiercely. "He says yes, yes, he will find you your twelve."

Nawzad, Helmand—May 5, 2005

We got five. They were drowsing in the HAVA basement when our little expedition arrived early the next morning. When Yaqub and Engineer Akbar woke them up, they grouchily confirmed that they were the only guards in the building.

I turned in weary exasperation to Rick Breitenstein, our newly arrived deputy team leader. "Well, normally I'd just say screw it, and drive out with whatever security we've got. Nawzad is kind of unknown territory, though."

The mountainous district of Nawzad ("newborn") was farther off the beaten track than anywhere else we'd worked to date. Kajaki, Sangin, and Musa Qala were all on major provincial roads that connected the national highway to distant backwaters like Baghran or Deh Rawud. The roads into Nawzad didn't lead anywhere but Nawzad. The area's main tribe, the Isakzai, was largely outside the governor's patronage network. Their corner of Helmand had a reputation for unruliness and banditry; we had heard rumors back in December that the Babaji carjackers had taken refuge in Nawzad.

Other than that, I hadn't heard anything about the place until April, when Yaqub declared that we could get 1,400 workers cleaning karez systems there. "This is an area that needs so much help," Yaqub insisted with passion. "The walaswal is a very good man, very cooperative. He says security will be no problem." I was a little dubious, but I figured the rumors I'd heard weren't as reliable as whatever Yaqub was seeing on the ground. I knew we needed the workers to meet our targets. I would also be glad to help a northern district that wasn't part of the Akhundzadas' domain, so our project didn't look like the governor's tribal slush fund.

It wasn't until Carol had already given Yaqub the green light to hire supervisors in Nawzad that I began finding out the more worrying details. First, on April 23, Yaqub mentioned that we would need more employees than usual to manage this activity, because our karez sites were spread out over such a large area. "The four valleys we will work in are quite far apart, quite remote, you know," Yaqub explained blandly. "It simply wouldn't be possible for any engineer to manage two of them."

"Did you and Akbar actually go out to these valleys?" I asked, with a nagging sense of logistical disaster.

"We saw some of the central one when we visited the district center," Yaqub replied. "But Joel, you know we do not have time to always visit all the sites. Our engineer candidates know the area very well. We only have a few hundred workers in each valley. It should not be a problem."

A week later, I met Ghulam Mahmud, Engineer Akbar's recommended manager for Nawzad: a gaunt hill-man with a scraggly gray beard, jaundiced eyes, and roughly twelve long teeth. He had no formal engineering training, but a lifetime's experience whittling tunnels deep underground as head of a traditional karez repair team. I liked him, and thought our work planning was going well—until Ghulam Mahmud mentioned the need for motorcycles, so our sixteen local supervisors could actually visit all their karez sites on a regular basis. Dismayed, I pointed out that in our other activities, the supervisors lived close enough to the sites to get there on foot or by bicycle. Ghulam Mahmud gave an amused wheeze. "In Nawzad, the distances between the karezes are so great! And the roads are too narrow to take cars. No, our supervisors will need motorcycles."

This was pointing nowhere good. We were launching this activity by hearsay, in remote ravines that could only be effectively monitored by men on motorbikes. But it was a bad time to hit the brakes; promises had been made, supervisors hired, and work was due to start in two days. I promised Ghulam Mahmud that the following Thursday, we would come to Nawzad to see the issues firsthand.

So here we were, throwing in our long-awaited deputy team leader Rick Breitenstein at the deep end. Within days of his arrival, Rick got to visit the cutting (or, I worried, collapsing) edge of our project. I knew he was eager to see it. A meticulous Missourian with a taut, clean-shaven face and dark hair shorn almost to the scalp, Rick was another of Chemonics' adventurous young troubleshooters. He had managed projects in Iraq, Jordan, and Kosovo, and had come out to Afghanistan on a couple of short-term stints. I didn't really think he'd be deterred by the fact that we only had five sleepy-looking police escorts.

"Nawzad has become quite calm," Yaqub declared reassuringly. "The new walaswal has brought things under control. We should not worry about traveling there."

"I'd like to see what we're doing there," Rick agreed.

"Right—let's go." I hopped into one car with Yaqub and Rick, Engineer Akbar and Raz Muhammad into another, and the guards into a blue pickup truck. As our convoy rolled into the salt-encrusted plains around Nad-i-Ali, I glanced over at Yaqub. "You said it's *become* quite calm?"

"Four months ago, there was a different walaswal," Yaqub clarified with mild distaste. "He was always fighting with the district police commander. Both of them were from Nawzad, you see, and they came from different families. Always their men were shooting at each other and blaming it on Taliban. We could not have worked in Nawzad, back then."

"But that feud's over now?" Rick said, brow furrowed.

"The governor finally got fed up with all their fighting," Yaqub smiled, "and replaced them both with people who were not from Nawzad. The new walaswal is from Marja district. He has had a very impressive effect in such a short time. You would not know it is the same place."

Our Land Rover jounced north across the Kandahar-Herat Highway and up a long, stony wash toward the barren hills. The five young gunmen appeared to wake up, whooping and waving their Kalashnikovs from the dust-drenched bed of their pickup as the driver accelerated past us. We began to see villages on either side of the track, enclosed gardens with unusually lush, full tree canopies bursting out above their earthen walls. There was no visible water anywhere in this undulating desert, but karez lines dotted the slopes, and occasionally we heard the *whut-whut-whut* of gas-powered pumps draining deep wells.

Rick was full of questions about our work—how we picked our activities, how we made our payrolls, how we kept on top of things in the field. As we talked, I realized that of all the odd things, I was feeling jealousy. After months spent yearning and pleading for Washington to send out a deputy team leader, here he was—just when I had finally grown comfortable in the role. I was going to miss the conspiratorial glances with the Haji, the frenzied planning sessions with Yaqub and Akbar, the payroll work with Raz. I was sorry to leave the game when I felt like I'd pretty much figured out the rules.

After about three hours on the road, we arrived at Nawzad bazaar, driving down a queue of earthen buildings with rounded, irregular edges and tiny windows. The bazaar got its water from a karez that had mostly caved in, leaving a deep trench where plastic bags and other refuse mingled with the stream. At the small district headquarters, Yaqub introduced Rick and me to the walaswal of Nawzad—a tall, energetic Pashtun with a cropped black beard and a magnificently bulbous nose. Raz Muhammad greeted him with unexpected warmth. It turned out that the walaswal had previously worked for the Ministry of Culture in Lashkargah, where he had provided Raz with a loudspeaker for a big Pashto poetry reading in the city's football stadium.

The district administrator was overflowing with ideas for development projects in Nawzad. "Our tomatoes," he said earnestly, "are famous throughout the south. I want to build a factory here for processing and drying tomatoes." He also wanted road repairs, a better water supply for the bazaar, and electricity from Kajaki. He was familiar with our work in his home district of Marja, where we had been employing three thousand men since January, and he hoped that as a start we could do something similar in Nawzad. "People here are very poor, and they have been fighting for a long time. They need something to hope for. I want to keep their hands busy with peaceful tasks."

His enthusiasm was infectious; unlike some district chiefs, he really seemed to have a plan for his area that went beyond maintaining stability and patronage. Rick thanked him, and we walked over together to the office space he had given us. Our five new employees were bustling noisily around the small room, brandishing timesheets and other paperwork. On one wall hung a hand-drawn map of Nawzad's four regions, with all our karez sites carefully marked. Ghulam Mahmud introduced the other "engineers"—all, like him, senior community figures with karez repair experience—and they began to report on their first few days of work.

I drifted over to the map and pointed to our most distant worksites, in the long double valley of Gorz-wa-Tizni. "Excuse me, Ghulam Mahmud. We have a single pay site for everyone in both valleys?"

"Absolutely," our managing engineer agreed. "The pay site is in Tizni valley, at a good and central place. Maybe two hours' drive from here."

"This other valley here—it's Gorz valley? Will everyone from Gorz willingly travel to Tizni to be paid?"

"They will come. This is not a problem."

"How long would it take someone to get from here"—I pointed to the farthest karez in Gorz valley—"to the payroll site?"

The engineers conferred. "Maybe eight hours," one of them finally said. "Seven or eight."

My eyebrows hit my hairline. There were simply too many ways for this to go wrong, and I was sick of dealing with them by word of mouth. "We're going to go see that pay site."

There was a flutter of discomfort and incredulity as my statement was translated. "Sir, it is too far. At least two hours! You will not be able to get back to Lashkargah before dark." Ghulam Mahmud looked positively alarmed, and I felt a twinge of unease at the recollection that we only had five gunmen escorting us. Yaqub's brow furrowed with displeasure as he conferred with the doubtful walaswal, and Rick looked on impassively. Then I caught Raz Muhammad's eye, saw him nod appreciatively. I pointed to the map again.

"Gentlemen—just from looking at this map, I can tell you that if our plans break down, Gorz-wa-Tizni is the first place it'll happen. We need to have a look so we can plan appropriately. On the way we can check out the karez work that's already going on. If we leave right now, we can still be back home by dusk."

"No lunch then," Yaqub said in a brisk tone, recalling his own interest in seeing the far-flung valley. "Very well. Let's go, if we are going to do this thing."

The walaswal nodded mildly. "We will eat when you come back."

We jolted north out of the fertile oasis of Nawzad town and onto a broad, uneven expanse of gravel and scrub. Two angular mountain walls hovered to either side, just far enough for the dust and distance to shade them purple. After an hour of driving through this rugged desert, our driver appeared to succumb to a suicidal impulse, easing us directly over the brink of a cliff. I broke off talking with Yaqub and flailed for the handhold above the door, while our Land Rover inched down a series of switchbacks so steep and narrow that I couldn't see them from the backseat.

Rolling from outcrop to outcrop, we finally reached the base of the bluff and found ourselves in a deep river gorge. The "road" here was only a faint trace on the rounded stones and sand. High, crumbling rock faces penned us in, broken by innumerable side ravines. *This is God's own ambush country*, I thought with dismay. It was the only road into Gorz-wa-Tizni.

After forty interminable minutes exposed at the base of the gorge, we crawled up the east slope and arrived in the lowest inhabited reaches of Tizni, a broad highland vale slanting toward a central stream. There were few houses on our side of the water. On the steeper far bank, walled compounds clung castle-like to sharp juts or sprawled across tablelands too rugged or dry for cultivation. As the parched, jagged mountain slopes converged on the stream, they turned from shades of sepia to bright green—and pink. Virtually all the cultivable land was bursting with poppy, grown as overtly as anywhere in Helmand. Farmers with black turbans and long, matted beards regarded us incredulously as we drove past.

Ghulam Mahmud waved us off the road at our first worksite, marked by the familiar double X of a wooden windlass. The karez was only six to eight feet deep at this end, and for long stretches it was more trench than tunnel. The slopes were gray with recently shoveled mud, but there were no workers to be seen anywhere.

The shamefaced engineer for Gorz-wa-Tizni ran off to the village to find the local supervisor responsible for this site. Our handful of guards fanned out to take the high ground. Raz, who would be responsible for delivering tens of thousands of dollars along this road, joined me and distractedly said,

"Mr. Joel, do you know the meaning of *wailiodet*?" I assumed it was a Pashto word I hadn't learned yet, but he corrected me, spelling out what he meant: V-A-L-L-E-Y-O-F-D-E-A-T-H.

I stared at him, unable to reconcile the morbid question with his perplexed look. "Uh . . . why do you ask, Raz?"

"Khair Muhammad told me this joke: What is the meaning of love? Land of Sorrow . . ."

"Yes, I've heard it."

Ten minutes later, the local supervisor arrived on his motorcycle. He explained guardedly that he had let the men off a little before noon because they needed to work in their own fields. We explained that we would only pay someone who worked a full day, and that if we ever again found a whole crew absent, they would not be working with us anymore—especially their supervisor. Rick and I tried to look and sound stern; Yaqub was volubly scolding in his translation. We let them off with a warning this time, though, to limit the chances that someone would take a shot at us on the long ride back.

By the time we had finished laying down the law, it seemed unwise to press on to the pay site, still another forty minutes up the poppy-blanketed valley. I joined Akbar and Raz in their Land Cruiser for the ride back to town. "Engineer-sahib, we have a major problem in Nawzad," I said cheerlessly. "Not counting the Taliban presence." I thought of the dour villagers in black turbans of paj fabric, and wondered whether they would give us a chance to win them over.

Akbar nodded, clicking his teeth together in thought. "We are not in control."

"We've expanded too quickly. But we can't just tell the people we've changed our minds and stop work." I considered for a minute. "Someone from Lashkargah needs to come here for long enough to make sure that not only our engineers but all the supervisors understand our expectations. And travel through every valley, to make sure we can supervise our worksites properly and pay everyone effectively. It has to happen soon. Maybe we could ask Gran, if you think he knows all the rules well enough."

There was silence from the front seat for a few minutes. Then: "It should be me," Sayed Akbar said, with only the faintest hint of reluctance. He straightened his shoulders and nodded. "I am the chief engineer. I will come back at the beginning of next week, and will stay until everything is right."

God bless you, Akbar. "Thank you, Engineer-sahib. I know we can trust you to get the job done." Akbar smiled, inclined his head dismissively. "I'd like to send a paymaster with you, to make sure the pay plans are realistic. Raz, what resources do you think we'll need to safely make payroll here?"

"That was on my mind, sir," Raz said as we drove around another blind corner. "With money, I believe when we come here we will need twenty-eight men."

He spoke with such dispassionate precision that I had to repress an abrupt, crazy urge to laugh. "Twenty-eight men it is, Raz. All thirty, if you need them."

"No, sir," Raz corrected me. "More than four vehicles, and we will get in each other's way if there is trouble. Seven guards is the most you can fit in a vehicle. So, twenty-eight men. But each vehicle must have at least one heavy machine gun and one rocket launcher. Otherwise, we will all be killed."

On our return to district headquarters, we were ushered upstairs for a very late lunch of naan, rice, and greasy lamb soup. We debriefed the other engineers, and told them that Akbar would be spending next week here to get everything shipshape. The walaswal joined us, declaring with visible pride that when he first arrived in Nawzad, he would not have allowed us to ride up into Gorz-wa-Tizni without dozens of armed men. Given that his pacification campaign was still only three or four months old, we didn't find this quite as comforting as he had intended.

Hearing about the absentee work crew, the walaswal's face flushed and his voice turned steely. He warned our engineers that he would be sending his own men to double-check their work, and promised to provide us with as many of his district police as we needed on payday. After the shock of finding just how remote and potentially dangerous the far reaches of Nawzad were, it was good to remember that we had a competent district chief on our side.

We were moving into new territory in these hard-to-reach mountain ravines. Because of its helpful walaswal and its relative proximity to Lashkar-gah, Nawzad was the best test case we were going to get. If we couldn't make our project work here, then we were never going to make it in Baghran or other equally distant valleys.

On the drive home, we stopped for prayers when the sun was low in the sky, casting a rusty light over the river valley and rapidly descending hills around us. When everyone was finished, we stood for a moment appreciating the landscape. "You know, my dream would be to start a project like ours in Deh Rawud," Yaqub confided. "Would that not be wonderful? To show the brothers and cousins of Mullah Omar the benefits of peace and development."

"We are already in Deh Rawud," Raz remarked, *sotto voce*. "This place has mountains, and poppy, and very many Taliban. What more does he want?"

Defining Success

Shahr-i-Zohak, Bamiyan—May 11, 2005

The entrance to Bamiyan was defended by a grand rampart of reddish crags—in places a dull magenta, in others the fierce pink of a sunburn, streaked with orange and silver where the jagged carapace had cracked away to expose the innards of the mountain. Further into the Bamiyan valley, these cliffs softened into hills of velvety dust below peaks made placid and blue by the snow. Here at the valley mouth, the rocks stood sheer and naked.

I would never forget driving into Bamiyan province for the first time with my friend Jon, almost a year earlier, rapt at the barbed ridges and knobs that soared above the road. The cliff wall looked like a precarious castle, carved over the millennia by wind and snowmelt. And then, at the convergence of the Bamiyan and Kalu rivers, the illusion had become breathtakingly real: The precipice above the river was crowned by ruddy towers and walls, worn down by the elements but unmistakably human. Ever since, the tourist in me had longed to come back and scramble up to the ruined city. And now I was back—with an improbable companion.

"Are you sure he knows where the land mines are?" my father murmured dubiously, nodding to our guide. We had picked up a scribbled note from the police commander of Bamiyan, giving us permission to explore the ruins of Shahr-i-Zohak—as long as we took along a guard to help us avoid the mines. Unfortunately, the guards at the closest highway checkpoint had never climbed up to the cliff-top city, and had no idea where the land mines were. So we had asked the first farmer we saw, a black-mustached, thin-bearded Hazara who promised to guide us to the peak for Af 500.

"I'd bet he *thinks* he knows where the mines are," I said cheerfully. "Even in Afghanistan, no one's going to risk losing a leg for ten bucks."

Dad shot me a wry look. "Your mother definitely would not approve of this."

My father came to Kabul every couple of years for board meetings of an international Christian development agency that ran clinics and poverty relief projects around Afghanistan. This time he had set aside a weekend to travel with me to Bamiyan, in the spectacular central Afghan highlands. So I took three days' vacation and drove up to Kabul. During those days, Dad and I got to be tourists: two pale-skinned, brown-bearded Americans in kamiz partoog, asking our driver to stop the Land Cruiser every few miles so my father could pull out his binoculars and identify the local birds.

We had already visited Bamiyan's most famous ruin, the cave city where the world's largest Buddha statues had once stood. The remains of Shahr-i-Zohak were less well known, but no less striking. Zohak had been a key outpost of Bamiyan's early Islamic kingdoms: a thriving city at the junction of two rivers, with a seemingly impregnable citadel atop the sheer red plateau. It briefly repelled the onrushing hordes of Genghis Khan in 1221, when the Mongol leader's favorite grandson died trying to capture the citadel. In revenge, Genghis Khan swore to leave nothing alive in Bamiyan. Starting with Shahr-i-Zohak, he slaughtered every human and animal in the valley.

Like so many other Afghan strongholds, Zohak's natural defenses would have made it a nightmare for any attacking army. The red cliffs were too sheer and brittle to scale on any side except the east, where a steep fall of rubble sloped halfway up the rock face. The strategists of Shahr-i-Zohak had covered that slope with tier after tier of stone battlements and ornate brick towers. The single road into the citadel wound up the fortified hillside, tunneled through a vertical outcrop, and continued as a narrow track clinging to the face of the precipice, fully exposed to the crenellated walls above. The only good way to capture Zohak would be waiting for the defenders to run out of water—a long game, if the defenders had had the basic foresight to keep their cisterns full. I wondered if Genghis Khan had taken the patient course or thrown lives away on a frontal assault.

As we ascended the debris-strewn trail, the broken towers around us testified to the many skills of Bamiyan's long-extinguished civilization: foundations that had survived centuries of erosion, crisply octagonal walls, friezes and diamond patterns adorning the brickwork. At the top of the cliff, we looked out across an empty tableland rising to a low mountain peak. There were walls above us, ringing the summit, and more fortifications toward the edge of plateau below.

The young farmer pointed to the edge of the trail, at a single stone with a streak of bright scarlet paint. "He says we should stay to the path here," our driver Zabi superfluously informed us. The minefield cut us off from the lower battlements overlooking the main Kabul-Bamiyan road. During the war against the Russians and the Taliban, the local Hazara militias had used that area of Shahr-i-Zohak as a strategic base. My father scanned the unreachable walls with his binoculars, snapped some pictures. I cringed at the thought of an invading army bombarding the ancient ruin to drive out its defenders.

When I asked our Hazara guide, through Zabi, whether the city had been damaged in the war, he nodded impassively. "He says the mujahidin found a book buried in the old city," Zabi translated, "a book of a thousand years, the history of Afghanistan. It was too beautiful. But they found it when the snow had started to come." Shaking his head, Zabi pulled pages out of an imaginary book, one by one. "They burned it. It was so big, it lasted until the snow was gone."

I mulled over that parable as we climbed toward the peak. The centuries-old earthworks at the summit were crowned with a battered artillery piece, its skinny green barrel jutting into the sky. We stood there at our destination for long minutes, soaking up the desolate splendor around us.

Before coming to Afghanistan, I had never really understood how much of the world's color was buried under a comfortable cladding of grass and trees. In these arid mountains, nothing hid the vibrant palette of dirt and rock. One ridgeline was a rich pomegranate hue with shining slate-dark veins, its neighbors rusty orange and vermillion. Around us the curious alchemy of the earth was made visible: an overhang of reddish stone crumbling into inexplicably purple rubble, or silver scars on the landscape that faded along their edges to drab yellow and ochre dust. Whatever its color, the naked rock was luminous, throwing back the sunlight with added force. The small white clouds scudding across the sky cast startlingly intense shadows, like dusk falling on a few isolated crags at a time. Along the valley floor, the ribbon of lush greenery glowed all the more vividly for the riot of color in the sterile cliffs.

I looked over at my father, wanting to share my exhilaration with him. We had been climbing mountains together since I was three years old in Nepal. "It's a funny thing, both of us winding up here," I said at last, inadequately but with feeling. "Who'd have thought it four years ago? When I was just killing time as a temp in New York?" I had spent years waiting for a vocation to find me before heading into development.

"Who'd have thought it," Dad echoed with a grin. He had likewise worked in mundane jobs in the States before hearing the call and going to Nepal in 1979. He had been the same age then that I was now. My young and inexperienced father was thrown headlong into a leadership position, managing a young team of peers from around the world. I had often thought of Dad when I was floundering in a similar predicament. I thought of the hydroelectric dam he and his team had finally completed, and the glint of lightbulbs visible on the Himalayan hills at night.

"Guess I'm following in your footsteps after all," I suggested—and felt an odd dissonance. At the time I shrugged it off, but I had plenty of time to think it over during our long, jolting drive back to Kabul. There was a profound difference between what had brought my father to Afghanistan and what had brought me here. The more I probed it, the less comfortable I felt. It wasn't about overt religiosity (neither my father nor I were preaching our Christianity in the streets), but about commitment and service.

In the Nepal mission community where I grew up, the typical foreign missionary stayed a minimum of four years, with most staying in Nepal closer to a decade and many dedicating their whole adult lives to the place. They learned the language and culture, built relationships with their neighbors, funded their own work, and lived with relatively few luxuries. Like Afghanistan, Nepal had strict laws against preaching and conversion, which meant that Christian missions in the country focused on service; the missionaries were doctors, teachers, engineers, foresters, and other professionals. Dad was working with a similar group here: religiously driven idealists who lived simply and made a long-term commitment to the country, its people, and their problems.

Being a USAID development professional was rather different. I knew some long-term "missionaries" of secular development, committed like Dick Scott of Helmand to a particular place over decades of work. But the typical consultant came for a few months, maybe a year or two, before flitting on to the next contract. The consultant might learn the language if it was a regionally useful one like Spanish, Mandarin, or French, but not a local one like Nepali, Urdu, or Pashto. Instead of service, the system was pervaded by an ethos of entitlement: By and large, USAID's consultants expected to be treated like any other professional, with generous financial benefits, business-class flights, and Western-caliber houses or hotels.

Obviously, you couldn't run USAID as a voluntary agency; that was the Peace Corps. And I didn't begrudge my friends and colleagues our comforts and benefits. I knew personally how precious they could be after an exhausting month of work. But nor was I surprised that Afghans didn't consider this the best use of the finite development money promised to Afghanistan by foreign countries. Every pricy perk, from their perspective, could only be justified by a proportional benefit to Afghanistan—and many of the benefits brought by foreign consultants were far from clear or uncontroversial.

Had I given Afghanistan its money's worth? As a junior Chemonics administrator, my monthly pay didn't put much of a dent in our project budget, but like all U.S. government contractors in Afghanistan, I enjoyed plenty of added allowances. Danger pay raised my salary by a quarter. "Post diff," the hardship money for working in a disagreeable post, justified another one-quarter hike. The State Department had set a hundred-dollar per diem for meals and incidental expenses in Kabul. This bore no relationship to the actual cost of living in Kabul; I could have eaten three meals a day in fine foreign-run restaurants and still struggled to spend $100. Outside Kabul, the per diem was $50, which was just as detached from the real cost of food. These were simply the extras the government felt it had to offer to get qualified people to come to Afghanistan.

In exchange for the money, I'd given a lot of effort but rather less time. After six months in Helmand, I felt like I had reached the point where I had a grip on things—and now I was leaving. I was part of the turnover problem: the projects that reported to seven different USAID officers in two years; the consultants who came just long enough to identify a problem but not long enough to solve it; the PRT colonels who made promises to tribal elders, then forgot to mention them in their handover reports. The lack of continuity meant that all kinds of reconstruction projects were constantly being thrown back to square one.

I talked about loving the country—its landscapes, its history and culture, my Afghan friends—like any passionate tourist. But how much was I actually helping it?

After eight hours of driving, Zabi, my father, and I descended at last into the steep ravine where Chemonics had built three dams—where seventeen months earlier I'd stared at the serrated rocks and dreamed of Bamiyan. There remained so much I hadn't seen, so much more I could do if I took the time. I rolled over crazy plans in my head, wondered if I could talk Fiona into coming back to Afghanistan with me.

The Ghorband valley became a broad draw, and the mountains on either side of us fell away into the Shamali Plain. A fierce wind greeted us, bending the trees back and lashing the fields. There was a mesmerizing splendor to the ripe wheat in the wind, thousands of kernel-heavy stalks all flung back and forth in waves, their tassels scuffing and seething against each other. The sun hovered low over the mountains behind us, casting a red-gold light on the tumultuous fields. From the midst of the wheat, a flock of small birds burst abruptly into flight, startled by our passage. They described a breathtakingly perfect arc in the air, each bird gleaming with the sunset, sparks hurled from the glowing field. They were framed for an instant by poplars, and then before I could utter a sound, we drove past the gap in the trees and the birds vanished again.

That conjunction of movement and sunlight was fleeting and anything but exotic, yet it resonated with me as powerfully as all the grandeur of Bamiyan. For an instant, I had felt the powerful harmony behind the chaotic motion of a multitude: wheat stalks flailing in all directions but blending into waves following the wind; dozens of birds circling in scattered, imperfect unison. The world was pregnant with such harmony, such beauty, even if I could only see it for a moment.

I did my best to hold on to that vision as I returned to Lashkargah to wrap up my assignment.

Kajaki, Helmand—May 16, 2005

The ridgeline above us was covered in tall, yellow-brown grass and unmarked gravestones, with a few lonely martyrs' flags fluttering atop flimsy-looking poles. Where the graveyard stopped, the opium poppy began: thousands of swaying, spindly stalks whose seedpods showed the first black scratches of the harvest. Our young police escorts strolled out into the field, idly snapping off the dark, engorged poppy bulbs, splitting them open, and thumbing the light green seeds into their mouths. I discreetly munched some fresh seeds myself, found them disappointingly bland and gummy.

This was the last morning of my last Afghan road trip. I looked down the slope to the molehills of Haki Jehannum, the familiar "little hell" karez in the Zamindawar highlands, and felt a moment of furious regret that I was only retracing my steps. I had been hankering for one last exploration to wrap up my time in Afghanistan. Instead, here I was with Rick, interviewing more karez cleaners and poppy farmers—while somewhere off in the crags to our north, Yaqub and Raz were driving to Baghran.

They had left the Queen's House in Kajaki at dawn, with two of our road engineers and a full squad of the governor's police. They would spend at least six hours jolting through the unforgiving, arid ravines north of Musa Qala.

In the late afternoon, they would arrive in the district center and meet the Rais-i-Baghran, the most elusive and rebellious of Helmand's warlords. The next morning, they would drive out another seven and a half hours to several remote villages to survey possible projects. Then they would drive back, reaching Lashkargah on the third day. All those hours on the road wouldn't be wasted. We hoped to get a couple of thousand men working to repair the track between Musa Qala and Baghran; by May 18, our engineers would be painfully familiar with its bumps and craters.

I thought back to my last conversation with Raz, in the garden of our Kajaki office. "Yaqub is going to come back and give us all the reasons that we should start work in the farthest bits of Baghran right away. I need you to look for the reasons that we can't. Find the problems—security, payroll, management—and think of ways to deal with them."

"Yes, sir."

"I know getting money up there is going to be hell." I tried to imagine sending a payroll convoy with a hundred thousand dollars on a nine-hour drive through isolated, high-walled valleys with no detours. "You tell me what we'll need to do it safely."

"We will find a way," Raz solemnly declared, with what was either remarkable optimism or fatalism.

"I wish I was going with you," I confessed. It wasn't just the adventurer in me, wanting to charge off into more obscure, mountainous corners of the map. Baghran would be the zenith of our project, if we could pull it off. International development efforts had barely touched Baghran; it was too remote, too Taliban-friendly, too poor and mountainous. I wanted to witness us turning that around, even if I wouldn't actually get to see our activities there. That was how the Afghan reconstruction was supposed to work: bringing development to forsaken, impoverished districts that had never had any reason to support the government.

Raz shook his head. "I think it is better that you do not. It is not a safe place for you Americans."

"Yeah, Ms. Carol said that, too." They were right. I would add nothing to the Baghran mission, except another target. My time would be much better spent introducing Rick Breitenstein to our Kajaki activities.

So instead of reveling in what our project might soon accomplish in wild new territory, I got to look at what we had accomplished already—through the eyes of a skeptical outsider. Rick and I had brought a guest to Kajaki: Adam Pain, a bespectacled, sandy-haired British development scholar who had spent years studying the livelihoods of Afghan farmers. Pain was researching a paper on the official eradication campaign and our alternative income work. Despite his politesse, he was clearly not terribly impressed by either.

"You said this district has 'light to moderate' poppy cultivation?" Pain asked as we walked back from the field to our convoy.

"Seeing it now, I'd call it moderate," I admitted. On my previous trips to the highlands of Zamindawar, I had noticed less poppy than in lower Kajaki and Sangin. With the poppies now a gangly three feet high, many more fields were visible atop ridges, behind low walls, or in folds in the landscape.

"Quite a lot, I'd say," Pain suggested, glancing around.

"Moderate by Helmand's standards," I said ruefully. Somehow I didn't think Sher Muhammad was going to achieve his promised 80 percent reduction. Given the news from eastern Nangarhar province, though, maybe that was just as well.

Nangarhar had consistently been one of the top three opium producers in Afghanistan over the last decade. In 2003, it had even beaten Helmand to the top of the rankings. To general surprise, this year its new governor (a burly thug from Kandahar) had successfully convinced most of the tribal elders not to plant poppy. Nangarhar's crop had accordingly plummeted by something like 90 percent, without much need for eradication. This was touted as a huge success—but it had some troubling consequences.

Another USAID contractor, Development Alternatives Inc., was providing cash-for-work in Nangarhar. By all accounts they had pushed as hard as we had to get something like fifteen thousand men simultaneously at work. And it was a drop in the bucket. Tens of thousands of Nangarhari petty farmers, sharecroppers, and laborers were directly hurt by the poppy ban. They were selling their cattle and mortgaging their tiny plots of land to get by, or spilling out into other provinces in search of work. Even without the violence of eradication, the sudden removal of poppy from the province was hitting its economy hard, and the bandage of cash-for-work couldn't stem the flow.

It was somewhat ironic that the success of our program might depend on the failure of the governor's eradication efforts. If Sher Muhammad had actually eliminated 80 percent of Helmand's poppy, all our efforts would not have been enough to compensate rural Afghans for what they were losing.

Meanwile, Adam Pain's questions were making me uncomfortably aware of how little we knew about our project's full impact. "Do you know how much of the poppy around here is irrigated by karez, and how much by private pumps?" Pain asked intently. The field we had just visited had been fed from a well by a gasoline-powered water pump. Such private wells lowered the water table, and could potentially cause the local karezes to dry up. They were a sign that the field owner probably had enough guns and money to ignore the rest of the village.

"Uh, personally, I don't," I said.

"The *interesting* thing about opium," Pain said with a note of professorial reproach, "is the way it's tied into local structures of power. All very relevant to what your project is doing here. You're having all these workers repair karez systems—but how will that help if local commanders are taking all the water?"

"We're a short-term project," I said defensively. "Our priority is the cash—getting it out there, plugging the gap from eradication. We try to pick activities that are more useful than just digging holes in the ground. But sure, most of the jobs are maintenance on canals and dirt roads, not stuff that will have a long-term impact."

"Maintenance for whom, and by whom?" Pain pressed. "Whose land is irrigated by the karezes you repair? Are your workers landowners themselves, or landless laborers? If you're trying to plug the gap from poppy . . . that poppy means very different things to people who have land and people who don't."

We just didn't know. I thought regretfully back to when Khair had suggested getting that information. Yaqub always asked the communities to include the needy and landless in their work crews, but we didn't really check up on it. Many shuras traditionally gave preference to landowners and powerful local clans when they were sharing out resources.

As a result, I realized, we knew roughly how many people we had paid, but not how many people we had helped. We hadn't been systematically asking our thousands of workers about their needs—their land, their assets, their debts—so we didn't know whether we were meeting those needs. That would have been an enormous task, and we didn't have the time or the staff to do it. We didn't know if we were helping the people whose need was greatest. We didn't know what effect we were having on Helmand's labor market, or opium market. We knew the number that mattered—two and a half million work days—and that's what we had charged toward.

As we jolted through the dust back to Lashkargah that afternoon, we could see the harvest was over in central Helmand. The farmers were scything down the much-scarred poppies, collecting the seeds to press into oil and for next year's crop. Donkeys trudged past our Land Cruiser, laden with great bundles of dried poppy stems to be stored as *konjara*, animal fodder. I gazed out at the remnants of the opium season, and wondered again whether I'd done much good during my too-short time here.

I had taken great personal pride in the fact that we were on track to hit our target. It was easier, now that I was leaving, to detach myself a little and see the limitations of the game we'd been playing. Pete Siu, that young prodigy of development, had left with similarly mixed feelings about the projects he had led.

"Out in the field, yes, there were some results. Some good results," Pete had told me. "Because you throw enough money at a problem, there are bound to be some results. But that whole process became quickly mired in spin—fulfilling the never-ending need for increasingly ambitious stories and numbers for the politicians and donors. And pretty soon, what was real, what was fantasy, and what was a possibility mixed together. What made us better people at the end of the day," Pete concluded, "was really the change we made in the staff, the friends around us. Their success became our success."

I was glad that we'd given Ehsan, Raz, and the others a chance to show their qualities and take on new leadership roles. I was glad that we'd given Khair the chance to learn computer mapping in Kabul. I was glad that Rubina and Safeena had built up their skills to the point where they could have kept the office running in our absence—and positively elated to see them sweetly but flatly uphold the rules against older or American men. I didn't feel I could claim credit as a mentor for any of that, but I was glad to have encouraged them in those opportunities.

What about opportunities for others—for the intended beneficiaries of our project? We still didn't know how much of Sher Muhammad's eradication would turn out to be an optical illusion, so we didn't really know how much damage we were supposed to be fixing. But by the time I left at the end of May, I guessed that we would have paid out more than four million dollars, for more than one million labor days, to more than twenty thousand workers all over Helmand. With that much money thrown at the problem, we surely helped some people. Yet I found myself wishing that we had monitored the project closely enough to know how many we'd helped—and to know honestly whether we had done some degree of damage. I wondered uneasily if we had really eroded the voluntary hashar system, or if our activities had strengthened the hand of landowners against the landless poor.

Ray Baum, with typical practicality, had articulated what our simple but daunting goal meant back at the beginning of the project: "We've just got to get things started quickly. We can adjust them later if we need to." Ever since then, we had been running hard, all our resources stretched to the limit, measuring our success in simple numbers and fixing problems as we ran into them.

Over three days in May, we finally hit the problems that would break us.

It began that evening, when Charles boisterously greeted our return with, "Don't suppose you've heard yet. Akbar's dug up some serious corruption in Marja—Engineer Yusuf's bit."

Three Days in May

✻

HAVA Building, Lashkargah—May 17, 2005

Like many of our engineers, the short, wizened Yusuf lived in a slightly different world from the rest of us. The Hazara engineer buried himself in numbers and schematics; getting him to answer a question was a strenuous chase, as his conversation wandered irrepressibly off into the problems of managing his thousand workers in Marja district. More problematically, like a cross between an eccentric professor and Malcolm X, Yusuf's smile and chatter masked a confrontational resentment at his people's long oppression at the hands of the Pashtuns. Yusuf bridled suspiciously at being told what to do by his Pashtun fellow engineers or by Habibullah, and his relationship with our police escort force was disastrous.

"The police do not do what I tell them," Yusuf had repeatedly complained to me, while his guards protested that the grizzled Hazara engineer gave them unreasonable orders. Their mutual loathing had reached its peak in April, when Yusuf had spotted a road accident involving a Pashtun and a Hazara, stopped his pickup truck, and told his police guards to arrest the Pashtun. When the man scoffed at the idea, Yusuf had shrilly commanded the police to shoot him. The Bolan police, Pashtuns themselves, had been unamused. "If Yusuf pulls that shit again, they say they're going to kill him," Charles had told me incredulously. "Can you fire him before he fucks us all?"

When I'd asked Yusuf about the incident, his eccentric smile had hardened. "Mr. Joel, the police are bad men. They do not help the people, especially my people."

"The police are all we have to keep our project safe, Engineer," I had replied wearily but forcefully. "If they are not protecting you, that is one thing. But you can't tell them to arrest anyone—or shoot anyone. If you do it again, your job will be over."

I was fond of Yusuf, though I'd ruefully expected that sooner or later he would force us to fire him by picking one fight too many. To hear him accused of corruption came as a shock. As soon as I got to the office, I met with our chief engineer, Sayed Akbar. "Engineer-sahib—what's happened in Yusuf's bit of Marja?"

"I heard about it two days ago, Joel," Akbar began with his usual air of strained calm. "From the walaswal of Nawzad. He is himself from Marja, you remember?"

"I remember," I confirmed. Akbar had spent the previous week driving around rugged, remote karez sites in Nawzad, belatedly ensuring that all of our work crews understood the rules and were following them. The trip had confirmed that Nawzad was riskier than any of our previous worksites— a real gamble on our project's ability to win hearts and minds. When Charles had asked Akbar's usually unflappable driver about the trip, the driver had just put his head between his hands and whimpered, "Taliban. So many Taliban."

At the end of the Nawzad trip, Akbar told me, he had mustered all of our local engineers for a final pep talk with the confident, reformist walaswal. "I will not be taking any money from this project," the bulbous-nosed district chief had declared sternly. "I am not like the walaswal of Marja. There will be no false names on the payroll in Nawzad. And if I am not taking money, none of you can take money either."

Akbar had been shocked by the cavalier reference to corruption in Marja, the central Helmand district where we were employing three thousand men. Yesterday, as soon as he got back from Nawzad, Akbar had headed to Marja to make inquiries. He had so far turned up nothing amiss with the walaswal, but a throng of people had queued up to complain about one of Engineer Yusuf's five local supervisors: a tribal elder named Mir Ahmad.

Akbar had heard with increasing horror that for more than a month, Mir Ahmad had been skimming money from his workers and using his position with our project to demand bribes from other Marja landowners. Sometimes Mir Ahmad had claimed extra cash or gifts in the name of Engineer Yusuf. At the beginning of the opium harvest, Mir Ahmad had redirected twelve laborers to work in his own poppy field. When nine of them had refused, Mir Ahmad had fired them and replaced them with his relatives.

"We paid twelve guys to *harvest poppy*?" I buried my face in my hands. "Akbar, why didn't anyone tell us about this earlier? Why didn't it get back to our other monitors or engineers?"

"Mir Ahmad is a powerful man in Marja," Akbar said flatly. "When I left to drive back to Lashkargah, there were a hundred men around my Land Cruiser. I got in, but they would not let me go. They were pushing the vehicle and shouting, 'We want Mir Ahmad. If you take away Mir Ahmad, we will not work.' I said to them, 'We do not need your Mir Ahmad, and we do not need you,' and said to my driver to go." There was an audible edge of anger in Akbar's voice, and pride as well. "They let us go."

I stared at him, impressed and aghast. "Engineer, did anyone say that Yusuf himself was part of all this? Has anyone claimed that he took a bribe?"

Akbar clicked his teeth together pensively. "No. No, I do not think he is corrupt. But I think he is crazy, so crazy he might not know what has happened around him."

It was hard to say whether Yusuf confirmed that impression at his dismissal hearing later that morning. As we described the evidence of corruption in his district, the eccentric Hazara engineer began distractedly searching through the pockets of his waistcoat and shirt. He finally produced a mini tape recorder, held it out, and triumphantly pressed the PLAY button. The sounds of a man and woman singing a nasal duet filled Carol's office. Yusuf's face fell, and, muttering to himself, he began rewinding through the tape, playing other brief snatches of pop music.

Carol finally cut in. "Engineer Yusuf—what are you doing?"

"These problems you have found are not only with my people," Yusuf declared, his eyes shining. "The other engineers in Marja are part of it too. Listen, you will hear. I have it all here." He hit PLAY. This song had slightly more prominent percussion.

"Engineer, if you knew about these problems in *anyone's* work force, you should have said something to us long ago," Carol said severely, as Yusuf continued to scan his tape. "If other engineers have been corrupt, we will find them and fire them. But you're responsible for your own supervisors."

Yusuf never found the recording that would have incriminated his colleagues, nor did he offer any coherent explanation of what had gone on in Marja. After we had given him his walking papers and escorted him out of the building, Rick and I reconvened to talk about what needed to happen next.

"Akbar and I will head out to Marja and see what else we can dig up," Rick said bleakly. "See if any of this mess does implicate other engineers—or the walaswal."

"If it does . . ." I shook my head. "We'll need to talk to Governor Sher Muhammad, get the walaswal replaced if we can. Regardless, we're going to need to let the governor know about this. There's got to be some kind of consequence for what Mir Ahmad's done."

Rick nodded, looking apprehensive. "How far do you think this goes?"

"We probably don't have any other engineers who are as paranoid and isolated from the people as Yusuf," I reflected. "In other districts, we'd probably have heard complaints about this kind of extortion earlier. But I don't know, Rick. I sure hope I'm not leaving you to clean up a stable of corrupt supervisors and engineers. I'm worried that we've expanded without adding enough monitors out in the field." I thought about how much time I'd spent setting up the offices, logistics, and pay systems for our expansion—and how little time I'd been able to give Khair and his department.

"We'll step up the monitoring and see what we catch."

"I'll tell Khair the good news," I said, grinning despite myself. Our ambitious, bossy monitoring officer was the obvious choice to head up an expanded gadfly squad. I headed down to talk to him, in the office he shared with Johannes and Rensje.

Khair was working intently on his computer mapping program, feeding in data from his long-bearded young assistant, Zaki. "Joel, I understand everything about this program now," he said proudly when he saw me, gesturing at the web of fine blue lines that was taking shape on the computer screen. "Soon we will have maps of our work in Nad-i-Ali and Marja."

"Looks great, Khair." For a moment, I forgot the corruption issue. "You know, we need to send Zaki or Nabi up to Kajaki to map what we've done there. It'll take them a good week at least."

Khair raised his hands helplessly. "I cannot send them anywhere. Ms. Carol and Yaqub Roshan have told us to take readings for every drain in Babaji. They want a map they can use to plan the new work there."

"Ah, hell," I sighed. It made sense—an accurate computer map of Babaji would be ten times more helpful than the elaborate pencil-and-crayon sketches we'd been working from since we'd left the main HAVA canals. But it meant we definitely wouldn't get the guys up mapping Kajaki or Darweshan before I left.

"Some of the drains in Babaji are very small, Mr. Joel," a querulous Zaki informed me, holding his hands about three feet apart. "I will be there for a month if I take the measurement of them all. How do I know which ones I need to measure?"

"Just do the big ones for now," I suggested resignedly. "When Yaqub Roshan gets back from Baghran, he can go out there with you and tell you what to do." Yaqub had been enthusiastically involved in the restart and expansion of our Babaji work; nothing short of the Baghran expedition could have pulled him away. I was sure he'd be more than happy to head out to the field and declare which drains we should fix. "But I didn't come here to talk about drains and maps. Have you heard about our problems in Marja?"

"Some things," said Khair, his eyes lighting up. Our idealistic young imam was clearly already eager to get a squad of corruption hunters reporting to him.

Before I could give any more details, Charles appeared in the doorway. "Joel—got another problem," he reported, with a flat urgency I had rarely heard in his voice before.

"I'll be back," I told Khair, and followed our security chief out to his office.

Charles spoke as soon as the door closed. "We just got a call from our boys in Darweshan. The payroll convoy got hit by a bomb."

"Lord." My stomach contracted as I mentally reviewed the four heavily guarded paymasters who had driven south the previous day. "Who's hurt?"

"No casualties, from the sounds of it." Charles looked to Farid, who nodded his relieved confirmation. "Someone remote-detonated a bomb under the lead security car in the convoy. The explosion was under the front of the pickup and flipped it right over, but no one was hurt. The police jumped out, pissed as hell, and arrested everyone they could see."

"So the bomber must have set it off a second too early."

"Less than a second, mate," Charles corrected me, grim-faced. "You can't push a button much more accurately than that. Our boys just got lucky."

I exhaled windily. "We all got lucky. Doesn't sound like it was meant to be a warning shot. What's our theory on who did it?"

Farid spoke up. "There is talk about Taliban crossing the border in lower Helmand, with motorbikes and Kalashnikovs."

Charles nodded. "I reckon the crocs have taken a snap at us."

As after the Babaji carjacking, I found myself coldly angry rather than afraid. "What's our response?"

"For now, I'm recommending to Carol that we suspend work down south and call all our engineers back to Lashkargah, pending the police investigation," Charles replied. "It'll give us time to figure out what kind of trouble we're in."

"Sounds right. What about the rest of our operations? Do we stop Johannes driving north?" Our Dutch engineering advisor was about to head off on an overnight trip to Kajaki.

Charles shook his head pensively. "Yaqub checked in from Baghran this morning, and it sounds like everything's quiet up there. Just because the bastards can set off an IED in Darweshan doesn't mean they can hit us in Kajaki. So far Sher Muhammad and his little brother have kept the north pretty well in hand. Let Johannes decide if he still wants to go." He gave a sharp laugh. "I reckon it'll take more than an explosion to change his mind."

Charles was right; Johannes listened gravely to our account of the Darweshan bomb, then left for Kajaki as planned. Later that afternoon, in his office, Khair and Zaki exchanged glances. "Miss Rensje?" Zaki said hesitantly, his face grave. "This is the time when Engineer Johannes would ask you if you want some tea."

"But he is not here," Khair joined in. "So it is our job to fetch you the tea. We will act as your husband for this afternoon." He began to laugh, and even Zaki smiled through his dense black beard. A couple weeks ago, he hadn't been able to look Rensje in the eye, and now he could handle a joke about being her spouse *in loco Johannes*. He'd come far. Rensje laughed as well, and accepted the tea.

Lashkargah, Helmand—May 18, 2005

The next morning, I had to begin reluctantly letting go of the big, glaring issues in Marja and Darweshan. Carol and Rick would lead the effort to deal with those; it was time for me to pack my bags, both metaphorically and literally. Though I wasn't due to depart Lashkargah for another eleven days, I was moving back to the RAMP house, yielding my place in our main staff house to a new visitor, Homaira Nassery. After lunch, I cleared out my room and said my good-byes to the house guards, cleaner, and cook.

Our Istanbul-trained chef, Ali Asghar, looked more downcast than I had ever seen him. He chided me unhappily for not telling him I was leaving, so he could have cooked a proper farewell dinner. "He wants you to know," translated Homaira, "that he thinks you're a very good man. He has never heard an angry word from you. He wishes you weren't leaving." I hugged him, told him he was a fantastic cook and a damn good man, and promised to come back again at least once before I left for Kabul.

I headed to the RAMP bungalow, greeted the guards, and dropped off my bags in the room where I'd lived from November to February. Before sitting down to get some report writing done without distractions, I brought out my guitar and strummed a few chords. My old friend, the weathered Uzbek guard-cum-laundryman, appeared at the window with a delighted grin. I serenaded him with some Barenaked Ladies and Rich Mullins. He gave a high-pitched hoot of laughter and vanished.

"I'm going to miss you guys," I said quietly to the vacancy where he had been. Then I set aside my guitar and cracked open my laptop.

A few minutes later, my mobile phone trilled at me; it was Farid. "Mr. Joel—we need you in the office now."

I could tell from his unadorned insistence that something was seriously wrong. "Okay, Farid—I'll be right there." He hung up without saying anything more. My mind gingerly brushed against and flinched away from the worst possibilities as I ran to the car: Raz and Yaqub killed in Baghran, Johannes in Kajaki, another bomb down south.

As our Land Rover was backing out of the driveway, my phone rang again. It was Charles. "You'd better come back to HAVA, mate."

"Farid called me. I'm on my way." I hesitated, wondering if I should ask for details.

Charles filled the silence. "We got word from Babaji that someone shot up the monitoring team. At least one of our boys is dead. Not sure who, yet."

I felt like I'd been punched in the chest. *Zaki was in Babaji today.* "Ah, God."

"I'll tell you the rest when you get here."

Minutes later, I was running up the stairs of our headquarters, past small huddles of our staff sharing horrified whispers. The cluster of senior staff in Carol's office looked much the same. Charles saw me and strode over; his voice was measured, professional. "The engineer who found them says we've got five bodies out there, ambushed and shot at close range. Two of our monitoring guys, one old HAVA engineer, a driver, and one Bolan police guard."

"Two monitoring guys?" I hadn't expected that. *Did Nabi go along to help take the drain measurements?* "Where's Khair?"

Nabi appeared in the doorway, and I knew who we had lost. Nabi's scarred face was contorted further with grief, and his hands were trembling. I immediately walked over and put my arms around him. He began sobbing into my shoulder.

"My teacher has died, sir. He was the best of my teachers. I will never know a man who was more kind and brave. And Zaki was like my brother. Who has done this? Why would they do this?"

All I could think of was Khair talking about his son and daughter, how his proud, aggressive, fastidious veneer would relax into paternal warmth. I remembered how he had wrestled with me for more time to visit his family in Pakistan—and how after each visit he would grill me again on our life insurance policy for Afghan staff. Once I had thoughtlessly told Khair not to worry about it, that everything was taken care of. His eyebrows had almost shot off his forehead. "You may say not to worry, Mr. Joel, but I am every day in danger, and what will *you* do for my family if I am killed?"

"Khair was a brave man, Nabi," I said hoarsely. "So was Zulu. So are you. I'm so sorry."

I held on to our scarred monitoring assistant until his sobs subsided. Then Carol beckoned me over. "We've got too many upset people milling around here. Can you close the office for the rest of the day? Tell everyone that tomorrow morning we'll meet here and tell them everything we know." I made the rounds of our distraught staff and gently sent most of them home to their families.

When I returned to Carol's office, Rick was asking, "Shouldn't our guys have had more than one guard with them?"

Charles's blunt features were creased in anger. "Yesterday, the Bolan commander lost his father-in-law to a gunfight—also, it turns out, in bloody Babaji. So today he and most of his force were out around the district. There was only one guard left at the station to escort our monitoring boys."

"I told Mian Khair Muhammad, do not go today, there are not enough police," Farid cut in, "but he said, 'Why do we waste the one day we can work?'"

I felt sick. Even if Khair had gotten two or three guards as usual, it wouldn't have been enough to deter a well-planned ambush. And even if he'd had no guards, Khair would probably still have gone to Babaji. We all regularly traveled without adequate protection, and our examples said more than our words.

"The police are all over Babaji now," Charles continued grimly. "The Bolan commander is out for blood. He's arresting everything in sight."

"What happened out there?" I burst out.

"We don't know much yet," Charles answered. "Our five guys were out measuring drains all morning. One of our engineers found their car this afternoon, in an out-of-the-way bit of Babaji, with the bodies close by. Some witnesses say they saw six armed strangers on motorbikes riding out of the area. Doesn't sound like the car was shot up—the attackers must have stopped it and ordered everyone out. The keys were still in the ignition. Khair's camera and satellite reader were on the backseat."

I could feel fury closing my throat, thick and warm. "I can't wait to have somebody tell me that this was just a random crime—nothing that should prevent us going back to work in Babaji tomorrow."

"We're stopping work everywhere, not just Babaji," Carol declared flatly. "I've asked Engineer Akbar to call back our field engineers, and we're postponing all payrolls until we know we can make them safely."

For the rest of the day we dispatched news of the murders and our response around Helmand, Kabul, and Washington, D.C. Our travelers returned safely, a few at a time—Johannes from Kajaki, Yaqub and Raz from their triumphant but now moot Baghran mission. Late in the afternoon, our Darweshan engineers arrived at the office, anxious and grave. As I welcomed them, I realized dizzily just how fast our project was collapsing: major corruption discovered one day, a bomb the next, then a lethal ambush. Any other day, these men would have been the main focus of our attention. Today, they were almost an afterthought. The engineers had little to add to what we already knew about the Darweshan bomb. We thanked them and sent them home to their families.

As the sun sank low above the Helmand River, Yaqub strode in, looking at once sorrowful and purposeful. "The police have brought the bodies of our friends back from Babaji to the Bost Hospital. After the death certificates are written, the families will collect the bodies there."

"Should any of us go there?" I asked uncertainly. I had no desire to see the bodies, but I wanted to honor the dead and support my surviving friends.

Yaqub wagged his head in a diplomatic but firm negative. "There will be many strong feelings, much anger. I think if there are Americans there, someone might cause problems." Less than a week earlier, much of Afghanistan had been wracked by anti-American riots, linked to rumors of the Qur'an being flushed down a toilet in Guantanamo Bay. Lashkargah had stayed quiet, but we could imagine local provocateurs using these attacks to spur new violence. "I will go," Yaqub continued. "And tomorrow, we will all go to the burials. That will be the best way for you to show your respect."

Carol agreed, weary but decisive. "Everyone else—we've done what we can for today. Let's close up and go home."

The RAMP guesthouse guards, so cheery when I had left after lunch, now looked frightened and somber. I slumped into a chair on the back porch, my grief curdling into a kind of numb bewilderment. My two fellow guests, American consultants for Chemonics' long-term alternatives project, came out to join me. We knew that today's events would completely upend their plans, but we couldn't talk about it. Instead, as the sky went dark and our carpenter-cook brought out the oily lamb du jour, we argued fiercely about U.S. politics—a surreal distraction, distancing us from the events unfolding here in Lashkargah.

When my mobile phone rang, I leapt up and hurried to a corner of the moonlit garden. It was Charles, businesslike and bitter. "Farid called from the hospital. They had a big crowd down there: relatives, friends, guys from our project and the government. There was a lot of crying and a lot of shouting, but Roshan and Haji and Akbar kept things in hand. Now the families have picked up the bodies. Most of the crowd's broken up."

"Sounds like it went about as well as we could expect."

"Except that Khair Muhammad isn't from Helmand, and his parents are desperate to get the body up to Kabul as soon as possible. There's a relative of Khair's at the hospital, who's dead set on taking him up tonight."

"What—overnight?" I could understand the parents' yearning to bury their devout son according to Muslim tradition, within a day of his death. Still, even at my most reckless, I wouldn't have chosen to travel from Lashkargah to Kabul in the dark.

"Some of our boys have volunteered to go along, and they say the governor's already arranged a security escort." Charles's voice was taut. "It's not a question of us sending the body up, mate—it's a question of whether we try to stop them. There are a lot of very angry, very sad Afghans down there. I don't recommend we try."

"Right," I said, troubled but sympathetic. "Well, if the governor's police are willing to escort them, that's something."

"Yaqub and Haji both say that a funeral convoy is sacred," Charles offered. "Everybody wants to be able to get their people in the ground in twenty-four hours. Hitting a funeral car is something you just don't do."

"Sounds right," I acceded.

"Get your rest, mate. There's funerals in the morning."

Nawa-i-Barakzai, Helmand—May 19, 2005

Yaqub and I arrived late for Zaki's burial. Our monitoring assistant had lived in Nawa-i-Barakzai, a densely farmed district in the Helmand River floodplain roughly an hour's drive southwest of Lashkargah. After getting lost a few times, our little convoy of Land Rovers and pickups finally halted on the poplar-lined canal bank opposite the bereaved family's compound. Small clusters of women were arriving on foot to pray with Zaki's mother and wife. As they noticed our strange cars, they rolled the mesh mask of their burqas down over their faces and ducked quickly through the household door. We crossed the slender footbridge toward the house and saw a crowd of solemn bearded men trudging up the track to our right, pallid dust swirling behind them.

"They say they have just come from the graveyard," Yaqub informed me regretfully. "Zaki is buried. We should sit with his family for a while."

One by one, we processed into the white-plastered guest room of the compound, bowing to clasp the hands of Zaki's father and brother and offer our condolences. All I remember of Zaki's father are his cracked, muscular, trembling hands and the web of his face, grief scribed fresh over a palimpsest of ancient pains. Yaqub and I were followed by a dozen young Afghan colleagues, many of them weeping openly. When we were seated cross-legged on broad, dusty toshak cushions around the room, Zaki's thickly bearded, obviously pious brother led us in a prayer. I understood none of it, but passed my hands in front of my face at the end with everyone else, and dazedly said, "Amen."

As Yaqub began praying, I thought back to our all-staff meeting in Lashkargah that morning. It had been short; Carol and Rick had explained what little we knew about the Babaji attacks, and then proposed that everyone split up to attend the funerals of the Helmandis killed in the attacks. Yaqub and I had led a contingent to visit Zaki's burial. As our little convoy had sped through the desert, made a wrong turn in a marshy lowland, and eventually rolled into Nawa-i-Barakzai's heavily populated terrain of canals and orchards, I had felt a slight anxiety pressing against my numbness. I was pretty sure Charles hadn't realized just how far out of Lashkargah Zaki's funeral would take us. We had grabbed only two or three armed guards on our way out, which more than ever seemed dismally inadequate for our protection. Yet I hadn't pushed us to turn back. Paying our respects seemed more important than self-protection, at that point.

I wasn't entirely surprised when, after less than half an hour sitting with Zaki's family, we saw two more vehicles screech to a halt at the canal and a squad of our Kajaki guard force leap out. One of our young colleagues hurried out to speak with them, then returned and conferred with Yaqub. "Charles has ordered us back to Lashkargah now," Yaqub said, sounding slightly vexed. I could almost hear Charles's voice: *What are you thinking, fucking off halfway to bloody Iran with only two shooters?* We stood and made our apologetic good-byes to the bereaved, promised we would do what we could to help.

As we drove off, my mind stayed on Zaki's brother: his strong, aching gaze fixed on mine, his mute demand for justice. Our newly arrived driver's frenetic chatter and the growing horror on my companions' faces only slowly penetrated my awareness. "What's Saber saying?" I asked Jawed, Haji Habibullah's adroit young assistant. "Is Charles very angry with us?"

I had never seen Jawed look quite so shaken. "In Lashkargah, they are saying that everyone who went with Khair Muhammad's body to Kabul is dead."

"What?" I said blankly.

"They say there was an attack on the highway north of Kandahar."

"No," I retorted, with stupid conviction. "If something had happened in the night, we would have heard earlier this morning. Rumors like this always start after something bad has happened. Don't believe it. Not yet."

I'd expected to see fury in Charles's eyes when we got back to headquarters in Lashkargah. Instead, I saw sheer relief, terrible in its implications. Our armed Kajaki police were swarming all over our office, their Kalashnikovs at the ready. Rick said quietly, "There's been another ambush. We thought they might have got you too."

"Khair's convoy?" I said, horror seeping through my disbelief.

Charles's face was bleak. "The bastards followed them and took them out in the middle of the night."

My mind reeled as I thought over the volunteers who had accompanied Khair's body. Two rental car drivers, driving in shifts. The engineer who had discovered the bodies in Babaji. And my gentle Hazara friend Ehsan, who knew Kabul well and had gone along to guide them through the streets. "What do we do?"

"We're getting out, mate," Charles replied flatly. I realized what it meant that our office was almost totally empty, even though most of our staff should have returned from the funerals by now. "Get your things. If what we're hearing from Zabul is true, we've been sitting here like bloody ducks for too long already. They're gunning hard for us. We don't know how many more attacks they're planning. We can't defend this building and we can't defend the houses. The expats are heading to the PRT, and we've told the Afghan staff to head home until they hear from us."

I began clearing out my desk, still not entirely grasping the extent of the calamity. Ten minutes later, the truth was brutally driven home by a phone call from Noor Khan, a Kandahar-based journalist who had driven to Zabul to investigate the attack and found my business card in Ehsan's pocket. When I'd hung up, I looked over, shattered, to Charles and Farid. "That was eye-witness confirmation. We've got six men dead in Zabul." Four volunteers, two relatives. That brought our total loss to eleven men in two days.

Charles cursed vainly. A haggard-looking Farid got on the phone, trying to find out what had happened to the pickup of armed guards who had driven out of Lashkargah with the funeral convoy. Charles called the PRT, futilely requesting helicopters to pick up the bodies, and trying to persuade the dubious colonel that, yes, we were being targeted—we couldn't assume that three attacks in three days were a coincidence. I finished packing my things, tried to take in the reality that my friends were dead, our work in meltdown.

"I'm ready to go," I told Charles raggedly.

"All right, mate." Charles let out a long breath, then said, "Johannes just called from the PRT. He's asked if someone can bring a few of his things from the staff house. Could you and Yaqub stop over there?"

As we drove the familiar streets, I felt we were broadcasting our vulnerability, as if every passerby could hear my deafening pulse. A roadside bomb, a drive-by shooting—how easily we could be erased. Our staff house guards opened the gate with agonizing slowness, while I waited for a black-turbaned assassin with a rocket launcher to appear at the end of our mud-walled street.

When I walked into the house, Ali Asghar came out of the kitchen. From the questioning tension in his face, I knew our Hazara chef had heard something of the rumors.

"Ehsan," I said, spreading my hands in a simple, helpless gesture of grief, wishing I knew any language to express what I was feeling. I had seen the two of them chatting while Ehsan worked on the boiler or the kitchen plumbing; I knew they were friends. "Ah, Asghar. Ehsan."

Ali Asghar uttered a brief noise, somewhere between a groan and a wail, and retreated into the kitchen. Standing still was suddenly unbearable. I began pacing around the house, seeing everywhere the things Ehsan had fixed or put in place, the corners where he and I had leaned while chatting about God or family. Ali Asghar reemerged, tears streaking his face, and spoke with devastated bewilderment.

Yaqub translated, his voice aching with sympathy. "He says Ehsan had been so happy. Ehsan was engaged to be married in Kabul."

Ehsan hadn't told me that. Something shifted inside me, a gasp that convulsed more than just my lungs, and tears finally rolled down my cheeks as well.

In Limbo

The PRT's new commander, Colonel Jim Hogberg, kindly made room for our shattered flock of refugees inside his garrison fort. Everyone with a rich-world passport slept on canvas cots in the barracks, just down the hall from the Texas National Guard troops. Our non-local Afghan staff who would have to be evacuated by air to their home provinces stayed in the walled-off corner of the base where the PRT received native visitors. It was an odd echo of an Afghan household; we family members were ushered inside, while the outsiders were kept in a comfortable but carefully quarantined guest room.

The inside of the PRT base was a barren limbo of raked gravel, with no view of anything beyond four gray walls, towers, and gun turrets. The grumble of generators filtered, incessant, into every corner of the space. Next to our barracks was an outdoor garbage pit with a five-foot concrete wall. From the first evening, this drab "PRT Bar" became the unlikely nerve center of our project-in-exile. Some of us would pace nearby, talking on satellite phones or mobiles, while the rest of us leaned our notebooks and paper cups of Chivas Regal against the garbage pit wall and tried to regain our bearings.

Our immediate priority was evacuation. Carol headed up to Kabul on the first available plane to deal with USAID and the embassy. We flew out nearly all of the other expatriates and all the non-local Afghan staff within a day or two of the attacks. Yaqub Roshan and I stayed on to help Rick and Charles shut everything down. I was mutely grateful not to be torn away in the first shock of tragedy. While I didn't expect that the police investigation would turn up much, I was raging to find out whatever we could about the murders. And I had some good-byes to say.

Karam Baba Graveyard, Lashkargah—May 21, 2005

It felt odd but good to leave the PRT unprotected and on foot—a small defiance, a reassertion of freedom, to walk the two minutes' distance to Lashkargah's sprawling cemetery. A few mourners broke away from the crowd of hundreds to meet us among the rough-edged grave markers and pebbly cairns. I embraced my tearful friends, bowed with hand on my heart to the people I didn't know. Some of our younger staff looked stricken and dazed, but most wore their grief with bleak familiarity.

Ehsan's body arrived in the bed of a small truck, on a welded iron funeral frame draped in thick shrouds of velvet and gold. His friends and family closed around it, brought forth a figure tightly and anonymously swaddled in white cloth. Tears blurred my vision and my shoulders shook as I joined the procession. *He looks so small. Surely he wasn't so small.* "Allah, Allah," groaned the young man next to me. All around me, people were moaning, swaying, praying, sobbing. I had been braced for the reek of death, but I couldn't smell a thing; the sun seemed to have blasted all scent from the cemetery.

My friend's grave was about five feet deep, with a slightly narrower trough at the bottom to receive his corpse. Two men climbed into the breach, bore the austerely wrapped body down with great care. One of them then took clay tiles from a stack beside the grave and began building a simple peaked roof over the trough. When Ehsan's body was hidden from view, friends and family began circling to cover the tiles with handfuls of dirt.

I wiped my face and walked over to meet Ehsan's brother, a bespectacled older version of my friend. He and his aged, wispy-bearded father had arrived from Kabul late the previous afternoon. They looked like they hadn't slept in days. Yaqub took the father's hands, spoke with an empathy and heartfelt distress that needed no translation. The old Hazara replied, his voice uneven and desolate. At his words, a wail went up from several of the young men nearby; Farid and Ali Asghar wept as though they were about to physically snap in two.

"He tells us that the day before the murders, he took Ehsan's wedding clothes to his fiancée for tailoring," Yaqub told me unsteadily. It was Afghan tradition, the special wedding suit embroidered in part or whole by the bride and her family. "They were to be married in two months. Now what is he to tell her?" I put my hand over my eyes, felt my own sobs start again.

The searingly prophetic Haji Habibullah launched into an oration, silver beard jutting out around his scowl. Afterward he joined us, bowing slightly as he clasped our hands with sorrowful warmth. "I said that the people who did these killings are the enemy of God and the enemy of Afghanistan," he declared, eyes still smoldering. "I said Ehsan was our brother, and you people are our guests who have come to help us, and anyone who tries to attack you is a criminal for attacking the guest. And anyone who remains silent about such crimes is also a criminal."

"Thank you, Habibullah," I replied bleakly. "Anyone talking yet?"

Habibullah raised his hands in a bitter, helpless gesture. "The Bolan police have arrested two hundred people in Babaji. They say they will not let them go until they find out who did the killings. But I think this is just like the jacking. These people will never tell us anything true. We should never have trusted them, Mr. Joel."

I couldn't say anything. Even as I released my grief for my gentle friend, I was also swept away by anger verging on hatred—for everyone who had assured us that Babaji was safe, for whoever had carried out the murders and everyone who would cover their tracks, for the police whose idea of investigation was mass hostage-taking. As the funeral assembly slowly broke up, I spotted Farid out of the corner of my eye, talking to Charles. We had heard that he had identified a suspect the previous afternoon. I hurried over, ravenous for the details.

"We were doing *fatiha*, the prayers for the dead, at the big mosque," Farid explained, grimly composed. "At the football ground afterward, we were talking about the killings, and I saw one man listening to us. He wore a black turban, and he had a new Honda motorbike. I asked if anyone knew who he was. No one knew him. But someone said, 'I saw him at Bost Hospital, when the bodies of our friends were there.'"

I glanced over sharply at Charles. We were working on the theory that the Zabul attacks had been orchestrated by an enemy who had been at the hospital and overheard the plans. Many of the mourners had not been particularly discreet in organizing Khair's midnight funeral convoy.

"This man saw us looking at him and left. So I followed him to the animal market," Farid continued. "Then I hurried to the Bolan commander and told him what I had seen. He sent police along with me, and we arrested the man at the animal market. I am sure he was Taliban—not the kind who is fighting or the kind who is preaching against the government, but the quiet third kind who is always watching, always collecting information. And I am sure he was involved in our case."

"Good work, Farid," I breathed. "Can we trust the Bolan commander on this?"

"He is so angry. The young guard who was killed in Babaji was close to him. Very close. Not a relative. But, you know, it is traditional . . ." Farid searched delicately for words. "He was really handsome and polite. A good officer."

"I get it," I said.

"The young guard was also from a very poor family. Now his mother has come to the Bolan commander, saying, Where is my son, where is my son," Farid continued in somber tones. "The commander will do anything to find out who killed our men."

"He's probably got the electrodes hooked up right now," Charles agreed harshly.

I loathed torture, both for its wickedness and its appalling ineffectiveness. No American policy roused more outrage in me than the blurring of lines that had led to Abu Ghraib. But in that moment of vertiginous, savage satisfaction, even if it had been in my power to spare the suspected Talib, I wouldn't have. My fear of a city of anonymous enemies and my sick abhorrence for the men who had killed and threatened my friends were more robust than my moral and religious convictions. I wanted the prisoner to talk. I wanted to *know*.

Governor's Office, Lashkargah—May 22, 2005

Four days after the murders, I saw Governor Sher Muhammad for the last time. Rick, Farid, and I headed to his office, where the sympathetic wali ushered us into a curtained conference chamber and called for tea. "You should know that right now, people across upper Helmand are meeting to memorialize your dead workers. They do not want your project to stop."

"We don't want to stop either," Rick affirmed fervently. "But we cannot send our people to the field when they are clearly targeted for murder."

Sher Muhammad wrinkled his nose in disgust. "You know that Babaji is full of drug smugglers and Gulbuddin's men. It is not a good place. The rest of Helmand is not like that. This is only the second problem you have had in six months."

"It is a big problem, wali-sahib." I tried to keep the anger out of my voice. "The sharwal and the shura, who promised to protect us, need to find out who was behind these attacks."

"It was the Taliban, the enemies of the country," the governor said, easily, almost dismissively. "We will catch them. But still you should not stop working." He paused in contemplation, eyes bulging and earnest. "Listen.

We will give ten guards to every engineer, minimum. The district heads will tell us when we need more because of special dangers. Perhaps you can also provide a per diem to the intelligence police to identify those dangers."

"No, we won't," I said with sharp despair. "We need to rely on the district heads, police, and Amniyat to tell us of danger whether or not we're paying them!"

Sher Muhammad shook his head, slouched wearily in his chair. "By God, it is not easy to keep peace in Helmand. I only have so many brothers! Most of the work I do myself. A computer cannot do more than I do. I have resigned three times, but Karzai does not let me go." I didn't believe him, but I momentarily felt sorry for him—prematurely aged, with deep shadows below his eyes. Then our warlord governor glanced up with a companionable smile. "It was not good that your men only had one policeman with them. Next time we will send more men, with more guns. Our workers may still be killed. But if you know you killed some of the enemy too, you feel better."

Only one policeman. We would hear that a lot over the next few days, from the thuggish Helmand provincial police commander, the politely aloof captain of the Amniyat, the defensive elders of Babaji. *Why did your men have only one guard? Why was your security so weak?* We could counter by blaming the Bolan police for their unexpected absence that day; or argue that we had been trying to deter petty criminals rather than serious assassins; or appeal to the security guarantee we had received, with fresh signatures from the mayor of Lashkargah and the Babaji shura. But I began to realize how much of my vindictive wrath was just my mind shouting down its buried guilt.

• • •

"There's no fucking chance we're just going to bring on another hundred of Sher Muhammad's police and keep going with business as usual," Charles swore cheerlessly that afternoon at the PRT Bar. "USAID, Chemonics—they need to understand what it means that we've been targeted down here. This isn't just about numbers of guards. We've got to bring in the professionals, real private security companies, none of this USPI bullshit. That's going to cost a few million dollars, and it's going to take time."

"The delay's going to upset them more than the cost," I predicted blackly, leaning against the garbage pit. "This project has always been about time—about how quickly we can hit our targets."

"Well, now we're the bloody target, mate," Charles retorted. "If we keep rushing about, we're just going to get shot up again."

Rick looked troubled. "Did you find out anything this morning in Babaji?"

Charles nodded; while we had been meeting with the governor, he had donned a flak jacket and rode out with a squad of Texas National Guardsmen to see the site of Khair's murder for himself. "It's all rolling terrain up there. Lots of vegetation, lots of ditches, lots of cover. And everyone was lying low—not a kid or a dog in sight. The PRT boys were shitting themselves. We'd have had no maneuverability at all if we'd been hit." His voice grew fiercer. "To set up an ambush in that kind of terrain, you'd need to know where your target is coming from, on which road, at which time. No way did this attack happen without inside help from Babaji."

"We knew the place was a snakes' nest," I said bitterly. "Drugs, feuds— but I'll bet you the police will just conclude that Taliban outsiders did this. No one's going to dig too deep in Babaji."

"The Bolan commander just might," Charles countered. "He'll have seen what happened to his 'favorite officer' up there. Looks like the kid made a run for it into a wheat field. The killers hunted him, pinned him down, and finally shot him in a drainage ditch about a hundred yards from the car. He ran out of bullets. Poor bastard only had one clip. The rest of our boys had a chance to run as well, and got shot in the legs." I tried in vain not to imagine the scene.

We were also piecing together the story of the funeral convoy. Five armed guards had accompanied the car as far as Kandahar. Then they had stopped, and reportedly told Ehsan and the other volunteers to wait in town until morning. I could imagine the state of mind that led our friends to reject that advice—the same dogged, numb determination to honor the dead that I had felt driving out to Zaki's wake. Their car was followed from Kandahar by a white Corolla, which sped through a checkpoint just behind them at 4:00 a.m. in the middle of Zabul province. The attackers hit the pickup with a rocket-propelled grenade, shot the driver dead in his seat. They then forced the other passengers from the wrecked car, murdered them, and looted the bodies.

The Zabul killers could have been bandits or random insurgents, with no link to the Babaji attacks. That was the convenient theory, backed by the PRT, the governor, and others with a strong interest in reviving our project as soon as possible. We were pressing ahead with the more unsettling theory that the murders were related. The Helmand intelligence police, who had claimed custody of the Talib arrested by Farid, said they had turned up "a connection" to Zabul. We heard similar things from the PRT and police in Zabul. And there was the evidence from Khair.

"Some friends at the hospital hid money in Khair's funeral wrappings," Charles said, his jawline tight and angry. "That's not the usual custom, according to Farid. There's no reason for Afghan bandits to open a casket and search a corpse, unless they knew there was money there. But these ones did. And afterward they shot up the casket. These bastards knew exactly who they were hunting, and they wanted to send a fucking clear message." Then he added the detail that overwhelmed me. "And they shot Ehsan in the eyes. Because he was Hazara. That's another message for you."

All I could see was the face of the gentlest young Afghan I knew—a man who would barely raise his voice in his own defense, let alone a fist. I maintained my composure long enough to get away to the abandoned gravel flats behind our barracks. Then I sank on my heels and trembled, dry-eyed and nauseous. I was horrified by the brutality of the murders, revolted at the desire for vengeance they had roused in me, seething at my own powerlessness.

A few hours later, when I was halfway recovered, Charles found me near the mess hall. I thought he might have more news to share, but he just walked along with me for a few moments quietly before speaking. "It's hard when something like this happens. Especially the first time. Hits different men different ways. Some of them get loud and pissed off, go shooting off their mouth at anyone who crosses them. Some of them bottle it up and can't let it out." He glanced over at me. "You wouldn't happen to be one of those quiet ones, would you, mate?"

"No," I said, fooling neither of us. "I mean, what is there to say? It hurts."

"Yaqub's a quiet one, too. He's taking it pretty hard that he didn't stop the car from leaving the hospital that night. The man's about ready to take a jump off the PRT Bar and end it all." I felt a sudden surge of affection for Yaqub, whose own grim experiences in the Communist era had done nothing to harden his heart. "The PRT's got a counselor who's said he'll talk to anyone who needs it. He's a good man. You might want to take him up on it."

I should have. Instead, I called Fiona, who hid her own terror and helplessness while I flailed on the phone. And I stalked around the PRT, craving activity and motion, trying to defer the inevitable idle moments that illuminated just how little we could do.

HAVA Building, Lashkargah—May 23, 2005

"My specialty," Rick declared to our assembled staff, "is working in conflict zones. I have worked in Kosovo, the Middle East, Iraq, and now Afghanistan. This is the third time I've been on a project suspension for security reasons. At no time were there discussions of *ending* those projects. And we are not discussing ending this project." He was interrupted by the deafening clamor of a helicopter landing in the stadium across the street. Our staff glanced out the window, muttering in surprise. "That is not a taxi to take the rest of the expats out of Lashkargah," Rick loudly, gamely insisted. We later found out that it was a British interdiction helicopter, whisking a local opium kingpin off to Kabul for prosecution.

We had gathered the whole team together in our office to explain the situation and to give them a forum to talk about whatever was on their minds. Rick wanted to reassure them that the project wasn't over, that we were only shutting things down for a short time while we strengthened our security. He also told them that each bereaved family would receive ten thousand dollars, with additional life insurance money for the Chemonics employees. I looked around at the sea of anxious, grieving, or hard-eyed faces. Over the next hour, our Afghan colleagues let us know what they thought without restraint.

"Our people lay in Zabul for seven hours after they were killed. Does Chemonics not have the power to send a helicopter to get the bodies back?"

"When we lost our first vehicle in the Babaji area, you said you wouldn't start work again unless the vehicle was returned. But you went ahead and started work."

"What kind of action will be taken against the Lashkargah sharwal and the Babaji shura, who gave us an official signed commitment that was then broken?"

"We do not have good security in this building. Only today I arrived with a satellite phone and a big box, and no guard searched me or questioned me."

Beyond debating our own mistakes and deficiencies, the meeting kept circling back to one crippling absence: the lack of a police force that could protect our workers, investigate murders, and punish the guilty within the bounds of law. "Not one of the guards we get in the districts is an officially trained policeman or soldier," objected the shovel storekeeper. "The walaswal has collected them on the basis of family relationships or work done for him in the past."

"The police we have now are just hired from the streets—robbers and criminals are brought in and given arms," echoed our manager from distant Musa Qala. "We need official police, who are trained to respect the project and the engineers."

We won't find those police in Helmand, I thought dolefully. Sher Muhammad and his militias had maintained a significant degree of order in the province, but they also filled the space where professional, accountable law enforcement might take root.

"When we are seeing clearly that the criminals are here in Babaji, why can't we take action against them?" raged one of our engineers. "Our loss and our killing doesn't mean anything, because you won't tell the governor or the commanders what to do."

"We are not a police force," Rick replied steadily. "We cannot investigate and we cannot arrest anyone for this crime. We are an aid organization. We are doing everything we can to apply high-level pressure. I understand your frustration, and I feel it as well. But we can't form a militia out of these men here and go get these guys."

• • •

That day, the informants finally began coming in. Shortly after the team meeting, Yaqub beckoned Charles, Habibullah, Rick, and me back to an isolated office room. His voice was oddly thick, his face pale. "A villager is here with some information that I think may be important. Do you know the old man from Babaji, the one who cried at every meeting?"

Elder Priam. "Of course," I said eagerly. "Has he brought us some news?"

"No." Yaqub shook his head. "No, but we have news of him. On the day of the attack, our young friends were measuring drains near his house. He invited them to have lunch with him. It was on their way from lunch that they were killed." Yaqub paused eloquently. "The villager says the old man's nephew left very quickly from lunch on a motorbike."

"You aren't serious." I struggled to reconcile the accusation with the weeping old farmer who had pleaded so obstinately for us to return. Was it thinkable that Elder Priam's tears had always been bait for a trap? Perhaps our early denials had embittered him, pushing him to a vengeful about-face. Perhaps he had been sincere, but ended up helping the assassins for one of a dozen unknown reasons. Perhaps he was just being framed by a malicious neighbor.

"The killers knew exactly where in Babaji to find our men," Yaqub reiterated. "This same informant tells us that two days before the killings, maybe twenty Taliban came to Babaji from Pakistan, with the mission to kill development workers. They say that the men were asking about Yaqub Roshan—about me." I understood why Yaqub looked so ashen. "Everyone knew I was helping in Babaji. They did not know I would be in Baghran for these few days. They were planning to invite *me* for lunch."

We called the informant in and grilled him for details. "I will tell the whole truth," he whispered, "but I value my own life also." By the end of his story, I wasn't completely convinced of Elder Priam's guilt, but I heatedly wanted the old man arrested for questioning. Ironically, despite being an obvious suspect, neither he nor his family had been among the two hundred people seized by the police.

Our next informant, to my continuing surprise, was Elder Odysseus. He glanced around as he entered the room to make sure the curtains were closed. I gestured at a chair and the shrewd leader of the Babaji delegations seated himself, looking only slightly nervous at the circle of hostile faces. Habibullah translated his words, with Yaqub occasionally jumping in.

"I have told all my neighbors what a terrible crime this was," the elder began, with a show of grave defiance. "The police arrested me, because I made people angry, but I told them I would keep arguing, no matter where. I have told them, and the Amniyat, and the PRT who was responsible for the crimes."

"And just who is that?" grated Charles.

"The Taliban," Elder Odysseus said simply, and began rattling off a list of names, one after another, all preceded by "Mullah" in good Talib fashion. He named a shopkeeper in the bazaar who had provided the AK-47s, and one of our workers in Babaji. He confirmed that the men had been targeting Yaqub, denied that any of the killers had been related to Elder Priam. "Some people in Babaji knew when they were coming together to discuss and organize for this attack. I have told their names to the PRT. Now the killers are all gone to Washir."

"Why didn't anyone tell us beforehand?" I demanded. "You had just told us how safe we would be in Babaji."

Elder Odysseus threw up his hands. "I told you we did not have the means to provide protection. I said how much we needed the work. When you came back, and I saw the engineers only had two guards, I said they should bring more. I said this to Engineer Roshan."

"And I asked if you had heard about any threats or problems," Yaqub recalled. "You said no."

"No. I had heard nothing then. I just knew this neighborhood was strange." The gaunt-cheeked elder sat stiffly in his chair. "We have . . . grievances against the government. They will not protect Babaji, and the criminals who did this have no mercy on us. I tell you, we are as upset as if this had been our own families. We have told everything to the PRT. If my own father was involved, I would have given you his name."

"This man fought with Gulbuddin before," Habibullah said with abrupt disgust. "He will give all these Taliban names, but we do not know whether his own people did this." I watched intently as the Haji confronted Elder Odysseus in Pashto. The ambush of the funeral convoy and desecration of the corpse certainly fit Gulbuddin Hekmetyar's style of horrifying, taboo-violating attacks.

Elder Odysseus shook his head with weary bitterness, as if confronted by a deep but half-forgotten grudge. "The party of Gulbuddin is dead in Helmand. Where is Commander Hafizullah? He runs an aid organization. Umar works for the Ministry of Rural Development. Mir Wali has given his allegiance to Rabbani. The party of Gulbuddin is nothing now. This was Taliban."

"As long as we're being honest here," I said dryly at the end of our questioning, "do you know who stole our car back in December?"

"Robbers," Elder Odysseus responded at once. "There is no connection."

PRT Base, Lashkargah—May 24, 2005

I had been struck by Elder Odysseus's assurances that the PRT already knew everything he was telling us. We had known that Colonel Hogberg was (understandably) being more generous with his accommodation than his intelligence, but I wondered what conclusions he was drawing from all the reports we didn't see. The following afternoon, I got a disheartening glimpse into the PRT's investigation.

It began by sheer coincidence—a walkie-talkie crackling to life on the belt of the soldier in the toilet stall next to me. The caller was a Texan guardsman on gate patrol. "We've got a guy out here who says he has some information about the Chemonics killings." My pulse sped up when he gave a familiar name: a Helmandi power broker who might well know about the murders.

Another voice echoed over the radio. "Okay, bring him in to the hutch. I'll meet you there in five minutes."

They clearly weren't about to invite any Chemonics observers, but I couldn't pass up on the chance to hear what this man had to say. I quietly left the toilets and headed to the trailer nearest the gate. When I opened the door, the nervous informant looked up and recognized me. I greeted him cordially in Pashto; he seemed immensely relieved to see a familiar face inside the American fortress. Then I turned to the slightly baffled, camouflage-clad Afghan translator. "My name's Joel Hafvenstein—I'm here to participate on Chemonics' behalf."

By the time the American interrogator arrived, I was seated at the table like I belonged there. I had seen the PRT's military intelligence and CIA guys stalk around the base with their shaggy blond beards and sunglasses, and knew that most of them were as young as me, or younger. This was one of the young ones. I just nodded to him, and after a moment of startled disorientation, he decided not to question my presence.

"It was the Taliban who did these killings," the wide-eyed, sweating informant began. "It is because of elections—they want to make too much trouble before the elections to parliament later this year." He gave us a list of names of the major Taliban of Helmand, highlighting the ones who were allegedly involved in the murders. Only one name matched the list we'd got from Elder Odysseus—and once again, none had any relation to the weeping Elder Priam.

I assumed the American interrogator across from me was also cross-checking the names against a much larger list and feeding them into a broad understanding of Helmand's opaque criminal undercurrents. Then our informant added, "The mayor is also trying to find out who killed these people."

"The mayor of Lashkargah?" the young American responded suspiciously. "Why would he get involved with this? What's his interest?"

"The mayor is head of the district, not just the city," I said, trying to hide my disbelief. "Babaji is part of his jurisdiction." If military intelligence had this poor a grasp of the overt structures of power, so much for the undercurrents.

The American interrogator grunted. As he continued questioning, I wondered if he was deliberately omitting the relevant questions because I was in the room. The alternative only slowly dawned on me: that he knew hardly anything about the case, and cared little more. "What else have these 'Taliban' done?" he queried impatiently at one point.

"They did a lot of stuff," the informant responded. "They took Chemonics' vehicle and ran away, back in December." I shook my head skeptically, but he insisted. "Even that first time, they threatened your engineers. The only reason they didn't steal the vehicle this time was that they were in a residential area, not a desert."

A half-hour later, I left the trailer feeling a sort of dull self-contempt. How had I fooled myself into thinking we would ever know who committed these crimes? We couldn't get a consistent story on any point from any two people, and we didn't have the power to follow up on any of them. The police were either responding with clumsy mass vengeance or simply covering their rears. And at PRT intelligence, as in USAID, the kids were running the show.

• • •

"Mr. Joel?" The roar and hiss of the wind almost overwhelmed Haji Habibullah's voice on the phone. "I am at the gate. I have the translations."

Dusk tinges of orange and indigo were seeping into the hazy sky as I hurried to the PRT's main entrance. The Haji stood at the far end of the base's security cordon: two heavy iron booms, a metal detector, a long avenue winding through concrete blast barriers, and an inner and outer sentry hut, both manned by Afghan gunmen. Habibullah's lips were pursed, and when I reached him, he spoke with mournful vehemence. "I hate to see you like this. You come to the gate and have to walk out here to meet me. It is like you are in some prison."

"The safest kind of prison." I glanced around the dry moat of barbed wire. "I'm sorry you have to wait here, Haji-sahib. I'd invite you in if I could."

"It is nothing." Habibullah handed me a sheaf of papers, which I tucked gratefully under my arm. They were our employees' death certificates, translated into English for the life insurance company. "Do you have anything else for me, Mr. Joel?"

We stood there for a while in the blowing dust as I tried to think of something. Finally I shook my head. "No, Haji-sahib. I don't think there's anything else to do."

The sad-eyed Haji clasped my hands, bowed across the boom gate. These days, we ended every meeting as if it would be our last. "*De khuday paman*, Mr. Joel." Go with God. He trudged to his Corolla, and I turned back to the barricades.

That night in our rooms, I reviewed the certificates, which included all the nightmarish details I hadn't wanted to witness at the hospital. The dead in Babaji had been shot in the legs while trying to run, then finished off with shots to the chest and abdomen. *There was looking burning area too and it was considerable.* "Tracer," Charles guessed with clinical detachment. In any other context, the contorted Afghan-English syntax would have gotten a chuckle out of me. *His intestinal were out of his stomach which is considerable. The mentioned points were the cause of his deadness.*

I couldn't bear it. Each murder had some physical detail that set my mind writhing, those brief and monstrous superfluities: Khair's legs, Ehsan's eyes. I had read enough human rights reports and spoken to enough torture victims to know that these were small cruelties, in a country where violence and torture had long been key tools for demonstrating power. Still I choked on the horror my friends must have felt, shuddered at the pictures that flared across my mind.

I knew the murderers had acted to appall, to create precisely the rage and terror I was feeling. My own impulses to answer brutality with brutality, my momentary willingness to condone torture, would only feed into their game. No amount of viciousness by our police would overwhelm or deter this enemy. Meanwhile, the police's arbitrary mass arrests and torture of prisoners were sapping the Karzai government's most vital asset—the loyalty of its people. Justice should have been our tool against the killers. Within a week of the attacks, though, it was clear that no one in Helmand had the interest and capacity to solve the murders justly.

If vengeance was heinous folly and justice out of reach, what was left?

That final night, I sat up numbly for hours with Rick, tallying all our remaining afghanis so he could hand them back to the hawaladar for safekeeping. As the bundles of aid money sprawled into a multicolored cairn, I let go and drifted on the sounds of our prison. The whir and clatter of our cash-counting machines. The din of rotors in the blackness outside, where a military helicopter touched down invisibly from its clandestine mission. The throaty, defiant voice of Johnny Cash on Rick's stereo, singing about all the people who died in the belief that we were on their side.

Helmand at War

Lashkargah, Helmand—May 25, 2005

I left the PRT base for the last time on a cloudless, dusty morning with Yaqub and our recently hired Afghan-American road engineer, Muhammad Kabir Azamy—the final stragglers with U.S. passports, bound at last for Kabul. As our convoy rumbled through the middle of Lashkargah, Azamy leaned abruptly toward the window. "I used to live in this house." It was one of the old brick tract homes built for American engineers, its signature 1950s architecture now barely visible behind a high mud wall. "When I worked with HAVA before the war, the government gave my family this house to live in. One of my sons was born here." Azamy's eyes came alive with memories, but his seamed face remained melancholy. "I am sure now some commander is living in it.

"You know, they used to call this place Little America. There were no walls in Lashkargah, then. It was the law of the engineers who built the city: no walls. So many trees, and women walking in the streets without veils." Azamy shook his head in reverie.

"We lost it. We were divided, all of us fighting each other for so long. The walls went up, the trees were cut down. Now we cannot get back to the way things were."

I listened with a knot in my throat, unsure of what to say. Azamy painted a simple, poignant picture: a bright moment of civilization created by American good intentions and lost because of Afghan violence. On a much smaller scale, maybe that was the story of our project, too.

Or maybe there were less comfortable reasons that America's Afghan successes kept succumbing to disaster. Americans in Afghanistan tended to set grand targets and sprint straight at them. Our ambition and optimism were not entirely blind. The engineers who brought vast amounts of water to Nad-i-Ali in the 1950s knew about its possible soil salinity troubles. The CIA men who lavishly armed Gulbuddin in the 1980s understood that he was a power-hungry, fanatical drug trafficker who loathed America no less than Russia. The State Department reports on today's opium economy noted that eradication without alternatives might drive farmers into the Taliban camp.

America didn't deny these potential problems; it just ignored their scale and significance. Our policies focused relentlessly on the greater good—turning the desert green, toppling the Afghan Communists, slashing poppy cultivation—while trusting that bad consequences could be managed as they arose. In each case, we were reluctant to take a slower, more cautious approach, lest a window of opportunity be lost. We measured our success in simple numbers like acres irrigated, Communists killed, poppy fields eradicated; we didn't take the time to understand and address the deeper context of those numbers. And so America's work in Afghanistan was overturned not only by hostile external forces, but also by the foreseeable side effects of our own policies.

America was hardly alone in this record of fleeting triumphs and great stumbles. We could write similar stories of Little Russia, Little Pakistan, Little Iran, the moments and places where one country partly transformed Afghanistan into its own image. Each had ultimately collapsed, with an Afghan backlash financed and supported by other foreign powers. Each had left its enduring mark on the country. But no one outside or inside Afghanistan had yet succeeded in producing what ordinary Afghans craved most: stability, security, a road to self-sufficiency.

The Lashkargah airstrip was surrounded by its usual constellations of ragged, rowdy children that morning. They gazed on from a prudent distance as our armored Texan escorts made an orbit of the runway, tossed down a green smoke canister, signaled the PRT Air pilot to land. I wondered, with an ache of receding opportunity, what if any stories those children would tell about Little America. I wondered how much we had affected them, beyond the spectacle of our flights. *Khair, there's something I'd like you to check up on.*

Then I was hugging Charles and Rick in an absurdly abrupt good-bye, climbing aboard the Beechcraft plane, and rising out of Helmand in a tight, dizzy spiral.

• • •

I left Afghanistan at a time when Washington and the UN were cautiously celebrating a minor victory in the war on opium. The final numbers for 2005 weren't in yet, but it looked like national poppy cultivation would be about 20 percent below the 2004 record—the first shrinkage since the Taliban had lost power. "We're finally moving in the right direction," I heard from relieved counter-narcotics workers in Kabul. "Now we've got to keep the momentum going."

Yet after six months in Afghanistan's opium heartland, I was convinced that America was charging in the wrong direction. We were devoting vast resources to the problem of poppy cultivation while ignoring a more fundamental problem: the wretched state of the Afghan police. As long as the police remained a ragtag bunch of warlord-run militias, ordinary Afghans would not know security—and the lack of security was the great undertow eroding everything America was trying to accomplish in Afghanistan, including our narcotics policy.

The Afghan police were helpless to prevent the extraordinary wave of violence that swept the country in 2005. In the weeks after I left, all across once-calm Helmand, de-mining agencies were bombed, PRT patrols ambushed, local officials assassinated. In neighboring Kandahar, an eloquently anti-Taliban mullah was shot dead in broad daylight, in the middle of town. Three days later at his funeral, a bomb killed twenty people, including Kabul's respected police commander. Tellingly, the investigation of this high-profile murder was as amateurish and shambolic as anything we had seen in Babaji.

As the summer of 2005 ground bloodily onward, even optimists had to admit that these hardly looked like the last-ditch, desperate blows of a dwindling insurgency. While the U.S. military focused on storming their remote mountain strongholds, the resurgent Taliban were carrying out ambushes and bombings in previously stable areas. They aimed increasingly at soft targets: aid workers, teachers, religious leaders. NATO could tout the number of insurgents it had killed in the far corners of Uruzgan or Zabul, but the Taliban boasted a far more significant and alarming body count of assassinated *munafiqun*—traitors.

While winter usually brought a lull in fighting, the months after November 2005 saw an unremitting wave of suicide bombs. By the spring, Helmand had disintegrated into violence so ceaseless and dire that the rough-and-ready stability of my time there seemed as remote as the golden age of the 1970s. By spring 2006, it was also clear that the temporary dip in poppy was going to be overturned by a new record crop, both in Helmand and the country as a whole.

Lashkargah's obviously inadequate 110-man American PRT was replaced in June 2006 by a confident British force thirty times its size, which promised a new strategy of spreading "inkblots" of security and development. The Taliban responded at once with ferocious assaults that left the British reeling and reduced Helmand's proposed inkblot areas to scorch marks. The insurgents also attacked the recently arrived Canadians in Kandahar and the Dutch in Uruzgan, trying to inflict enough casualties to destroy political support for the war back home.

I followed all this horrifying news from London, trying to reconcile what I was reading with the Helmand I knew. The government buildings where we had chewed over ideas and savory pilau with shura members; the starkly beautiful slopes around the Kajaki reservoir; the muddy tracks our men had repaired; the earth-walled villages where we had blithely hired thousands of laborers—all were now seeing regular pitched battles and NATO air strikes. A shaky-sounding Farid commiserated with me on the phone: "Do you remember the days when Yaqub Roshan could get into a pickup and drive to Baghran with only six police? Oh my God." The Rais-i-Baghran had cut off his rapprochement with the government, and was once more enthusiastically assisting the Taliban. I reminded Farid of my impromptu motorbike ride in lower Kajaki with two guards and no interpreter. Farid began laughing uncontrollably, unable to say anything but, "Oh my God. Oh my God."

• • •

Afghanistan badly needed a professional army and police force to defend against this Taliban resurgence—though the ultimate source of the problem, most Afghans agreed, was across the border. "Look at the map," a Helmandi friend pronounced flatly. "It is the regions that touch Pakistan that have these problems. Pakistani intelligence has never stopped helping the Taliban. They want Afghans to be ruled by uneducated mullahs, so we will be easy to control." President Karzai openly accused Pakistan of trying to destabilize his country, and threatened to return the favor.

President Musharraf continued to angrily reject the accusations. Yet a host of witnesses confirmed that the onslaught in Afghanistan was being openly orchestrated by militants in the Pakistani cities of Quetta and Peshawar. The insurgents' bold, coordinated assaults and their painstaking campaign to encircle Kandahar in 2006 showed a remarkably advanced level of strategic planning, intelligence, and communications. The Taliban had always relied on the Pakistani military for those capacities in the past. Within a year of the attacks on our project, only the most optimistic or diplomatic observers would still describe Pakistan's policy toward the Taliban as a selective blind eye. The evidence suggested, rather, that the Pakistani government was one of the main forces stoking the insurgency across the border.

Pakistan's basic interests in Afghanistan had never changed. Musharraf's government wanted a pliable neighbor that wouldn't try to redraw the border, sponsor Pakistani ethnic separatists, or allow India a platform for mischief. The new Karzai regime was unreliable on all three counts. Meanwhile, plenty of Pakistani officers were profitably immersed in the Afghan war economy, whether in guns, drugs, or smuggling. All of those interests were best served by keeping Afghanistan unstable.

The Bush administration couldn't respond by just consigning Pakistan to the axis of evil. Musharraf still offered America measured but vital cooperation in tasks like rolling up al-Qaeda and restraining nuclear proliferation. Getting Pakistan sincerely to reverse its decades-old policies toward Afghanistan would be a colossal diplomatic challenge. It wasn't simply a question of offering the right sticks and carrots, but also of trying to change the factors that made a strong Afghanistan threatening to Pakistan—a process that would require some difficult concessions on the Afghan side as well.

That meant the Taliban insurgency was here for the long haul. NATO couldn't knock it out by sheer military might, by search-and-destroy missions, or by cutting off its drug money—not as long as the militants enjoyed an untouchable haven in the tribal zones and as much support as the Pakistani military deemed prudent. America needed to refocus its strategy for the long haul. We needed to defend and secure the areas that the Kabul government could control, and win over ordinary Afghans in those areas by providing prosperity and protection.

So far, America had put a lot of resources and effort into building a new Afghan army, which would be vital for confronting large insurgent forces (and keeping Afghan warlords in line). But the army wasn't built to meet the security needs of ordinary Afghans. It couldn't protect them from assault, theft, rape, or extortion. It couldn't investigate murder or trafficking. As the Taliban carried out more kidnappings, school burnings, and attacks on civilian targets, the police-shaped hole in Afghanistan's security became ever more glaring.

• • •

I could see that hole most clearly, personally, and painfully when it came to the choices it forced on development agencies targeted by criminals or insurgents. I thought back to the stark response of Médecins sans Frontières, clos-

ing all of its Afghan projects to protest the lack of any investigation or prosecution after its staff members were killed in June 2004. "The inaction of the
Afghan authorities sends a signal of impunity for the murderers," MSF had
angrily stated. If the police and other government authorities were too corrupt or weak to protect aid agencies, what could the agencies do when they
were explicitly targeted except pull out?

The murders of our staff, likewise, were never seriously investigated before or after I left. There was a flutter of activity in May 2005. USAID director Patrick Fine, who had given our team such a candid and scathing greeting
in November, flew down to Helmand to "express his concern" to the governor—I hoped with equal candor. The Kabul police sent down an inspector,
General Akbar, to inquire into the murders.

Nothing came of any of it. The Bolan commander handed over his top
suspects (including the man Farid had arrested) to the Amniyat in Lashkargah, who questioned and released them all. "I reckon the guy running the intelligence police made a phone call to someone more senior and got the order
to let the bastards go," Charles said bitterly. Down in the Darweshan area,
the district police identified a likely suspect in the bombing of our convoy: a
former Taliban intelligence officer, who was reportedly having trouble getting poppy labor for his fields. By the time Charles had reached the police
station, this suspect too had been released. "A few dozen of his neighbors
came and asked the police to let him go. Said he was a nice guy, that they'd
got the wrong man." Charles gave an incredulous bark of a laugh. "A nice
guy. He's pissed off into the mountains now."

Within two weeks, all of the random prisoners from Babaji were freed,
apparently without yielding a single lead. One by one, the shura members
who had signed our security guarantee shrugged it off, saying, "The attack
didn't happen in *my* village." Elder Priam, who couldn't say that, bristled fe-
rociously at any suggestion of responsibility and remained untouched by the
police. It turned out that his cousin was a militia leader in Babaji, on the
Akhundzada side of the area's bitter feud. The well-meaning General Akbar
from Kabul nosed around for a couple of days and gave us his report in five
simple points:

1. No one in the Helmand police force was qualified to carry out an
   investigation.
2. General Akbar could not send a qualified officer to conduct an
   investigation because he could not protect him.
3. Governor Sher Muhammad did not have time to see him.

4. The Helmand police commander was uncooperative.
5. The people of Babaji had roughly eighty thousand automatic weapons and would not permit an investigation.

It was hard to illustrate "impunity" any better than that.

But unlike Médecins sans Frontières, the United States government wasn't about to pull its development workers out of southern Afghanistan. That would be too serious an admission of defeat. Most major American policy makers acknowledged, at least by way of lip service, that the way to beat the insurgency was to win ordinary Afghans' hearts and minds with reconstruction projects. The British and other NATO allies believed even more passionately in the decisiveness of development. So also, to judge from their target list, did the Taliban.

These facts led to a growing tough-mindedness at USAID. "Look, there's a reason you consultants in Afghanistan get danger pay," one official said bluntly—though Taliban attacks almost never hit foreign consultants, and the Afghan staff who were in danger enjoyed no such bonuses. At a Washington conference, a brusque senior USAID manager spoke about "acceptable casualties" for development projects in southern Afghanistan. "I was stunned," an aid agency director told us afterward. "That's just not language I was comfortable with." Any organization working in a war zone had to recognize the risk of death, of course, but there was a world of difference between planning for acceptable risks and planning for acceptable casualties.

Some of USAID's contractors declined to play ball. The team repairing the Kajaki Dam insisted that before they began real work, they needed NATO troops to establish a secure five-kilometer perimeter to protect their camp from mortar fire. Security had to come first, reconstruction second. Chemonics, by contrast, was petrified of losing its USAID money to rival contractors who were ready to work to the last Afghan. The company was desperate to get its projects restarted and prove to USAID that it could still meet its targets under fire.

Jim Graham obstinately refused to be hurried. "Acceptable casualties" was the antithesis of everything about him—his fierce loyalty toward his team, his insistence that we not sacrifice our health and sanity to the job. "Until we have militarized our 'development' project," Jim repeated with weary bitterness, "the project's operations will remain locked down." Charles was negotiating with private security companies to set up a robust, expensive defense platform that wouldn't rely on Afghan police. In the meantime, Jim refused to head back to work under USPI's dubious protection. He suggested that the project's ambitious targets had to change, given the security situation. He also recommended that they not resume work in the chaotic lead-up to the September 2005 parliamentary elections.

All this was too much for Chemonics' executives, who unceremoniously sacked Jim for obstructing the project. This had a predictable effect on the morale and effectiveness of the rest of the expatriate team; most quit or were dismissed within a few months. The company eventually replaced Jim with Ray Baum, our swashbuckling Go Team leader.

• • •

I was torn and not a little angry as I followed these struggles over how best to protect USAID development workers. I remembered Charles's initial comment—"You guys don't want to be out there bringing jobs at gunpoint, right?" I was still intensely uncomfortable with the militarization of development. Now it was accelerating, even though the U.S. government had no institutions that were particularly good at it. The PRTs tried clumsily to do development projects while USAID contractors tried clumsily to protect themselves, all in the name of getting schools and cash-for-work into the most dangerous provinces in the country.

On the one hand, it felt like the kind of mistake America had made before in Afghanistan: the setting of a target and sprinting at it despite all obstacles, determined to hit it before a window of opportunity closed. Maybe we should be stepping back and asking what exactly we hoped to achieve by bringing "development" to places where there was no functioning government or security. Why not begin with a campaign to secure and develop the areas of relative peace, places where development agencies could work without bringing their own army? Why not begin, above all, by putting serious effort and resources into reforming the police and prosecuting the traffickers and criminals in government?

On the other hand, maybe places like Baghran and Deh Rawud wouldn't accept police or government, however reformed, unless that government was already providing benefits like roads, clinics, or electricity. Some kinds of development work could produce lasting results even under fire. We might not have the luxury of doing things in the safest order.

Even if that were the case, "acceptable casualties" was not a principle that we could just graft onto a reconstruction project along with a higher security budget and danger pay. When I was hiring our Afghan staff, especially field workers like engineers and paymasters, I had assured them that we wouldn't knowingly send them into places where the risk of attack was too great or our security inadequate. That was the norm for development work.

If we were going to change that norm, we would need to change it explicitly. We would need to tell every person we hired, "We will be heading into the nastiest places, the Baghrans and the Babajis, because the American and Afghan governments are determined to win over the people there. We can be fairly sure that this will bring attacks from insurgents, criminals, and drug traffickers. We will go with the best security money can buy, but we know it won't prevent every attack." We would need to build a culture more like that of a police or army squad, where planning for "acceptable casualties" was a tragedy but not a betrayal. We couldn't just assume that Afghans who took USAID jobs were willing foot soldiers in the escalating war over development.

In reality, the militarization of development as currently practiced by most PRTs and USAID projects tended to involve much *less* travel into insurgent-friendly areas. The foreign staff would bunker down in a secure fortress, hire Afghan contractors to carry out quick-impact projects, make a couple of heavily armed monitoring visits if they thought it was safe, and bring back photos and numbers to declare success. I thought about the corruption that our relatively hands-on project had experienced in Marja, where a dozen of our workers had ended up harvesting poppy. I just couldn't imagine how development-from-the-bunker could possibly avoid graft on an even more scandalous scale.

Ultimately, we had no good model for carrying out development in a place where we were being targeted for murder. Most organizations that tried wound up at one of two dead ends: a retreat or a bunker.

That impasse made the creation of a professional Afghan army and police all the more vital. Only they had a chance at establishing and expanding the islands of security where international development agencies—and more importantly, Afghan teachers, development workers, and local officials—could produce lasting benefits.

• • •

In June 2005, some audacious Afghan counter-narcotics officers raided Governor Sher Muhammad's mansion in Lashkargah, with support from America's Drug Enforcement Agency. They discovered the largest single cache of opium the DEA had found anywhere in Afghanistan—nine metric tons, enough to make well over a ton of heroin. Sher Muhammad coolly replied that he had confiscated it from drug traffickers, and was only storing it until he could dispose of it properly. President Karzai chose to accept this excuse. No amount of evidence, it seemed, could bring down the wily wali.

Sher Muhammad Akhundzada was a perfect illustration of the main obstacle to both police reform and counter-narcotics work in Afghanistan: the indispensable warlord. All across Afghanistan, the police were dominated by thugs and traffickers, but as long as they kept their regions more or less quiet, the Kabul government was loath to crack down on their criminal activities. President Karzai seemed determined to keep as many power brokers as possible bound into his government. The most punishment a warlord could expect was being shuffled into a distant, weaker position if he failed to meet government expectations in his current one.

Eventually the nimble Sher Muhammad did fall victim to this shuffle. His aura of indispensability began to flicker as his province collapsed into carnage. Then, six months after the 2005 harvest, the UN's annual opium report revealed that Helmand's poppy fields had dwindled by a paltry 10 percent—nothing like the 80 percent Sher Muhammad had promised, or even the 30 to 40 percent estimated by Kabul's inspectors. The UN satellites showed a surge in remote districts like Nawzad or Baghran, largely offsetting the governor's mild eradication. Helmand had still produced fully a quarter of Afghanistan's opium.

In December 2005, the British government quietly insisted that President Karzai remove the tainted Sher Muhammad before Britain took over the Helmand PRT. Karzai appointed his old friend to the upper house of the Afghan parliament, replacing him as governor with a lackluster but honest technocrat. To keep the Akhundzadas inside the fold, Karzai gave the post of deputy governor of Helmand to the ex-wali's red-bearded, limping younger brother, Amir Muhammad. Senator Sher Muhammad headed irritably off to Kabul, joining a score of other alleged traffickers in parliament—including Mir Wali and Amir Dado from Helmand.

In spring 2006, as poppy cultivation in Helmand reached new heights and the Taliban advanced across the province, a desperate Karzai sent Sher Muhammad back to Lashkargah—not as wali, but as warlord. The president wanted to know if the former governor could enlist an "auxiliary police" force to fight the insurgents. Sher Muhammad, who had complained about arming our twenty guards, confidently declared that he could muster five hundred gunmen within a week.

His new militia wouldn't include the Akhundzada gunmen we knew best. Our former Kajaki guard captain, Hayat Khan, was a casualty of the spring 2006 eradication campaign. A self-proclaimed Taliban group had ordered the farmers of lower Helmand to plant poppy and promised to protect them from the police tractors. Deputy Governor Amir Muhammad sent Hayat Khan's squad police south to confront the interlopers and eradicate their poppy. The Taliban-hating captain died as he had lived, clashing bloodily with insurgents near the grand narco-bazaar of Baramcha on the Pakistan border. Hayat Khan's hawk-faced, sullen nephew inherited his command and withdrew the surviving police to Kajaki. "Now people are saying that the nephew joined the Taliban and is fighting against the government," a Helmandi friend reported bleakly.

• • •

Helmand needed more reliable police than Sher Muhammad Akhundzada could possibly provide. That was illustrated all too painfully in the lives of my Afghan friends in the months after I left. Farid and Raz both received death threats for their work with the Americans; Nazar, our canny logistics officer, spent three months recovering from a beating by a militia commander's thugs, after he accidentally bumped into the commander's Land Cruiser on his motorbike. The Helmand police offered no meaningful protection against any of this violence.

Unfortunately, the West's police reform program still barely existed. The German government continued to run its officer academy in Kabul. In 2006, the American government expanded its meager training program to a few more provincial centers, including Lashkargah. One of my friends worked there for a while. I asked him how many Helmandi police had gone through the classroom during his months there. "It was a slow start . . . fourteen, and then fifty police," my friend replied diffidently. All of the trainees had been from Lashkargah; training the rural police who were facing insurgents on a daily basis was still a pipe dream. "They didn't do good in attendance. One day we had eight instructors and four students."

To create an Afghan police force that was protective rather than predatory, the Karzai government and its foreign sponsors would have to do a lot better than that. They would have to confront the powerful warlords who currently used the police as a home for their militias and an escort service for their opium convoys. They would need to reform the Ministry of the Interior, setting up new branches for public complaints and corruption investigations. They would need to phase out the existing militias and organize new police units—as they had done with the Afghan National Army. Western countries would need to send field-based mentors to be embedded with the police units, instead of just funding classroom training. They would also need to provide equipment, and a level of pay high enough to discourage extortion and bribe-taking.

All of this was a huge, daunting, messy task; there was no way it would be done quickly or soon. Yet that was true of everything we were doing in Afghanistan—certainly of rebuilding the army, or of our ill-fated efforts to take on the opium trade. And police reform was a more fundamental problem than counter-narcotics.

We had come to Helmand thinking of opium as the local currency, and had tried to replace it with cash. But *security* was the real currency of Afghanistan. The traumatized population of Helmand would trade almost anything for it, follow anyone who could offer it. Afghans desperately wanted a government that could protect them from violence, theft, and extortion. If the police couldn't provide that protection, the people would fall back on a second-best option: warlords, opium traders, Taliban. And in the absence of security, they would keep planting poppy.

Badakhshan

Dear Joel:

Now that the honeymoon is over, how about spending two to five months in
lovely Badakhshan? . . . Security is the best in the country. The apricots are
in bloom, the sun is out and the birds sinning.

I laughed out loud when I first got Jim Graham's invitation. It was the spring
of 2006, and going back to Afghanistan was the furthest thing from my new-
lywed mind. Fiona and I had been married on January 14, 2006, seven and a
half months after I left Helmand. ("If I had known you were leaving us so
long before your marriage, I would have stolen your passport," Haji Habibullah had grouchily informed me.) I had been writing ever since I got to England, to pay the bills and purge the ghosts, and expected to keep writing for
the next year or so. Fiona and I planned to work in Asia again eventually, but
not for a while—and I had promised her that if we went anywhere, it would
be together, to a place where we both wanted to work.

Meanwhile, within six months of being fired from Chemonics, Jim had
been rehired by another USAID contractor to run their alternatives-to-
poppy program. It was basically the same job, but in the northeastern
province of Badakhshan instead of southern Helmand. Jim had already
brought in Johannes Oosterkamp to have a look at the local irrigation systems, and he was talking to USAID about hiring Charles for a security assessment. Now he wanted me to recruit and train Afghan managers for a new
cash-for-work department.

I told Jim that it sounded tempting, but I didn't think it would fit in with our lives right now. Still, I mentioned the invitation to Fiona, and she unexpectedly replied, "See if he could use you for six weeks—and ask how reliable their Internet connection is." Fi's job, with an Oklahoma-based international reforestation group, was flexible enough that she could take six weeks working part-time by e-mail. She had lived the terrors of Afghanistan vicariously along with me; for both our sakes, she wanted a chance to see the side of the country that I loved.

Badakhshan was safe by Afghan standards, I told our uneasy family and friends as we began making plans. It was the one province that had always remained entirely free of Taliban control, and the insurgents had no reach there today. "So all we have to worry about are tribal feuds and drug lords," I admitted dryly. I knew there were aid agencies working comfortably all over Badakhshan; many had been operating there in relative safety since the Afghan-Soviet War. Fiona spoke with a couple that were interested in having her as a part-time volunteer. The northeast seemed about as friendly a place for development work as anywhere in the country.

But as Jim Graham was always ready to point out, "First and foremost, these projects are about drugs, not development." On May 30, a week before we were due to fly out to Afghanistan, Rick Breitenstein e-mailed me. Though he was still working with Chemonics in Lashkargah, Rick was writing to find out if *I* was safe. "I heard the Alternative Livelihoods Project in Badakhshan was hit by an IED and two people were killed."

The news came as an almost physical blow—it was as if we were about to fly back into the same disaster I had left. Jim's voice was flat and raw as he confirmed the murders to me over the phone. "We've now lost thirteen people in fifty-four weeks. USAID needs to think seriously about how they're doing this whole alternative livelihoods thing."

The attack had come in a secluded valley, Derayem, which was filled mountain to mountain with poppy. A few staff from Jim's project had been driving around the district, taking photographs and satellite readings of repaired canals. At a culvert just outside Derayem town, a concealed bomb took out the lead Land Cruiser. The two Afghans in the front died; the two Americans in the backseat survived with minor fractures. I remembered Charles's bleak comment on the Darweshan blast: "You can't push a button much more accurately than that." Eventually an Afghan police detachment had driven up to Derayem to rescue the survivors. The German commander of the Badakhshan PRT had refused to send any of his troops because the situation was too dangerous.

No one seriously attributed the attack to insurgents. The only question was whether the murderers had mistaken the vehicle for a drug eradication team, or had knowingly targeted the USAID alternatives-to-poppy project. We knew that the investigation was unlikely to turn up any culprits, or any solid answers. A haggard Jim asked me to postpone our trip for a couple of weeks, while he and his team figured out what their next steps had to be.

In the end, perhaps inevitably, they decided that most of Badakhshan was still safe enough to continue their work as planned. "We're tightening up the security we've got," Jim told me simply, "and I've got Charlie Watt coming in on the next plane. We aren't sending our people to any district where we think there's serious danger. If you're still willing to come, we could still use the help."

For a few days more, Fiona and I agonized and prayed, dithered and questioned. The illusion of relative safety was gone. We had to decide how much we were willing to risk for a chance to see if we could work in the country together. I wasn't convinced that cash-for-work was a particularly productive use of Western development money, but USAID required it, and it now seemed more important than ever to back Jim up in his insistence that we plan our activities without any "acceptable casualties." At the end of the day, Fi and I still felt it was worth going to accomplish whatever we could. On June 19, we flew out to Kabul.

The trip didn't offer much by way of reunion with old friends. By the time we arrived, Jim Graham himself was on extended medical leave in the States, and Johannes was due to depart in a week. Several of my young friends from Helmand tried to make time to meet us in Kabul, but found themselves stuck in the south. Raz, now ebulliently bearded and turbaned and working in a different city, wasn't able to get any time off work. Nabi had a job as a translator for a distant military outpost. Farid was holed up in a bunker to escape the insurgents who were trying to kill him—though thankfully, Charles soon succeeded in finding him a safer job outside Helmand.

Impatient to see me again and to meet my now perfectly respectable wife, Haji Habibullah implored me to find a flight down to Lashkargah. When I unhappily but firmly demurred, he tried to find some safe way of coming up to Kabul himself. "As you know, the present situation in southern Afghanistan, it is very dangerous," the disconsolate Haji finally explained. That was an understatement; the grand clash between the Taliban and the incoming British army was getting under way, with dozens of mostly Afghan casualties every week. "There are no flights this week and the road situation is not secured. We will have to pray God to save us until we see each other once again."

"Inshallah, Haji-sahib," I replied, aching to hear our resourceful old patriarch so hopeless and downcast.

The only friend from Helmand Fiona and I met during our single day in Kabul was Yaqub Roshan. He seemed to have pulled through the horror of the previous year; the Zabul killings were now just one more of the many streaks of sadness set against his jovial, irrepressible passion to rebuild Afghanistan. He had finally found a proper government liaison job, between Chemonics and the Ministry of Counter-Narcotics in Kabul. Yaqub was clearly still feeling the tug of the wilder corners of the country, though, and we reminisced for hours about our travels in Kajaki, Musa Qala, and Nawzad. "It was good that we were there, Joel," Yaqub said wistfully. "Our jobs were the one good thing the government brought in some of those Taliban areas."

"It wasn't enough," I countered somberly. "Just look at those places now. The government has got to bring more than just cash-for-work. Better police. And real alternatives to poppy, not just short-term filler."

My Afghan-American friend sighed and nodded reluctantly. "Still—I will always be a little sad that we could not work in Baghran. Or in Deh Rawud. Who else will bring help to such places?"

Faizabad, Badakhshan—June 21, 2006

The next morning, Fi and I were off into unfamiliar territory again, flying northeast from Kabul. Fiona was wearing her pale blue headscarf and voluminous clothes, and staring out the airplane window with some apprehension. The craggy terrain below us rippled past in drab shades of gray, with ice glazing the heights. Far off to the east were the gigantic, azure peaks of Chitral, looming higher than the clouds, higher than our plane. "It's all so barren," Fiona murmured at last—and my memory was wrenched back to my first flight over the Hindu Kush, gazing into the desiccated crags, wondering whether I would find more in Afghanistan than emptiness and danger.

Our initial weeks in Badakhshan felt a lot like my first trip to Kabul in 2003, thanks to the tight security after the Derayem murders. We always traveled by vehicle, and mostly kept to the circle between the office and the staff house. We spent most of our time hemmed in not only by compound walls but by the steep, gritty slopes that enclosed Faizabad, the little provincial capital.

I looked on as Fiona was engulfed by a storm of claustrophobia and isolation similar to what I had felt when I first reached Afghanistan. The two of us stayed in an air-conditioned room with misted glass windows and heavy curtains that blocked the view but not the ever-present dust. From the staff house roof, we could see the stars and the stony ridgelines, but high panels screened out our view of the town around us. Twice, Fi and I went for walks around the block to have tea with our neighbors; the security guys strongly advised us against walking the extra few blocks to the bazaar.

The strictures on women added to Fiona's general sense of alienation, though as a Westerner she could get away with half-compliance. She befriended the Afghan women in the office, joined them for a wedding celebration, went clothes shopping with them in the bazaar. "It's so strange to see the burqa come down as soon as they step outside the office," she said pensively. "I sit beside Maliya in the car when she pulls her burqa over her face—and then the woman I'm talking to is indistinguishable from all the other women around. Women can't recognize their friends on the street, unless they recognize their voices or the hem of their clothes."

The burqa was just as widespread among the Taliban-loathing Tajiks of Badakhshan as it had been among the Taliban-sympathizing Pashtuns of Helmand. In part, this was because conservative readings of Islam and gender crossed ethnic and political boundaries. But in part, the veiling was one more consequence of Afghanistan's pervasive lack of security. "When the Communists were in control of Faizabad," one of my male Afghan colleagues reminisced, "women walked around the city with their faces uncovered. Then the mujahidin drove out the Russians—and there were hundreds of weddings in Badakhshan. All these gunmen came into town, and when they saw a girl they liked, they would demand to marry her. Who could say no? Fathers veiled their daughters to keep the commanders and gunmen from knowing whether she was beautiful." He shrugged sadly. "Before the burqa goes, the guns will have to go."

The walls, the guns, the threat of bombs, the confinement of women—what had I invited Fiona into? I had hoped to show her the side of the country that I loved. But my closest Afghan friends were trapped in a war zone, and in supposedly safe Badakhshan, it seemed that all Fi was seeing was Afghanistan at its most repressive and forbidding.

• • •

Charles Watt arrived in Faizabad not long after we did. The blunt-featured New Zealander seemed gentler than I remembered, even from the days before our disastrous retreat in Helmand. I wondered if he was just toning it down for Fiona, but she clearly liked him even in his rougher-edged moments, and he had the same ease when he and I were alone. "I'm a little rusty, mate," he admitted one evening with a rueful grin. "I have to put all this on the shelf when I'm at home. Otherwise my wife would divorce me, and my kid would grow up scared of me. Or be a mite scary himself."

If he was rusty, it didn't show in his work. Charles quickly whipped out a security plan and began building on the project's existing guards and resources. At first, our conversations focused on immediate needs, how to protect the program from drug-related violence. Inevitably, that led to talk about the collapse of our Helmand project, and to the question that I had been wanting to ask Charles in person: "So what do you think happened to us?"

"We put together some of the picture, mate," Charles replied grimly. "We can't know for sure, but I can tell you my best guess."

My old hunger for information blazed up again. "Shoot."

"When USAID and the PRT gave up on the investigation, I went around and dug up what I could—informants in Helmand, people with the right connections in Kabul and Kandahar. A lot of people had something to say. Back in those days, it was a pretty high-profile hit." In today's Helmand, eleven people killed by the Taliban scarcely counted as news.

"The Taliban who killed our boys left a trail," Charles continued, warming to the tale. "There were twenty of them, coming in on motorbikes across the Pakistan border; the border guards on both sides were ordered to look the other way. All twenty were seen in Garmser, down south, two days before the murder. Then they went to Babaji, and stayed with the old crying man who had our boys over for lunch."

I listened unhappily. My old anger hadn't entirely died, but I had no illusions that it would accomplish anything here. Plus, I was skeptical that Babaji had any reliable sources, let alone ones who knew what went on inside Elder Priam's house.

"Of those twenty Taliban, only six went after our guys. That says a bloody lot. It means they knew our guys only had one guard, and they knew a place to make a clean hit. Those six killers were spotted a day later in Farah province. The second crew hung around, sniffing for their second hit." Charles paused to lend his next words emphasis. "Those were the terms of their contract—it was a two-hit contract."

"Wait," I said, head spinning. "A contract made by whom?"

Charles inclined his head. "I think the basic story is pretty simple, mate. We had fourteen thousand workers in Helmand during the harvest season. That was making it hard for some powerful people to bring in their opium. They were willing to look the other way until we threatened their profits, but once we hit the magic number of workers—and we don't know exactly what number that was—they called in a gang of Taliban to get rid of us. And police all over the province looked the other way. That's what I was told, and I believe it."

I frowned, tried to reorient myself to the idea. "But we were hearing about excess labor coming out of Nangarhar. We were sure that whatever we were doing, we weren't actually starving the opium labor market."

"There was a big poppy crop in Kandahar," Charles countered darkly. "The workers from Nangarhar weren't making it to Helmand. Not enough of them, anyway, not to the landowners who took out the contract on us."

For some reason, the irony of the theory overwhelmed me. *They were contractors, determined to hit their targets.* It was the jargon of our project, turned bloodily on its head. I wondered if the assassin squad had won praise for their quick deployment and flexible implementation. I also wondered who we would threaten most by hitting a "magic number" that unacceptably shrank the labor pool. The drug lords should have been able to beat our wage levels; but the Taliban insurgents were currently paying young Helmandis five dollars a day to attack the best-equipped armies in the world. Our four-dollar wage might have looked pretty competitive to them.

I wasn't willing to accept the story at face value—not after our time in the PRT watching the contradictory rumors multiply in the wake of the murder. Still, the fact that it was plausible spoke volumes about the tangle of criminality, insurgency, and government corruption in Helmand.

• • •

But that wasn't the last word. After two weeks stuck in Faizabad, I started riding around rural Badakhshan with a handful of Afghan colleagues to launch cash-for-work activities. Fiona headed even farther afield, into the heights of the Pamir mountains, volunteering with an agency that was hunting for medicinal plants. She spent weeks meeting with the shuras of far-flung villages, surveying their traditional medical knowledge and carefully collecting plant samples for the University of Kabul lab. On the back roads of Badakhshan, Fi got to see more of what drew me to Afghanistan: the people's cheer and resourcefulness, their hospitality despite grinding poverty, the beautiful ferocity of the terrain, the intense camaraderie of work in a volatile land.

We left notes for each other on our travels. Our paths didn't cross often, but once we managed to meet up for lunch in the valley of Baharak. Fi looked utterly exhausted but happy as she related the many challenges and little triumphs of the past week. Surrounded by Afghan development workers, we conducted our reunion without touching each other—though I slipped once and brushed her hand in a moment of thoughtless reassurance. Then I had to leave for another district shura meeting, and my wife was off to the Tajikistan border.

Meanwhile, I was on the road for between five and twelve hours a day, which was grueling but marvelous. Each district of Badakhshan had its own distinctive character. Steep Shuhada was a spectacular canyon lined with golden wheat terraces, dark cherry orchards, and hot springs. The Jurm valley was broader and more barren, interrupted by deep green wedges of forest and field where nourishing streams broke out of the mountains. In the fertile highlands of Khash, the streams were densely lined with a reed used for classical Persian calligraphy pens, and the roads were brazenly lined with poppy fields. We drove past the sites of grand mujahidin massacres, and lunched near the centuries-old shrine of a warrior saint.

The main road connecting Badakhshan to the outside world followed the Kokcha River through a glorious wilderness: dun and silver mountains leaping up at unbelievable angles, sawtooth ridgelines stippled with wild pistachio trees, broad deltas of flood-tossed stone and sand bursting from small side gorges. Periodically the river valley widened enough to allow villages, forests, and fields (including rice paddies, a particularly extravagant contrast with the desert landscape). For most of its length, though, the Kokcha was pent up between high cliffs of dense-packed pebbles and dust. The road was an eight-foot-wide shelf chewed away by landslides above, the river below, and the groaning Russian Kamaz trucks plying its rutted surface. In places the road swooped up so steeply that our Land Cruiser strained to crest the rise; I had no idea how the trucks loaded with four tons of watermelon made it.

During these weeks of work on the road, I became friends with the ever-resourceful Engineer Zafer and the brilliant young Shafaq, who would be running the cash-for-work program. I bonded with the drivers, swapping wedding stories and jokes and singing songs to pass the time between towns. With wicked grins, they introduced me to *shoor chai*, the standard breakfast tea of Badakhshan—a salty brown broth with gobs of floating curd. It reminded me of the Tibetan tea I used to drink on treks in Nepal, and to my hosts' delight, I downed bowls of the stuff with naan every morning. I would gladly have spent my life in such places, with such people.

We avoided districts where there was poppy harvesting or other clear dangers. Our only encounter with the province's traffickers came on the road southwest of Faizabad, when we drove past two new Land Cruisers surrounded by fretful-looking gunmen. They turned out to be heroin smugglers with a flat tire. Waving down the second car in our convoy, they requested the use of its spare as far as the Tajik border. Our stolid engineer told the traffickers that he was heading in the wrong direction for Tajikistan, and would probably need the spare tire himself. They waved him on glumly.

"Those were Nasirmad's men," our driver informed us, the anxiety in his voice quenching my amusement. Nasir Muhammad, generally known by the shortened form of his name, was the dominant warlord and opium trafficker of Faizabad. The German PRT relied on his "police" to guard their base on the outskirts of town. In some ways, clearly, Badakhshan wasn't that different from Helmand.

Yet before leaving the province, I found a difference that stayed with me. The high mountain district of Tagab could have grown poppy in its steep terraces, but by the accounts of all my Afghan coworkers, it was basically opium-free. And that turned out to be one of the least impressive things about Tagab.

It was the last region that Engineer Zafer and I visited. The previous day we had driven around the broad valley of Kishim, one of Badakhshan's most fertile regions and a plentiful poppy producer. The many-branched ravines of Tagab extended back from a gap in the hills around Kishim, rising swiftly toward dusty purplish-gray peaks. As we juddered along the dirt road, I realized that the majority of passersby returned my smiles and nodded or raised a hand in greeting. I hadn't seen that in other valleys like Jurm or Khash, where the farmers eyed passing vehicles suspiciously—and I certainly hadn't seen it in Helmand. Tagab seemed to be an area where the villagers welcomed Westerners in Land Cruisers as a positive sign, not a potential threat.

Thanks to its gimlet-eyed and unrelenting leader, Tagab was also a place where those Westerners in their Land Cruisers could be made very uncomfortable. Haji Awrang was a small man, fine-boned and fine-bearded, whose relaxed, disarming smile did not quite soften the intensity of his stare. He appeared to be an extraordinarily rare creature: a former mujahidin leader who had come out of the Afghan-Soviet War without a reputation for monstrosity, surrendered his guns and opium, run for parliament, and was focused on delivering legal development to a constituency that admired rather than feared him.

When Western aid agencies praised Afghan leaders as "focused on development," they usually meant that those leaders were happy to cooperate with the aid agencies' agendas. Awrang flintily insisted on setting the agenda, monitoring every donor project in Tagab to prevent any corruption or mismanagement. If he found that a Western organization was being lazy in its own monitoring, or had hired a known drug trafficker or other undesirable, he would expel its project from Tagab.

Our project was hardly immune from his skepticism. "The United States claims that it is spending sixty million dollars on alternative livelihoods in Badakhshan," Awrang said with a sardonic grin. "I think it has given a sixty-million-dollar loan to an American company. I will be watching to see how much of that borrowed money the company spends on the people of Badakhshan. I will tell the Afghan parliament what I find, and I will tell USAID. I am sure that USAID wants its companies to be accountable."

Topping off the sense that Awrang was too good to be true, he was also an ardent conservationist. All across Badakhshan, we had spoken to shuras who mourned the loss of the once-extensive forests on the mountain ridges. "The Soviets began bombing the trees, because the mujahidin could hide there," Engineer Zafer had explained to me. "The people decided that if the forests were going to be burned by the Soviets, they would cut down the trees and sell them first. So now the forests are gone." In Tagab, Haji Awrang had declared a ban on cutting wild trees, and we could see the results: small, tough saplings fighting their way back up the colossal slopes. He had also banned fishing in the rivers (to keep the fish supply sustainable downstream) and hunting wild animals, such as the famous Marco Polo sheep in the high passes (in the extraordinary hopes of one day attracting ecotourism).

Tagab was safe. Every Afghan I spoke to agreed that if I had wanted to walk from one end of the district to the other, I would be fine. Awrang's deal with the people didn't depend on force or threats, but on his continued supply of benefits and his own reputation for honesty. As far as I could see, he was trying to cast himself as the new Ahmad Shah Massoud, and wanted to keep his reputation untainted by corruption and poppy. In parliament, many of his allies and one-time military comrades were traffickers; but by all I could discover, Awrang was genuinely determined to make Tagab work without poppy.

Nothing I had seen in Helmand had prepared me for this—and I was leaving before I could investigate it, before I had any way of knowing whether this spectacular little cluster of valleys could be all that it promised. Haji Awrang saw my hope and invited me to stay in Tagab for an extra day. I asked him if I could bring my wife back to show her the medicinal plants of the valley. So in our last days in Afghanistan, Fiona and I drove up the boulder-lined track into Tagab.

Haji Awrang sent us up to visit a lake in the remote snowy passes. We spent the night enjoying the warm hospitality of the people of Chishma, a high-altitude tent village that only existed during the summer months. They served us gritty bread with four or five varieties of yogurt (the mainstay of their diet). Long after we thought the meal was over, they produced a painstakingly cooked chicken and rice with curd. We sat up by crisp starlight and oil lantern, talking about their flocks and their families, about when Fiona and I planned to start having children, and about their idea (taken from Haji Awrang) that one day they would build a hotel here for guests to come and see the mountains and the sheep.

In the early morning, an extraordinary luminosity clung to the hillsides and filled the high ravines. It was the ever-present dust: that inescapable powder that filled our nostrils, parched our lips, and whitened everything that stood still for an hour or two. By mid-morning the dust clouds blowing in off the steppe would once again be one of the great nuisances of Afghan life. For a few hours after dawn, though, the dust softened and transfigured the mountains, creating one radiant continuum between the rock and the sun.

My friend Jahan in Kabul had shared with me an Afghan proverb: "Mountains can never reach each other despite their bigness, but humans can." In this light, I almost believed that the mountains could reach each other. And even in the hot, disenchanting glare of noon, there would still be the people—tiny and resolute against the massive crags, reaching out across the gulf that separated us, pulling me willingly back in.

Sources

Unless otherwise noted, all figures on the opium economy throughout the book are derived from the Afghanistan reports of the UN Office on Drugs and Crime (www.unodc.org/afg/).

Yaqub: For historical background on Afghanistan, ancient and modern, I am indebted to Louis Dupree's *Afghanistan* (1973) and Barnett Rubin's *The Fragmentation of Afghanistan*, second edition (2002), with Nancy Hatch Dupree's *An Historical Guide to Afghanistan* (1977) an invaluable short resource. Many thanks to Professor Houchang Chehabi of Boston University for my introduction to the region's history.

USAID's education work in Afghanistan was critiqued by Craig Davis in "'A' is for Allah, 'J' is for Jihad," *World Policy Journal* (Spring 2002) and by Ann Jones in *Kabul in Winter* (2006).

Into the Minefield: All quotes from Amir Abdurrahman come from his autobiography, *The Life of Abdur Rahman, Amir of Afghanistan*, 2 vols. (1900).

A Million Dollars a Mile: Figures for the Kabul-Kandahar Highway project are derived from GAO and USAID reports.

The Place of the Soldiers: The quote (page 80) from Arrian is from E. J. Chinnock's 1893 translation of the *Anabasis Alexandri*, available online at http://websfor.org/alexander/arrian/intro.asp. My discussion of HAVA is informed by Nick Cullather, "Damming Afghanistan: Modernization in a Buffer State," *Journal of American History* (September 2002).

The Babaji Abduction: Regarding the hawala system, I am indebted to Roger Ballard's 2003 paper, "Hawala Transformed: Remittance-Driven Transnational Networks in the Post-Imperial Economic Order" (www.arts .manchester.ac.uk/casas/papers/hawala.html).

The Warloards' Vendetta: On the history of the Akhundzada family, see Antonio Giustozzi and Noor Ullah, "'Tribes' and Warlords in Southern Afghanistan, 1980–2005" (Working Paper no. 7, Crisis States Research Centre, September 2006).

New California: The short-sightedness of the original Helmand Valley project was chronicled not only by Cullather (cited above) but also by Aloys

Michel, "The Impact of Modern Irrigation Technology in the Indus and Helmand Basins of Southwest Asia," in *The Careless Technology* (1973). The Eric
Newby quote (page 157) is from the delightful *A Short Walk in the Hindu Kush*
(1958).

Good Cop, Bad Cop: Thanks to Jonathan Griswold for sharing his master's
thesis, "The Origins of the Afghan National Police and the Modern Afghan
State" (2007), with me as I wrote about the history of Afghanistan's police
force. On the Pakistani trucker mafia and the Taliban in Spin Boldak, see
Ahmed Rashid, *Taliban* (2000).

The Royal Bungalow: Antonio Maria Costa's quote on robbing banks is
from an IRIN interview of August 24, 2004. For a response, see Adam Pain
and David Mansfield, "Opium Poppy Eradication: How to raise risk when
there is nothing to lose?" (Afghanistan Research and Evaluation Unit, August
2006, www.areu.org.af). For a good overview of these and other counter-narcotics issues, see the UNODC/World Bank report, "Afghanistan's Drug Industry" (November 2006). For a discussion of principles of counterinsurgency,
see John Nagl, *Eating Soup with a Knife* (2002).

Back on Track: The Senlis Council's reports and proposals are available at
www.senliscouncil.net. See also David Mansfield, "An Analysis of Licit
Opium Poppy Cultivation: India and Turkey" (2001, www.geopium.com).
Figures on morphine consumption are from the 2005 Narcotic Drugs report
of the International Narcotics Control Board (INCB). For a discussion of alternative livelihoods in Thailand and elsewhere, see the UNODC report,
"Alternative Development: A Global Thematic Evaluation" (December
2005) and Adam Pain and David Mansfield's "Alternative Livelihoods: Sub-
stance or Slogan?" (October 2005, www.areu.org.af).

Gunfire in the Backyard: On the failures of police reform, see Vance Ser-
chuk, "Cop Out: Why Afghanistan Has No Police" (American Enterprise In-
stitute, July 2006), and the GAO report, "Afghanistan Security: Efforts to
Establish Army and Police Have Made Progress, but Future Plans Need to
Be Better Defined" (June 2005).

Defining Success: Since my departure, the danger pay and post differential
allowances for Afghanistan have both been raised from 25 percent to 35 percent. On the impact of reduced poppy cultivation in Nangarhar, see David
Mansfield, "Opium Poppy Cultivation in Nangarhar and Ghor" (December
2006, www.areu.org.af).

Helmand at War: Sarah Chayes's *The Punishment of Virtue* (2006) gives a
first-hand description of the amateurish follow-up to the Kandahar
bombing that killed the Kabul police commander.

Index

A

Abdurrahman, Amir, 55, 164
and "Durand Line," 198, 202
police force of, 190
Afghanistan. *See also* specific
provinces, projects
agriculture in Kunduz region,
146–47, 148–49
alcohol and drug use in, 123,
181–82
Amu Darya River, 154–56
attitudes of students in, 17–18
attitude toward Hazaras, 34
borders of, 54–55
communists in, 18, 19
condition of Kabul, 31–35
drought in, 36, 127
economy of, 235–36
Friendship Bridge, 153–54
invasion by Soviet Union and
resistance, 19–24
Kabul-Kandahar Highway, 67,
68–70
Kuchi nomadic group, 75–76
mineral wealth of, 18–19
monarchy in, 16–17
old empire in Ghazni, 70–71

police force of, 149–50, 190–92,
245–47, 306, 308, 314–15
poppy eradication in, 214–16,
257, 273, 305–6
poppy farming in, 10–11,
234–35
reconstruction projects in,
12–13, 34–35, 60, 64–65,
304–5, 311–12
relationship with Pakistan,
198–201, 308
Shamali Plain, 46–47
social values in, 177, 182, 183
statue of Buddha in, 48
Taliban in, 24, 33–34, 36–39,
71–72, 306, 307–8
UN disarmament campaign
in, 149, 211
winter 2005 in, 150, 194, 196
Afghanistan Quick Impact Project,
28, 34–35, 48
Akbar, Sayed, 95, 218, 220, 222
corruption in Marja, 277–79
in Darweshan area, 231–32
in Nawzad district, 264, 278
Akhundzada, Amir Muhammad,
224, 225, 313, 314

Akhundzada, Nasim, 129, 130
Akhundzada, Rasul, 130, 131
Akhundzada, Sher Muhammad,
131, 132, 229–30, 312–13
abduction of engineers, 111–12
ambushes of AIP team, 293–94
and drug trade, 192–93
police of, 191, 211
and poppy eradication, 210–11,
213, 224, 257
reconciliation efforts of, 228, 248
Alauddin, 81
Alexander the Great, 80
al-Saffar, Yaqub bin Laith, 81
Alternative Income Project. *See also*
Hafvenstein, Joel, 9,
11–13, 203
abduction of engineers, 110–14
ambushes of team, 283–85, 288,
295, 296–97, 309–10, 321–22
bombing of convoy, 281–82
in Darweshan area, 231
evacuation of team, 290
expanding in north, 227–28
high-profile visitors, 248–50
in Nawzad district, 261–62,
264–65
payrolls of, 108–10, 132–33,
168, 220–21, 258
relationship with HAVA, 206
relationship with PRTs, 206–7,
208–9
results of, 104–5, 162, 239–40,
241, 273–76
returning to Babaji, 251–52
road projects, 228, 247–48
security for, 121, 124–25,
127–28, 171, 258, 259

start-up team for, 86, 89–90,
91, 98, 136
Alternative Livelihoods Project,
203, 234
attack in Badakhshan, 317–18
Amanullah, King, 39
Amu Darya River, 154–56
Ansari, Haji, 108, 168
Anwari, Sayed Hussain, 62
Aqa, Khan. *See* Khan Aqa
Aral Sea, 154
Ariaspans, 80
Asghar, Ali, 119, 122, 282, 289
on opium harvesting, 255, 256
Augustine, Eugene, 102, 206,
207, 209
Awrang, Haji, 324–25
Azamy, Muhammad Kabir, 304
Aziz, Zulaikha, 28, 40, 62

B
Badakhshan Province, 317, 323,
324
Baghrani, Abdul Wahid. *See* Rais-i-
Baghran
Bamiyan Province, 266–67
Barno, David, 248
Baum, Ray, 7–10, 29, 311
and Alternative Income Project,
61, 65, 66, 86, 89–90, 275–76
and Alternative Livelihoods
Project, 203
hiking Kabul's boundary wall,
51–54
and housing, 87
and Khan Aqa, 103
and security, 84, 85, 101–2, 107
and underage workers, 105

bin Laden, Osama, 200, 232
Breitenstein, Rick, 259, 260, 261, 317
  ambushes of team, 284, 293, 295, 296–97, 298
  corruption in Marja, 279–80
  and Kajaki projects, 272
Brezhev, Leonid, 18
Britain
  and Afghanistan's borders, 54–55, 198
  defeats in Afghanistan, 164
  poppy eradication program, 193
Brydon, William, 164
Burqas, 38, 39–40, 320
Bush, George, 11

C

Chemonics International. *See also* specific projects, 9, 208
Afghanistan Quick Impact Project, 28
  alternative livelihoods projects, 60–61
  Peru project, 92
  reaction to ambushes, 310–11
  Rebuilding Agricultural Markets Program (RAMP), 28
Costa, Antonio Maria, 214

D

Dad Muhammad Khan, 130, 131, 212, 247, 313
Dado, Amir. *See* Dad Muhammad Khan
Daud, Prime Minister Sardar, 17, 18, 39
Dawari, A. K., 83–84, 87, 205–6

de Beir, Hélène, 158, 159–60
Development Alternatives Inc., 273
Dostum, Abdul Rashid, 153, 155
Downie, Nick, 67
Dupree, Louis, 80
Durand, Mortimer, 198
DynCorp, 246

E

Ehsan, Muhammad, 184–86, 218, 289, 291

F

Fine, Patrick, 63, 64–65, 309

G

Genghis Khan, 81, 267
Germany, and Afghan police reform, 245–46, 314
Ghaznavi, Sultan Mahmud, 71
Graham, Jim, 91, 96–97, 100, 121–22, 162, 240
  abduction of engineers, 110, 114
  and Alternative Livelihoods Project, 203
  on expanding project, 188, 209
  firing of, 310–11
  and Hafvenstein, 125–26, 135–36, 137
  handling payroll, 109, 110
  project in Badakhshan, 316, 317, 318
  and security, 107, 124
  and underage workers, 105
Gran, Abdul Ghani, 103–4, 105
  abduction of engineers, 112–13
  and security, 106–7
Griswold, Jon, 158–60

Guier, Dave, 59–60, 169, 203, 205
  arrival of, 194, 195, 196
  with PRT and Babaji elders,
    206–7

H
Habibullah, Haji, 77–78, 79,
    84–85, 88–89, 98, 109, 178
  abduction of engineers, 110,
    111, 132
  ambushes of team, 291–92, 299
  and Babaji elders, 188, 189
  and car bomb, 204–5
  and Christmas dinner, 115, 116,
    118–19, 122
  finding housing, 236
Hafvenstein, Joel
  abduction of engineers, 110,
    111–14
  and Alternative Income Project,
    58–60, 61, 66, 98–100, 162,
    272–76
  ambushes of team, 1–3, 283–89,
    291–303, 321–22
  at arch of Bost, 137–38
  and Babaji elders, 188–89
  in Badakhshan Province,
    316–21, 322–26
  in Balkh Province, 150–52, 153,
    154, 155, 156
  in Bamiyan Province, 158,
    266–69, 270–71
  and Baum, 7–9
  bombing of convoy, 281–82
  and car bomb, 204–5
  and Chemonics, 9–10, 11
  and Christmas dinner, 115,
    116–19, 122

corruption in Marja, 277–80
  in Darweshan area, 231–33
  and Ehsan, 184–86, 291
  engagement of, 169–70
  finding housing, 87–89, 236–37
  and Graham, 96–97
  and Griswold, 158–60
  handling payroll, 108–10,
    132–33, 168, 219–22
  hiking Kabul's boundary wall,
    51–54, 55
  hiring for project, 93–96, 105–6,
    238–39
  and Khair Muhammad, 133–35,
    237–38
  in Kunduz Province, 143–49
  in Musa Qala, 223–25
  in Nawzad district, 259–65
  in Pakistan, 196–97, 201–3
  and Quick Impact Project,
    26–31, 48
  and Roshan, 14–15
  in Sangin and Kajaki, 212–14,
    216–19, 225–27, 271–72
  and security, 84–85, 100–102,
    106–7, 121, 171–73, 175
  in Shamali region, 46–48
  trip to Helmand Province,
    67–69, 70, 71, 72–75, 76–79
  trip to Kabul, 163, 164–67
  and Yee, 240–41
Hawala system, 108
Hayat Khan, 191, 244–45, 313–14
Hazaras, 34, 118, 186
Hekmetyar, Gulbuddin, 18, 22–23,
    51, 112
  attack on Kabul, 33
  and drug trade, 129, 130, 215

Pakistan support for, 199
Helmand-Aghrabab Valley Author-
    ity (HAVA), 82–83, 206
security for, 172
Helmand Province, 9, 70, 80–83,
    115–16
    arch of Bost, 137–38
    Bolan and Babaji, 104
    Bost Hotel, 110–11
    canal grid in, 156–58
    flood in, 194
    Kajaki and Sangin, 212, 216–17
    Lashkargah, 77
    lower Helmand, 231
    Musa Qala, 223–24
    Nawzad district, 259, 260, 261,
        263
    poppy farming in, 12, 129–30,
        212–14, 315, 325
    poppy harvest in, 255–57, 258,
        274–75
    social values in, 177–78
    violence in, 306, 307
    warlords in, 128–29, 130–32
    Zamindawar, 219
Hizb-i-Islami. See Hekmetyar,
    Gulbuddin
Hogberg, Jim, 290, 300
Homes, David, 133, 167–68, 176

I
India, opium production in,
    235, 236
Ivey, Ron, 60, 240

J
Jan, Abdul Rahman, 114, 243, 244
Jurat, Din Muhammad, 150

K
Kabul. See also Afghanistan
    boundary wall of, 51, 52, 54
    condition of, 31–35
    Kabul-Kandahar Highway, 67,
        68–70, 163
    Taliban in, 36–41
Kandahar. See also Afghanistan,
    74, 75
British defeats at, 164
riots in, 257–58
violence in, 306, 307
Karezes, 219
Karzai, Ahmad Wali, 229
Karzai, Hamid
    and Akhundzadas, 229–30
    anmnesty offer, 72
    on border question, 200
    and Kabul-Kandahar
        Highway, 69
    and poppy eradication, 11, 216
    reforming police force,
        314–15
Khair Muhammad, Mian, 133–34,
    194, 237–38, 239, 280
    murder of, 283–84, 286
    values of, 177, 178–79, 180
Khalilzad, Zalmay, 64, 65, 69,
    248–49
Khan, Dad Muhammad. See Dad
    Muhammad Khan
Khan, Haji Homayoon, 236–37
Khan, Hayat. See Hayat Khan
Khan, Noor, 2, 288
Khan Aqa, 85, 103, 206
Khan Muhammad "Khano," 243
Kramer, Bob, 91–93, 101, 136
    on PRT, 208

Kuchi (nomadic group), 75–76
Kunduz Province, 143–44, 145, 146

L
Lashkargah. *See also* Helmand
    province, 1, 77, 82, 83, 304
    attitude towards America, 7, 8
    gun fight in, 242–44
Louis Berger Co., 69–70, 217

M
Mackay, Fiona, 169, 317
    in Badakhashan, 319–20,
        322–23, 325
Mahmud, Ghulam, 260, 262, 263
Massoud, Ahmad Shah, 22, 23, 36,
    51
    and Pakistan, 199, 200
    and Shamali Plain, 46–47
Médecins sans Frontières (MSF),
    attack on, 158, 159, 160,
    308–9
Miller, Dan, 63, 65, 91
Mir Ahmad, 278, 279
Mir Wali, 130, 131, 132, 165, 210,
    313
Morrison-Knudsen Co., 81–82
Muhammad, Khan. *See* Khan
    Muhammad "Khano"
Muhammad, Mian Khair. *See* Khair
    Muhammad, Mian
Muhammad, Nasir, 324
Muhammad, Raz, 110, 133
    in Darweshan area, 231–33
    handling payroll, 220
    and Kajaki Dam, 225–26
    in Nawzad district, 264–65
    on police, 190–91

    projects in Baghran, 271–72
    values of, 177, 178, 179, 180
Munaf, Abdul, 188–89, 209
Musharraf, Pervez. *See also*
    Pakistan, 200, 307

N
Nabi, Muhammad, 238–39
Najibullah, Muhammad, 18, 20,
    23, 24, 37
Nassery, Homaira, 282
Newby, Eric, 157

O
Omar, Mullah. *See also* Taliban, 36
    and Kandahar, 74
    and opium production, 131,
        214–15
    Pakistan support for, 199, 200
Oosterkamp, Johannes, 194, 224,
    230–31, 282
    and Alternative Income Project,
        60, 61–62
    project in Badakhshan, 316
    and security, 102
Opium poppy. *See* also Helmand
    Province, 10–13
    in Balkh Province, 150–51
    eradication campaign, 210–11,
        213, 214–16, 224, 257, 305–6
    harvesting and distributing,
        255–57, 258
    in Nangarhar, 273
    pay for harvestors, 128, 258
    proposal to legalize, 234–36

P
Pain, Adam, 272–73, 273–74

Pakistan
  and Afghan resistance, 21–22
  relationship with Afghanistan,
    198–201, 308
  and Taliban, 307–8
Pashtuns, 16, 80–81
  and antigovernment insurgency,
    72
  attitudes on religion, 183–84
  and Pakistan, 198
  social values of, 176–82
Police force. *See* Afghanistan
Poppy. *See* Opium poppy
Provincial Reconstruction Teams
    (PRTs), 65, 102, 232–33, 290
  ambushes of AIP team, 300–301
  relationship with AIP team, 206,
    207–9
  replacement of, 306–7

Q
Qaderi, Habibullah, 249, 250

R
Rabbani, Burhanuddin, 17, 18, 22
Rais-i-Baghran, 223, 228–29
Rebuilding Agricultural Markets
    Program (RAMP), 28, 58, 62,
    64, 68
Rhodes, Todd, 101
Rizk, Ashraf, 61
Roshan, Yaqub, 9, 14–15, 17–19,
    20–25, 138, 318
  and Alternative Income Project,
    61, 66, 187–88, 247
  ambushes of team, 285, 286,
    287, 298, 299
  finding housing, 87–88

  in Kajaki, 217, 218–19
  in Musa Qala, 223, 224
  on Nawzad district, 259, 260–61
  on Pakistan and Afghanistan,
    199
  and payroll, 221–22
  projects in Baghran, 271–72
  on returning to Babaji, 251–52
Russia. *See also* Soviet Union
  and Afghanistan's borders, 54–55
  and Kandahar-Herat Highway,
    75

S
Sangerwal, Daud, 58–59
Scott, Dick, 85–86, 108, 117, 136,
    187, 193
  on floods, 194
Senlis Council, 234, 235
Sher Muhammad. *See* Akhundzada,
    Sher Muhammad
Singer, Rick, 96, 120
Siu, Pete, 28–29, 43
  and Alternative Income
    Project, 61, 65, 66, 86,
    89–90, 98
  on Khair Muhammad, 134
  mentoring staff, 49–50
  and Quick Impact Project,
    48–49
  on results of projects, 275
  on road projects, 47, 247–48
  trip to Helmand, 73, 74–75
Soviet Union, 199
  and Aral Sea, 154
  and Friendship Bridge, 153–54
  invasion of Afghanistan,
    19–20, 23

Swanberg, Ken, 144, 145–46,
151, 152
and Amu Darya River, 154,
155, 156

T
Taliban, 24, 71–72
ambush of AIP teams, 321–22
ambush of MSF workers,
158, 160
collapse of, 248
in Kabul, 33, 34, 36–37, 39–41
and Kabul-Kandahar
Highway, 69
in Kandahar, 74
and opium production,
214–15, 216
and Pakistan, 199–201
restrictions on women, 37–38
resurgence of, 306, 307–8
and Shamali Plain, 46–47
and *shorombe*, 151
and statue of Buddha, 48
turbans of, 221
and warlords, 131
Tashqurgan Gap, 148
Thailand, opium production in,
236
Timur-i-Leng, 81
Truss, Reggie, 208
Turkey, opium production in,
235, 236

U
United Nations, disarmament
campaign, 149–50, 211
United States. *See also* specific
agencies

and Afghan police reform,
246, 314
development policies of, 304–5,
311 12
and poppy eradication, 216
United States Agency for International Development (USAID).
See also specific projects
and Afghan police reform, 246
and Baum, 8
cash-for-work projects, 9, 11–13,
60, 63–66, 91
consultants in, 269–70
dams and canals in Helmand,
81–82, 157–58
and Kabul-Kandahar Highway,
69–70
reaction to ambushes, 310–12
United States Protection and Investigations (USPI), 68, 70,
72–73, 101, 102
Kabul troops of, 150
policies of, 143, 146
Uruzgan Province, 71

V
van Neck, Rensje, 231, 239

W
Wahid, Abdul, 130, 131
Wali, Mir. *See* Mir Wali
Walters, John, 248, 249, 250
Watt, Charles, 100, 127–28,
170–71, 173–74
ambushes of team, 283, 284,
286, 288–89, 294, 295–96,
309, 321–22
bombing of convoy, 281–82

finding housing, 236–37
on IED threat, 228
project in Babakshan, 318,
 320–21
on returning to Babaji, 252
and security, 1, 2, 171–73, 175,
 192, 244–45, 246–47
Women, under Taliban, 37–38,
 39–41

Y
Yar, Khaliq, 133, 194
Yates, Jeff, 120, 123–24, 125

Yee, Carol, 89–90, 98, 203
 ambushes of team, 284, 285
 and Babaji issue, 251
 corruption in Marja, 279
 finding housing, 87, 88
 and Hafvenstein, 86, 240–41
 hiring women, 95

Z
Zabul Province, 71
Zahir Shah, King, 16, 17, 110
Zaki, Abdul Qader Khan, 239